The Restoration of God's Dwelling and Kingdom

Peter Nyende has written here a stimulating, well-researched and clearly developed biblical theology of God's kingdom and dwelling that has captured the heart and breadth of the biblical story. In line with Irenaeus and the early church's first catechisms, Nyende faithfully presents the Christian faith in Scripture as one story of God's purpose to restore his good creation to again be his kingdom where he can dwell among his people. This book will bring new insight but will also draw you to take your place in the biblical story. Highly recommended!

Michael W. Goheen, PhD
Professor of Missional Theology,
Mission Training Centre, Arizona, USA

Written out of passion for the well-being of the church and his students, Peter Nyende carefully unfolds a full Bible theology that shines a light on the central concern of Scripture – the kingdom of God. With clarity and precision, he draws the two testaments together to provide his readers with an overarching view of God's plan for the world. This well-researched contribution to biblical theology centres Scripture and avoids overspecialization and technical jargon. Nyende is a rising star in African biblical studies whose work is a gift to the church around the globe.

Gene Green, PhD
Professor Emeritus of New Testament,
Wheaton College and Graduate School, Illinois, USA

This book is a significant contribution to academic and non-academic debates on the nature of biblical theology. Prof. Peter Nyende makes a painstaking effort to highlight the canonical, symbolic and typological interconnectivity of the Old and New Testaments. This is vividly illustrated through his passionate engagement with the thought-provoking theme of how God's dwelling and kingdom are being restored. The subject of "Restoration of Fortunes" is of vital importance to the African biblical theologizing exercise at both scholarly and non-scholarly levels. Such an exercise takes due cognizance of issues of holistic salvation embracing the material as well as spiritual wellbeing of communities and individuals.

The quest for divine intervention is a non-negotiable component of the African existential reality.

Prof. Nyende deserves commendation for guiding us through subject matter that is critically needed in our post-modern and increasingly secularized world. Those training for pastoral ministry will find it a priceless resource material.

John David Kwamena Ekem, PhD
Kwesi Dickson-Glibert Ansre Distinguished Professor of Biblical Exegesis and Mother Tongue Hermeneutics,
Trinity Theological Seminary, Accra, Ghana
Pro Vice-Chancellor, Methodist University Ghana

Peter Nyende embarks on a biblical theology that approaches the written word of God as a single coherent story in which God's dwelling and kingdom constitute the main plot. The book substantiates this view with different types of exegesis, including symbolic, intertextual, typological, literary and canonical readings. This interpretation of the word of God represents a landmark work for evangelical audiences and others.

Jean-Claude Loba Mkole, PhD
Global Translation Consultant, United Bible Societies, Kenya
Research Associate, University of the Free State, South Africa

A story is sweeter when told at one sitting than in smaller pieces. Here Professor Nyende tells the Bible story in a unified manner focused on the theme of "the earth, God's dwelling place," and especially on its restoration. Professor Nyende does not limit this to the incarnate Christ but begins with God's first relationship with humankind in Genesis and extends this to the eternal future in Revelation. Careful exegesis is brought alongside simplicity in expression of thought in a manner that means this book will bless both the theological scholar and the believer in the church. I highly recommend it for all of us.

Samuel Ngewa, PhD
Dean of the Graduate School,
Africa International University, Kenya

The Bible is a large and complicated book, and we can read particular books and isolated texts in the Scriptures and fail to understand the larger framework of all sixty-six books. Professor Peter Nyende has written an astute and accessible biblical theology, tracing the storyline of the scriptural narrative. Nyende also addresses matters that are sometimes missing from Western studies in biblical theology and his own contribution is warmly welcomed as part of the ongoing conversation. To sum up, this is a wonderful resource for pastors, teachers and for all who desire to understand the whole plan of God.

Thomas Schreiner, PhD
James Buchanan Harrison Professor of New Testament Interpretation,
Southern Baptist Theological Seminary, Kentucky, USA

I greatly appreciate the holistic approach advanced by Dr. Nyende. The canonical relationship of Scripture favors a two-testament Bible. It is to be expected that there are many threads suggesting typological connections revealing the nature, plan, and love of Triune God. As God is One-in-Three, we must expect a great diversity revealing an organic unity. This book will encourage a theological and canonical integration much-needed in our churches. After all, the church and the word of God manifest the reality of God's revelation in Jesus Christ.

Willem VanGermeren, PhD
Professor Emeritus of Old Testament and Semitic Languages,
Trinity Evangelical Divinity School, Illinois, USA

The Restoration of God's Dwelling and Kingdom

A Biblical Theology

Peter Nyende

© 2023 Peter Nyende

Published 2023 by Langham Global Library
An imprint of Langham Publishing

www.langhampublishing.org

Langham Publishing and its imprints are a ministry of Langham Partnership

Langham Partnership
PO Box 296, Carlisle, Cumbria, CA3 9WZ, UK
www.langham.org

ISBNs:
978-1-83973-735-0 Print
978-1-83973-841-8 ePub
978-1-83973-843-2 PDF

Peter Nyende has asserted his right under the Copyright, Designs and Patents Act, 1988 to be identified as the Author of this work.

All rights reserved. No part of this publication may be reproduced, stored in a retrieval system or transmitted, in any form or by any means, electronic, mechanical, photocopying, recording or otherwise, without the prior written permission of the publisher or the Copyright Licensing Agency.

Requests to reuse content from Langham Publishing are processed through PLSclear. Please visit www.plsclear.com to complete your request.

Unless otherwise stated, Scripture quotations are from the New Revised Standard Version Bible, copyright © 1989 National Council of the Churches of Christ in the United States of America. Used by permission. All rights reserved.

Scripture quotations marked (ESV) are from The Holy Bible, English Standard Version® (ESV®), copyright © 2001 by Crossway, a publishing ministry of Good News Publishers. Used by permission. All rights reserved.

Scripture quotations marked (RSV) are from the Revised Standard Version of the Bible, copyright © 1946, 1952, and 1971 National Council of the Churches of Christ in the United States of America. Used by permission. All rights reserved.

Scripture quotations marked (NIV) are taken from the Holy Bible, New International Version®, NIV®. Copyright © 1973, 1978, 1984, 2011 by Biblica, Inc.™ Used by permission of Zondervan.

British Library Cataloguing-in-Publication Data
A catalogue record for this book is available from the British Library

ISBN: 978-1-83973-735-0

Cover & Book Design: projectluz.com

Langham Partnership actively supports theological dialogue and an author's right to publish but does not necessarily endorse the views and opinions set forth here or in works referenced within this publication, nor can we guarantee technical and grammatical correctness. Langham Partnership does not accept any responsibility or liability to persons or property as a consequence of the reading, use or interpretation of its published content.

In loving memory of my mother Decima Wesa Nyende (1939–2001)

Contents

	Preface xiii
	Abbreviations xv
1	Introduction 1
2	Dawn and Loss of God's Dwelling and Kingdom 13
3	The Restoration of God's Dwelling and Kingdom via Israel. ... 35
4	The Restoration of God's Kingdom through David's Dynasty ... 63
5	Failure in the Restoration of God's Dwelling and Kingdom ... 97
6	An Interlude: The Promises and Delay of Israel's Restoration ... 117
7	The Restoration of God's Kingdom via Jesus 151
8	Israel's Restoration and the Restoration of God's Kingdom ... 187
9	Restoration of God's Dwelling via Jesus 219
10	Conclusion. 243
	Bibliography 247
	Subject Index. 253
	Scripture Index 257

Preface

My commitment to write this book took place with the first biblical theology class I taught at Nairobi Graduate School of Theology (NEGST) in 2006. Students of that class loved its content, describing it as eye-opening. At the end of the course, as is typical in classes where student satisfaction is high, they thanked me for it. But one student went beyond gratitude and requested if I could write a book based on my class lectures. In his view, the content merited a wider audience. His request was enthusiastically supported by his colleagues, some of whom said they would be the first ones to buy the book. I promised that I would write a book in due course.

This book has therefore been delayed for fifteen years. Despite my desire to write it I just could not get the time I needed to do so. Theological education in Africa is demanding of its practitioners. Not only are we expected to be teaching in class as well as involved quite closely with the practical training of students, but we are also expected to be actively involved in the life of the church. Under these circumstances, setting aside time to write for extended periods of time is usually very difficult. It was the COVID-19 pandemic, painful as it was, that afforded me an extended period of time away from seminary, church and other responsibilities to write and complete this book.

My approach in writing this book has not betrayed the spirit of my 2006 class. As I did in that and all my subsequent classes, I have ensured that the Bible is supremely the primary subject of study. This is why the book is characterized more by Bible references and textual quotes and less by references from scholarly books on the Bible's content. It is for the same reason that I have privileged the context of the Bible over extra-biblical contexts to enlighten my exegesis of its individual texts. I have tried to underline the latter by referring to the Bible often as literature. This reference is meant to engender the view that the Bible is a literary whole, whose individual parts, like a piece of good literature, must be made sense of within the whole. By no means, however, do I neglect biblical scholarship, nor extra-biblical sources; rather I refer and engage them relatively sparingly, where I have considered them vital in my exegesis of a given Bible text.

I am especially indebted to Joyce Carlson, my neighbour in Karen, Nairobi when I taught at NEGST, and the godmother of my firstborn son. Out of her generosity she read, and commented on, all the first drafts of the chapters of my manuscript. Her eyes caught numerous errors in the drafts. But crucially, the clarity of my writing in this book has been greatly improved by her editorial skills and command of the English language.

I cannot forget the enormous debt I owe my wife, Josephine, who afforded me in this pandemic and without complaint many days of time alone in my study to write this book. Her forbearing companionship is a blessing without measure.

Lastly, although he always knows before we express ourselves, I would like to thank the one in whom "we live, breath and have our being" for enabling me to honour the commitment I made to my students to write this book, albeit fifteen years on. He knows the end from the beginning, and everything has a time in line with his plans and purposes. To him be reserved always the ultimate glory and honour for our efforts whose fruits see the light of day.

Abbreviations

AJET	*African Journal of Evangelical Theology*
BA	*Biblical Archaeologist*
BBR	*Bulletin of Biblical Research*
Bib	*Biblica*
BibInt	*Biblical Interpretation*
BICS	*Bulletin of the Institute of Classical Studies*
b.Sukk	Babylonian Talmud, Tractate *Sukkah*
CBQ	*Catholic Biblical Quarterly*
ESV	The English Standard Bible
FRLANT	Forschungen zur Religion und Literatur des Alten und Neuen Testaments
GND	Good News Bible
HTR	*Harvard Theological Review*
HUCA	*Hebrew Union College Annual*
ICC	International Critical Commentary
J. Hist. Geogr.	*Journal for Historical Geography*
J. Hist. Int. Law	*Journal of the History of International Law*
JAOS	*Journal of the American Oriental Society*
JBL	*Journal of Biblical Literature*
JBQ	*Jewish Biblical Quarterly*
JSJ	*Journal for the Study of Judaism in the Persian, Hellenistic and Roman Periods*
JSNT	*Journal for the Study of the New Testament*
JSNTSup	Journal for the Study of the New Testament: Supplementary Series
J. Theta Alpha Kappa	*Journal of Theta Alpha Kappa*
JTS	*Journal of Theological Studies*
LXX	Septuagint
m. Yoma	Mishnah, Tractate *Yoma*
m. Sukk	Mishnah, Tractate *Sukkah*

MQR	*Mennonite Quarterly Review*
Neot	*Neotestamentica*
NCB	New Century Bible
NEB	New English Bible
NIV	New International Bible
NICOT	New International Commentary on the Old Testament
NRSV	New Revised Standard Bible
NSBT	New Studies in Biblical Theology
PPR	*Philosophy and Phenomenological Research*
RSV	Revised Standard Bible
ResQ	*Restoration Quarterly*
SJT	*Scottish Journal of Theology*
Tradition	*Tradition: A Journal of Orthodox Jewish Thought*
TSAJ	Texte Und Studien Zum Antiken Judentum Series
VT	*Vetus Testamentum*
WBC	Word Biblical Commentary
y. Sukk	Jerusalem Talmud, Tractate *Sukkah*

1

Introduction

The Discipline of Biblical Theology

This book in the field of biblical studies falls in the area of biblical theology. The subject of study in biblical theology is the content of the whole Bible and not just a section of it. For this reason, biblical theology studies are based on the view that biblical literature constitutes a single cohesive book. Whole-Bible studies based on the perceived unity of the scriptures have been the defining characteristic of biblical theology since its introduction in the academic study of the Bible by the Swiss theologian Johann Gabler in the eighteenth century. In 1787 Gabler offered a lecture[1] in which he advocated a method of studying the Bible as a source of Christian doctrine and ethics. His method entailed studying the content of the whole Bible which was based on his perception of its unity in regard to its timeless truths.

Biblical theology studies usually proceed in either of two ways. The first is by reading the content of the Bible as a single coherent whole and on that basis articulating its message. A few examples will suffice here. For Schreiner,[2] the Bible's message is about God as king and thus his kingdom's inevitable triumph. Pate and his colleagues[3] interpret the Bible's message as revolving around sin, exile and restoration. For Beale and Kim,[4] the Bible's message is

---

[1]. Laurence Eldredge and John Sandys-Wunsch, "J. B. Gabler and the Distinction Between Biblical and Dogmatic Theology: Translation, Commentary, and the Discussion of His Originality," *SJT* 33 (1980).

[2]. Thomas R. Schreiner, *The King in His Beauty: A Biblical Theology of the Old and New Testament* (Grand Rapids, MI: Baker Academic, 2013).

[3]. G. Marvin Pate, J. Scott Duvall et al., *The Story of Israel: A Biblical Theology* (Downers Grove: InterVarsity Press, 2004).

[4]. G. K. Beale and Mitchell Kim, *God Dwells Among Us: Expanding Eden to the End of the Earth* (Downers Grove: InterVarsity Press, 2014).

about "God's dwelling among us" while William views the Bible's message as a redemptive narrative within the framework of covenants.[5] We should note, however, that there are biblical scholars who have used this procedure but limited their reading of the Bible's message to the Old Testament. An example of this is Dempster,[6] who considers the Old Testament message to be about dominion and dynasty.

The second way in which biblical theology studies proceed is through studying what the content of the whole Bible says about a select topic or theme. For example, what the Bible says about "worship" is discussed by Ross,[7] "mission" by Kostenberger,[8] "covenants" by Robertson,[9] "stewardship" by Blomberg,[10] "mystery" by Beale and Gladd,[11] and "race" by Hays.[12] In addition, we also have this procedure applied to what only the Old Testament says about a given topic. For example, what the Old Testament says about Israel's gospel, faith and life;[13] "sin" is considered by Lam,[14] while "God and gods," "creation," "God's people," "the future and the nations" is examined by Routledge.[15] From the content of the New Testament alone, "God" is looked at by Hurtado,[16] and

---

5. Michael Williams, *Far as the Curse is Found: The Covenant Story of Redemption* (Phillipsburg: P&R Publishing, 2005).

6. Stephen G. Dempster, *Dominion and Dynasty: A Theology of the Hebrew Bible* (Downers Grove: InterVarsity Press 2003).

7. Allen P. Ross, *Recalling the Hope of Glory: Biblical Worship From the Garden to the New Creation* (Grand Rapids: Kregel Academic and Professional, 2006).

8. Andreas J. Köstenberger with T. Desmond Alexander, *Salvation to the Ends of the Earth: A Biblical Theology of Mission* 2nd ed. (Downers Grove: InterVarsity Press 2020).

9. O. Palmer Robertson, *The Christ of the Covenant* (Phillipsburg: P&R Publishing, 1980).

10. Craig L. Blomberg, *Christians in an Age of Wealth: A Biblical Theology of Stewardship*, Biblical Theology for Life (Grand Rapids: Zondervan, 2013).

11. G. K. Beale and Benjamin L. Gladd, *Hidden But Now Revealed: A Biblical Theology of Mystery* (London: SPCK, 2014).

12. J. Daniel Hays, *From Every People and Nation: A Biblical Theology of Race*, NSBT (Downers Grove: InterVarsity Press 2003).

13. John Goldingay, *Old Testament Theology: Israel's Gospel*, Vol. I (Downers Grove: InterVarsity Press 2003); John Goldingay, *Old Testament Theology: Israel's Faith*, Vol. II (Downers Grove: InterVarsity Press 2006); and John Goldingay, *Old Testament Theology: Israel's Life*, Vol. III (Downers Grove: InterVarsity Press, 2009).

14. Joseph Lam, *Patterns of Sin in the Hebrew Bible: Metaphor, Culture, and the Making of a Religious Concept* (Oxford: Oxford University Press, 2016).

15. Robin Routledge, *Old Testament Theology: A Thematic Approach*, Library of Biblical Theology (Nottingham: Apollos, 2008).

16. Larry Hurtado, *God in New Testament Theology*, Library of Biblical Theology (Nashville: Abingdon Press, 2010).

"God, salvation, the church of God, and ethics" is studied by Dunn.[17] The procedure I have taken for this study is the first one mentioned: I will discuss the message of the whole Bible by reading all of it as a single coherent book (more on this later).

I have written this biblical theology book in order to help students of the Bible acquire a general knowledge of all its content. Biblical theology is foremost among the disciplines of biblical studies that fosters knowledge and understanding of the content of the whole Bible. It does so in two distinct ways. The first is through enabling one to have an overview of the content of the whole Bible and not just a part of it. In biblical theology the study of the Bible does not end with the study of a text, or a book, or even a set of books. Other books of the Bible must be taken into account or studied as well for a study to be a biblical theology study. For a study to be classified as biblical-theological, one deliberately studies all the books of the Bible in an integrated manner in order to have a general picture of the content of the whole Bible. It is only when one has such a picture of the Bible that it can be said s/he has attained the ends of biblical theology.

The second way biblical theology fosters Bible knowledge is by the usefulness of the general picture of the content of the Bible one acquires for interpreting its individual parts (its verses, or texts, or books, or even set of books). The general picture helps to foster biblical knowledge by acting as the primary context for interpreting individual parts of the Bible by giving one a standpoint from which to view them. The general picture of the Bible also enables one to make sense of individual parts of the Bible in relationship to the rest of the Bible's content. It can also provide clues about the content, concerns, and intentions of individual parts of the Bible one is studying and thereby help in interpreting them.

We should note here that the need for whole-Bible readings in the academic study of the Bible is also strongly justified by specialisation in biblical studies, which denies students of the Bible a good grasp of the content of the whole. The common practice in academic studies is for scholars to specialize in and teach only a small section of the content of the Bible divorced from the whole. Specialization is practised to enable detailed studies of Bible texts, as is made clear in the response I received to a biblical theology article I submitted to a biblical studies journal for a publication consideration. The editor candidly emailed thus. "Your sweep of the canon in this biblical theology article is

---

17. James D. G. Dunn, *New Testament Theology: An Introduction* (Nashville: Abingdon Press, 2009).

commendable. It is not usually what . . . reviewers approve in their reviews. Usually our readers prefer more detailed engagement with particular texts, secondary literature, etc." However, although atomized studies of the Bible allow for more detailed studies, they do not usually lead to biblical literacy. They lack the context provided by a general picture of the content of the Bible within which to interpret their detailed individual study and/or relate it to other books of the Bible. It is therefore my hope that this book, like others in the same subject area, will promote knowledge of the content of the whole Bible in academic studies.

My hope here is personal. When I started my pastoral training and theological studies in university in the early 1990s, my study of the Bible was disjointed by specialization. We studied books of the Bible as autonomous units without deliberate recourse to the overall content of the Bible, or to other books or texts of the Bible except, on some occasions, those of a similar genre. Interpreting a book of the Bible in relationship to the content of other books of the Bible was usually not done. The practice in survey or introductory approaches to the Old Testament and New Testament were no different, because we surveyed the books of the Old Testament and the New Testament individually or in groups of similar literature or common authorship. If we were studying groups of books under the same literature or authorship in the Old Testament, we did not relate them to the New Testament and vice versa. The closest we came to studying the Old Testament and the New Testament together were in quotations of Old Testament prophets in the Gospels.

My lack of a general grasp of the Bible's content was often found out by the lectionary of Bible readings used for preaching in my Anglican church. The lectionary required me to relate texts of the Bible one to another generally, and the Old Testament to the New Testament, which I struggled to do. When I started teaching the Bible as a theological scholar and educator, I was determined to help my students have a better grasp of the Bible, and use that knowledge to preach, than I had been afforded. This desire is what eventually led me to invest in biblical theology and become its advocate for the theological education of clergy and prospective pastors. Opportunities subsequently came for me to write up courses in biblical theology and be involved in teaching them. This book is an expanded version of material I have developed in my more than fifteen years of teaching biblical theology classes in African theological colleges and faculties of theology in African Christian universities.

Looked at from another perspective, the reason I have written this biblical theology book is because I wish to have my biblical scholarship serve men and women training to pastorally serve churches. Such a goal is in tune with the ends of biblical theology. Biblical theology unambiguously aims to serve the church by informing the faith and life of clergy and the laity. This is already alluded to in Gabler's desire to bring the fruits of his unified study of the Bible for use in doctrine (faith) and ethics (life). Biblical theology leads naturally to application and, thus, it is where ecclesial concerns and interests are catered for most in biblical studies. To use the series NSBT[18] as an example, their titles in the series sound more like sermon headings than titles of academic biblical literature. These titles, for example, include: *Possessed by God*, *Christ Our Righteousness*, *Hearing God's Word*, *From Every People and Nation*, *The Temple and the Church's Mission*, *God has Spoken in His Son*, *Bound for the Promised Land*. Indeed biblical theology studies are usually undertaken from a confessional perspective and, to their credit, can be drawn from for faith and living by Christians in the academy and elsewhere. These conclusions may not apply in other areas of biblical studies even where they are motivated, or informed, by confessional persuasions.

As an African Bible scholar I have more to say here. The numerical strength of Christianity in Africa is celebrated and so is the boldness of its faith as well as its fervour. However I am also acutely aware of the need to have Christianity in Africa's faith and life informed by the Bible. Not all therein is biblically informed nor hospitable to the Bible's message. In fact, the challenge of folk African Christianity, by which I mean a Christian faith informed more by traditional African beliefs than by the Bible, always looms large. Critical to bringing about an African Christianity informed by the Bible are pastors of African churches who regularly teach the Bible's content to African Christians. However they cannot play this role if they themselves are not biblically literate. The fruits of biblical studies, therefore, must be made available for the education and training of those who pastor African Christian congregations. A study like this one can help towards that end.

This Book's Approach to Biblical Theology

Before I explain the content of my book in outline, it is important that we point out significant aspects of my approach to biblical theology in this book. The first is general to biblical theology: as already mentioned, I read the content of the Bible as a single coherent book. I do so by reading the Bible as a story.

---

18. With over 60 volumes so far, books in the series are published by Apollos and Inter-Varsity Press.

This story has a discernable plot, beginning, unfolding, and coming to an end, having resolved the chief problem it presents. The chief problem, as we shall see, is the world ceasing to be God's dwelling and kingdom as intended. This story of the Bible comes out from reading all its parts in relationship to the rest of the content of biblical literature. For this reason, I focus my reading on the canon of the Bible as is. I do not engage at length with issues that are of importance in monographic biblical studies such as sources, composition, dating, and transmission. I only engage with them to the extent that they are necessary in enlightening a reading under discussion in the story.

The second is that my study of the Bible is informed by symbolic readings, whereby the content of biblical texts are understood through the deeper meaning they are perceived to represent, as much as by historical-literary readings. Although a significant proportion of the Bible communicates by means of symbolism, the need for symbolic readings is more acute in this study because the Bible's story line cannot be isolated with clarity in Genesis, and traced through the rest of biblical literature, solely by historical-literary interpretations. Symbolic readings are needed to do this. By nature symbols do not communicate directly but indirectly; they are brief and only allude and imply rather than state. It is therefore upon the one looking at the symbols to make them explicit.

The third is that the Bible itself, and not scholarly literature, is the primary content of discussion in the book. This is in order to have undergraduate and graduate students of the Bible (who are the primary target audience of this book) to engage first hand with the Bible's content. I do not ignore scholarly literature altogether, but keep it at a minimum by limiting references and/or use to where scholarly sources are crucial in enlightening the biblical material under discussion. This approach accounts for the mass of Bible references and actual quotes in the book's discussion, and the relatively fewer references and quotes from scholarly literature. Although I try to be as exhaustive as possible, the Bible references and quotes I give are fundamentally illustrative of the point being discussed in the story.

The fourth is that the context to which I give the first priority for interpreting Bible words, terms, and phrases significant in our reading of the story of the Bible, is the preceding and succeeding content of the Bible itself. I rely more on the context of the usage of these words, terms, or phrases in biblical literature in understanding their meaning, and less on their lexicon and philological meaning. These key terms and concepts include "image of God," "kingdom of God," "God's rest" "blessings," and "curses." Giving priority to biblical context for interpretation further cements the examination of the whole Bible as the primary main content of the book which those reading it must reckon with and thus engage first hand with the Bible.

Lastly, I apply typology to relate the story of the Bible in the Old Testament with its further development and conclusion in the New Testament. My application of typology is to all significant entities in the story of the Bible in the Old Testament in relationship to their antitypes in the New Testament. These significant entities are: Israel, the Davidic kings, the land, Jerusalem, the temple, and God's and Israel's enemies. This means that I apply typology in the broadest sense to understand how the whole story of the Bible in the Old Testament continues and concludes in the New Testament.

Although typology relates the story of the Bible in the Old Testament logically with its continuation and conclusion in the New Testament, it is not a product solely of our historical-literary reading of the Old Testament, nor even of our symbolic readings. The basis for my use of typology to understand how the story of the Bible in the Old Testament continues and concludes in the New Testament is the New Testament itself. As we shall see, the restoration of Israel and the Davidic kingship promised in the Old Testament (and the corresponding restoration of God's dwelling and kingdom in the world) was fulfilled in Christ in the New Testament. This biblical theology book is thus a Christian biblical theology book in approach.

We will read the Bible as a story about the restoration of God's dwelling and kingdom in the world in the following order. We will begin in chapter 2 with the beginning of the story of the Bible in Genesis. We will argue, from our reading of the content of Genesis and related Old Testament texts, that God created the world to be his dwelling with human beings and a part of his kingdom. However, because of the disobedience of Adam and Eve, God's dwelling and kingdom in the world were placed in jeopardy. The world ceased to be his dwelling and a part of his kingdom (in a visible unambiguous sense). We will argue that creation and what it was meant for, together with humans' disobedience and its consequences, is the foundational starting point of the Bible's narrative. It both controls and is the basis for the story of the Bible. We will conclude the chapter by pointing out that in calling Abraham and promising him offspring, land, kings, and blessing to all nations, God set out to restore his residency and kingdom purposes for creation.

In chapter 3 we will demonstrate from my reading of Exodus, Leviticus, Numbers, Deuteronomy, the Psalms, and related Old Testament texts that God planned to restore his dwelling and kingdom in the world using Israel by virtue of their Abrahamic ancestry. The people of Israel as God's people would live with him and by his laws in the land. The "blessed" quality of life (blessings of abundant life) Israel would experience in the land as a result of their obedience to God would be the means by which God's dwelling and kingdom would be restored in the world. The blessings of abundant life would include abundance of food, herds and flock, the absence of barrenness and sickness, and security and peace in the land. The blessings of abundant life would attract other nations to YHWH (who would be dwelling in Zion) because they would desire the blessings of abundant life he had granted Israel. Trips to Zion would then lead them to the knowledge of YHWH and to obedience of his laws (just as Israel had). As a result, the nations would come under God's rule and receive the blessings of abundant life as a part of God's kingdom. This way God's kingdom and dwelling would be restored in the world. However if the Israelites would not live in obedience, curses would ensue. These curses would include hunger, lack, sickness, defeat by enemies, desolation of the land, and their destruction. In the end they would be expelled from the land, so that, rather than being an attraction to other nations, they would be an object of scorn.

In chapter 4 we will focus on the parallel but corresponding way that God intended to restore his kingdom through David's dynasty. The dynasty was a result of God's promise of kings to Abraham. I will argue from my reading of 1 and 2 Samuel, the Psalms, and related Old Testament texts, that David's dynasty was designed to be an instrument of restoring God's kingdom in the world. This design was indirectly pointed to by God "merging" David's dynasty with his own through the extraordinary promise he gave to David of an everlasting kingdom. This promise signalled the turning of the Davidic kingship into God's and consequently the making of the Davidic kings into his kings (God's anointed). Because of this, the Davidic kings would rule in justice and righteousness, and ensure peace and safety in the kingdom. They would also establish a universal reign, with YHWH's help, by subjugating nations and incorporating them into Israel. The nations, in becoming a part of Israel, would know YHWH and submit to his laws, thus become a part of his kingdom. God's use of the Davidic dynasty would depend upon his successors' obedience – their ruling in justice and righteousness. Their disobedience would lead to their dethronement.

In chapter 5 we will discuss Israel's disobedience and the Davidic kings' inability to rule in justice and righteousness. Through our reading of Samuel, Kings, and the pre-exilic prophets, we will discuss the extent of Israel's disobedience. We will do this by discussing the sins of idolatry and social injustice which are singled out as Israel's disobedience in the unfolding story of the Bible. On account of their disobedience, God's plan to restore his dwelling and kingdom in the world through Israel and the Davidic kingship was halted.

Instead judgement was proclaimed on, and befell, Israel, namely loss of land, death by the sword, famine and pestilence on the land, and captivity by foreign armies. God, through the curses foretold by Moses, had warned Israel of these judgements if they disobeyed.

As the story of the Bible unfolds we learn that Israel's destruction, which ended with the Israelites in exile, was not its end. This will be our subject in chapter 6. God, in honour of his promises to Abraham, proclaimed through the pre-exilic prophets the restoration of Israel. The restoration of Israel would result in the Israelites' return to the land, their restoration as God's people under a new covenant, the restoration of the Davidic kingship in a promised new David, and the restoration of the temple and Jerusalem as God's dwelling. Israel would return to the land with abundance, peace, and security under the new David. In the face of their delay, the promises of Israel's restoration would be repeated through the post-exilic prophets. They would further be repeated in the face of their prolonged delay in the book of Daniel.

This scenario meant that the Israelites would have received the blessings of abundant life on their return to the land. Their blessings would attract nations to YHWH in Zion because YHWH would dwell there and the nations would want his blessings of abundant life. Their flocking to Zion would make them know YHWH and obey his laws, thus experiencing abundant life as a part of God's kingdom. Alongside this, the promised new David would secure peace in the land and enforce social justice. He would also expand Israel as God's kingdom to the ends of the world by subjugating nations and incorporating them into Israel. The promises of the restoration of Israel and the Davidic kingship thus pointed to God's intentions to still use both in line with his promises to Abraham, to restore his dwelling and kingdom in the world.

However, we shall also discuss in chapter 6 the paradigm shift in the Second Temple period (or intertestamental period) of the Israelites' worldview. This paradigm shift is evident in translations of the Bible at the time and in Jewish devout literature – the LXX, Apocalyptic Literature, Pseudepigraphy, and Qumran texts. In this new worldview the world was perceived, in more drastic ways, as two dimensional: the earthly world and the heavenly (or non-material, spiritual) world. This was a cosmological dualism where the visible earthly world was populated with physical entities and human beings while the largely invisible heavenly world was perceived to be populated with spiritual realities and beings (some humanlike and some not). The Israelites in this period began to have elaborate beliefs in the spiritual restoration of God's dwelling and kingdom. These beliefs would provide a hospitable ground to the spiritual nature of Israel's restoration and corresponding spiritual restoration of God's dwelling and kingdom (which take place in Jesus Christ as is evident in the unfolding of the story in the New Testament). The spiritual nature of the restorations would lend themselves to the view that they were thereby typologically fulfilled. The earthly realities in the story of the Bible in the Old Testament are types that are restored in their spiritual antitypes in the development and conclusion of the story of the Bible in the New Testament.

We will show in chapters 7, 8, and 9 how the restoration of Israel as prophesied takes place spiritually (but typologically) in Christ, and how through him God is restoring his dwelling and kingdom in the world. God in Christ will ultimately restore his dwelling and kingdom fully in the world, resulting in a new creation, a new heaven and earth. More specifically, my focus in chapter 7 will be on the restoration of David's dynasty that took place in Christ. This new David sat on David's throne; not in the king's palace in Jerusalem, but at God's right hand in heaven. In the continuing story of the Bible in the New Testament, we will see that God was restoring his kingdom also through him (and will continue to do so until all his enemies are subjugated or destroyed). However, God's kingdom is not simply the earthly theocratic kingdom of Israel in Zion in the promised land. It is now both earthly and heavenly. Its subjects are not just the generations of those currently on earth, who believe in God and his son, the Lord Jesus, but believing Jews and gentiles from past generations as well who will all be together when the dead in Christ will be resurrected. Jesus Christ as God's king, the new David, will bring peace in the world and to all under his kingship by destroying all the enemies of God and his people.

In chapter 8 we will turn our attention to the spiritual restoration of Israel that took place, and continues to take place, in Christ. According to the unfolding story of the Bible in the New Testament, the people of Israel being restored as the people of God are those with faith in God and his son, the Lord Jesus Christ. Believing Jews and gentiles universally and transgenerationally are now the people of God, and not simply the physical descendants of Jacob. God has now, with believing Jews and gentiles, his promised new covenant. Despite this kind of restoration, the vocation of God's people remained the same: they are set apart for God's use to restore his dwelling and kingdom in the world as God's royal priesthood. We shall demonstrate from our New Testament reading that the kingdom of God does not grow in the world by the nations' attraction to Zion on account of Israel's blessings of abundant life. Rather, the kingdom of God grows now through believers' proclamation of the gospel which enables people who believe it and repent to enter the kingdom.

In chapter 9 our focus will be on the spiritual restoration of the temple and Jerusalem, that took place and continues to take place in Christ. According to the unfolding story of the Bible in the New Testament, God's dwelling once again with Israel is fulfilled by his dwelling first in Jesus the promised Davidic king. Subsequently, God dwells through his Spirit in believing Jews and gentiles individually and collectively. His dwelling in believing Jews and gentiles is on account of their oneness with Jesus, because he is the head of the body they are a part of, and he is the anglestone of God's house of which they are a part as living stones. God's dwelling with his people is enroute to the full restoration of his dwelling in the world with human beings, which he shall do in the Jerusalem above. Believing Jews and gentiles in some mystical sense have a residence in this new Jerusalem. The result is that for now, God's people have a sort of dual experience of on the one hand being God's dwelling on earth, and on the other dwelling with him in the heavenly realm. Ultimately, they will both dwell with God in the new Jerusalem when God brings the city and thereby makes the whole world his dwelling with humans.

2

Dawn and Loss of God's Dwelling and Kingdom

The key to understanding the story of the Bible lies in making sense of creation stories in Genesis and elsewhere. These stories are not a discourse with a lot of literary detail telling us everything we would like to know about how God created the world. Rather, they are brief stories imbued with numerous examples of symbolism, whose meanings are foundational for understanding the purposes of God for creation, what jeopardized those purposes, and God's plan for restoring those purposes. For this reason, these stories are foundational for the rest of the story of the Bible. From the symbolism in the stories of creation, we shall isolate God's purposes for creating the world before discussing what went wrong and how God responded to the crisis.

God's Dwelling and Kingdom in the World

God created the world to be his dwelling with human beings. This purpose is symbolized in the garden of Eden. In one of the two creation accounts in Genesis (Gen 2:4–24), the garden of Eden is presented in a number of ways as God's own dwelling. This portrayal is seen, for example, in God's full accessibility to human beings within the garden. The proximity and dialogue between God and human beings symbolized direct and unlimited access to God which human beings had. This kind of access to God was possible because humans were living with him in his dwelling. In other words, the garden of Eden was God's house, and human beings were living with him; as such they were in "the presence of the LORD God" (Gen 3:8).[1]

---

1. All quotations in this study, unless otherwise indicated, are from the NRSV.

Creation is also depicted as God's dwelling by the use of verbs that explain the duties of human beings in the garden; "the LORD took the man and put him in the Garden of Eden to till it and keep it" (Gen 2:15). The verbs to "work" (*ʾābad*) and to "keep it" (*shamar*) are used in subsequent biblical literature to describe priestly duties in the tabernacle and the temple. As such the words are associated with God's house. To give a few examples, YHWH said through Moses that, "the Levites shall keep guard (*šāmar*) over the tabernacle of the testimony" (Num 1:53; see also Num 18:4). The Levites also "shall keep watch (*šāmar*) over the furnishing of the tent of meetings" (Num 3:8). In the case of the sons of Gershon in relation to service in God's house, YHWH said, "This is the service of the clans of Gershonites in serving (*ʾābad*) and bearing burdens; they shall carry the curtains of the tabernacle and the tent of meeting" (Num 4:23–26). The use of *ʾābad* and *šāmar* to designate the duties of human beings in the Garden, therefore, implied that the Garden was God's dwelling in which human beings were to serve.

Creation's depiction as God's house is further seen when human beings sin against God: "And they heard the sound of the LORD God walking (*mithallēk*) in the Garden" (Gen 3:8). The hitapel form of the verb *halak* used for God's walking here (used in a participle form: *mithallek*) is a reflexive form that, as Hamilton observes[2] "suggests iterative and habitual aspects" and is therefore suited to communicate that God was taking a walk in his residence. The twinning of this verb with one's residence is also clarified in a promise which YHWH gave to the people of Israel in regard to dwelling with them, that contains the verb indicating God's movement within his residence. YHWH declared, "I will place my dwelling in your midst . . . And I will walk (*mithallēk*) among you" (Lev 26:11–12). Elsewhere Moses declared, "the LORD your God travels (*mithallēk*) along with your camp" (Deut 23:14) because God's house, the tabernacle, was in the midst of the people of Israel and was carried along wherever they went.

Creation's depiction as God's house is also seen in the design of the tabernacle and the temple in the Old Testament, both of which mirror the garden of Eden, suggesting that the garden was God's dwelling. Understanding the tabernacle and temple as replicas of the garden of Eden is supported by numerous similarities between the two and the garden of Eden. For example, the entrance to the tabernacle and temple was through the east (Ezek 43:1–4; 42:12; 44:1; 46:12; 47:1), which paralleled the entrance to the garden which was

---

2. Victor P. Hamilton, *The Book of Genesis Chap. 1–17*, NICOT (Grand Rapids: Eerdmans, 1990), 192.

on the eastern side (Gen 3:24). Cherubim icons guard the Ark (Exod 25:18), which is God's throne, corresponding to cherubim guarding God's Garden (Gen 3:24). Cherubim also adorn the tabernacle (Exod 26:1) and the temple (1 Kgs 7:27–38; Ezek 41:18–20). This correspondence is also seen in the biblical literature in references where, for example, a psalmist refers to himself as "a green olive tree in the house of God" (Ps 52:8). The psalmist also refers to the righteous as flourishing trees planted in God's house:

> The righteous flourish like the palm tree,
>   and grow like a cedar in Lebanon
> They are planted in the house of the LORD
>   they flourish in the courts of our God. (Ps 92:12–13)

Moreover, the similarities between the Garden and temple are seen in references to a river in Jerusalem where the temple was located:

> There is a river whose streams make glad the city of God,
>   the holy habitation of the most high. (Ps 46:4; cf. Ezek 47:1–12)

All these examples of the similarities between the tabernacle and the temple on the one hand, and the garden of Eden on the other, point to the view that the garden of Eden is God's house.

The garden of Eden is also seen as God's dwelling with human beings when it is referred to in biblical literature as God's garden. The following examples make this clear. The narrator in Genesis comments that Lot compared the Jordan valley with God's garden on account of the availability of water (Gen 13:10). YHWH through the prophet Isaiah talks of a time when Zion's waste places will become like YHWH's garden (Isa 51:3). YHWH also in his lament over Tyre refers to Tyre as once being in Eden, his garden (Ezek 28:13). If the garden of Eden was God's garden, then it must have been a part of his residence given the inextricable link between a house and its garden. The latter is dependent on the former; they cannot be disassociated.

To give a last example, creation is depicted as God's dwelling in the following words:

> And on the seventh day God finished his work which he had done, and he rested (*šābat*) on the seventh day from all his work which he had done. So God blessed the seventh day and hallowed it, because on it God rested from all which he had done in creation. (Gen 2:2)

A literal understanding of these words in relationship to the preceding story may lead one to conclude simply that God worked for six days to create the world and rested on the seventh. In biblical literature rest is the cessation of labour, so for example, "Six days shall work be done; but the seventh day is a sabbath of complete rest, a holy convocation; you shall do no work" (Lev 23:3). It could also be the cessation of labouring the land, "but in the seventh year there shall be a sabbath of complete rest for the land . . . you shall not sow your field nor prune your vineyard" (Lev 25:4). However, there is more to God's rest after he created the world besides what the literal understanding reveals; there is symbolism too that points to creation as God's dwelling. This symbolism is captured in a key text in later biblical literature that relates God's rest to his house. By means of a synonymous parallel poem, God's rest and residence are seen to naturally belong together in the words of YHWH thus:

> This is my resting place (*menuḥāti*) forever
> here I will reside, for I have desired it. (Ps 132:14)

Here YHWH's rest and house are indivisible because YHWH rests not in any other place but in his house (the temple). Moreover, God's house, the temple, is also referred to as YHWH's resting place by the psalmist when he pleads to God to take up residence there:

> Rise up, O LORD, and go to your resting place (*menuḥatekā*),
> you and the ark of your might. (Ps 132:8)

Creation, then, is presented as YHWH's house in which he appropriately rested after he completed building it. Walton aptly puts it this way, "He furbishes it, puts people in it, and takes his repose (Sabbath) in 1:1–2:3."[3]

We conclude this discussion by noting that the idea of the world as God's dwelling, although expressed in symbolic ways in the creation account, is not alien to subsequent biblical literature. We encounter the notion of the world as God's dwelling with humans (as an invisible reality) when in God's presence Isaiah hears angels proclaim that the whole earth is full of YHWH's glory (Isa 6:3). We also encounter the view of the world as God's dwelling in the desire of the psalmist that the whole earth should be full of God's glory (Ps 72:19; see also Num 14:21). In these cases, the earth is said to be God's dwelling in the same way as YHWH's temple is, which when it was built was filled with God's glory (a signal that he occupied it). Lastly, we encounter the notion of

---

3. John H. Walton, *Genesis*, NIV Application Commentary (Grand Rapids: Zondervan, 2001), 147.

the world as God's dwelling as a future hope, which is the destiny of the world, that the world will be full of the knowledge of YHWH (Isa 11:9; Hab 2:14).

Another purpose behind God's creation of the world was for it to be a part of his kingdom. This purpose is symbolized in God having a throne. In synonymous parallel poems, the psalmists brought together God's reign and seat as one and the same:

> God is king over the nations;
> God sits on his holy throne. (Ps 47:8)

> The LORD is king; let the peoples tremble!
> He sits enthroned upon the cherubim; let the earth
> quake! (Ps 99:1)

YHWH was also seen as ruling over all because his throne was established in heaven:

> The LORD has established his throne in the heavens,
> and his kingdom rules over all. (Ps 103:19)

The significance of the Psalter's view is the understanding that God's throne is the seat of his power, and where he reigns over his kingdom. This thesis is also clear when we consider that what takes place wherever God's throne is mentioned in Old Testament biblical literature has to do with some form of rule (commands, judgements, authorisations, and the like). In Micaiah's vision of God, for example, YHWH sat on his throne to "chair" his council: "I saw the LORD sitting on his throne, with all the host of heaven standing beside him . . . And the LORD said, 'who will entice Ahab'" (1 Kgs 22:19–20). In Daniel, too, we have the same event. In his vision of the Ancient of days seated on a throne, he saw him "chair" the court sitting in judgement (Dan 7:10). From his throne God issues commands and authorizes. It is also from his throne that God gave power to one "like a human being" (Dan 7:13) to rule and have an everlasting kingdom (Dan 7:13–14). In a vision of God, Isaiah saw YHWH seated on a throne (Isa 6:1) from where he was sent to the people of Israel: "Then I heard the voice of the Lord saying, 'Whom shall I send, and who will go for us?' And I said, 'Here am I; send me!' And he said, 'Go, and say to this people'" (Isa 6:8–9).

Since God's throne and house are inseparable, his house, therefore, is where his kingdom is and where he rules over it, and viceversa. Inseparability of God's dwelling and kingdom is also demonstrated in the design of God's house, the tabernacle and later the temple. Old Testament literature makes clear in a number of instances that the ark is God's throne or hosts his throne, which is his mercy seat.

> Make one cherub at one end, and another cherub at the other; of one piece with the mercy seat you shall make the cherubim at its two ends. The cherubim shall spread out their wings above, overshadowing the mercy seat . . . You shall put the mercy seat on top of the ark . . . There I will meet you, and from above the mercy seat, from between the two cherubim that are on the ark of the covenant. (Exod 25:19–22; cf. Num 7:89)

When the temple was built in Jerusalem the ark of the covenant was brought into the inner room (*debir*) under the wings of the cherubim; "the priests brought the ark of the covenant of the LORD to its place, in the inner sanctuary of the house, in the most holy place" (1 Kgs 8:6). This is because God would need his seat, the ark (1 Sam 4:4; 2 Sam 6:2) in his house. Indeed, after the ark was brought into the temple his glory filled it (which is an indirect way of saying that God occupied it).

Furthermore, the linkage between God's house and his throne is also evident in the Psalms. The psalmist declared:

> The LORD is in his holy temple;
> the LORD's throne is in heaven. (Ps 11:4)

By means of a synonymous parallel poem, the psalmist brought together as inseparable YHWH's house and his throne which are in heaven. In his mind God's throne and house were inextricably linked. The psalmist also referred to YHWH's temple as his footstool:

> Let us go to his dwelling place;
> Let us worship at his footstool. (Ps 132:7; see also Ps 99:5)

In doing so, he closely associated God's house with his throne. This intimacy is harmonious with the design of the temple which had his throne in the inner room as we pointed out above.

It is worth noting here that some of those who offered prayers to YHWH were also aware that God's throne was in his residence. King Hezekiah in his time of need, for example, addressed YHWH as "who are enthroned above the cherubim" (Isa 37:16). This reference alluded to God's house where the ark of the covenant was underneath the cherubim in the inner room of the temple.

Finally, the pronouncements of YHWH himself point to the intimate relationship between his dwelling and his throne from where he rules. Through Isaiah, for example, YHWH spoke of the temple as the place of his feet (Isa

60:13). YHWH through the same prophet spoke that "heaven is my throne and the earth my footstool" (Isa 66:1), thereby fostering an understanding of both as his residence to counter the notion human beings can build him a house. The proclamation from Micah that YHWH would rule from Mount Zion, his residence (Mic 4:7), made more sense when one was aware that God's throne is inseparable from his house. Through Ezekiel, YHWH refers to the temple as "the place of my throne and the place of the soles of my feet" when speaking to Ezekiel (Ezek 43:7). From this perspective, the remarks of Jesus that heaven is God's throne or where God's throne is, and the earth is his footstool (Matt 5:34–35) are clarified as meaning that heaven is God's house.

The yoking, therefore, of God's dwelling and throne point to God's design for creation, namely that God made the world to be a part of his kingdom where he intended to rule over the world from his dwelling. This intention is also found and supported by non-Genesis accounts of creation in biblical literature. These non-Genesis accounts of creation are within the context of the ancient Near Eastern worldview of a pre-existing world of chaos which preceded creation. Creation of the world was in essence a reversal of the chaos by some creative power of a deity who imposed his/hers/its kingship (order) by stopping the chaos. Although precreation is commonly referred to as a world of chaos, what is described transcends the literal meaning of the word to include various states such as darkness and fluidity, which are all hostile to the life which humans experience. As Clifford points out, "precreation in many ancient texts was a state of inertia, nonmotion, absence of key elements of society, nonsolidity, and total darkness."[4]

In biblical literature, there is reference to precreation in Genesis (Gen 1:2) as a "formless" (*tohu*), "empty" (*bohu*) and "dark" (*ḥišek*) and covered with deep water (*tᵉhom*). YHWH revealed to those having, or influenced by, this ancient Near Eastern worldview, that he is the creator. He imposed his kingship on precreation by reining in the chaos and simultaneously creating the world. YHWH did this through controlling the sea which symbolized a powerfully dangerous and unpredictable deadly force.[5] He also destroyed the creatures of chaos: the sea dragon (Leviathan), and the chaos monster (Rahab). The dragon and monster represented chaos personified in the ancient world,

---

4. Richard J. Clifford S. J., "Creation Ex Nihilo in the Old Testament/Hebrew Bible," in *Creation "ex nihilo": Origin, Developments, Contemporary Challenges*, eds. Gary A. Anderson and Markus Bockmuehl (Notre Dame: University of Notre Dame Press, 2017), 57.

5. See also Christopher Connery, "There Was No More Sea: The Supersession of the Ocean, from the Bible to Cyberspace," *J. Hist. Geogr.* 32.3 (2006).

by virtue of their taxonomic anomaly, evil and repulsion, and power.[6] Having imposed form on the sea and wedded it, and having destroyed the monster and the dragon, God created the world – day, night, the sun, moon, stars, the seasons (i.e. the world and all in it):

> God my king is from old,
>   working salvation in the earth.
> You divided the sea by your might . . .
> You crushed the heads of Leviathan;
>   you gave him as food for the creatures of the wilderness.
> You cut openings for springs and torrents;
>   you dried up ever-flowing streams.
> Yours is the day, yours also the night;
>   you established the luminaries and the sun.
> You fixed all the bounds of the earth;
>   you made summer and winter. (Ps 74:12–17)

> You rule the raging of the sea;
>   when its waves rise, you still them.
> You crushed Rahab like a carcass;
>   you scattered your enemies with your mighty arm.
> The heavens are yours, the earth also is yours;
>   the world and all that is in it –
> you have founded them. (Ps 89:9–11)

There are other references in biblical literature to creation of the world by YHWH out of precreation chaos (for example, Ps 104:5–9; Job 26:10–14; 38:8–11; Isa 51:9–10; Jer 5:22). The two we have quoted above suffice to clarify that creation and God as king are tied together in the sense that creation is a product of God's kingship, of his order and rule (and a part of it as well). As soon as God created the world, it became a part of his kingdom. In consequence, the dawn of his kingdom in the world coincides with the moment he created it.

As his dwelling and a part of his kingdom, the world had nothing hurtful. The world then was all "good" in God's sight and was characterized with delight ("out of the ground the LORD God made to spring up every tree that is pleasant to the sight" – Gen 2:9). It was also characterized with abundance. This abundance is symbolized by plenteous trees for food (Gen 2:9), by the presence of precious metal in gold, bdellium, and onyx (Gen 2:12), and by

---

6. See for more David D. Gilmore, *Monsters: Evil Beings, Mystical Beasts, and All Manner of Imaginary Terrors* (Philadelphia: University of Pennsylvania Press, 2003), 21.

rivers (Gen 2:10–14). In addition, the world was also to be characterized by life as symbolized by the tree of life (Gen 2:9) which was available amongst the many trees as well as in the rivers watering the garden. All this was because the world was then a part of God's kingdom and as such characterized by joy, abundance, and life ("abundant life" from here on).

Abundant life as the state of life in God's kingdom is alluded to in later biblical literature, albeit mostly expressed as the future destiny of God's people. Revelation best captures this state of life where "death will be no more; mourning and crying and pain will be no more" (Rev 21:4) when God's dwelling is once again with human beings. Abundant life is captured too in Isaiah when through the prophet YHWH talked of a world to come, where "They will not hurt nor destroy on all my holy mountain for the earth will be full of the knowledge of the LORD as the waters cover the sea" (Isa 11:9). YHWH, again, through Isaiah, talked of a coming time when he will host a feast for all peoples, destroy death and wipe away their tears (Isa 25:6–8). In Ezekiel's vision, such life is manifest in the abundance and life provided by the river that flowed from God's dwelling (Ezek 47:1–12).

Abundant life is also captured in Paul's discussion of the resurrection. He writes that God's kingdom is to be inherited by the imperishable: "flesh and blood cannot inherit the kingdom of God, nor does the perishable inherit the imperishable" (1 Cor 15:50). Rather, God's kingdom is to be inherited by glory and power, and has heirs who have a spiritual body, thus are not subject to weakness and mortality (1 Cor 15:42–44). Such abundant life is the opposite of the current experience of human life, which is one of weakness, dishonour and mortality, with their associated pain and misery. Paul teaches that like a seed, this experience of human life must be sown through death to give way to the experience of a new life, abundant life, by those who have believed the gospel at the resurrection when death is destroyed (1 Cor 15:50–57). In a different epistle Paul also alludes to abundant life as the quality of life in God's kingdom when he says, "For the kingdom of God is not food nor drink but righteousness and peace and joy in the Holy Spirit" (Rom 14:17).

Besides support of the notion of abundant life as a characteristic of the kingdom of God drawn from eschatological biblical texts, we also have a psalm that points to this. A psalmist expressed the conviction that abundant life was always to be found where God dwelt, in his kingdom:

> You show me the path of life.
> In your presence there of fullness of joy;
> in your right hand are pleasures for evermore. (Ps 16:11)

Humans as Kings over Creation

The last purpose behind God's creation of the world I wish to discuss is centred on the role of human beings within it. In the accounts of Genesis, the creation of human beings is distinguished from the rest of creation thereby making them unique. It is only human beings who are created in the image (*ṣelem*) and likeness (*dᵊmut*) of God (Gen 1:26–27). As I shall make clear, this nature of human beings symbolically communicates God's purposes for creation, namely, that God created human beings to rule over his creation according to his pleasure.

Image (*ṣelem*) in biblical literature is most commonly used to signify representation, with the most common type of representation being that of a deity, represented by a physical object. For example, we have references to images of Baal, the god of the Canaanites, within the worship sites of the Canaanites which YHWH commanded the people of Israel to destroy; "destroy all their cast images (*ṣelem*), and demolish all their high places" (Num 33:52). In the book of 2 Kings the people of Israel "went to the house of Baal, and tore it down; his altars and his images (*ṣᵊlāmāyw*) they broke in pieces (2 Kgs 11:18). In the prophets, images were referred to as idolatrous because the people of Israel fashioned and worshipped them and the gods they represented, instead of worshipping YHWH their God: "Did you bring me sacrifices and offerings the forty years in the wilderness, O house of Israel? You shall take up Sakkuth your king, and Kaiwan your star-god, your images (*ṣalmêkem*) which you have made for yourselves" (Amos 5:25–26). Image as the representation of deity is the prevalent use of image in biblical literature. Human beings therefore were made in the image of God in order to represent him in the world.

However, an entity cannot represent what it does not resemble in form or in function. There is no doubt about such a connection with human beings because they are also made in the likeness of God, which means, as we shall shortly see, in ways that resemble God. In biblical literature likeness means "similar to." For example, "King Ahaz sent to the priest Uriah a model (*dᵊmut*) of the altar, and its pattern, exact in all its details" (2 Kgs 16:10) of what he saw in Damascus, the capital of Assyria. In the narrative of Daniel's visions, Daniel was touched by one "in human form (*dᵊmut*)" (Dan 10:16), that is to say one who looked like a human being. As another example, YHWH through the prophet Isaiah asked rhetorically: "To whom will you liken (*damah*) God, or what likeness (*dᵊmut*) compare with him?" (Isa 40:18). Human beings were created to be representatives of God in the world, to whom, for this reason, they bear resemblance. The question that forces itself on us then is this: In what ways were human beings to represent God, and in what ways were they to resemble him? We answer this question below.

In the Genesis account of creation, God gives human beings dominion over the rest of creation immediately after declaring his intention to make those human beings in his own image. This sequence is repeated, but in the second instance the will and intentions are actualized, since God does create human beings in his image and immediately after commands them to rule over all creation:

> Then God said, "Let us make humankind in our image, according to our likeness. And let them have dominion over the fish of the sea and over the birds of the heavens and over the cattle and over all the wild animals of the earth and over every creeping thing that creeps on the earth."
>
> So God created man in his own image,
> in the image of God he created them;
> male and female he created them . . .
>
> and God said to them "Be fruitful and multiply and fill the earth and subdue it; and have dominion over the fish of the sea and over the birds of the air and over every living thing that moves upon the earth." (Gen 1:26–28)

Twice the narrative of the creation of humans in God's image is followed by God's command to humans to have dominion. Repetition of this sequence suggests that human beings were to represent God by ruling over creation. Interpreting the plot of the narrative in this way is supported in the first case by the use of the Hebrew verb for rule (*radah*). This verb, as Wenham explains, is a purpose clause which when taken into consideration renders Genesis 1:26 thus: "Let us make man in our image, according to our likeness, that they may rule the fish of the sea."[7] This conclusion is further supported by an interpretation of Genesis within the ancient Near Eastern background which, as pointed out by Middleton, show that kings as images of a deity guaranteed order on earth.[8]

Human beings representing God as rulers in the world is echoed too by the psalmist in a psalm related to creation:

---

7. Gordon Wenham, *Genesis 1–15*, WBC (Nashville: Nelson, 1987), 3–4.

8. J. Richard Middleton, *Liberating Image: The Imago Dei in Gen 1* (Grand Rapids: Bazos Press, 2005), 110, 119–21.

> When I look at your heavens, the work of your fingers,
>> the moon and the stars that you have established;
> what are human beings that you are mindful of them,
>> mortals that you care for them?
> Yet you have made them a little lower than God
>> and crowned him with glory and honour
> you have given them dominion over the works of your hands;
>> you have put all things under their feet,
> all sheep and oxen, and also the beasts of the field,
>> the birds of the air, and the fish of the sea,
> whatever passes along the paths of the seas. (Ps 8:3–8)

The psalmist against the background of the grandeur of the night sky wonders why God is mindful of human beings. The answer is clear: for royalty, to rule. To be created for royalty is an honour bestowed on humanity by God. The symbolism of the nature of human beings as creatures made in the image, therefore, is in communicating that human beings were created to represent God as rulers of his creatures in the world.

In the story of creation human beings were designed to live for God's pleasure. The implication of this design is that human beings were to be worshippers of God. Again, the sequence in the plot of the story where immediately after creating humans God gave them commandments concerning what they were supposed to do and not do, suggests that they were meant to rule according to his pleasure. In other words, human beings were required to act in certain ways and to play certain roles because they had been made in the image of God. The first set of commandments are in Genesis 1:28: "Be fruitful and multiply, and fill the earth and subdue it, and have dominion over the fish of the sea and over the birds of the air and over every living thing that moves upon the earth." The second set of commandments is in Genesis 2:15–17 when God placed the human in the Garden to care for it: "You may freely eat of every tree of the Garden; but of the tree of the knowledge of good and evil you shall not eat" (Gen 2:17). These sets of commandments are indicative of God not creating human beings to be his representatives as rulers in ways independent of him, but to do so according to his wishes by obeying him. In addition, human beings living in obedience to God would result in their ruling of the world as God wished, and thereby in their resembling him.

There is further support of the view that being made in the image and likeness of God symbolized that human beings were designed to rule the world according to God's pleasure. For example, in the interpretation of "image of

God" against the ancient Near Eastern background, there is evidence of a relationship between image and the deity it represents. For example, in Mesopotamian royal ideology "image" was not simply a replica of the deity it represented, but was believed to manifest the deity it represented. In the words of Herring, the image is a "mode of presencing"[9] the deity, or an extension of the deity's presence. If we apply this understanding to Genesis, then the rule over creation by human beings must correspond to that of God whom they represent, because they are the eyes, ears, mouth, being and action of God. Human beings as creatures created in the image of God carry out divine rule over creation, and not their own. In this sense, human beings become the likeness of God since they resemble, or imitate, God in their rule by ruling according to his pleasure. From this perspective the significance of filling the earth can be appreciated. If human beings are a mode of "presencing" God in the world then humanity is "to fill it with God's presence and is to exercise the creator's own divine rule over his creation."[10] We could thereby argue that, in essence, the significance of the command to reproduce lies indirectly in God telling humans to be his representatives in the world.

We conclude by noting that this notion of human kingship of the world intimately tied to God's rule symbolized in humans' creation in the image and likeness of God is not alien to biblical literature. Biblical literature points to a correspondence between the role of humans on earth as rulers and that of God as the ruler of the whole cosmos. On this account the rule of humans on earth is modelled on the rule of God in heaven as the psalmist's praise of God implies:

> The heavens are the LORD's heavens
> but the earth he has given to human beings. (Ps 115:16)

This is a plausible conclusion if the psalm is read against the background of Genesis 1:27–28. In the visions of John, mention is made of the reign on earth by those redeemed by God; "they will reign on earth" (Rev 5:10). Mention is also made that God's servants "will reign forever and ever" (Rev 22:5) with both contexts making it clear that they rule according to God's will and pleasure.

---

9. Stephen Herring, *Divine Substitution: Humanity as the Manifestation of Deity in the Hebrew Bible and the Ancient Near East*, FRLANT 247 (Gottingen: Vandenhoeck & Ruprecht, 2013), 18. See also Zainab Bahrani, *The Graven Image: Representation in Babylonia and Assyria* (Philadelphia: University of Pennyslvania, 2003).

10. Crispin H. T. Fletcher-Louis, "God's Image, His Cosmic Temple and the High Priest," in *Heaven on Earth: The Temple in Biblical Theology*, eds. T. Desmond Alexander and Simon Gathercole (Carlisle: Paternoster, 2004), 84.

The picture which we have, derived from the symbolism embodied in the story of creation, is that God made the world to be his dwelling with human beings, and a part of his kingdom. Consequently, creation was characterized by abundant life. Creation was also anthropocentric, for human beings were especially made to represent God in creation by ruling according to his pleasure.

Loss of God's Dwelling and Kingdom

Unfortunately, human beings did not follow God's commands for their roles and life in the world, thus compromising the purposes of God for creation. Their disobedience was symbolized by their eating from the tree of the knowledge of good and evil whose fruits God had commanded them not to eat. Disobedience jeopardized God's dwelling and kingdom purposes for the world as well as their vocation as kings over creation as God's representatives in the world.

The world ceased to be a dwelling place of God with humans, symbolized by the expulsion of human beings from God's garden. Cherubim were stationed at the east gate to guard against human entry back into the garden (Gen 3:23–24). Thus humans had no access any longer to God's dwelling. For this reason, the previous closeness between human beings and God, by virtue of humans dwelling with God, was lost. There was now a fear of God, a desire to get away from him, "the man and his wife hid themselves from the presence of the LORD God" (Gen 3:8) which was previously not the case. From then on in biblical narrative, access to God became occasional, mediated, and limited in frequency. It also became available only to a select few, mainly prophets and priests. There was also some sense that God cannot be seen by human beings without deadly results. For this reason, for example, Hagar celebrated her vision of God without destruction; "'You are El-roi', for she said, 'Have I really seen God and remained alive after seeing him?'" (Gen 16:13). When Isaiah saw God, he cried apprehensive of his doom: "woe is me! I am lost, for I am a man of unclean lips, and I live among a people of unclean lips; yet my eyes have seen the King, the LORD of hosts! (Isa 6:5).

We pointed out earlier that dwelling and kingdom are yoked. The world ceasing to be God's dwelling with humans meant that it ceased also to be a part of God's kingdom. In consequence the world was no longer "good," and characterized by abundant life as it was before. Instead, it became a place characterized by death as symbolized by the inability of humans to have the fruits of the tree of life which were previously available to them (Gen 3:22). It also became a place characterized by pain, symbolized by the hardship humans would encounter in the course of their lives:

> Cursed is the ground because of you
> in toil you shall eat of it all the days of your life;
> thorns and thistles it shall bring forth for you. (Gen 3:17–19)

Pain, as a characteristic of the world, is also symbolized by the cursing of the earth, whose effects would, in principle, see the ground unable to flourish as before and yield abundant food for the use and enjoyment of humans. Where there was an abundance of pleasant trees that were all good for food (Gen 2:9), there would now be thorns and thistles (Gen 3:18). Humans were also condemned to hardship: "By the sweat of your face you shall eat bread" (Gen 3:19). They were also condemned to tilling the ground (Gen 3:23) contrary to enjoying it by tending it and caring for it.

It is worth noting here that God continued to exercise his sovereignty over all things in the world even though the world was no longer a part of his kingdom. We have many passages in biblical literature proclaiming the kingship of God particularly in the Psalms with pronouncements such as, "The LORD is king forever and ever" (Ps 10:16), or "For God is king of all the earth" (Ps 47:7; see also Pss 29:10; 47:2). Stating that the world was no longer a part of God's kingdom means that the manifestation of God's reign through humanity's experience of the blessings of abundant life – as seen when he created the world – is, save in limited ways, lacking in the world.

The world ceasing to be a part of God's kingdom also meant, correspondingly, that humans ceased to be God's representative in the world by not ruling according to his pleasure. In this regard there are those who have pointed out that beyond disobedience to God, the eating of the tree of the knowledge of good (*tôb*) and evil (*ra'*) is itself symbolic of humans' rejection of ruling as his representatives, in favour of doing it on their own. This view is on the understanding that distinguishing between what is good and what is evil was a matter for God and not human beings. As McConville explains, "the exercise of fundamental judgement about things is in reality a divine prerogative."[11] The determination of good and evil as belonging to God is alluded to in the commands of Moses when he exhorted the Israelites to "do what is right and good in the sight of the LORD" (Deut 6:18) in conjunction to keeping God's commandments (Deut 6:17). In addition, God as the determinant of good

---

11. J. Gordon McConville, *Being Human in God's World* (Grand Rapids: Baker Academic, 2016), 44.

and evil is confirmed by Solomon's prayers to discern between good and evil, which he could not do but asked God who determines it to help him know it (1 Kgs 3:3–9). This conclusion is further supported by the perception of David to be a divine being (*mal'āk*, an angel of God) because he could distinguish good from evil: "'The word of my lord the king will set me at rest'; for my lord the king is like an angel of God, discerning good and evil" (2 Sam 14:17; see also 2 Sam 19:27). Furthermore, in biblical literature, good is associated with obedience to God's laws and evil with the rejection of the same (Isa 5:20–24; Amos 5:13–14).

In eating from this tree, therefore, human beings were rejecting their place under God, and seeking autonomy from him and in ways that would rival him. It was "assuming divine autonomy in discerning and deciding what is beneficial to life and what is detrimental."[12] It was such a likeness with God that was off-limits to human beings. If humans were to have been given this particular role as part of their representation of God, they would transcend being his representatives and become gods in their own right. Such a role was contrary to the vocation which God gave human beings as his representatives. Reading the temptation narrative in this way makes a great deal of sense given the nature of the temptation. It was at its root about humans knowing good and evil and thus becoming like God. The serpent set it forth directly: "for God knows that when you eat of it your eyes will be opened, and you will be like God, knowing good and evil" (Gen 3:5). Adam and Eve fell for it – as well as for the lie that they would not die. From this perspective we may conclude then that the significance of the command not to eat from the tree of the knowledge of good and evil was indirectly a command to human beings to represent God by ruling according to his pleasure; a command that humans rebelled against.

The consequence of eating of the fruit of the tree of the knowledge of good and evil was that human beings would face death: "for in the day that you eat of it, you shall die" (Gen 2:17). The immediate form of death was metaphorical in terms of the quality of life which ensued. Instead of abundant life, human beings would now encounter life as harsh and difficult. We should note that ultimately such a quality of life would be a source of literal death, hence the inextricable connection between the two. Understanding death as metaphorical is supported by later biblical literature. In Deuteronomy, for example, life (blessings) and death (curses) were held out as possibilities for Israel depending on whether they would obey the law or disobey it:

---

12. James Luther Mays, "The Self in the Psalms and the Image of God," in *God and Human Dignity*, eds. R. Kendall Soulen and Linda Woodhead (Grand Rapids: Eerdmans, 2006), 37.

> See, I have set before you today life and prosperity, death and adversity. If you obey the commandments of the LORD your God . . . then you shall live and become numerous, and the LORD your God will bless you in the land that you are entering to possess. (Deut 30:15–16)

To obey the law was to choose abundant life by means of God's blessings: to name a few, abundance, health, longevity, and security which together would bring fullness of life (Deut 28:1–14). To disobey the law was to choose death and evil which would be manifest in curses, a quality of life characterized by, to name a few, scarcity, diseases, and vulnerability which would hasten death if not bring it (Deut 28:15–68). This outlook is echoed earlier in Leviticus. If the people of Israel would obey God's commandments, they would have YHWH's blessings of abundant life by means of rains, bounteous yields and great harvests, lack of hunger and so on (Lev 26:3–13). To the contrary, if the people of Israel disobeyed God's commandments, they would incur YHWH's curses (death) by means of lack of rains, death itself, desolation, plagues, sickness and so on (Lev 26:14–39).

Literal death as a consequence of disobedience followed the metaphorical one. Cain killed his brother Abel (Gen 4:8–16), Lamech, out of revenge, killed someone and declared that he would avenge seventy-sevenfold when wronged (Gen 4:23–24), and human beings beginning with Adam himself began to experience death literally (Gen 5:4–31). In the final analysis, humans' disobedience turned the world into, first, a place of hardship, and, second, into a place characterized by emotions, thoughts, and actions all of which did not bring joy and life but strife and death (both literally and metaphorically). Such was the extent of strife and death that YHWH himself had to reckon with it. He saw that the wickedness of humans was great "that every inclination of the thoughts of their hearts was only evil continually" (Gen 6:5). According to the story of the Bible the world was corrupt and filled with violence (Gen 6:11). There is an emphasis that the state of the world has turned into one that was unpleasant and horrible; "and God saw that the earth was corrupt; for all flesh had corrupted its ways upon the earth" (Gen 6:12). What God saw was the opposite of what he saw when he created the world; "God saw everything that he had made and indeed, it was very good" (Gen 1:31). The purposes of God creating the world were unravelled by humans' disobedience.

Abraham and Restoration

In the unfolding story of the Bible, there are indications that God acted to restore his dwelling and kingdom purposes for the world. Noah found favour in God's sight (Gen 6:8) so that when God rid the world of human beings by means of a flood, he and a small number of people were saved. This salvation offered hope that the world would once again be God's dwelling and a part of his kingdom.

It was in Noah and his sons that God first intended to restore the world to his kingdom. Therefore, just as he did with Adam and Eve, God commanded Noah and his sons to "Be fruitful and multiply and fill the earth" (Gen 9:1, 7). Just as it was with Adam and Eve, the command to be fruitful and multiply must have had in view humans' vocation to rule the world under YHWH by populating it and thus, as we discussed, filling it with God's presence. This is the reason why, just as with Adam and Eve, Noah and his sons were God's representatives in the world as his image bearers, "for in his own image God made humankind" (Gen 9:6). As God's representatives, they too were given dominion over the rest of creation, although not in the words of "subdue and rule" but in the following words "The fear and dread of you shall rest on every animal of the earth, and on every bird of the air, on everything that creeps on the ground, and on all the fish in the sea; into your hand they are delivered" (Gen 9:2).

Noah and his sons were also commanded not to murder (Gen 9:3–6). The command not to murder is significant because it is not just about them not committing murder, but also living in the world for God's pleasure, and consequently representing God in the world by ruling according to his wishes. We derive this significance from the fact that murder is not just simply an act of taking away life. It invariably carries with it emotions and thoughts displeasing to God. These emotions and thoughts include jealousy, cover-ups and dishonesty, hatred, bitterness, anger, greed, selfishness, and vengeance. It seems that this command was intensified in the command not to eat meat with an animal's blood because blood symbolized life, which they were not to take away:

> I give you everything. Only you shall not eat flesh with its life, that is, its blood. For your own lifeblood I will surely require a reckoning: from every animal I will require it and from human beings, each one for the blood of another, I will require a reckoning for human life. (Gen 9:3–5)

On this basis we can presume that just like Adam and Eve, Noah and those who were saved from the flood were to be God's representatives in the world according to the pleasure of YHWH.

According to the story of the Bible, however, the world did not become a part of God's dwelling and kingdom characterized by abundant life. On the contrary, it was still characterized by strife and death as symbolically seen in the actions of Noah and Ham and the subsequent ill will of Noah towards his grandson on account of his son Ham, by cursing him: "Cursed be Canaan; lowest of slaves shall he be to his brothers" (Gen 9:25).

In addition, human beings also rejected their role of ruling according to God's pleasure as was the case in Adam and Eve's eating from the tree of the knowledge of good and evil. This time, however, the rejection was seen in their desire to build a tower that reached the heavens. This desire was informed by their wish for a name: "let us build us build ourselves a city, and a tower with its top in the heavens, and let us make a name for ourselves" (Gen 11:4). In all likelihood making a name for themselves is a desire for immortality, which was a preserve for God. However, this immortality was not in the form of their persevering existence (which was beyond their power) but, rather, through some form of remembrance; of one living in the memory of those subsequent generations who hear about him/her. This form of immortality was priced, as the psalmist extols it, as a preserve for the righteous and not the ungodly:

> For the righteous will never be moved;
>   they will be remembered forever. (Ps 112:6)

It was even desired for a Davidic king, probably with the stability and good of the kingdom in view:

> May his name endure forever,
>   his fame continue as long as the sun. (Ps 72:17)

As for the preacher it seemed, such immortality was, very discouragingly to him, beyond the reach of both the wise and poor:

> The wise have eyes in their head,
>   but fools walk in darkness.
>
> Yet I perceived that the same fate befalls all of them. Then I said to myself, "What happens to the fool will happen to me also; why then have I been so wise?" . . . For there is no enduring remembrance of the wise or of fools, seeing that in the days to come all will have been long forgotten." (Eccl 2:14–16)

To the extent then that the desire to build a city that reached the heavens was for the people's name, it is likely symbolic of their desire to be like God. This desire to be like God may also be symbolized in the prospective building that would have reached the clouds, as the abode of God did (see Isa 14:14). Like Adam and Eve, they were not content with their role as God's representatives by ruling according to his dictates, but wanted to be like him and rule as such. Implicitly God pointed out that the effects of their desire to rule by themselves would be far worse if they were united: "Look, they are one people and they have all one language; and this is only the beginning of what they will do" (Gen 11:6). Confusing their languages was therefore God's way of breaking their unity and thereby forestalling their implied rebellious potential when they were united.

After the story of the tower of Babel, the story of the Bible turns to Abraham the son of Terah (Gen 11:26). YHWH called Abraham out of his ancestral home and from his family to go to a land he did not know. YHWH promised Abraham offspring, kings, land, and blessing to all nations:

> Now the LORD said to Abram, "Go from your country and your kindred and your father's house to the land I will show you. I will make of you a great nation, and I will bless you and make your name great, so that you will be a blessing. I will bless those who bless you, and the one who curses you I will curse; and in you all the families of the earth shall be blessed. (Gen 12:1–3)

> Behold my covenant is with you, and you shall be the father of a multitude of nations. No longer shall your name be Abram but your name shall be Abraham for I have made you the father of a multitude of nations. I will make you exceedingly fruitful, and I will make you into nations, and kings shall come from you. (Gen 17:4–6 ESV)

Through God's promises to Abraham, the stage was then set for the story of the restoration of God's dwelling and kingdom in the world through Abraham and Sarah, and their offspring on the land. Beginning from Genesis 18, this story occupies the rest of the Bible. Accordingly, the rest of the Bible's content revolves these promises: around Israel's journey to the land, Israel in the land, Israel in the land under the Davidic kingship, Israel in exile from the land, Israel back in the land but under foreign rule, and in Jesus, who is a Davidic king, and believing Israelites and gentiles, God's new people (the new Israel), who are formed in his wake.

One of the promises God gave Abraham hints at his intention to use him to restore his dwelling and kingdom in the world. This is the promise that all nations will be blessed through him. We discussed earlier that curses, when viewed from the perspective of their use in biblical literature, denote a quality of life that does not belong to God's kingdom and brings or hastens death. It is a state of living which is hostile to life. The opposite is the case with blessings, as alluded to earlier: blessings denote abundant life, the quality of life in God's kingdom. In consequence, Abraham becoming a blessing to all nations meant, in principle, that through him and his offspring the world would experience abundant life as it did in the beginning, by once again becoming a part of God's kingdom (see below). For this reason, blessings and abundant life are inextricable as terms referring by implication to the quality of life in God's kingdom, and thus to the presence of the kingdom of God. The blessing of nations through Abraham and Israel implies abundant life, and abundant life implies God's kingdom (thus my use of "blessings of abundant life" to imply the presence of God's kingdom throughout this study). Put differently, all nations being blessed through Abraham and his offspring was to say that all nations would come under God's kingdom and dwell with him as it was in the beginning. In the next chapter we shall discuss how this blessing to all nations was designed to take effect in the land through the promised offspring (Israel) and kings (the Davidic kings).

It is important to note here that the same promises of offspring and kings were also given to Sarah the wife of Abraham:

> As for Sarah your wife, you shall not call her Sarai, but Sarah shall be her name. I will bless her, and moreover I will give you a son by her. I will bless her, and she will give rise to nations; kings of people shall come from her. (Gen 17:15–16)

Consequently, Sarah became an integral part of God's dwelling and kingdom restoration plans because the promised offspring to Abraham would have to come from her womb. It is for this reason that the other children who Abraham had with other women besides Sarah were not considered as his offspring according to promise.

On the other hand, Israel was included in the promise of land which God gave Abraham:

> On that day the LORD made a covenant with Abram, saying, "To your descendants I give this land, from the river of Egypt to the great river, the river Euphrates, the land of Kenites, the Kenizzites, the Kadmonites, the Hittites, the Perrizzites, the Rephaim, the Amorites, the Canaanites, the Girgashites, and the Jebusites." (Gen 15:18–19)

Including Abraham's offspring in the promise of land implied that the blessing of all nations which God intended by Abraham would be fulfilled through both Abraham and his offspring, and not exclusively through Abraham. From Abraham we would have a nation according to God's promise, and through this nation God's promise of blessing-to-all-nations, given exclusively to Abraham, would be fulfilled. As we shall subsequently demonstrate in our study of the unfolding story of the Bible, the blessing of all nations which God intended to carry out through Abraham in the land, he would actually carry out through Abraham's descendants. Doing so would not nullify his promise to Abraham as the one through whom all the nations of the world would be blessed. This is because his descendants were his offspring, a part of him, according to God's promise, and therefore designed by God to be included in what he would do through him.

The above understanding is clarified by the inclusion of Abraham's offspring in the blessing-to-all-nations promise given to him: "and by your offspring shall all the nations of the earth gain blessing for themselves" (Gen 22:18; also Gen 26:4). Consequently, Abraham's offspring were, together with him, an integral part of God's dwelling and kingdom restoration plans as part of the promises given by God to Abraham. Being the product of God's promise to Abraham ensured that his offspring were together with him an integral part of God's restorative plans.

We conclude by noting that the rest of Genesis goes on to show God's faithfulness in keeping his promises to Abraham. There are a number of examples here. Abraham nearly lost his wife twice to another man before she had the chance to bear him the promised offspring (Gen 12:10–20; 20:1–18). He also nearly lost the land to Lot (Gen 13). In the story of Isaac, YHWH granted Abraham's son a wife and opened her womb to bear a child without whom God would have failed to keep his promise to Abraham (Gen 25:19). Isaac was led by God to Gerar to escape famine (Gen 26); had he died from it, God would have failed to keep his promise. Though Jacob was Esau's younger brother, the promise of offspring which God gave to Abraham was kept through him and not his older brother as was the custom (Gen 25:21–23). Ultimately, Jacob's name changed to Israel (Gen 32:28). It was from him that the offspring of Abraham had their name since all his sons were children of the promise from whom the twelve tribes of Israel trace their ancestry (Gen 49). For a last example, God preserved the offspring of Abraham before they became numerous in number by protecting them from famine through Joseph who was taken away to Egypt to prepare the way for their refuge there (Gen 37–46).

3

The Restoration of God's Dwelling and Kingdom via Israel

In concluding our last chapter we noted that it is through Abraham's grandchild, Jacob, the second born of his son Isaac, that the fulfilment of God's promise of offspring to Abraham is tracked. Jacob's children settled in Egypt where they became very many throughout the land (Exod 1:1–7). For this reason they were oppressed by the Egyptians. However God responded (Exod 2:23–25) and delivered them from the Egyptians through Moses, his prophet. He led them to the land he had promised them (Exodus, Leviticus, and Numbers). Israel entered and settled in the promised land, where they would dwell first under the leadership of men filled by God's Spirit (Deuteronomy, Joshua, and Judges) and later under the Davidic kings (1, 2 Samuel and 1, 2 Kings). In this chapter we will discuss how the fulfilment of God's promise of offspring and land to Abraham was meant to bring about the restoration of the world as a part of God's kingdom.

Israel and Restoration of God's Kingdom

Across the Red Sea and beyond, God guided the offspring of Israel and eventually led them to the foot of Mount Sinai (Exod 19). God's words through Moses at the foot of that mountain were fundamental to understanding Israel's vocation, within the perspective of God's promise to Abraham that all nations would be blessed through him.

> Now therefore, if you will indeed obey my voice and keep my covenant,
> you shall be my treasured possession among all peoples,
> for all the earth is mine;

> and you shall be to me a kingdom of priests, and a holy nation.
> These are the words that you are to speak to the people of Israel.
> (Exod 19:4–5)

It is apparent that this message was expressed in Hebrew poetic form. As such it contains clauses that ought to be read together for the message to be understood well. First YHWH tells Israel that if they obey his voice and keep his covenant (we shall discuss the synonymity of "keeping my covenant" with obeying God's voice in the conclusion to this section), they will become his most treasured possession (*sᵊgullâ* – used from here on). However, becoming YHWH's *sᵊgullâ* does not mean that other nations are not his because, as is pointed out in the clause which follows, all the earth (or nations) belong to YHWH. The meaning therefore of Israel becoming YHWH's *sᵊgullâ* if they obeyed him is that they would become, of all his possessions, his most treasured. Essentially Israel would be amongst God's property "his crown jewel, his masterwork, the one-of-a-kind piece."[1] Israel would become uniquely of extreme value to God.

Understanding Israel as God's *sᵊgullâ* is supported in later biblical literature. David referred to his *sᵊgullâ* which he brought to God's house in the context of his other possessions of gold, silver, bronze, iron, and wood; "Moreover, in addition to all I have provided for the holy house, I have a treasure (*sᵊgullâ*) of my own . . . because of my devotion to the house of my God I give it to the house of my God" (1 Chr 29:3). The preacher indirectly pointed out that it was customary for kings to have prized possessions amongst their possessions; "I also gathered for myself silver and gold and the treasure (*sᵊgullâ*) of kings (Eccl 2:8). Such an understanding is also supported by virtue of the fact that references in biblical literature to Israel as God's *sᵊgullâ* are always mentioned in comparison to other nations. For example "the LORD your God has chosen you to be for his own possession (*sᵊgullâ*) out of all the peoples that are on the face of the earth" (Deut 7:6; also Deut 14:2; 26:18).

Second, YHWH declared that Israel was to be a royal priesthood. Israel's royal priesthood would be a consequence of being God's *sᵊgullâ*. This conclusion is made clear when this clause, "and you shall be to me a kingdom of priests, and a holy nation," is considered as a parallel clause to the first one, "you shall be my treasured possession among all peoples." In keeping with Hebrew poetry's synthetic parallelism, the second clause should be viewed as advancing the thought of the first one by further defining it. Thus the message in plain

---

1. John I. Durham, *Exodus*, WBC 3 (Nashville: Thomas Nelson, 1987), 262.

terms would be understood as: "you will become my *sᵉgullâ* and therefore a royal priesthood and a holy nation." Israel as a holy people being the parallel to royal priesthood in that clause, is thus also a consequence of being God's *sᵉgullâ* (although it is not the subject of our discussion here).[2] Concretely, the designation of Israel as a royal priesthood because the nation was God's *sᵉgullâ* set Israel apart from all other nations (thus it was a holy nation). It also defined Israel's fundamental vocation: to be a blessing to all nations. Israel's vocation is in keeping with God's promise to Abraham because Israel was his offspring and a recipient with Abraham of the promise of land. To this we turn now.

In biblical literature priests had three distinct roles. First, they were attendants in God's house in ways similar to courtiers in the king's palace. This is clear in their designation as temple servants (Joel 1:13; see also Ezra 2:43; 2:58; Neh 3:26) and as God's servants: "Come bless the LORD, all you servants of the LORD, who stand by night in the house of the LORD" (Ps 134:1; see also Ps 135:1–2; Jer 33:21; Joel 1:9; 1:13; 2:17). It is also made clear in the view that they offered service in God's house (Exod 28:43; 30:20; 35:19; 39:41; Joel 1:13; Ezek 44:16; 45:4; 46:24) and in descriptions of their work revolving around service in God's house (Exod 28:43; Num 18:2; Deut 21:5; Ezek 44:16–17). Such was the extent of the role of priest that one Bible commentator noted, "'serving in the holy place' and 'priesting' are synonymous."[3] This understanding is supported by ancient Near Eastern apprehensions of priests as persons who waited on a god or gods residing in a temple: "In this abode there are servants who attend on him and fulfil his wants, the whole cult being designed essentially to provide for the needs of the deity."[4] In biblical literature the priests replaced old bread on the table (Lev 24:5–9) and dressed the lamps on the lamp stands every morning and evening, keeping them burning day and night (Exod 30:7–8; Lev 24:1–4; Deut 33:10).

Second, priests had a distinct service they offered in the temple: priests offered sacrifices, and presided over the sacrifices that others offered. Offerings of sacrifices are quite prominent. After the ordination of Aaron and his sons, God through Moses gave elaborate instructions on sacrificial offerings (Exod 29:10–18; 29:38–46; 30:1–10). There are also graphic descriptions of various

---

2. For a brief discussion on this see, Pancratius C. Beentjes, "'Holy People': The Biblical Evidence," in *A Holy People: Jewish and Christian Perspectives on Religious Communal Identity*, eds. M. Poorthius and J. Schwartz (Leiden: Brill, 2006).

3. Peter J. Leithart, "Attendants of Yahweh's House: Priesthood in the Old Testament," *JSOT* 85 (1999), 17.

4. M. Haran, "Priests and Priesthood," in *Encyclopedia of Judaism*, eds. Alan J. Avery-Peck, Jacob Neusner, and William S. Green (Leiden: Brill Academic, 1999).

types of sacrificial offerings to be brought by people to God, and presided over by his ministers the priests (Lev 1–7).

Third, priests represented the people before God. This can be seen in the symbolism in the vestments of the high priest. Aaron bore the names of the tribes of Israel on his priestly garments whenever he approached God in the temple's holy of holies: "So Aaron shall bear the names of the sons of Israel in the breastpiece of judgement on his heart when he goes into the holy place, for a continual remembrance before the LORD" (Exod 28:29). This symbolism of the high priest's vestments points to his intercessory role to bring the whole of Israel before God. Although they did not intercede for the whole of Israel, interceding for people to a lesser extent must also have been the role of other priests given this background.

We return to the relationship between Israel as God's *sᵉgullâ* and the Israelites' role as a royal priesthood. Israel among all nations was privileged to be a royal priesthood in the ways noted above by virtue of being YHWH's *sᵉgullâ*. As Hamilton succinctly points out, "Because they are the Lord's *sᵉgullâ*, Israel is able to stand before God, to enter into his presence, in a way no other people can."[5]

Priests were also supposed to give God's words to the people by means of "the Urim and Thummim" (Deut 33:8). Due to a paucity of relevant literature from the Bible and related contexts, there is no definitive answer to what exactly Urim and Thummim were beyond some sort of physical objects. They were closely associated with priests and knowledge of the will of God: "he shall stand before Eliazar the priest, who shall inquire for him by the decision of the Urim before the LORD" (Num 27:21; see also 1 Sam 28:6; Ezra 2:63). Consequently, as bearers of the Urim and Thummim (Exod 28:30; Lev 8:8), priests were to reveal God's will to people. Priests also declared God's word through the teaching of God's law: "you shall teach the people of Israel all the statutes that the LORD has spoken to them through Moses" (Lev 10:11; see also Deut 33:10; Ezek 44:23–24). God judged them through the prophets for not doing so (Jer 2:8; 18:18; Hos 4:4–6; Mal 2:7) or doing it for hire (Mic 3:11).

The priests' roles of offering, and presiding over, sacrifices to God and giving his word to the people, throw into sharp relief their function as mediators. The implication of those two priestly roles is that they mediated between YHWH and his people. This is captured so well in the words of De Vaux, that he is worthy of a full quotation:

---

5. Victor P. Hamilton, *Exodus: An Exegetical Commentary* (Grand Rapids: Baker Academics, 2011), 355.

> When the priest delivered a message, he was passing on an answer from God; when he gave an instruction, a *torah*, and later when he explained the Law, the *Torah*, he was passing on and interpreting teaching that came from God; when he took the blood and flesh of victims to the altar, or burned incense upon the altar, he was presenting to God the prayers and petitions of the faithful. In the first two roles he represented God before men, and in the third he represented men before God; but he is always an intermediary... The priesthood is an institution for mediation.[6]

Understanding priests as mediators between God and humans, as an implication of their roles, is captured directly in later biblical literature. In an extended reflection of its kind in the New Testament on the ministry of Jesus as a high priest who represents believers before God with mercy and sympathy (Heb 2:17–18; 4:14–16), the author of Hebrews states that "For every high priest... is appointed by God to act on behalf of men in relation to God" (Heb 5:1 ESV). To this we may add Paul's epistle to the Romans, where he understands his vocation as an evangelist to the gentiles as a priestly one because he represents God before gentiles by delivering his gospel of Christ to them. The goal of his proclamation is to have gentiles come to God, or approach God, in ways that are acceptable. In Paul's words, God has given him grace "to be a minister of Christ Jesus to the gentiles in the priestly service of the gospel of God, so that the offering of the gentiles may be acceptable" (Rom 15:16). Lastly in a direct quotation of Exodus 19:4–5, the purpose of royal priesthood is understood in the first epistle of Peter to be one of representing God to humans: "But you are a chosen race, a royal priesthood, a holy nation, God's own people" (1 Pet 2:9). In the epistle, the particular way of representing God is by the declarations of his wonderful deeds: "in order that you may proclaim the mighty acts of him who called you out of darkness into his marvellous light" (1 Pet 2:9).

Since Israel was to be a kingdom of priests, we should understand the nation's priestly vocation metaphorically as a nation that was to represent God to other nations – but how was it to be executed? Crucially, how was it related to the restoration of all nations to God's kingdom by their blessing through Israel (and thus through Abraham as alluded to in the last chapter)? We already pointed out that according to Exodus 19:4–5, the vocation of Israel as a kingdom of priests was contingent upon their obedience. By keeping God's

---

6. Roland De Vaux, *Ancient Israel: Its Life and Institutions,* trans. John McHigh (London: Darton, Longman & Todd, 1961), 375.

laws, Israel would experience the blessings of abundant life, having become a part of God's kingdom. The blessings of abundant life would be the means by which Israel would act as God's representative to other nations, and influence them to know YHWH and submit to his rule. Submitting to God's rule would make these nations become a part of his kingdom. In the language of blessings, Israel would be the first nation to be blessed with abundant life by God, and thereafter, as priests, used by God to spread his blessings of abundant life to other nations. This understanding of the priesthood of Israel is clarified in a section of Moses's address to Israel. Moses stated:

> Behold, I have taught you statutes and rules as the LORD my God commanded me, that you should do them in the land which you are entering to take possession of it. Keep them and do them; for that will be your wisdom and your understanding in the sight of the peoples, who, when they hear all these statutes, will say, "Surely this great nation is a wise *and* understanding people." For what great nation is there that has a god so near to it as the Lord our God is to us, whenever we call upon him? And what great nation is there, that has statutes and rules so righteous as all this law that I set before you today. (Deut 4:5–9)

From these words, we learn that Israel's obedience is valued for, and viewed from the perspective of, its impact on other nations. Such a perspective would logically be the case if Israel's obedience was connected to their blessings of abundant life as part of God's kingdom, which would thereby be the means of impacting other nations. It is precisely this connection that is being made by YHWH in this message through Moses his prophet. For this reason, if the Israelites kept God's laws on the land, they would be blessed, and other nations would take notice and consequently admire their laws and their God. Notice and admiration would naturally draw them to YHWH in Zion where he dwelt, because of their desire to share in Israel's blessings which YHWH alone could give. Their coming to Zion would lead to their knowledge of YHWH and obeying his laws (just as Israel was doing). As a result, these nations would have submitted to God's rule and received the blessings of abundant life as a part of God's kingdom. In the end, God's kingdom would be restored in the world by virtue of Israel's blessings of abundant life. The blessings of abundant life would have been the means by which Israel would become God's representatives to the nations of the world, causing them to know YHWH and consequently submit to his rule. This is the very reason for which YHWH designated Israel to be his name, praise and glory if they obeyed him (Jer 13:11).

It is important we bear in mind that the nations' knowledge of YHWH as God (the holy and/or most high) was critical to their turning away from their own gods and idols to submit to, and worship, YHWH. The blessings of abundant life enjoyed by Israel would force the nations to reckon with YHWH, who was responsible for them, and come to terms with his sovereign power as either exclusive (thus making YHWH holy in their eyes), or greater than their gods (thus making YHWH the most high). This knowledge would in turn make them abandon their gods and idols to submit to (obey his laws) and worship YHWH. This direct relationship between knowing YHWH and obeying him is clear in biblical literature. Knowing God was critical in making Israel obedient. YHWH accused the Israelites of disobeying him because they did not know him (Hos 4:1–3; Joel 2:26–27; Jer 4:22; 9:1–6).

God's laws were absolutely instrumental in the Israelites' fulfilment of their vocation on the promised land. For this reason, God gave the people of Israel his laws before they entered and settled on the land he had given them – laws that could be classified broadly as religious, ceremonial, ethical, civic, and criminal in nature. It was at the foot of Mount Sinai after God defined the identity and vocation of Israel that he gave them his laws and made a covenant with them. According to Exodus, God gave Israel his laws starting with the Ten Commandments (Exod 20:1–17), and then followed by laws concerning slaves (Exod 21:1–9), murder (Exod 21:12–17), violence (Exod 21:18–32), restitution (Exod 21:33–36), theft (Exod 22:1–15), seducing a virgin (Exod 22:16–17), sorcery, bestiality, and sacrifices (Exod 22:18–20), malice, injustice, false reporting, bribery, oppression of strangers (Exod 32:1–9), sabbaths for land and humans (Exod 23:10–12), feasts of unleavened bread, of harvest, and of ingathering (Exod 23:14–17). The whole content of Leviticus is virtually God's laws. These laws concerned offerings (Lev 1:1–6:7), priests and offerings (Lev 6:8–7:37), eating of holy things (Lev 10:12–20), clean and unclean animals (Lev 11), purification of women after childbirth (Lev 12), leprosy (Lev 13–14), secretions (Lev 15), day of atonement (Lev 16), animal killing and blood (Lev 17), sexual immorality (Lev 18), various laws on behaviour and attitude (Lev 19), punishments of various disobedience (Lev 20), feasts (Lev 23), Jubilee and sabbatical years (Lev 25), and vows (Lev 27).

After the generation that was given these laws had been wiped out, Moses gave God's people his laws once again before they made entry into the promised land: "Beyond the Jordan in the land of Moab, Moses undertook to expound this law as follows" (Deut 1:5). When he repeated the laws to them, he insisted that the same must not only be memorized and kept in their hearts: "give heed to the statutes and ordinances that I am teaching you to observe" (Deut 4:1), but he also directed that they must be taught to their children, "make them known to your children and your children's children" (Deut 4:9; also Deut 6:6–8). The centrality of God's laws to the people of Israel was not in any doubt. It should be clear to us by now that this was on account of the absolute necessity of obedience to these laws by Israel if they were to fulfil their priestly vocation in the land.

Curses would befall the Israelites in the land if they would not obey God's laws. The curses God promised would fall on them if they disobeyed him included insecurity, diseases, low crop yields, famine, and slavery (Lev 26:14–39; Deut 28:15–68). The ultimate end of the curses would be Israel's destruction: "All these curses shall come upon you, pursuing you and overtaking you until you are destroyed, because you did not obey the LORD your God" (Deut 28:45). The curses would also result in Israel's loss of the land. "You shall therefore keep all my statutes and all my ordinances, and observe them, so that the land to which I bring you to settle in may not vomit you out" (Lev 20:22; also Lev 18:28), or "you shall be plucked off the land which you are entering to possess" (Deut 28:63). It would also result in the exile of the few who would escape destruction: "The LORD will bring you, and your king whom you set over you to a nation that neither you nor your ancestors have known" (Deut 28:36; see also Deut 28:49–57).

Based on the consequences of disobedience – the loss of land and exile – we can conclude that the purpose for which God gave Abraham and Israel the land was for its use to bless all nations, that is, for its use to restore the world to his kingdom. This was the fundamental significance of the land, and justified their special inheritance. The land was the site on which the Israelites, being Abraham's offspring, would fulfil their priestly vocation, thereby becoming a territory of God's kingdom, and thus experiencing abundant life; a purpose well expressed by a psalmist:

> He gave them the lands of the nations,
>> and they took possession of the wealth of the peoples,
> that they might keep his statutes
>> and observe his laws. (Ps 106:44–45)

If Israel lived in obedience, the land would act as a magnet to bring other nations to God's kingdom, which was its purpose. If the Israelites would not fulfil their priestly vocation by obeying God in the land, they would be expelled from it, and, rather than being an attraction, they would be an object of scorn to other nations. The land was therefore to Israel a means to an end and not an end in itself.

The land's destiny as the beginning of the restoration of God's kingdom is hinted at in Deuteronomy, Exodus, and the Psalms. When Moses gives the law a second time to the people of Israel, he refers to the land God promised them as the rest (*mᵊnûḥah*): "for you have not yet come to the rest and to the inheritance which the LORD your God gives to you" (Deut 12:9). This reference in biblical literature clearly identified the promised land with YHWH's *mᵊnûḥah* (rest). The significance of this identification lies in the indivisibility of God's rest and dwelling, which we pointed out earlier. As God's *menuhāti*, the land was to be God's dwelling, and as such a part of his kingdom. In Exodus the song that Moses sang to YHWH refers to the land as the place which God made his house by his own hands:

> You bought them in and planted them on the mountain of your
>   own possession,
>   the place, O LORD, that you made your abode,
>   the sanctuary, O LORD, that your hands have established.
>   (Exod 15:17)

However, the land could only be God's dwelling and kingdom if the Israelites fulfilled their priestly vocation by obeying God. Without obedience, their land inheritance would become untenable as was the case with their forebears:

> For forty years I loathed that generation
>   and said, "They are a people whose hearts go astray
>   and do not regard my ways"
> Therefore in my anger I swore
>   "They should not enter my rest (*mᵊnûḥātî*)." (Ps 95:10–11)

Israel failed repeatedly, as we shall see in the next chapter, to keep God's laws, and was not blessed; it did not become a part of God's kingdom in the land. Consequently, the nation was not a blessing to other nations, because the Israelites could not play their role as priests by representing God to the nations through the blessings of abundant life, and influence them to want to know God who dwelt in Zion and to submit to his rule. In the course of their failure to keep God's laws, however, YHWH offered them chances to begin obeying him and thus fulfil their priestly vocation through their blessings of abundant life. Jeremiah's prophecy best captures such chances:

> If you return, O Israel,
>   says the LORD,
> if you return to me,
>   if you remove your abominations from my presence,

> and do not waver,
> > and if you swear, "As the LORD lives!" in truth, in justice,
> > > and in uprightness,
> >
> > then nations shall be blessed by him,
> > > and in him they shall boast. (Jer 4:1–2)

Since Israel did not turn back to YHWH and obey him, the curses pointed out by Moses befell the Israelites and they were accordingly destroyed, lost the land, and a remnant was exiled. However, mention was made of Israel's prospective priestly vocation, signifying God's intent to keep his promise to Abraham by using his offspring to restore the world to his kingdom. The servant songs in Isaiah which were given when a remnant of Israel was in exile can be understood as a reiteration of Israel's role as God's representative to the nations, to bring them under his kingdom. If we take it that the servant songs are about Israel, then it is clear that Israel's role as God's servant (a label used for priests as noted earlier) has to do with their impact on other nations. YHWH reminds his discouraged people, to whom he intends to restore their land, of their vocation in the servant songs: "I have given you as a covenant to the people, a light to the nations" (Isa 42:6) and "You are my witnesses says the LORD" (Isa 43:10). Accordingly, Israel was to be instrumental to God in drawing nations out of darkness and bondage to light and freedom (Isa 42:7). Israel as God's servant (priests) and witness are indeed a light for the benefit of the nations (Isa 42:6): "I will give you as a light to the nations, that my salvation may reach to the ends of the world" (Isa 49:6). However, Israel could fulfil this priestly vocation only through obedience to God.

From the discussion above, it clear that Israel's vocation in the land was to be a kingdom of priests representing God to the nations. God gave Israel the land in order for them to represent him to other nations and, as Abraham's offspring, lead them into his kingdom. However, they would represent God only if they were obedient to his laws, since their representation of God to the nations would be through the blessings of abundant life. Obedience would make them become a part of God's kingdom and thus have the blessings of abundant life which characterizes God's kingdom. By virtue of those blessings, nations would be drawn to YHWH in Zion where he dwelt because of their desire to want to share in Israel's blessings which YHWH alone could give. Their coming to Zion would lead to their knowledge of YHWH and obeying his laws (just as Israel was doing). As a result, these nations would have submitted to God's rule and received, too, the blessings of abundant life as a part of God's kingdom. In the end, God's kingdom would be restored in the world by virtue of Israel's blessings of abundant life. It is in this way that Israel as Abraham's offspring would become a blessing to all nations and bring about the restoration of God's kingdom in the world.

Before we move our discussion of the restoration of God's dwelling and kingdom in the world further, it is important that we note two things: the language of covenant, and Israel's sonship as alternative ways of communicating Israel's priestly vocation which we have just discussed. We examine both below.

Covenant and Sonship and Restoration of God's Kingdom

Israel's vocation is expressed in the context of "covenant." The words of YHWH, which we discussed as fundamental to understanding Israel's vocation, mention covenant ($b^ərît$): "Now therefore, if you will indeed obey my voice and keep my covenant" (Exod 19:5). Moreover, covenants are mentioned in numerous places in biblical literature with the Sinai covenant (which we are concerned with here) mentioned most. Understanding the purpose of covenants and their various elements (or components) is therefore essential in contributing to our articulation of the story of the Bible. More specifically, understanding covenants helps one to make sense of biblical literature concerning "covenant," and thus to integrate them into the story of the Bible. In particular, understanding the Sinai covenant leads to the isolation of God's laws and their obedience as the obligation imposed upon Israel if they were to become YHWH's $s^əgullâ$ and thereby a royal priesthood and holy people. Isolating (by means of the Sinai covenant) God's laws and the necessity of Israel to obey them as central to fulfilling his vocation is what integrates biblical literature on covenant with the story of the Bible.

The treaties from the period of the bronze-age of the Near Eastern Hittite Empire of the fourteenth to the twelfth centuries BC[7] have been of significant assistance in making sense of the Sinai covenant. This is because the treaties were close in time, and correspond, to the Sinai covenant, so understanding their purposes and their various elements enlightens our understanding of the Sinai covenant. In terms of purpose, generally speaking, covenants were meant to secure and order relationships by legal means in both private and political spheres. In regard to Hittite suzerainty treaties, the relationship would

---

7. Two classic works on these treaties and the understanding of *berit* in the Old Testament are George E. Mendenhall, *Law and Covenant in Israel and the Ancient Near East* (Biblical Colloquium, 1955), and Dennis J. McCarthy, *Treaty and Covenant*, trans. E. A. Speizer (Rome: Pontifical Biblical Institute, 1963).

be between a powerful king (the Hittite Emperor) called the *suzerain*, and a kingdom or group of a lesser state, called the *vassal*. The specific purpose of the political alliance was to secure the allegiance and faithfulness of the *vassal*. In the words of Mendenhall:

> The primary purpose of the suzerainty treaty was to establish a firm relationship of mutual support between the two parties (especially military support), in which the interests of the Hittite sovereign were of primary and ultimate concern.[8]

When the purpose of suzerainty treaties is applied to the covenant between YHWH and Israel, YHWH was the *suzerain*, and the people of Israel the *vassal*. The purpose of God in the Sinai covenant was, in the first instance (as reflected in our earlier discussion on the vocation of Israel), to secure Israel's obedience to his laws in order to bless the nation with abundant life – that is, to dwell with the people of Israel and make them a part of his kingdom. In the second instance, and consequently, God would be able to use Israel to bless other nations: to bring them into his kingdom and dwell with them.

The Hittite suzerainty treaties had six distinct elements in their structure, each with specific goals to achieve. The first element was the "preamble" in which the *suzerain*, the author of the covenant, identified himself. The focus of the history was "upon the majesty and power of the king,"[9] presumably to show his vast superiority over the *vassal* with whom he makes a covenant. The second element was a "historical prologue" where the past relationship between the two parties was recalled. The goal of this history was to make the *vassal* to be "obligated to perpetual gratitude toward the great king because of the benevolence, consideration, and favour which he had already received."[10] In addition, the prologue was also meant to justify "the imposition of obligations on the second party . . . depriving that party of the ability to contest the validity or legality of the treaty."[11] The third element was "stipulations" where details of "the obligations imposed upon and accepted by the vassal"[12] were given. The goal of the obligations was to protect the interests of the *suzerain*. The fourth element was "provisions for deposit in temple and public reading"

---

8. George E. Mendenhall, "Law and Covenant in Israel and the Ancient Near East," *BA* 17.3 (1954), 56.

9. Mendenhall, 58.

10. Mendenhall, 58.

11. Amnon Altman, "The Role of the 'Historical Prologue' in the Hittite Vassal Treaties: An Early Experiment in Securing Treaty Compliance," *J. Hist. Int. Law* 6.1 (2004): 45.

12. Mendenhall, 59.

of the covenant. A deposit of the covenant in a house of a deity was for its protection by the deity. Periodic public readings were to remind the *vassal* of his obligations because the covenant was not the responsibility of an individual within it but a collective responsibility of the kingdom or the group. The fifth element was "list of witnesses" who were gods, although it could also include nature, such as the sun and moon, or/and heaven and earth. It was believed that the gods would be responsible for enforcing the covenant. The last element in *suzerain* treaties was "curses and blessings." Blessings were believed to be bestowed on the *vassal* by the gods if they carried out the obligations enshrined in the covenant, and curses unleashed on them by the same gods if they failed to carry out their obligations.

When we examine these elements in the Sinai covenant, Exodus 19:4 contained, albeit in summary, the "historical prologue." YHWH recalled the gracious acts he did for Israel in delivering him from Egypt and leading him out of that nation: "You have seen what I did to the Egyptians, and how I bore you on eagle's wings, and brought you to myself." The outcome of this act, we can say, was to bring about perpetual gratitude from Israel and justify the obligations imposed on them by YHWH. Exodus 19:5 contained "stipulations," the obligations which were imposed upon Israel but without any details given at the time: "Now therefore, if you will obey my voice." These stipulations, as our previous discussion on Israel's vocation shows, were in the interests of God's kingdom. Still under "stipulations," YHWH obliged himself to make Israel his *sᵉgūllâ*, as a consequence of which they would be a royal priesthood and a holy nation. YHWH's obligation, however, was contingent upon Israel carrying out its obligations. Exodus contained, indirectly, a provision for deposit in the temple and public reading because mention is made of "the book of the covenant" whose material was read out to the public (Exod 24:7).

The people of Israel collectively accepted the obligations imposed on them by YHWH, the *suzerain*, which was a requirement under "stipulations" in the covenant:

> Moses came, summoned the elders of the people, and set before them all these words that the LORD had commanded him. The people all answered as one, "Everything that the LORD has spoken we will do." Moses reported the words of the people to the LORD. (Exod 19:7–8)

It is on account of their acceptance of the stipulated obligations, if we follow the plot of the narrative, that the covenant would soon after come into force. YHWH appeared on the mountain, identified himself, and gave them his laws in detail (Exod 20–23). The people of Israel accepted their detailed obligations: "Moses came and told the people all the words of the LORD and the ordinances; and all the people answered with one voice, and said, 'All the words that the LORD has spoken, we will do'" (Exod 24:3). Moses once again read God's laws, but this time from "the book of the covenant." The people of Israel for the third time in the narrative accepted their obligations in their covenant with YHWH (Exod 24:7–8). Subsequently, sacrifices were made by which the covenant came into force: "See the blood of the covenant that the LORD has made with you in accordance with all these words" (Exod 24:8; see also Ps 50:5).

According to other biblical literature this covenant between YHWH and Israel was renewed. It was renewed in the land of Moab (Deut 29:1), in Shechem (Josh 24:25), during the reign of Jehoiada (2 Kgs 11:17), and during the reign of Josiah (2 Kgs 23:3). Some of suzerainty covenants' elements not seen in the Exodus narrative of the covenant are evident in the renewals of the Sinai covenant. For example, a provision for deposit in the temple and public reading is found in the renewal in the land of Moab when Moses commanded the Levites to "Take this book of the law, and put it by the side of the ark of the covenant" (Deut 31:26). We also should note that some of the elements in the Sinai covenant seemed to have been expanded upon in the renewals. For example, "curses and blessings" were elaborated in the covenant renewal in the land of Moab (see Deut 28), while a historical prologue was given in more detail at the covenant renewal in Shechem (Josh 24:2–13). It is therefore safe to presume that virtually all the elements of *suzerain* treaties were contained in the Sinai covenant. The reason we do not see all of them in Exodus is because we have a narrative about the covenant and not "the book of the covenant" itself.

It is clear that when the relationship between YHWH and Israel is looked at through the lens of suzerainty covenants (which biblical literature compels us to), the pre-eminent element of the Sinai covenant is "stipulations," the obligations that YHWH imposed upon Israel. This pre-eminence highlighted God's laws and their obedience as of first importance in his covenant with the people of Israel. Everything hinged upon Israel carrying out its obligations in the covenant, because the interests of YHWH to use Israel on the land to restore his kingdom could not be served without it. The Israelites' obligations in the covenant were of such fundamental importance that their disobedience to God's laws was synonymous with their breaking, or not keeping (or unfaithfulness to), the covenant:

> They have turned back to the iniquities of their ancestors of old, who refused to heed my words; they have gone after other gods to

serve them; the house of Israel and the house of Judah have *broken the covenant* that I made with their ancestors. (Jer 11:10; also Jer 31:31–32; Ezek 17:18–19; Hos 8:1, emphasis added)

They did not *keep God's covenant*,
>but refused to walk according to his law. (Ps 78:10; also Pss 25:10; 103:18, emphasis added)

But as Adam they *transgressed the covenant*;
>there they dealt faithlessly with me. (Hos 6:7, emphasis added)

It must be also because of the fundamental importance of the laws in God's covenant with Israel that "the book of the covenant" was also called "the book of the law" in Deuteronomy (Deut 28:61; see also Deut 29:21; 30:10; 31:26; Josh 1:8; 8:34; 2 Kgs 22:11).

The importance of God's laws in his covenant with Israel is also the reason why the commandment to obey God's voice was paired with "keeping the covenant" in the opening words from God in the text fundamental to Israel's vocation: "Now, therefore, if you obey my voice and keep my commandment" (Exod 19:4). "Obey my voice" and "keep my covenant" were not different prerequisites but similar, because they both communicated the same requirements from YHWH. This is because, as we have seen, keeping the covenant is obeying God's voice. In other words, the people of Israel would be obeying YHWH's voice if they lived according to his laws, which would also simultaneously mean, in covenant terms, that they were keeping the covenant. To put it in plain language, this is what God told Israel: *You will be my "sᵉgullâ" and thus a royal priesthood and a holy nation if you fulfil the obligations of following my laws as stipulated in the covenant I am making with you.* In keeping the covenant, the people of Israel would experience blessings of abundant life in the land, which would attract other nations to Zion and bring them under God's kingdom to experience the blessings of abundant life as well.

We turn now to the vocation of the Israelites expressed in Israel's "sonship." In biblical literature YHWH refers to Israel as his son. We first encounter this in Exodus where, through Moses, YHWH told Pharaoh that Israel was his firstborn son: "Then you shall say to Pharaoh, 'Thus says the LORD: Israel is my firstborn son'" (Exod 4:22). YHWH through Hosea the prophet referred to Israel as his son: "When Israel was a child I loved him, and out of Egypt I called my son" (Hos 11:1). Through the same prophet YHWH let it be known that after he had judged Israel, a judgement that would include their temporary rejection as his people (Hos 1:8), they will be referred to as "sons of the living

God" (Hos 2:1). YHWH claimed Israel as his son because he formed him, having established the nation as a people in keeping his promise to Abraham:

> Is he not your father, who created you,
> who made you and established you? (Deut 32:6)

Israel's status as God's son had a bearing on how the people of Israel lived, and thus on their role as God's representatives in the world. As God's son, Israel was supposed to reflect the nature of God in the manner of its living. The significance of its status was implied in Moses's inspired words to the people of Israel when he accused them of betraying God (as their father), by their corrupt ways which were contrary to God's:

> The Rock, his work is perfect,
> and all his ways are just.
> A faithful God, without deceit,
> just and upright is he;
> yet his degenerate children have dealt falsely with him,
> a perverse and crooked generation. (Deut 32:4–6)

The command, "You shall be holy for I the LORD your God am holy" (Lev 19:2; 20:7; 20:26) was YHWH's motivation to Israel to follow his laws, which was based on Israel reflecting his nature, as his son. If God was holy, so was Israel; if God was without deceit, just and upright, so was Israel. However, this fact was also a possibility that needed to be realized. Israel would be God's representative, a royal priesthood, to the nation to the extent that it was true to its status as God's son, by obeying God's laws.

However YHWH did not just refer to Israel as his son, but as his firstborn son. We noted this in Exodus. Despite Israel's fortunes, YHWH persisted in referring to him as his firstborn:

> For I am a father to Israel,
> and Ephraim is my firstborn. (Jer 31:9)

In the ancient Near Eastern world, a firstborn son was considered as preeminent, and as one's might and pride (Gen 49:3). Firstborn children were therefore distinguished and of special importance amongst one's sons. From this perspective we can understand why it took the slaying of the Egyptians' firstborn children to convince pharaoh to let the Israelites leave his empire. More importantly, it follows that a firstborn was also first in rank amongst other sons, or a cut above them. For this reason the firstborn's siblings were subject to him, and he could lead them. This is why YHWH's election of Jacob, who was the younger brother of Esau the firstborn of Isaac (Gen 25:23), was a stark reversal of the order of things as perceived in that world. This view of firstborn children accounts for YHWH's claim on all the firstborn of Israel as his. They belonged to him and were to be set aside for him: "Consecrate to me all the firstborn; whatever is the first to open the womb among the Israelites, of human beings and animals, is mine" (Exod 13:2; also Exod 22:28–29; Num 8:17).

From an international perspective, Israel was God's firstborn amongst other nations; the first in rank and taking precedence above the others. Consequently, just as the firstborn children of Israel amongst the Israelites especially belonged to God, so the people of Israel in the league of nations especially belonged to YHWH. Two texts make this very clear:

> When the most high apportioned the nations,
> when he divided humankind,
> he fixed the boundaries of the peoples
> according to the number of their gods;
> the *LORD's own portion* was his people,
> Jacob his allotted share. (Deut 32:8–9, emphasis added)

> For you are a people holy to the LORD your God; it is you the LORD has chosen out of all the peoples of the earth to be his people, *his treasured possession*. (Deut 14:4, emphasis added)

Israel, therefore, was God's portion for the sake of serving him in relation to other nations. This observation is clarified by the replacement of Israel's firstborn with the Levites. The Levites were chosen by YHWH to serve him in his house in the place of all the firstborn of Israel:

> I hereby accept the Levites from among the Israelites as substitutes for all the firstborn that open the womb among the Israelites. The Levites shall be mine, for all the first born are mine. (Num 3:12–13)

If YHWH did not replace the firstborn of Israel in this way, they would have been the ones serving in his house because they were his portion. Israel, then, was God's portion, his *sᵉgūllâ*, for the sake of becoming YHWH's royal priest amongst the nations. All this was also to the extent that the Israelites obeyed God's laws (as YHWH himself had said – Exod 19:5). If they reflected God's nature through obedience, they would have the blessings of abundant life in the land as a part of God's kingdom. Abundant life in the land would attract other nations to Zion, and bring them under God's kingdom, causing them to experience the blessings of abundant life as well.

Through our exegesis, we have established the vocation of Israel directly from YHWH's words through Moses, and indirectly from his covenant with

Israel, and through Israel's sonship status. We turn now to consider how God intended to restore his dwelling with humans in the world through Abraham and his offspring on the land.

Temple, Jerusalem, Land, and Restoration of God's Dwelling

According to the unfolding story we find in the Bible, God commanded Moses to have the people of Israel build him a sanctuary (*miqdāš*) once he had made clear Israel's vocation on the land and made a covenant with them. The sanctuary was to be his dwelling. This point is emphasized by the tabernacle's design coming from YHWH himself and not from a human being. Even the decor within the sanctuary was according to God's design:

> And have them make me a sanctuary, so that I may dwell among them. In accordance with all that I show you concerning the pattern of the tabernacle and all its furniture, so you shall make it. (Exod 25:8–9)

It therefore should not be a surprise that the design of the tabernacle had numerous parallels with his dwelling in the garden of Eden. This correspondence was also present in the tabernacle's successor, the temple. The temple also naturally inherited the tabernacle's decor, such as the ark. Accordingly, we can identify at least eight parallels between the tabernacle and temple on the one hand, and the garden of Eden on the other thus:

Element in Tabernacle/Temple	Garden of Eden Parallel
1. Presence of cherubim: cherubim icons guarding the ark (Exod 25:22), and adorning both the tabernacle (Exod 26:1) and the temple (1 Kgs 7:27–38; Ezek 41:18–20, 25).	Cherubim guard the garden (Gen 3:24).
2. Seven branched lamp-stand (*mᵊnôrah*), made of gold and styled on flowers and almond tree (Exod 25:31–40); door to the *dᵊbîr* carved with palm tree and flowers (1 Kgs 6:29–35).	Representing YHWH and the tree of life in the garden (Gen 2:9), and depicting the garden.

3. The molten sea on the south east corner of the temple (1 Kgs 7:23–26) and the ten stands of bronze with ten lavers atop with five on the south side of the temple and five on the north side of the temple (1 Kgs 7:27–39; Ezek 47:1–2).	Water flowing from the garden of Eden (Gen 2:10).
4. Two pillars of bronze topped with lilies, pomegranates, and tangled branches with one on the south and the north of the temple (1 Kgs 7:15–22).	Suggestive of the tree of the knowledge of good and evil (Gen 2:17), and of the tree of life in the garden (Gen 2:9).
5. Human servants, the priests serving in the tabernacle and temple (Num 1:53; 3:23, 29, 35; Zech 3:7; Mal 2:1–9).	Adam and Eve serving and taking care of the garden (Gen 2:15–17).
6. Vegetation engraved on the walls and doors of temple (1 Kgs 6:29, Ezek 40:31, 34, 37; 41:18–20, 24–26).	Garden setting in the garden of Eden.
7. Gold plating on the ark (Exod 25:11), the table (Exod 25:24) the *mᵉnôrah* (Exod 25:31), and in the *dᵉbîr* (1 Kgs 6:19–22).	Representing gold, a precious metal found in the garden of Eden (Gen 2:11–12).
8. Entrance is from the east (Ezek 43:1–4; 42:12; 44:1; 46:12; 47:1).	Entrance to the garden from the east (Gen 3:24).

Furthermore, this parallelism is seen in the psalm's metaphoric language where human beings were referred to as trees in the temple which corresponded with trees in God's Garden:

> The righteous flourish like a palm tree,
>   and grow like a cedar in Lebanon.
> They are planted in the house of the LORD;
>   They flourish in the courts of our God. (Ps 92:12–13; also Ps 52:8)

Where a river was said to flow in Jerusalem (where the temple was) corresponds with the river in the garden of Eden: "There is a river whose streams make glad the city of God, the holy habitation of the Most High" (Ps 46:4–5; see also Ezek 47:1–12).

These parallels denote a continuity between the garden of Eden as God's dwelling, and tabernacle and temple as his dwelling with the people of Israel. In other words, the parallels between the garden and the tabernacle demonstrate that God's dwelling with humans in the garden was being restored in the tabernacle, and later the temple. The parallels reflect the plan of God to restore his dwelling with human beings in the world, starting with Israel.

Before the tabernacle and subsequently the temple, Moses and the people of Israel had known Mount Sinai as God's dwelling. This is the mountain explicitly referred to as "the mountain of God" (Exod 3:1). Upon that mountain God called Moses as his chosen instrument to deliver the people of Israel from Egypt (Exod 3:1–12). It is on that mountain that YHWH more than once asked Moses to ascend in order to talk to him (Exod 19:24; 24:1–3, 12–18). It was also on this mountain that YHWH made his presence felt definitively amongst the people of Israel in thunder, fire, lightning, thick smoke, a cloud, and with a loud trumpet sound before revealing the *torah* to them (Exod 19:16–25; Exod 20:1–23:33; Ps 68:8). In time, the people of Israel moved from Mount Sinai to the promised land. YHWH moved with them by changing his abode to the tabernacle which he had commanded them to build.

When the tabernacle was built, it was covered by a cloud and filled with God's glory: "the cloud covered the tent of the meeting, and the glory (*kābôd*) of the LORD filled the tabernacle" (Exod 40:34). Both the cloud and God's glory signified that God had taken up residence in the tabernacle for the following reasons. The people of Israel had become accustomed to associating a cloud with God's presence. God had led them by a pillar of cloud when he delivered them from Egypt. The cloud covering the tabernacle would then have been a sign to the people of Israel that God was there. As regards God's *kābôd*, usage of the term points to some visible manifestation or appearance of God. For example, Moses wished to see God's *kābôd*, by which was meant to see God (Exod 33:18). In answer to his wish, God showed him a part of him that he could bear (Exod 34:5). Ezekiel, too, saw YHWH in a vision and referred to the vision as the *kābôd* of YHWH (Ezek 1:28; 3:23). God's *kābôd* filling the tabernacle would have been some sort of manifestation of YHWH in the tabernacle that was visible to the people of Israel. As Smith has pointed out in his study of bodily representations of God in the Old Testament, "the divine body as experienced by both Moses and Isaiah (and others) is not represented as flesh; it appears to be a body of "glory" (*kābôd*) manifest on earth."[13] Thus it could be talked of as "the aura or effulgence of divine (i.e. YHWH's) presence,"[14] the physical manifestation to human beings of the presence of God.

YHWH's manifestation in the tabernacle would have signified to the people that he had occupied his house. In the larger scheme of things it had

---

13. Mark S. Smith, "The Three Bodies of God in the Hebrew Bible," *JBL* 134.3 (2015): 481.
14. Smith, "Three Bodies of God," 488.

become YHWH's new house with the people of Israel, not Mount Sinai where they first encountered his dwelling. From then on YHWH led the people of Israel by moving out of his residence or by staying put:

> Whenever the cloud was taken up from the tabernacle, the Israelites would set out on each stage of their journey; but if the cloud was not taken up from the tabernacle, they did not set out . . . For the cloud of the LORD was on the tabernacle by day, and fire was in the cloud by night, before the eyes of all the house of Israel at each stage of their journey. (Exod 40:36–37)

The same events which occurred in the tabernacle were witnessed when the temple was built. After Solomon finished building the temple (1 Kgs 7:51), he asked Israel's leaders to bring the ark of the covenant into God's house. Subsequently the temple was filled with a cloud and the *kābôd* of God: "And when the priest came out of the holy place, a cloud filled the house of the LORD . . . for the glory of the LORD filled the house of the LORD" (1 Kgs 8:10). The temple then became God's final residence amongst the people of Israel.

Now back to Mount Sinai as God's initial dwelling before he took up residence amongst the people of Israel. Mountains in ancient Near Eastern cosmology were viewed as dwellings of deities. Because they were permanent and reached to the clouds, mountains were understood to be places where the nether world, earth and heaven met (thus the fulcrum, the *axis mundi*, of the world) and therefore believed to be the dwelling place of divinities.[15] As such, mountains were the "hot spots" of encounters and communications between humans and divinities. By virtue of this perception, as we see in biblical literature, YHWH's dwellings on earth were viewed as mountains. This is seen in various places. First, the place where God appears to Abraham (Gen 22:9–14) and to David (2 Chr 3:1) are mountains. Second, in a prophecy concerning the king of Tyre, YHWH refers to his dwelling in the garden as his mountain: "the holy mountain of God" (Ezek 28:14). A psalmist too refers to God's city dwelling as a mountain: "Great is the LORD and greatly to be praised in the city of our God, His holy mountain" (Ps 48:1–2; see also Ps 2:6) – even though the two are not literally mountains. Third, in prophetic messages the temple would be transformed as the highest of mountains (Mic 4:1–2; Isa 2:2–4). It was also referred to as high and lofty (Ezek 17:22–23) although it was

---

15. See for example, Mircea Eliade, *Patterns in Comparative Religion* (Cleveland: Meridan, 1958), 367–87; Richard J. Clifford S. J, *The Cosmic Mountain in Canaan and the Old Testament* (Cambridge: Harvard University Press, 1972); and Robert L. Cohn, "The Mountains and Mount Zion," *Judaism* 26 (1977).

not literally a mountain, nor high and lofty. Fourth, and most significantly, the temple as YHWH's abode, was at times referred to as "Mount Zion" although it was not a mountain: "Remember Mount Zion, where you came to dwell" (Ps 74:2; see also Pss 3:3–4; 15:1; 24:3; 99:9; Isa 4:5; 8:18; 56:6–7). The temple then, as the mountain where God dwelt, Mount Zion, was immovable and permanent (Ps 125:1). According to the psalmist, it was also ultimately after Mount Sinai, God's immovable and everlasting abode amongst Israel:

> O mighty mountain, mountain of Bashan;
> > O many-peaked mountain, mountain of Bashan!
> Why do you look with envy, O many-peaked mountain,
> > at the mount that God desired for his abode,
> > where the LORD will reside forever?
> With mighty chariotry, twice ten thousand,
> > thousands upon thousands,
> the LORD came from Sinai into the holy place. (Ps 68:15–17)

Since God's dwelling was in Jerusalem (also called Zion – 1 Kgs 8:1), the city was also God's dwelling. YHWH's own words in Joel point to this: "So you shall know that I, the LORD your God, dwell in Zion, my holy mountain (Joel 3:17). A psalmist too refers to Jerusalem as God's holy habitation (*mishvanē*):

> There is a river whose streams make glad the city of God,
> > the holy habitation of the Most High. (Ps 46:4; also Ps 135:21)

According to another psalmist, the city was indeed chosen by God as his habitation: "For the LORD has chosen Zion; he has desired it for his habitation" (Ps 132:13; see also Ps 76:1–2). Furthermore, because God's dwelling was in Jerusalem, Zion was also understood as God's city:

> The LORD loves the gates of Zion
> > more than all the dwellings of Jacob.
> Glorious things are spoken of you,
> > O City of God. (Ps 87:2–3; see also Pss 48:1–2, 8; 101:8)

The land too, just as the city, was also God's dwelling because of his house in Jerusalem. In our earlier discussion, we mentioned that the land was referred to as God's rest (*mənûḥah*), or God's dwelling (Deut 12:9; Ps 95:11). The land was God's dwelling because he was to live there with the people of Israel to whom he gave it. This view is supported by the relationship between the tabernacle, as God's house, and God's dwelling with the people of Israel. The reason YHWH gave Moses for building the tabernacle was "so that I may dwell among you"

(Exod 25:8). Since the people would eventually live throughout the land, God's permanent house amongst theirs was a manifestation of his living with them wherever they were in the land, in the same way that his pitched house in the camp was wherever they were in the wilderness.

We find more support for the land being God's dwelling on account of his house from Leviticus, Numbers, and the Psalms. We already mentioned that the hitpael form of the verb *halak* when used for walking can be used to communicate movement in one's dwelling. It is this verb which is used in Leviticus to denote God's movement amongst the people of Israel: "I will place my dwelling in your midst . . . And I will walk (*hithallaktî*) among you" (Lev 26:11–12). YHWH would be able to *hithallaktî* amongst the Israelites because they were in his house. The land, therefore, was God's dwelling with the people. The reason God commanded the people of Israel not to pollute the land makes clear as well that the land was his dwelling: "You shall not defile the land in which you live, in which I also dwell; for I the LORD dwell among the Israelites" (Num 35:34). Without God's house amongst the houses of the people of Israel in Jerusalem, the land would not be his dwelling with them. A psalmist was most likely informed by this view when he used for land a notion that would usually apply to God's house. He talked of God's *kabōd* filling the land, which would have signified his taking up residence there (as we shall later demonstrate), as he did with both the tabernacle and temple:

> Surely his salvation is at hand for those who fear him,
> > that his glory may dwell in our land. (Ps 85:9)

The view of the land as God's dwelling is also evident in the inspired song of praise to YHWH as a mighty warrior who delivered Israel from all her foes. The praise song starts with the praise of YHWH for delivering Israel from Egypt and concludes with praise to YHWH for bringing Israel victoriously to, and settling them in, the land thus:

> You brought them in and planted them on the mountain of
> > your own possession,
> > > the place, O LORD, that you made your abode,
> > the sanctuary, O LORD, that your hands have established.
> (Exod 15:17)

Land in this hymn is referred to as God's dwelling. The view here is that YHWH planted the people of Israel in his dwelling in order to live with them. In biblical literature, the land as the place where God plants Israel is also found in YHWH's word to David: "I will appoint a place for my people Israel and will plant them, so that they may live in their own place" (2 Sam 7:10). The language of planting the people of Israel on the land reinforced the view that the land was indeed God's dwelling by reminding them of the garden of Eden, God's dwelling with human beings at creation. It should then not surprise us that Israel's dispossession from the land was interpreted by the narrator of the books of Kings as being cast away from YHWH's presence (2 Kgs 24:20), that is, from YHWH's house.

God's dwelling with the people of Israel in the land was not incidental but designed to fulfil his blessing-to-all-nations promise to Abraham. His living with Israel in the land was a first step towards restoring his dwelling and kingdom in the world. The people of Israel would approach YHWH in his house through all manner of prayers such as thanksgiving, praise, and petition, as the prayer of Solomon suggests: "Hear the plea of your servant and of your people when they pray towards this place" (1 Kgs 8:30). The psalms provide a helpful window to look through for pictures of Israel's temple life. We see that in the temple the people of Israel offered praises to God, "O LORD, our Sovereign, how majestic is your name in all the earth" (Ps 8:1; see also for example Pss 29; 33; 65). They would also offer individual and communal thanksgiving, "I love the LORD, because he has heard my voice and supplication" (Ps 116:1; see also for example Pss 107; 118; 138). They would also offer specific petitions relative to their troubling personal or national circumstances:

> O LORD, how many are my foes!
> Many are rising against me; many are saying to me,
> "There is no help for you in God." (Ps 3:1–2; see also for
> example Pss 13; 22; 71)

The people of Israel would also bring sacrifices and feasts to YHWH in the temple as prescribed through Moses (Lev 1:1–7:19; 16; 23). This is evident in some psalms:

> Your solemn processions are seen, O God,
> the processions of my God, my king, into the sanctuary –
> the singers in front, the musicians last, between them girls
> playing tambourines:
> ... There is Benjamin, the least of them, in the lead,
> the princes of Judah, in a body,
> the princes of Zebulun, the princes of Naphtali. (Ps
> 68:24–27; see also Pss 122:1–2; 132:6–7)

Consequently, YHWH would respond to their approaches. For example, a self-pitying psalmist envied the arrogant and the wicked, but when he approached God in the temple he understood their end and was delivered from his envy: "until I went into the sanctuary of God; then I perceived their end" he confessed (Ps 73:17). Another psalmist talked of the delight and of the epiphany found in the temple thus:

> All people may take refuge in the shadow of your wings.
> > They feast on the abundance of your house,
> and you give them drink from the rivers of your delights.
> > For with you is the fountain of life; in your light we see
> > light. (Ps 36:7–9)

King Hezekiah found help in YHWH against the prospective invasion of the Assyrian king, Sennacharib, when he approached him in the temple and "prayed to the LORD" (Isa 37:15). YHWH responded by telling him through Isaiah the prophet that the Assyrian king would not enter the city for God would defend it (Is 37:21–34). These and such like experiences must have been the reasons why the psalmists longed for visits and even residence in the temple. A psalmist, for example, longed for God's house and there to behold his face:

> As a deer longs for flowing streams, so my soul longs for you O God.
> > My soul thirsts for God, for the living God,
> When shall I come and behold the face of God? (Ps 42:1–2)

Another confessed his love for it: "O LORD, I love the house in which you dwell, and the place where your glory abides" (Ps 26:8; see also Pss 84:1–7; 122:1–2).

The experiences in the temple and the help from God that they received were also reasons that made some psalmists have eschatological-like hopes of living in God's house forever: "One thing I asked the LORD, that will I seek after; to live in the house of the LORD all the days of my life" (Ps 27:4; see also Pss 23:6; 27:4–5; 65:4).

After approaching God through their own individual initiatives or according to prescribed pilgrimages, the people of Israel were then to go back to their homes and daily lives to live in obedience to God. Going to God's house and living according to his laws were linked:

> O LORD, who may abide in your tent?
> > Who may dwell in your holy hill?
> Those who walk blamelessly, and do what is right,
> and speak the truth from their hearts;
> > who do not slander with their tongue,

and do no evil to their friends. (Ps 15:1–5; also Ps 24)

The people of Israel would then experience, as we have discussed, the blessings of abundant life on the land (Lev 26:3–13; Deut 28:1–14), as a result of living by God's laws in their daily lives. The Israelites would thereby fulfil their priestly vocation by representing God to the nations through the blessings of abundant life. The nations would then be attracted to YHWH in Zion where he dwelt, because of what the nations would have seen YHWH do for Israel on the land. Solomon's prayer after he finished building the temple was in harmony with this plan of YHWH:

> Likewise when a foreigner, who is not of your people Israel, comes from a distant land because of your name – for they shall hear of your great name, your mighty hand, and your outstretched arm – when a foreigner comes and prays towards this house, then hear in heaven your dwelling place . . . so that all the people of the earth may know your name and fear you, as do your people Israel. (1 Kgs 8:42–43)

The nations would then flock to Zion to also encounter YHWH and be exposed to his law and ways. This state of affairs is implied in the praises of the psalmists:

> Great is the LORD and greatly to be praised in the city of our God.
> His holy mountain . . . is the joy of all the earth" (Ps 48:1–2; see also Ps 76:1; Ps 87).

God's plan is clearly expressed in the prophets albeit as an eschatological prophecy. YHWH spoke through Isaiah thus:

> Many peoples shall come and say
> "Come, let us go to the mountain of the LORD,
>   to the house of the God of Jacob;
> that he may teach us his ways and that we may walk in his
>   paths."
> For out of Zion shall go forth instructions,
>   and the word of the LORD from Jerusalem. (Isa 2:3; also
>   Mic 4:2)

Zion as God's dwelling would have become a conspicuously attractive place to the nations of the world. The nations would be coming to Zion to know YHWH and to learn about his laws or ways. They would then go back to their lands and kingdoms to live according to God's ways and thereby come under God's kingdom.

As we demonstrated in our last chapter, God's kingdom and dwelling are integrated. To be in God's house is to be in his kingdom, and to be in his kingdom is to be in his house. This being the case, the natural outcome of nations flocking to Zion, knowing YHWH, and going back to their lands to live by God's laws would have been the expansion of not only God's dwelling but his kingdom too, from the land of Israel to other nations. God would dwell in other lands to the extent that they had come to know him and were exposed to his laws, by which they were living. In the end the whole world would be God's dwelling with human beings and a part of his kingdom, experiencing thereby blessings of abundant life. The nations would have been blessed through Abraham and his offspring on the land. This outcome of becoming a part of God's kingdom through Israel's blessings of abundant life is apparently encapsulated in the hopes of the psalmist:

> All the ends of the earth shall remember and turn to the LORD;
> and all the families of the nations shall worship before him.
> For dominion belongs to the LORD,
> and he rules over all nations. (Ps 22:27–28; see also Pss 50:1–2; 99:1–3)

However, this plan to restore God's dwelling in the world was dependent on the obedience of the people of Israel. YHWH through Moses had made it clear that if they followed his statutes and kept his commandments, and faithfully observed them (Lev 26:3) he would, amongst other blessings, dwell with them (Lev 26:11–12). The same had been repeated to Solomon by requiring obedience from him for God to dwell with Israel: "if you walk in my statutes, obey my commandments by walking in them, then . . . I will dwell among the children of Israel" (1 Kgs 6:12–13). So God's plan first to make Israel a part of his kingdom and dwelling, and then from them extend the same to the whole world, was based on their obedience. Unfortunately, as we shall see later in our study, Israel failed to do so; but God acted in his faithfulness to the promise he gave to Abraham.

4

The Restoration of God's Kingdom through David's Dynasty

In the last chapter we examined the grand scheme of God in the unfolding story of the Bible to restore his dwelling and kingdom in the world, through placing the people of Israel in the land and by dwelling with them there. We consider in this chapter an additional, but complementary, way in which God intended to restore the world to his kingdom. This additional way is through the kings of Israel, and it is tied to the promise which God gave to Abraham that he would be a father of kings (hereafter referred to as "the promise of kings"). We will consider the fulfilment of this promise and the way it was also meant to bring about the restoration of the kingdom of God in the world, and thereby make Abraham a blessing to all nations.

David's Dynasty, the Promised Kingship

The land of Israel was meant to be God's dwelling with the people of Israel and a part of his kingdom if they obeyed him. Blessings of abundant life on the land as a consequence would attract other nations to Israel, and more specifically to Zion, causing them to come under the kingdom of God. However, in the unfolding story of the Bible, there is more to how God intended to restore his kingdom in the world through Abraham and his offspring than this. In a very direct way, God intended to be the king of Israel, and Israel to be his kingdom. This intention is reflected in God's covenant with Israel.

Going back to suzerainty covenants, of which the covenant between YHWH and Israel was one, the *suzerain* was king over the *vassal*, regardless of whether the *vassal* had a ruler or not. The *vassal* was bound to his kingship through the obligations imposed upon him and to which he consented. The *vassal* was also bound to the *suzerain* as his king through exclusive loyalty. A *vassal* could not acknowledge more than one *suzerain*. Acknowledging another *suzerain* would only occur if the *vassal* was rebelling against a current *suzerain*. In addition, the *vassal's* king was an agent of the *suzerain*. As demonstrated in the study of Tagger-Cohen,[1] Hittite rulers understood themselves to be the rulers over all their state territory as granted to them by the gods, but they could grant rulership to *vassal* kings or governors.

YHWH's covenant with the people of Israel implied that he made Israel his kingdom. As one Old Testament scholar observed over a century ago, "The real beginning of the kingly rule was when Yahweh bound the tribes of Israel into a community by the formation of a legal covenant."[2] On the basis of the covenant, Israel became the dominion of God, the kingdom of YHWH, as a first step in YHWH's intentions to be *suzerain* over all the nations of the world. Levenson summed this up quite well thus: "If the language of covenant makes clear the suzerainty of God, it also sheds a new light on the identity of Israel. Israel is the kingdom of God."[3] This inference is confirmed by the words of Moses when he referred to the commencement of the covenant as the time when God became the king of Israel (note that Jeshurun was a term referring to Israel [see Deut 32:15; Isa 44:2]):

> The LORD came from Sinai,
>   and dawned from Seir upon us . . .
> when Moses commanded us a law,
>   as a possession for the assembly of Jacob.
> Thus the LORD became king in Jeshurun when the heads of the
>   people gathered,
> all the tribes of Israel together. (Deut 33:1–5 RSV and ESV)

In the unfolding story of the Bible, Israel was indeed God's kingdom. At the beginning of Israel's life in the land, God led the people by means of judges (*šōpəṭîm*), whose role was mostly a military one (Judg 2:16). Soon after, the people of Israel started to agitate for an earthly monarchy (*melek*) to lead them.

---

1. Ada Taggar-Cohen, "Biblical Covenant and Hittite *ishiul* reexamined," *VT* 61 (2011).

2. F. B. Denio, "The Kingdom of God in the Old Testament," *The Old Testament Student* 6.1 (1886), 71.

3. Jon D. Levenson, "Covenant and Commandment," *Tradition* 21.1 (1983), 46.

They asked Gideon, one of the judges who defeated the Midianites, to become their king and establish a dynasty:

> Then the Israelites said to Gideon, "Rule over us, you and your son and your grandson also; for you have delivered us out of the hand of Midian." Gideon said to them, "I will not rule over you, and my son will not rule over you; the LORD will rule over you. (Judg 8:22–23)

Gideon's rejection of their request was based on his knowledge that Israel was God's kingdom. To Gideon, being king of Israel or turning Israel into a kingdom ruled by his dynasty would be a rejection of YHWH's kingship over Israel and the breaking of the covenant.

The desire of the people of Israel to have an earthly king from among their own persisted, as seen from the point of view of the narrator of the book of Judges. The book of Judges dwells on the individual charismatic leadership offered to the people of Israel by its judges against the twin threats of idolatry and external aggression. The judges of Israel before Abimelech (Judg 3:7–8:28) were more effective in delivering the people of Israel from idolatry, and securing peace. The judges after Abimelech (Judg 10:1–16:31) were not as effective as seen in the idolatrous practices during their leadership and in their lack of securing peace for Israel.

The impression created is that the judge-leadership of Israel was increasingly beginning to fail. Accordingly the narrator of the book offered the view that this problem of judge-leadership would only be resolved by Israel becoming a monarchy. Thus twice as a commentary to explain Israel's idolatry, violence and murders, and sexual violence, the narrator remarks: "In those days there was no king in Israel" (Judg 17:6; 19:1). Ultimately the narrator faults the state of Israel on its lack of a monarch: "In those days there was no king in Israel; all the people did what was right in their own eyes" (Judg 21:25). The solution, therefore, to Israel's problems was to have a king.

Against the background of Israel's push for a king, the odd story of Abimelech in the book of Judges (Judg 8:29–9:57) as king of Israel may have been intended to qualify the earthly monarchy needed in Israel.[4] Abimelech was the son of Gideon and did not lead Israel as judge, but did so conspicuously as king (*melek*). After slaughtering all his brothers except Jotham, he was made a king by the citizens of Shechem (Judg 9:6). His rule was a very short period

---

4. See for more Brian P. Irwin, "Not Just Any King: Abimelech, the Northern Monarchy, and the Final Form of Judges," *JBL* 131.3 (2012).

of three years characterized by violence and destruction, and by hostility and internal strife. He became the leader of Israel by usurping power, and not by the Spirit of YHWH coming upon him. In the end his reign, unlike that of the judges, ended in God's judgement on his murders and the wickedness of his supporters (Judg 9:56–57). Abimelech was the only king amongst the judges, but he provided Israel with leadership far worse than that of any judge before and after him. Although Israel wanted a monarch in the place of judge-leadership, Abimelech's reprehensible kingship was a lesson on what kind of monarchy was unsuitable for Israel.

Israel's desire to have an earthly king continued to grow. During the leadership of Samuel the judge, the people of Israel unanimously requested an earthly king to rule over them in the way kings ruled nations (1 Sam 8:5). The request was a rejection of YHWH's rule: "and the LORD said to Samuel, 'Listen to the voice of the people in all that they say to you; for they have not rejected you, but they have rejected me from being king over them'" (1 Sam 8:7; see also 1 Sam 12:12). Although God granted the people of Israel their request, he warned them of its disastrous consequences (1 Sam 8:10–18). God's warnings were an indication that he was against their request to have an earthly monarch. Their desired earthly monarch could, therefore, not be the onset of the fulfilment of the promise of kings given to Abraham.

The direct relationship between the people of Israel's desire for an earthly monarch and their rejection of YHWH's kingship here should not lead us to conclude that God's kingship over Israel and an earthly monarch in Israel were mutually exclusive. The desire for an earthly king was fundamentally a manifestation of the people of Israel's rejection of YHWH's kingship. It was for this reason that it displeased God. Yet how could God reject wholesale an earthly monarchy for Israel when he had already promised that their ancestor Abraham would be a father of kings? Even the people of Israel did not see an earthly kingship and YHWH's kingship as mutually exclusive. For this reason psalmists referred to YHWH as their king:

> Sing praises to God, sing praises;
> sing praise to our King, sing praises.
> For God is the king of all the earth;
> sing praises with a psalm. (Ps 47:6–7; also Pss 44:4; 48:2; 74:12; 89:18; 98:6)

YHWH was recognized as king despite the presence of an earthly king whom the psalmists recognized as theirs and prayed for fervently. We therefore consider below how the promise of kings which God gave to Abraham was fulfilled and how it was designed to restore the kingdom of God in the world as intended at creation.

The first hint towards the fulfilment of this promise in biblical literature appears in the blessings Jacob gave to his children. Jacob's blessing of Judah envisages him as one from whom Israel's monarchy would come:

> The sceptre shall not depart from Judah,
> nor the ruler's staff from between his feet. (Gen 49:10)

As a prophecy, this blessing pointed to kings coming from Judah, to a royal family from the tribe, in time to come. We must therefore begin our tracing of the fulfilment of the promise of kings given to Abraham from here. The promise was now limited in fulfilment to the house of Judah.

The second hint towards the fulfilment of the promise of kings to Abraham were the prophecies of Balaam. In his first prophecy, he refers to Israel's earthly king by means of a comparison. Israel's king would be higher than the king (or kings)[5] of the Amalekites, "his king shall be higher than Agag" (Num 24:7). In his second prophecy, Balaam prophesies of a royalty that would arise from Israel who would have dominion over Israel's neighbours:

> A star shall come out of Jacob,
> and a sceptre shall arise out of Israel;
> it shall crush the borderlands of all the Shethites . . .
> One out of Jacob shall rule. (Num 24:17–19)

The third hint is in Hannah's thanksgiving to YHWH for her child, Samuel (1 Sam 2:1–10). Hannah was a barren woman who in pain prayed to God fervently, and repeatedly asked him to grant her a child. YHWH answered her prayers. A little while later, Hannah brought the child Samuel to Eli for God's service. Upon leaving Samuel in God's house she offered a prayer which focused on God's kingship in the world. Central to this kingship was justice. On the one hand, YHWH granted justice to the poor, the lowly, the oppressed, while on the other, he judged the arrogant, the rich, and mighty and those opposed to him. In her prayer, which was a synonymous parallel poem, Hannah praised YHWH for he who would raise up a temporal king (his anointed) to rule Israel – a king whom YHWH would give power and strength to rule according to his will:

---

5. This is either the king of the Amalekites, or kings of the Amalekites if we understand "Agag" as the common title for the kings of the Amalekites as some have suggested (see 1 Sam 15:8, 32).

> The LORD will judge the ends of the earth;
> he will give strength to his king,
> and exalt the power of his anointed. (1 Sam 2:10)

Hannah must have been moved by God's spirit to offer this prayer to God for she praised him for his future king at a time when there was no king in Israel. We can only conclude then that her prayer was a revelation, a prophecy about God's prospective king in Israel.

Our comprehension of the prophecies examined above should be viewed in relationship to the promise of kings which YHWH gave to Abraham. They were reminders that God was going to fulfil his promise of kings to Abraham in due time. In the unfolding story of the Bible, Jacob's prophecy narrowed down the fulfilment of the promise to the house of Judah, while Hannah's prophecy encapsulated the essence of God's kingship which would be furthered by his king in Israel (we shall revisit both of these observations later).

As already noted, the beginning of Israel's earthly monarchy came after the people of Israel settled in the land which God promised them, from their desire to have an earthly monarch like other nations. Although YHWH gave them what they asked for, it was, as we noted, a rejection of YHWH as their king (1 Sam 8:7; 1 Sam 10:19). Asking for an earthly king was an act of great rebellion: "the wickedness you have done in the sight of the LORD is great in demanding a king for yourself' (1 Sam 12:17). This explains why there was a hesitancy in the biblical narrative to view Saul as purely God's elect as king over Israel. The question of who exactly placed Saul at the head of the nation of Israel remains ambiguous. Was it YHWH, or Samuel the prophet, or the people themselves who were asking for a king? On the one hand, Saul, it seems, was God's choice: "Do you see the one whom the LORD had chosen?' (1 Sam 10:24). On the other hand, he was also the people's choice, not God's: "See, here is the king whom you have chosen" (1 Sam 12:13). Moreover it was Samuel, and not God, who set him up as the king: "I have listened to you in all that you have said to me, and have set a king over you" (1 Sam 12:1). Further still, God did not anoint him to be king (*melek*) over Israel but anointed him to be a military ruler (*nāgîd*) of Israel: "The LORD has anointed you ruler (*nāgîd*) over his people Israel" (1 Sam 10:1).

Israel's rejection of YHWH as its king implied that King Saul was not the beginning of the fulfilment of God's promise of kings to Abraham. It is for this reason that, as we mentioned, God warned the people of Israel of disastrous consequences of having their desired earthly king (1 Sam 8:10–18). In the wider scheme of God's plan to restore his kingdom in the world, Saul's monarchy was, therefore, not the chosen instrument to bring about the restoration. Ultimately, and soon after, God repented of making Saul the king (1 Sam 15:11; 1 Sam 15:35), rejected his kingship over Israel (1 Sam 15:26), took it away from him, and gave it to David (1 Sam 15:28). It is towards the end of the reign of David that we encounter the onset of the fulfilment of the promise of kings given to Abraham. We turn now to that kingship.

After rejecting the kingship of Saul YHWH told Samuel the judge that he had provided for himself a king amongst the sons of Jesse:

> The LORD said to Samuel, "How long will you grieve over Saul? I have rejected him from being king over Israel? Fill your horn with oil and set out; I will send you to Jesse the Bethlehemite, for I have provided for myself a king amongst his sons." (1 Sam 16:1)

These words were a contrast to the setting up of the kingship of Saul. While with Saul, the people of Israel insisted on having a king for themselves so that the king given to them was considered as their choice, with David YHWH took the initiative to provide a king. In addition, while the choice of Saul's kingship was ambiguous, YHWH alone chose David to be king from among the sons of Jesse. David as YHWH's choice is highlighted in biblical literature:

> He chose his servant David,
>   and took him from the sheepfolds;
> from tending the nursing ewes he brought him
>   to be the shepherd of his people Jacob,
> of Israel, his inheritance. (Ps 78:70–71; also Ps 89:3, 19;
>   1 Kgs 8:16)

The distinctions between the two kingships are then clear. The dividing line between them is about what God wanted, and not what the people desired. As noted by McKelvey, "The Lord chose Saul as king for Israel in accord with their desire (i.e. a king like the nations), but God chose David according to his purposes."[6] For this reason although David, like Saul, was not free from sin, his fortunes were different from Saul's. These contrasts between the kingships of Saul and David indicated that the fulfilment of the promise given by God to Abraham was in David.

David was eventually made king in Hebron (2 Sam 2:4). Initially he was king only over Judah but later over the whole of Israel (2 Sam 5:3). He made Jerusalem the capital of Israel (2 Sam 5:6–10). Towards the end of his life David

---

6. Michael G. McKelvey, "1–2 Samuel", in *A Biblical-Theological Introduction to the Old Testament: The Gospel Promised*, ed. Miles V. Van Pelt (Wheaton: Crossway, 2016), 215.

contemplated building YHWH a permanent house. The word of YHWH that coincided with David's plan revealed both the fulfilment of the promise of kings given to Abraham, and its use towards the restoration of God's dwelling and kingdom in the world.

According to the biblical narrative, David revealed to Nathan, the prophet, his wishes to build God a house. Nathan, in full agreement, gave him his blessing before God's word on the matter came to him by night, putting a stop to David's plans:

> The LORD declares to you that the LORD will make you a house. When your days are fulfilled and you lie down with your ancestors, I will raise up your offspring after you, who shall come forth from your body, and I will establish his kingdom. He shall build a house for my name, and I will establish the throne of his kingdom forever. I will be a father to him, and he shall be a son to me. When he commits iniquity, I will punish him with a rod such as mortals use, with blows inflicted by human beings. But I will not take my steadfast love from him, as I took it from Saul whom I put away from before me. Your house and your kingdom shall be made sure forever before me; your throne shall be established forever. (2 Sam 7:11–16)

God let David know that his intentions to build him a permanent house would be carried out by David's son. Instead of allowing David to build him a house, YHWH would make a house for David and would establish his kingship. Essentially the message of YHWH was the perpetuity of David's dynasty and throne. YHWH would through David's dynasty "establish the throne of his kingdom forever" (2 Sam 7:13, repeated in 7:16). YHWH promised to chastise future kings in the Davidic line if they sinned but, unlike the way he dealt with Saul, he would leave the throne untouched in David's house (2 Sam 7:15; see also Ps 89:4). David's house and kingdom would "be made sure forever" (2 Sam 7:16).

The promise of an everlasting dynasty and kingship to David is reiterated in Psalm 89 through the psalmist's inspired petition. The perpetual preservation of David's dynasty and kingship is expressed in that prayer in the language of covenant. The covenant YHWH made with David was identified by Weinfeld as a grant covenant.[7] Grant covenants, or royal grants, were promissory types of covenants common in the ancient Near East in the second half of the second millennium BC. In a grant covenant, the *vassal* was unconditionally granted, through an oath, a substantial gift (such as land or dynasty) by his *suzerain* as a reward of his loyalty. In this inspired petition, the psalmist, by some revelation, reveals that YHWH granted David by oath an everlasting dynasty and a throne:

> You said, "I have made a covenant with my chosen one.
> I have sworn to my servant David:
> 'I will establish your descendants forever,
> and build your throne for all generations.'" (Ps 89:3–4)

Together with this, the covenant God made with David was also unconditional (unrelated to the conduct of David's dynasty). If an heir of David erred, God would chastise him but not take the throne away from David's house:

> I will establish his line forever,
> and his throne as long as the heavens endure.
> If his children forsake my law
> and do not walk according to my ordinances,
> if they violate my statutes
> and do not keep my commandments,
> then I will punish their transgressions with the rod
> and their iniquity with scourges;
> but I will not remove from him my steadfast love,
> or be false to my faithfulness. (Ps 89:29–33)

The covenant between YHWH and David was clear. When David's heirs failed to follow God's law, they would be chastised. This stipulation was not exclusive to Solomon (as some readings of 2 Sam 7:11–16 conclude), but applied to all his descendants. Additionally the blessings YHWH promised to David under this covenant included the promise that David and his dynasty would prevail over their enemies (Ps 89:20–23), that they would enjoy YHWH's faithfulness and steadfast love (Ps 89:24), that they would bring order in the world (Ps 89:25), and as YHWH's firstborn would be exalted over all kings of the earth.

---

7. M. Weinfeld, "The Covenant of Grant in the Old Testament and in the Ancient Near East," *JAOS* 90.2 (1970). See also Scott W. Hahn, *Kinship By Covenant: A Canonical Fulfilment of God's Saving Promises*, The Anchor Yale Bible Reference Library (Yale: Yale University Press, 2019).

The promise of an everlasting kingship as a fulfilment of the promise of kings given to Abraham had been alluded to earlier in Jacob's prophecy to Judah that the monarchy would not depart from him (Gen 49:10): "The sceptre shall not depart from Judah . . . until (*ad*) tribute comes to him." Although translated as implying that Judah's house reign will have a point of culmination or even cessation, "until," in the NRSV (and some other versions of the Bible), the Hebrew word *ad* usually means "ever," or "forever" where it appears in biblical literature.[8] This being the case, other translations such as the one in GNB, "Judah will hold the royal sceptre, And his descendants will always rule," capture more accurately Jacob's prophecy that Judah's house would hold the kingship in perpetuity.

YHWH's promise to David of an everlasting dynasty and throne helps us to understand that the fulfilment of the promise of kings given to Abraham started with David. Since YHWH's promise of a perpetual dynasty and throne meant that the kings of Israel would come exclusively from David's house, it follows logically that this promise began to be fulfilled in David and thereafter through his dynasty. David's coming from the house of Judah fulfilled the prophecy of Jacob. This meant therefore that Saul could not have been God's choice for the onset of the fulfilment of the promise of kings to Abraham because he was not from the house of Judah. We should not be surprised by such a reading of Saul's kingship. The fulfilment of YHWH's promises to Abraham proceeded by God's election and not on the basis of human effort or desire. This procedure is basic to the unfolding story of the Bible.

YHWH chose Isaac by including Sarah in the promise of offspring to Abraham. Ishmael then was not his choice. YHWH chose Jacob but rejected Esau the firstborn of Isaac, as the one through whom his promise of offspring to Abraham would be fulfilled. From among all the nations of the world, God chose Israel to be his *sᵉgullâ*. Finally, YHWH chose Mount Zion to be his dwelling place with the people of Israel, and not Shiloh or any other place. A psalmist captured the unfolding of God's work through his election, and not through human desires and efforts quite well:

> He rejected the tent of Joseph,
> he did not choose the tribe of Ephraim;
> but he chose the tribe of Judah,

---

8. For more on *ad*, see Richard C. Steiner, "Four Inner-Biblical Interpretations of Genesis 49:10: On the lexical and Syntatic Ambiguities of עד as Reflected in the Prophecies of Nathan, Ahijah, Ezekiel, and Zechariah," *JBL* 132.1 (2013); and Hayyim Angel, "The Eternal Davidic Covenant in II Samuel Chapter 7 and its Later Manifestations in the Bible," *JBQ* 44.2 (2016).

> Mt Zion, which he loves.
> He built his sanctuary like the high heavens...
> He chose his servant David. (Ps 78:67–70)

Hardly any reasons for God's choices were given; they remain a mystery.[9] Thus Saul is rejected (not chosen) because of his sins; but David too sinned but was never rejected. Moving slightly forward in the story of the Bible, God promised to chastise erring monarchs but not take the throne from David's dynasty, but did not afford the same charity to Saul. Moreover, although Samuel intimates that YHWH had chosen David because in him, unlike in Saul, he had found a man "after his own heart" (1 Sam 13:14), that reason is incidental and not the fundamental reason behind YHWH's choice of David. It is an incidental reason because the choice of Judah, from whom David came, preceded the kingship of Saul which YHWH rejected. God could not have rejected Saul on account of his misdeeds and consequently elected David instead when he had already chosen Judah for Israel's monarchy before Saul was even born. There must have been therefore a more primary reason for God's choice of David which is not given in biblical literature.

David's Everlasting Throne and Restoration of God's Kingdom

Why did God promise David an everlasting dynasty and throne? The promise to David that his dynasty would rule Israel would have been sufficient to fulfil the promise of kings which God gave to Abraham. Our understanding of the role of David's dynasty and throne can only be satisfactory if we consider the significance of its eternity. This is critically important as a basis of comprehending the place of the promise of kings in the restoration of God's kingdom in the world. Unfortunately, biblical literature where David's dynasty and throne are mentioned do not explicitly or implicitly give us the significance of their perpetuity. We, therefore, have to look elsewhere in biblical literature for their significance. We will do so by drawing out what is implied by "everlasting" in biblical literature in settings where the word appears without reference to David's dynasty and/or throne. We will then apply that implication to David's dynasty and throne in order to understand its role in the restoration of God's kingdom in the world.

---

9. See for more Joel S. Kaminsky, *Yet I loved Jacob: Reclaiming the Biblical Concept of Election* (Nashville: Abingdon Press, 2007).

In biblical literature (the Old Testament particularly) the subject of eternity is used virtually in association with God only. YHWH alone in biblical literature is referred to as eternal (*ʿôlām*) and viewed as such (Gen 21:33; Deut 33:27; Hab 1:12). He is the "everlasting rock" (Isa 26:4; Jer 31:3). He alone is not subject to change or decay, or to coming into existence or becoming non-existent. For example, before creation God was and will be:

> Lord, you have been our dwelling place in all generations.
> Before the mountains were brought forth,
> or ever you had formed the earth and the world,
> from everlasting to everlasting you are God. (Ps 90:1–2; see also Deut 33:27; Isa 26:4; 40:28; Hab 1:12)

Even visions of God capture his permanence. In a unique vision of God by Daniel, God is foremost described, metaphorically, as "the ancient of days" (Dan 7:9). For this reason, what God is, his character (particularly some of its aspects that are of immense benefit to humans), and some of his properties, are singled out in biblical literature as everlasting. His steadfast love, for example, is everlasting (Pss 103:17; 89:2; 107:1; 1 Kgs 10:9). His mercies never end (Lam 3:22). His dwelling place, Mount Zion, remains forever (Ps 125:1; also Ezek 37:26–27), its doors are eternal (Ps 24:7), and he will rest there forever (Ps 132:14). His city, Jerusalem, is also everlasting (Ps 48:8). His kingship will never come to an end:

> The LORD sits enthroned over the flood;
> the LORD sits enthroned as king forever. (Ps 29:10; also Exod 15:18; Ps 10:16; Jer 10:10)

Neither will his kingdom:

> Your kingdom is an everlasting kingdom,
> and your dominion endures throughout all generations.
> (Ps 145:13; see also Dan 4:3, 34)

God's word is eternal: "For ever, O LORD, thy word is firmly fixed in the heavens (Ps 119:89 RSV). His pleasures are everlasting (Ps 16:11). His holiness is everlasting (Ps 93:5). His way is everlasting (Ps 139:24), and so is his salvation (Isa 45:17), joy (Isa 51:11; 61:7), and light (Isa 60:19–20).

There is more to eternity's association with God. What God gives can be everlasting, because God is everlasting. For example, he gave an everlasting covenant to Noah (Gen 9:16), and to Abraham (Gen 17:7, 13). He also promised to make an everlasting covenant with Israel (Isa 61:8; Jer 32:40). God will give his steadfast love to David and his descendants forever (Ps 18:50) and promises

David an everlasting priesthood (Ps 110:4). His judgements are everlasting (Ps 78:66) and so those on the receiving end of his wrath can come to everlasting ruin (Ps 52:5; Jer 25:9) and shame (Ps 78:66; Jer 23:40). In some cases, the everlasting aspect of something is by virtue of God giving it. This is the case with everlasting hills referring to the land which God gave Israel (Deut 33:15; cf. Hab 3:6); everlasting life (Dan 12:2), and everlasting righteousness which God will give the faithful (Dan 9:24); also everlasting shame and contempt on those who will incur God's judgement (Dan 12:2).

From the examination above, we can conclude that anything that is everlasting is either God himself, his character, or something which belongs to him or is closely associated with him. There is no notion in biblical literature that besides God there are other beings (and things associated with them) which exist in perpetuity parallel to God, without a relationship with God by virtue of which they are then everlasting. Even the cosmos or mountains, despite their seeming permanence (Hab 3:6), will not exist forever, but only God will:

> Long ago you laid the foundation of the earth,
>   and the heavens are the work of your hands.
> They will perish but you endure;
>   they will all wear out like a garment.
> You change them like clothing, and they pass away;
>   but you are the same, and your years have no end.
>   (Ps 102:25–27; see also Hab 3:6, 10)

This applies too to David's dynasty and throne. The dynasty and throne of David could not exist in perpetuity if they were not in some definite sense closely associated with God.

If our reflections are correct, then the implication of the perpetuity of David's dynasty and throne lay in their relation to God; David's dynasty and throne were everlasting because they were associated with YHWH. On one level this close association of David's dynasty and throne with YHWH has to do with the purpose of David's throne in relation to God's. The Davidic dynasty and throne were not chosen to exist for their own ends independent from YHWH's; they were inextricably linked intimately to YHWH's. The reason for this linkage was Israel. Having become, through the covenant, God's kingdom, Israel also became David's kingdom the moment God chose him to rule over it. God's kingdom, Israel, which had hitherto been in God's hands was thereafter in the hands of the Davidic kings (human kings), but not absolutely. This extraordinary phenomenon was only possible because David's throne was not simply a solitary human throne, but one attached to God's throne; David's dynasty was intended then to participate in YHWH's rule. In this sense the Davidic kings were kings of Israel as God's servants because God was Israel's true king.

Consequently, the heirs of David were to rule Israel according to the ways of YHWH because it was YHWH's kingdom. This role was its *raison d'être*, the purpose for its existence. The Davidic kings' rule over Israel as God's kingdom was to be done according to God's pleasure, and not according to human wishes. The Davidic kings were subject to God's kingship as his servants. In this way David's kingship would be used by God to restore his kingdom in the world. In covenant terms, God would be the great *suzerain*, and the Davidic kings would be God's *vassals* in his service to make other nations and kingdoms his *vassals*.

On another level the close association of David's dynasty and throne with YHWH as indicated by their eternity has to do with the eternity of God's kingdom, which Israel had become. The chosen king, therefore, also needed to be as everlasting as God's kingdom to be fit to rule it. This observation is apparent in some of the prayers of the psalmists for the king in which perpetual life is tied to their throne:

> Prolong the life of the king;
> > may his years endure to all generations!
> May he be enthroned forever before God. (Ps 61:6-7)

There are also allusions to the immortality of the Davidic kings in the Psalms. In a psalm that best epitomizes the king's immortality, the king is granted not only life but everlasting life:

> In your strength the king rejoices . . .
> > He asked for life; you gave it to him –
> length of days forever and ever. (Ps 21:1-4; also Pss 72:5; 72:17)

Unending life was not literally possible for David as a human being. An eternal earthly king ruling over God's everlasting kingdom would only be possible across generations by David transcending himself perpetually through his progeny. This is exactly what the promise to David of an everlasting house delivered.

Our conclusion above that the promise of eternity links David's throne to God's and prescribes, therefore, its role to rule Israel as God's kingdom and expand it to the whole world, is explicit in biblical literature in a number of ways. The first way biblical literature explicitly links David's throne to God and thereby prescribes its role is in revealing the status of the Davidic kings as sons of God. In the unfolding story of the Bible, this status is in fulfilment of the promise which God gave David concerning his son, Solomon. Although this promise was focused on Solomon, it was not limited to him. Since David's dynasty was its concern, the promise was meant to demonstrate that the closeness between YHWH and the Davidic kings (and not just between Solomon and YHWH) was analogous to the one between a father and his son. The divine-sonship status of the Davidic kings is confirmed in a psalm that was used during the coronation of a Davidic king. When an heir to the throne of David ascended his throne, he became from then on YHWH's son: "He said to me, 'You are my son; today I have begotten you'" (Ps 2:7). We also encounter the divine-sonship of the Davidic kings in Psalm 89 which contains an inspired petition centred on David's kingship. The psalmist alluded to the promise of divine-sonship which YHWH gave David as a heritage of his dynasty. He did so by reminding God of his words concerning David thus: "He shall cry to me, 'you are my father'" (Ps 89:26).

We discussed earlier that YHWH expected Israel as his son to live in ways that mirrored his own because a son resembles his father, or ought to be like him. This expectation, therefore, means that the father-son relationship between the Davidic kings and YHWH was meant to be reflected in the way they ruled Israel. A Davidic king was to replicate God's likeness in his rule by ruling Israel according to God's will. The rule of Israel by God's will was crucial in God's intentions to restore his kingdom in Israel and thereafter in the whole world. Without such a qualitative rule from the Davidic kings, the purpose of God would be jeopardized.

The second way biblical literature explicitly links David's throne to God and thereby prescribes its role is in showing the closeness between David's throne and YHWH's. Closeness between David's throne and YHWH's is seen by the symbolic portrayal of the proximity of David's throne to YHWH. The following psalm espouses this proximity and the reasons for it:

> The LORD says to my lord,
>   "Sit at my right hand
> until I make your enemies your footstool." (Ps 110:1)

The psalmist, by revelation of some sort, heard YHWH tell his lord to sit at his right hand. The context of the psalm indicates that the lord referred to was the king (a Davidic king, see also the same reference in Ps 80:17). The purpose of the closeness between the king's throne and YHWH's is for YHWH to support the king to subdue those who are against him (his enemies). Since the king was meant to rule according to God's will, all those who opposed his rule would, therefore, be God's enemies as well. As such, God would either defeat them, or subdue and bring them under the rule of the Davidic kings. Ultimately, God's kingdom would expand unimpeded through David's throne and dynasty.

In another sense, the closeness of David's throne and YHWH's is brought out in biblical literature by the direct identification of David's throne with God. David's throne is God's throne: "And of all my sons . . . he has chosen my son Solomon to sit upon the throne of the kingdom of the LORD over Israel" (1 Chr 28:5). This identification meant that those sitting on the throne of David were to rule Israel as God's kingdom, which is according to God's wishes and interests. This is further supported in biblical literature by the direct identification of the kingdom of Israel with the kingdom of YHWH. In his prayer to YHWH, David acknowledged that the kingdom of Israel was YHWH's: "yours is the kingdom, O LORD, and you are exalted as head above all" (1 Chr 29:11). This identification is also found in the remarks by certain people to Jeroboam who was resisting the dynasty of David: "And you think that you can withstand the kingdom of the LORD in the hand of the sons of David?" (2 Chr 13:8). If Israel is YHWH's kingdom, then its monarchy is meant to rule it as such, according to his wishes.

The third way biblical literature explicitly links David's throne to God and thereby prescribes its role is in the revelation that YHWH owns and uses the Davidic kings as his firstborn. In the inspired petition concerning David's kingship we looked at, the psalmist also reminded God that he promised to make David his firstborn: "I will make him the firstborn" (Ps 89:27). We mentioned in our discussion of Israel as God's firstborn that all firstborn belonged to God. For this reason the Israelites' firstborn, on the one hand, belonged to God, and, on the other, the people of Israel as a nation belonged to God as his firstborn in the league of nations. This worldview applied as well to the Davidic kings who thereby belonged to God. This is the reason why those seated on David's throne were referred to by YHWH as his, as "his king" (1 Sam 2:10; Pss 2:6; 18:50), or as "his anointed" (*māšiah*) (2 Sam 23:1; Pss 2:2; 20:6; 132:10; 132:17; Lam 4:20) which was an alternative way to refer to a king because kings were anointed. The reason the Davidic kings belonged to YHWH (as paralleled in the Levites' dedication to God's service in the temple as a substitute for Israel's firstborn) was so that they could serve God. That service would be in their dedication to rule Israel according to God's will – as his representatives – and thus advance his kingdom in Israel (as well as priesthood which we shall look at later).

Moreover as firstborn, the Davidic kings were also first in rank amongst the kings of the other nations:

> I will make him the firstborn,
> > the highest of the kings of the earth. (Ps 89:27)

According to YHWH's scheme, the Davidic kings were destined to rule not only Israel but the world. We, therefore, see that the Davidic kingship was not only to be used to restore God's kingdom in Israel but advance it abroad. The Davidic kings would lead other kingdoms as the firstborn amongst them, as a firstborn led his siblings. A psalmist's prayer for the king captures this universal reign as the vocation of the Davidic kings:

> May he have dominion from sea to sea.
> > And from the River to the ends of the earth . . .
>
> May the kings of Tarshish and of the isles render him tribute,
> > may the kings of Sheba and Seba bring gifts.
>
> May all the kings fall down before him,
> > all nations give him service. (Ps 72:8–11)

The universal reign of the Davidic kings (as a fulfilment of the promise of kings given to Abraham) is also evident in the blessing of Jacob who prophesied that nations would be subject to the monarchy from Judah:

> Judah will hold the royal sceptre,
> > And his descendants will always rule.
>
> Nations will bring him tribute
> > and bow in obedience to him. (Gen 49:10 GNB)

This outlook on Israel's monarchy is reflected too in Balaam's prophecy when he prophesied that Israel's monarchy would be higher than the monarchy of other nations:

> his king shall be higher than Agag;
> > and his kingdom shall be exulted. (Num 24:7)

Lastly, the Davidic kings' universal rule for God's kingdom sake is aptly captured in YHWH's words through his prophet Isaiah:

> See, I made him a witness to the peoples,
> > a leader and commander for the peoples. (Isa 55:4)

Davidic Kingship and Restoration of God's Kingdom

The task of the Davidic kings to rule Israel as God's kingdom, and thus advance it to the whole world, as signalled in the eternity of David's throne and dynasty, is more tightly defined in biblical literature in three specific roles of the Davidic kings. These are delivery of social justice, securing peace in Israel and subjugating nations, and priesthood. We discuss these roles in turn below.

We begin with social justice as a specified role of the Davidic kings, as brought out in the inspired thanksgiving of Hannah (1 Sam 2:1–10). Hannah's prayer prescribed directly the role of the Davidic kings and showed that the role corresponded to, and was modelled after, YHWH's kingship, in whose interest the Davidic kings ruled. As we pointed out earlier, Hannah offered a prayer whose content was God's justice in the world in relation to the soon-to-be-chosen Davidic kings (God's *māšîaḥ*). YHWH is judge, and so the pre-eminent role of his kingship is to deliver justice. In this thanksgiving YHWH grants justice to those at the bottom of the social hierarchy, including the feeble, the poor, the lowly and the oppressed. YHWH's justice is also seen in his judgement of the perpetrators of injustice, who are those higher up in the social hierarchy, including the arrogant, rich, and mighty:

> Talk no more so very proudly,
>   let not arrogance come from your mouth;
> for the LORD is a God of knowledge,
>   and by him actions are weighed.
> The bows of the mighty are broken,
>   but the feeble gird on strength.
> Those who are full have hired themselves out for bread,
>   but those who were hungry are fat for spoil.
> The barren has borne seven,
>   but she who had many children is forlorn.
> The LORD kills and brings life;
>   he brings down to Sheol and raises up.
> The LORD makes poor and makes rich;
>   he brings low, he also exalts.
> He raises up the poor from the dust;
>   he lifts the needy from the ash heap,
> to make them sit with princes,
>   and inherit a seat of honour. (1 Sam 2:3–9)

This role of YHWH's kingship, according to Hannah's prophetic prayer, would be furthered by "his king" (as we earlier discussed, a Davidic king).

The yoking of God's justice to a Davidic king is expressed by means of poetic parallelism thus:

> The LORD will judge the end of the earth;
> he will give strength to his king,
> and exalt the power of his anointed (*mᵉšîḥô*). (1 Sam 2:10)

In plain talk, YHWH would judge the world by a Davidic king through granting the king strength to be able to do so. The role of the Davidic kings was, therefore, to deliver justice.

The delivery of justice as integral to YHWH's kingship is found elsewhere in biblical literature. A psalmist, for example, praised God because his throne was founded on justice:

> The LORD is king! Let the earth rejoice;
> let the many coastlands be glad!
> Clouds and thick darkness are all around him;
> righteousness and justice are the foundation of his
> throne. (Ps 97:1–2; see also 89:14)

We should not understand the psalmist to mean here that YHWH's throne is founded on both justice (*mišpat*) and righteousness (*ṣedek*) because they virtually mean the same thing. This is why in biblical literature they are used synonymously as seen in their appearances in synonymous parallel poems (Amos 5:24; Isa 32:16; Prov 8:20), or, as in the psalm above, they are used as a pair (Isa 9:7; Jer 9:24; Hos 2:19). In other words, to act justly and to act rightly according to biblical literature is one and the same thing. YHWH's throne is therefore not founded on justice and righteousness, but on justice (or righteousness). I have preferred to use justice, rather than use justice and righteousness, or righteousness, because it is the most commonly used in biblical literature.

If justice is the foundation of YHWH's throne, then his kingship is based on justice. We can say then that, in an aggressive sense, YHWH's rule promotes justice. In a defensive sense, YHWH's rule defends justice. In a working sense, YHWH's rule delivers or executes justice. In other words YHWH's rule in the world is substantially ordered in the interest of justice. This is in keeping with God's nature for we read in biblical literature that YHWH "loves righteousness and justice" (Pss 33:5; 37:28; 99:4; see also Isa 61:8), and that he is "a God of justice" (Isa 30:18; Job 37:23).

Since, as revealed in Hannah's prayers, the Davidic kingship corresponds with YHWH's kingship, the role of the Davidic kings is, correspondingly, the delivery of justice. A psalmist understood this well as evidenced in his prayer for the king:

> Give the king your justice, O God,
>> and your righteousness to the king's son. (Ps 72:1–2)

Through Isaiah, YHWH says, in the context of the restoration of the Davidic kingship, that the Davidic king will fulfil this specific role effectively. He will establish his kingdom and hold it together with justice:

> . . . for the throne of David and his kingdom.
> He will establish and uphold it
>> with justice and with righteousness. (Isa 9:6)

In the context of the restoration of Israel, YHWH through his prophet Isaiah (and others) pointed to the execution of justice as the role of the Davidic kings. YHWH proclaimed that his king will not be impeded in delivering justice in the world:

> Here is my servant, whom I uphold
>> my chosen one, in whom my soul delights;
> I have put my spirit upon him;
>> he will bring forth justice to the nations . . .
> He will not grow faint or be crushed
>> until he has established justice in the earth. (Isa 42:1–4;
>> see also Jer 23:5–6; 33:15)

Solomon's prayer also indirectly pointed to justice as a role of the Davidic kingship. When Solomon was asked by YHWH what he desired, he prayed for wisdom to discern good and evil for the sake of delivering justice to Israel. The fact that God was gladdened by his prayer indicated that justice was a vital role given to the Davidic kingship. Solomon prayed thus: "Give your servant therefore an understanding mind to govern your people, able to discern between good (*tob*) and evil (*ra*)" (1 Kgs 3:9). If we go back to our earlier chapter, humans' desire to know good and evil was a rebellion against ruling by God's wishes, in order to rule by their own. Solomon, however, prayed to be enabled to deliver justice by what is good (God's wishes). It must have dawned on Solomon that as a man he could not by himself discern between good and evil to deliver justice. He needed YHWH to help him with discernment, which YHWH did. His judgement in the case of the woman whose child had been stolen by another was clear to all as a delivery of justice (according to what was good and not evil): "All Israel heard of the judgement that the king had rendered; and they stood in awe of the king, because they perceived that the wisdom of God was in him to execute justice" (1 Kgs 3:28). Elsewhere in biblical literature the queen of Sheba alluded to justice as the role of the Davidic kings. She acknowledged the love of YHWH for King Solomon whom she perceived was placed on the throne to "execute justice and righteousness" (1 Kgs 10:9) for the sake of Israel (his kingdom).

We need now to consider what justice meant for us to have a clearer understanding of the Davidic kings' role of delivering justice. The prayer of Solomon which we have looked at points to where the details of justice can be found. He desired to discern between good and evil for the sake of justice. If he was able to know what is good, he would deliver justice by promoting or defending the good, and by judging in the interest of the good. Justice, therefore, lay in *tob* (good) which YHWH determined and revealed; for which reason Solomon needed YHWH's help to discern. Because God had a covenant with Israel, *tob* must have been situated in the set of obligations he had imposed upon the people of Israel (i.e. in YHWH's laws to Israel). Those who lived by YHWH's laws did what was *tob* and those who did not did what was *ra'* (evil). This understanding is demonstrated in YHWH's charge against Israel of replacing good with evil by virtue of rejecting his laws.

> Woe to those who call evil good
>   and good evil,
> who put darkness for light
>   and light for darkness . . .
> Therefore . . . their root will be as rottenness,
>   and their blossom go up like dust
> for they have rejected the law of the LORD of hosts
>   and have despised the word of the Holy one of Israel.
>   (Isa 5:20–24 ESV)

This understanding of justice is also demonstrated in YHWH's appeal to Israel to do good, by which he meant to keep his law (the context of the proclamation showed), and not to love evil, by which (the context again showed) he meant to reject his laws (Amos 5:13–14). In regard to kings, those who used God's laws to rule and judge Israel would be doing good and thereby delivering justice, and those who did not would be doing evil and promoting injustice.

Not all of God's laws were about justice. Indeed YHWH's justice in biblical literature is a particular type of justice that we may call social justice. This social justice has a specific set of concerns and is binary in nature: justice to the suffering weak and lowly, and punishment/judgement to the culpable high and mighty in society. The dual nature of social justice as YHWH's justice is succinctly expressed by a psalmist:

> It is God who executes judgement,
>> putting down one and lifting another. (Ps 75:7)

It is also captured in the prophetic thanksgiving of Hannah:

> The LORD kills and brings to life;
>> he brings down from Sheol and raises up.
> The LORD makes poor and makes rich;
>> he brings low and he exalts. (1 Sam 2:6–7)

In the same thanksgiving by Hannah, more details are given on God's justice as social justice. Hannah praised God because he is the judge whose justice to the weak and lowly brings an end to their wretched state, while his punishment to the high and mighty sees them suffer the former fate of the weak and lowly:

> He raises up the poor from the dust;
>> he lifts the needy from the ash heap,
> to make them sit with princes,
>> and inherit a seat of honour. (1 Sam 2:8–9)

In addition, where justice is elaborated upon in biblical literature, its content is social justice. A psalmist in his praise of YHWH's kingship, for example, portrays his justice as social justice:

> Who is like the LORD our God,
>> who is seated on high . . .
> He raises the poor from the dust . . .
>> He gives the barren woman a home
> making her the joyous mother of children.
>> (Ps 113:5–9)

Another psalmist in a petition to God articulated social justice as YHWH's justice:

> How long will you judge unjustly
>> and show partiality to the wicked?
> Give justice to the weak and the orphan;
>> maintain the right of the lowly and destitute.
> Rescue the weak and the needy;
>> deliver them from the hand of the wicked. (Ps 82:2–4)

Also according to the Psalms, when YHWH stood to judge, social justice was the outcome:

> ... God rose up to establish judgement
> to save all the oppressed of the earth. (Ps 76:9)

To give a last set of examples of YHWH's justice as social justice, YHWH through the prophets instructed the people of Judah to seek justice (i.e. social justice), by helping the weak and lowly whose state is on account of the injustice meted on them by the powerful:

> ... learn to do good;
> > seek justice,
> rescue the oppressed,
> > defend the orphan,
> plead for the widow. (Isa 1:17)

Through the same prophet, YHWH's justice as social justice is seen in his impending punishment on the powerful for not giving justice to the weak and lowly:

> Ah, you who make iniquitous decrees,
> > who write oppressive statutes,
> to turn aside the needy from justice
> > and to rob the poor of my people of their right,
> that widows may be your spoil,
> > and that you may make the orphans your prey!
> What will you do on the day of punishment? (Isa 10:1–3; see also 33:13–15)

God's justice, therefore, was to be found in his laws whose concerns were with the downtrodden. These laws were meant to uplift them from their wretched plight, or at least ameliorate them. These were laws protecting the rights of the poor, prescribing the responsibility and help to be given to the orphan, the widow, and the outsider (Exod 22:21–24; 23:9–11; Lev 19:9–10; Deut 15:4–11; 23:25–26; 24:19–22). In this regard, the laws of the Jubilee and sabbatical years was especially important because their details were exclusively about social justice to individuals and families. The concern of the Jubilee was the redistribution of wealth to help particularly the weak and lowly, and to restrain the excesses and greed of the powerful which victimized the lowly (Lev 25:8–55).

The Davidic kings, therefore, had the role of delivering social justice by implementing, in their judgements and actions, God's laws concerned with the downtrodden. YHWH himself points this out. Through the prophet Jeremiah,

YHWH warns the Davidic kings of dire consequences if they do not execute their role of delivering social justice:

> Hear the word of the LORD, O King of Judah sitting on the throne of David – you, and your servants, and your people who enter these gates. Thus says the LORD: Act with justice and righteousness, and deliver from the hand of the oppressor anyone who has been robbed. And do not wrong or violence to the alien, the orphan, and the widow, or shed innocent blood in this place. (Jer 22:1–3; also Jer 21:11–12)

Through the same prophet, YHWH points to a certain Davidic king who, in the restoration of Israel, would deliver social justice perfectly by implementing the law on the Jubilee and sabbatical years which, as we said, was concerned exclusively with justice to the downtrodden at the expense of the rich and able:

> The spirit of the LORD is upon me,
> because the LORD has anointed me;
> he has sent me to bring good news to the oppressed,
> to bind up the brokenhearted,
> to proclaim liberty to the captives,
> and release to the prisoner;
> to proclaim the year of the LORD's favour,
> and the day of vengeance of our God. (Isa 61:1–2)

Social justice delivery as a role of the Davidic kings is also evident in the Psalter. In his prayer for the king, a psalmist prayed for him to be enabled to deliver social justice:

> Give the king your justice, O God . . .
> May he defend the cause of the poor of the people,
> give deliverance to the needy,
> and crush the oppressor. (Ps 72:1–4)

The oppressed poor and the wicked are also in special focus in the judgements of the prophesied Davidic king because that is the role expected of the Davidic kings. This Davidic king would execute social justice perfectly because he would offer justice without human limitations by having "perfect knowledge" of the situation of the downtrodden:

> He shall not judge by what his eyes see,
> or decide by what his ears hear;
> but with righteousness he shall judge the poor,

and decide with equity for the meek of the earth. (Isa 11:3-4)

The Davidic kings were therefore meant to be judicial kings imposing social justice in Israel by their judgements and actions.

We now look at the second role of the Davidic kings: securing peace in Israel and subjugating Israel's enemies. In biblical literature God is proclaimed as a warrior: "The LORD is a warrior . . ." (Exod 15:3; see also Zeph 3:17; Ps 24:8; Josh 5:13-15). Indeed, he is viewed as a warrior-king:

> O LORD my God, you are very great.
>> You are clothed with honour and majesty . . .
> you make the clouds your chariot,
>> you ride on the wings of the wind,
> you make the winds your messengers,
>> fire and flame your ministers. (Ps 104:1-4; also Pss 18:7-15; 68:17-18)

As a warrior-king YHWH uses war to punish nations and to either destroy his enemies (evil doers, idolators, those that are not subject/loyal to him, and the proud) or to subdue them in order to bring them into his kingdom. God's wars are, therefore, subordinate to the interests of his kingship. They are not simply wars for the sake of wars, or even as a display of might (although YHWH may be praised for his might which his wars demonstrate).

According to biblical literature God's war was at first cosmic. Within the ancient Near Eastern worldview, it was perceived that YHWH fought with the chaotic sea, and with Leviathan (the sea dragon) and Rahab (the chaos monster). As a result, God bound the waters and controlled them, and destroyed Leviathan and Rahab:

> Yet God my king is from old . . .
>> You divided the sea by your might . . .
> You crushed the heads of Leviathan;
>> you gave him as food for the creatures of the wilderness.
>> (Ps 74:12-14)

> You rule the raging of the sea; . . .
>> You crushed Rahab like a carcass;
> you scattered your enemies with your mighty arm. (Ps 89:9-10)

The linkage between God's fight with chaos and his kingship in biblical literature, as we made clear in our discussion on creation, is not incidental. God's victory over chaos came about because he imposed his kingship on precreation. The sea came under his control (Ps 65:7; 89:9; 104:9; Job 38:8) and he eliminated the threat of chaos by destroying the forces of chaos, Leviathan and Rahab. He thereby created the world, and the world simultaneously became a part of his kingdom. Moreover whenever the sea threatens to unleash chaos, God still imposes his kingship:

> You silence the roaring of the seas,
>   the roaring of their waves. (Ps 65:7)

> The floods have lifted up, O LORD,
>   the floods have lifted up their voice;
>   the floods lift up their roaring.
> More majestic than the thunders of mighty waters,
>   more majestic than the waves of the sea,
>   majestic on high is the LORD. (Ps 93:3–4)

In contemporary language, God is king of creation for he created the world and all that is in it, and he continually sustains it as king (Ps 104:10–13; 135:5–7; Jer 31:35).

God's cosmic war in biblical literature is followed by God's earthly wars which he also uses to punish the nations and/or to impose his rule in the temporal world. We see the use of war as a punishment in the Israelites' deliverance in Egypt, in their journey to the promised land, in their settlement on the land, and in their exile from it. In regard to Egypt, God waged war against the Egyptians (Exod 15:4–10; Ps 18:7–15) as a punishment for their oppression of the Israelites (Exod 3:7–9). Their sinking in the sea (Exod 15:10) was not only actual but symbolized their punishment, given the allusions in biblical literature between sinking in water and guilt (Exod 15:5; Ps 69:3, 16; Jonah 2:4).[10] In regard to the promised land, God waged war on its prior inhabitants as a punishment for their sins (Gen 15:16; Deut 9:4).

When Israel was settled in the land, the prophets warned the nations of YHWH's impending punishment by means of war for their sins. The Ammonites, for example, would be punished by war for their transgressions (Amos 1:13–15). Israel's neighbours would be punished by war (Joel 3:2, 9–12) because of their plunder of Israel (Joel 3:1–3). YHWH would use war to punish the Egyptians for their haughtiness (Ezek 31:1–11) using the king of Babylon: "I will strengthen the hand of the king of Babylon, and put a sword in his hand" (Ezek 30:24). The Babylonians, too, would be punished by YHWH by means of war for their harshness and pride (Isa 13:17–22).

---

10. See for more, P. Kyle McCarter, "The River Ordeal in Israelite Literature," *HTR* 66:4 (1973), and Robert M. Good, "The Just War in Israel," *JBL* 104.3 (1985).

Although the Israelites were God's people, they were not spared YHWH's punishment by means of war. God would punish them for their evil ways using the armies of foreign nations (Judg 2:11–14; Ps 106:40–42). The Israelites were warned, specifically, of YHWH's impending judgement through the Babylonian army who would come from the north (Jer 6:22–26; Hab 1:5–11; Ezek 9:1–11).

There is more to God's earthly wars in relationship to the restoration of his dwelling and kingdom in the world. His wars through the Davidic kingship were meant for the peace and security of Israel as a part of his kingdom. God's election of David and his line to be the kings of Israel meant, as we earlier argued, that YHWH's kingdom in the world was in human hands; but human rule over Israel was not absolute. As we pointed out, the Davidic kings belonged to God and had their throne close to his. They were also meant to be reflective of God's nature. God, therefore, intended to use the Davidic kings to rule Israel and establish his rule in the world. In consequence, his earthly wars to secure peace and security in Israel and expand the kingdom became the responsibility of the Davidic kings. It became the role of the Davidic kings to fight off Israel's enemies for her peace and security as an element of the blessings of abundant life. For this reason their fights were not common wars but wars in the interest of YHWH's kingdom: "kingdom wars." David, for example, "was fighting the battles of the LORD" (1 Sam 25:28). David seemed aware of this in his praise of YHWH:

> He trains my hands for war,
>   so that my arms can bend a bow of bronze . . .
> I pursued my enemies and overtook them;
>   and did not turn back until they were consumed.
> I struck them down, so that they were not able to rise;
>   they fell under my feet.
> For you girded me with strength for the battle;
>   you made my assailants sink under me. (Ps 18:34–39; also
>   Pss 18:50; 20:6; 45:5)

YHWH himself in his covenant with David confirmed this as a role of the Davidic kings by promising David, his *māšîaḥ*, that he would be by his side to enable him to defeat his enemies:

> The enemy shall not outwit him,
>   the wicked shall not humble him.
> I will crush his foes before him
>   and strike down those who hate him. (Ps 89:22–23; also
>   Pss 110:2; 132:18)

It is such an understanding of the role of the Davidic kings that informs a psalmist's prayers for the king (Ps 72:1–11) which associates him with peace: "In his days may . . . peace abound" (Ps 72:7). Without the king's defeat of Israel's enemies, that peace would not be forthcoming, something which the psalmist knew and prayed about thus:

> May his foes bow down before him
> and his enemies lick the dust. (Ps 72:9)

King Solomon seemed quite successful at this role. During his reign "Israel lived in safety, from Dan even to Beersheba, all of them under their vine and fig trees" (1 Kgs 4:25).

God's earthly wars were also meant to advance his kingdom beyond Israel to the whole world by subjugating resistant nations. Since God intended to use the Davidic kings to rule Israel and extend his kingdom in the world, it was the role of these kings to subjugate hostile nations by means of war (through YHWH's support) and bring them under their rule. The nations, in becoming a part of Israel would know YHWH, submit to his laws and thus become a part of his kingdom. We encounter this most strongly in the second Psalm:

> Why do the nations conspire
> and the peoples plot in vain?
> The kings of the earth set themselves,
> and the rulers take counsel together,
> against the LORD and his anointed (*mᵊšîḥô*), saying,
> "Let us burst their bonds asunder,
> and cast their cords from us." (Ps 2:1–3)

Nations that were conspiring to rebel against YHWH and the Davidic king were warned to take notice. The bond between the king and YHWH was very strong because the king was YHWH's son and his choice for his universal reign (Ps 2:4–8). For this reason no nation would be able to withstand the king:

> You shall break them with a rod of iron,
> and dash them in pieces like a potter's vessel. (Ps 2:9)

It was therefore wise of the nations to make peace with YHWH by serving him, which simultaneously meant being subject to his *māšîaḥ*, the Davidic king (Ps 2:10–11; see also Deut 20:10–20). The same is clear in the Psalmist's revelation concerning God's covenant with David, which included his promise to give the Davidic kings power to rule the world by subjugating and ruling the nations. The nations were symbolized in the chaotic forces of the waters (reminiscent of his YHWH's cosmic defeat, and control of the chaotic waters) which represented resistant and rebellious nations to the king's rule:

> I will set his hand on the sea
> and his right hand on the rivers. (Ps 89:25; cf. Isa 17:12–13)

The role of the Davidic kings to rule the world by subjugating resistant or rebellious nations by war (through YHWH's support) is revealed by other psalmists too (Pss 110:2, 5; 89:20–23).

Outside the Psalms this role is revealed in several places in biblical literature. In the prophecy of Balaam, the prophesied king of Israel shall bring to subjection nations that are his enemies (his political adversaries as well as those opposed to his rule as clarified in Thompson's study):[11]

> His king shall be higher than Agag,
>   and his kingdom shall be exalted . . .
> he shall devour the nations that are his foes
>   and break their bones.
> He shall strike with his arrows. (Num 24:7–9)

Zechariah's prophecy of the restoration of the Davidic kingship also points to the Davidic kings' universal reign achieved, in some cases, by war to subjugate resistant nations. It is through their subjugation by the prophesied Davidic king that peace is established in the world as an element of abundant life, which characterizes God's kingdom:

> Rejoice greatly, O daughter Zion! . . .
>   Lo, your king comes to you; . . .
> He will cut off the chariot from Ephraim
>   and the war-horse from Jerusalem!
> and the battle bow shall be cut off,
>   and he shall command peace to the nations;
> his dominion shall be from sea to sea,
>   and from the River to the ends of the earth. (Zech 9:9–10)

Historically it would appear that King David and King Solomon were relatively successful in subjugating other nations and ruling them by means of war. David recognized his universal reign (Ps 18:43–45). He expanded the realms of Israel to their furthest extent ruling over the Ammonites, the Moabites, the Edomites, the Philistines, and even over the northern empires of Geshur, Aram and Hamath through wars of subjugation. King Solomon

---

11. J. A. Thompson, "Israel's 'haters,'" *VT* 29.2 (1979).

consolidated this universal reign: "Solomon was sovereign over all the kingdoms from the Euphrates to the land of the Philistines, even to the border of Egypt; they brought tribute and served Solomon all the days of his life" (1 Kgs 4:21). Judging by Psalm 47, however, King Solomon seemed to have moved his universal reign towards its intended goal, the extension of God's kingdom. In this psalm, God is credited with Israel's victories in battle by which the nations became their subjects:

> For the LORD, the Most High, is awesome,
>> a great king over all the earth.
> He subdued peoples under us,
>> and nations under our feet. (Ps 47:2–3)

On account of their subjugation and rule by Israel, the nations went to Jerusalem to pay homage to the king, and to YHWH the ultimate king. They had become thereby, with Israel, subjects of God and thus a part of God's kingdom:

> God is king over all nations;
>> God sits on his holy throne.
> The princes of the peoples gathered
>> as the people of the God of Abraham.
> For the shields of the earth belong to God;
>> he is highly exalted. (Ps 47:8–9)

Psalm 47 is also critical to indicating that wars of subjugation that the Davidic kings undertook were intended to advance God's kingdom (i.e. they were "kingdom wars") to the extent that the Davidic kings and the Israelites were obedient to God's laws. Solomon's wars of subjugation were kingdom wars because it would appear that King Solomon and the people of Israel were obedient to YHWH in that period. Consequently the subdued nations became YHWH's subjects, and therefore a part of his kingdom. Wars unaccompanied by obedience would be "common wars," wars whose goal was not the extension of God's kingdom. Nations that would be subjugated and ruled through such wars would in the end not be subject to YHWH's kingdom and would not experience the blessings of abundant life; a situation which would defeat the aims of their subjugation by the Davidic kings. Common wars behind subjugation would simply be for the Davidic king, or for Israel, and would be an abusive and unjust use of the sword.

The Davidic kings were therefore warrior-kings with the role of first securing peace and security in Israel as God's kingdom. They were then to ultimately extend by subjugation the kingdom of God to the rest of the world.

We conclude our discussion of the role of the Davidic king with some comments on war, given contemporary difficulties with it. We need to understand that in the Bronze and Iron Ages and even later times, war at national level was the way of life which was tied to conceptions of society and attendant political organisation. War was therefore "a necessary means of defence and security,"[12] and a fundamental instrument for international order, control and domination, acquisition of wealth, vengeance, display of power, and so on. God's involvement with such a world to express his displeasure with evil, and fight against forces opposed to his ways, meant his involvement with physical war. However his involvement was limited to a circumscribed goal. It was exclusively for punishment and the restoration of his kingdom in the world which would result in abundant life. For this reason not all wars that Israel fought were God's wars ("kingdom wars"). This would apply to all wars Israel fought when the people were not obedient to YHWH and when the Davidic kings were not ruling with social justice (see Ps 81:11–16). Moreover, war in biblical literature is not revelled in or glorified. To the contrary, it is associated with destruction, pain, and bitterness – the very reason why it is one of the tools used by God to punish nations. Further still, God will bring war to an end when his kingdom is restored in the world.

We also need to understand that when God is described as a warrior, the focus is upon his action of punishing evil and reining in the forces opposed to his kingdom, and not on his physical wars. When the Bronze and Iron Age world changed, the manifestation of God's punishment of evil, and fight against those opposed to his rule, changed as well. In apocalyptic literature of the Old Testament and in the New Testament, as we shall later discuss, the forces with which God fights, and which he empowers his king to defeat, change from the nations to spiritual entities – Satan, demons (and evil spirits), and the flesh. These forces are the enemies of God, his king, and his people. His punishments also have changed accordingly, to be meted out fundamentally in the realm of the afterlife (through the resurrection) when God will judge all people.

The last role of the Davidic kings we discuss is priesthood. We see this in the priestly activities of David and Solomon. David's priestly activities are seen in 2 Samuel 6:12–19 where the activities of David correspond to those of a priest. David pitched the tabernacle in Jerusalem (2 Sam 6:17) which was a function of priests (Num 1:51). David offered a sacrifice to YHWH by himself (2 Sam 6:13) and offered burnt offerings and peace offerings (2 Sam 6:17); yet it was only the priests who offered sacrifices and presented offerings to YHWH on

---

12. Waldemar Janzen, "War in the Old Testament," *MQR* 46.2 (1972):162.

the people's behalf (Num 3:6–8; 6:16–17; 8:14–26). David "blessed the people in the name of the LORD of hosts" (2 Sam 6:18) which was a role designated for the priests (Num 6:22–27; Deut 10:8). David also wore a linen ephod (2 Sam 6:14), the dress of the priests (Exod 39:1–31). Solomon performed the duties of a priest, indicating that he too was a priest: "Three times a year Solomon used to offer up burnt offerings and sacrifices of well-being on the altar that he built for the LORD" (1 Kgs 9:25; 10:5). We mentioned in our discussion of priesthood that on account of their varied services for YHWH in his house, priests were also called the servants of YHWH. YHWH referred to David on numerous occasions as "my servant" (2 Sam 7:5, 8; 2 Kgs 11:32, 38; Ps 89:3, 20; Jer 33:26). David was also referred to by others as YHWH's servant (2 Sam 7:26, 29; 1 Kgs 8:24–26; Pss 78:70; 86:16; 132:10).

However, the most direct reference to the role of the Davidic kings as priests is in Psalm 110:

> The Lord has sworn and will not change his mind,
>   "You are a priest forever according to the order of
>   Melchizedek." (Ps 110:4)

This role is expressed as an oath, and reveals thereby a further detail in God's covenant with David. Since David, as an individual human being, could not be a priest in perpetuity, we should understand the Davidic kings to be priests according to this covenant. The covenant detail concerning God's promises to David which is provided in this psalm is not entirely new. In Psalm 89, the psalmist made it known that God had promised to make David the firstborn (Ps 89:27). As we pointed out, the Davidic kings' status as God's firstborn is indicative of their priesthood as God's portion (or *sᵉgullâ*) along the lines of the Levites (who replaced Israel's firstborn). What is new in this covenant detail is the kind of priests the Davidic kings will be: they are priests in the manner of (*dibrātî*) Melchizedek. The difference between Melchizedek, the priest who blessed Abraham and received his tithe offering from Abraham (Gen 14:17–20), and a Levite priest, was that Melchizedek was a priest-king. Such a priesthood is the one designed for the Davidic kings; they are priest-kings. As priests the Davidic kings would, in line with the role of priests we mentioned, attend to YHWH's house, offer and preside over sacrifices, and give God's word to the people. They would thus function as mediators between YHWH and his people.

Apart from the general association of priests with service in God's house which underlines their mediatorial role as representatives of God to humans (and viceversa), nothing is said of the precise way the Davidic kings would be mediators. However the book of Chronicles seems to give a picture of the Davidic kings as priest-kings who were meant, therefore, to lead Israel to worship YHWH in his house as well as offer leadership in the administration of worship. Being designed as world rulers, the Davidic kings were also meant to lead the nations, alongside Israel, in the worship of YHWH. Chronicles portrayed David as a king involved closely with worship in the tabernacle. He prepared a place for the tabernacle (1 Chr 15:1). He brought the ark of God into Jerusalem (1 Chr 15–16). He appointed the Levites, as YHWH's minsters, to be responsible for carrying the ark to the tabernacle (1 Chr 15:2). He also commanded the leaders of the Levites to appoint them as temple singers and music makers (1 Chr 15:16–24). He led the joyous procession when he brought the ark into the tabernacle in Jerusalem (1 Chr 15:25–29). He appointed some Levites as "ministers before the ark of the Lord" (1 Chr 16:4). He offered burnt and peace offerings in the tent, and blessed God's people (1 Chr 16:1–3). He also appointed Asaph and his brethren to offer a thanksgiving psalm to God (1 Chr 16:7–43). Moreover, David's association with the book of Psalms is a testament of his close involvement with worship in YHWH's house as a priest-king.

We conclude by summing up our discussion in this chapter. God's promise to Abraham that he would be a father of kings as a component of bringing about the restoration of God's dwelling and kingdom in the world through Abraham was fulfilled in David's throne and dynasty. Through his covenant with Israel, YHWH intended Israel to be his kingdom, and through it to restore his kingdom in the world. However, as signalled in the promise of an everlasting dynasty and kingship which YHWH gave to David, YHWH elected David and his dynasty to be the monarchy he would use to rule and advance his kingdom in the world. To rule Israel as God's kingdom the Davidic kings needed to be judicial kings, warrior-kings, and priest-kings. Specifically, they needed to judge Israel with social justice, fight off Israel's enemies (for peace and security as a component of the blessings of abundant life), and expand Israel's domain by subjugating resistant nations (in order to restore God's kingdom in the world).

However the Davidic kings' success as the earthly rulers of God's kingdom, responsible for its advance throughout the world, was not a given. It was only a potential because it was dependent on their obedience to God's laws. Without obedience, the blessings of abundant life brought through social justice would not be forthcoming. In the event that they managed to fight off their enemies, the land would still be devoid of the blessings of abundant life. Subjugation of the nations would also be futile because Israel itself (which they would come under) would not be a part of God's kingdom under the rule of an obedient Davidic king and blessed thereof with abundant life. Unfortunately, as we shall discuss in our next chapter, the Davidic kings did fail to rule in obedience to God's laws.

5

Failure in the Restoration of God's Dwelling and Kingdom

With Israel settled in the promised land under the Davidic kings, God had fulfilled his promise to Abraham of offspring, land, and kings. What remained in the unfolding story of the Bible was the fulfilment of the blessings-to-all-nations promise. If we recall our previous discussions, the Abrahamic blessings-to-all-nations promise meant the restoration of God's dwelling and kingdom in the world. More specifically, this meant the blessings of abundant life to all nations by virtue of their becoming, thanks to Abraham's offspring, part of God's kingdom.

However, the blessings-to-all-nations promise was contingent upon the people of Israel fulfilling their priestly vocation of representing God to the nations through their own blessings of abundant life, which required obedience. If the Israelites would live in obedience to YHWH, he would dwell with them and they would become a part of his kingdom, experiencing thereby the blessings of abundant life on the land. The blessings of abundant life would attract other nations to YHWH who dwelt in Zion and lead them to his knowledge and to obedience of his laws (just as Israel would be doing). As a result, the nations would come under God's rule and receive the blessings of abundant life as a part of God's kingdom. This way God's kingdom and dwelling would be restored in the world.

In a different but complementary way, if the Davidic kings ruled Israel in obedience to YHWH as God's kingdom, they would be God's *māšiaḥ*, thereby enforcing social justice on the land and ensuring abundant life's blessing of peace and security upon it. They would also defeat their enemies or subjugate them and incorporate them into the kingdom of Israel as God's kingdom. As such, subjugated nations would come to know YHWH, submit to his rule and together with Israel worship YHWH in Zion. This way too, God's kingdom and dwelling would be restored in the world.

We therefore examine in this chapter how Israel and the Davidic kings fared in relationship to obedience to God's laws. More precisely, we will first look at the failure of the Davidic kings and the people of Israel to rule and live respectively in obedience to God, their consequent loss of land, and their apparent end as a result of God's judgement.

Failure of the Davidic Kings and Israel in Narratives

The books of Kings narrate the conduct of the kings of Israel in relationship to their obedience to God in ruling Israel. Starting with Solomon, all the kings are assessed predominantly on whether they did evil or good/right in the sight of God. Since, as we earlier discussed, good (*tob*), or doing right, is associated with obeying God's laws, while evil (*ra'*) is associated with disobeying him, a king's assessment on the basis of whether he did good or evil is indicative of whether the king ruled in obedience to God's law or not. Obeying or disobeying God's law as the criterion of assessing the kings is confirmed in cases where the narrator of the books of Kings assesses them as keeping or forsaking YHWH's commandment (1 Kgs 18:18; 2 Kgs 10:31; 14:6; 17:13; 18:6), or as not walking in the way of YHWH (2 Kgs 21:22), or as sinning (1 Kgs 12:30; 16:31; 2 Kgs 10:31). According to this criterion, all kings of the northern kingdom ("Israel" from here on) did what was evil in God's sight for they all "followed the sins of Jeroboam" (1 Kgs 15:3; 16:31; 2 Kgs 12:28 etc.). In the southern kingdom (Judah), seven kings – Asa, Jehoshaphat, Jehoash, Azariah/Uzziah, Jotham, Hezekiah, and Josiah – were judged to have ruled in obedience, that is, they did what was right in God's sight (though it is only King Josiah who did so without qualification).

The details of the kings' disobedience given in the books of Kings are almost exclusively centred on worship. All the kings of "Israel" and Judah (with only the exception of Kings Hezekiah and Josiah) were either idolatrous themselves, or, if not, entertained Israel's idolatry. They disobeyed God by having and building high places (*bāma*), pillars (*matsebah*) and altars, by having and building houses for Baal, making and having asherim and other idols, by sacrificing children, and by consulting mediums and soothsayers. They also disobeyed God by introducing altars of Baal and an image of Asherah in the house of YHWH to co-exist with YHWH. We examine below these various elements of the idolatry of the kings of Israel.

According to the discussion in chapter 3, mountains were perceived in the ancient world to be places of residence for deities. Height was a significant factor behind this belief because mountains reached up to the heavens where it was believed gods dwelt. Though not as high, hills as raised places would have also, for the same reasons, been revered as potential abodes of gods. As such they would have attracted people as sites of cultic worship. Solomon, for example, went to Gibeon for cultic worship because "that was the principal high place (*bāma*)" (1 Kgs 3:3). If hills were not available, raised places would have been put up, and that is exactly what the kings of Israel did but for non-YHWH cultic worship. Solomon, for example:

> built a high place for Chemosh the abomination of Moab, and for Molech (Milcom) the abomination of the Ammonites, on the mountain east of Jerusalem. He did the same for all his foreign wives, who offered incense and sacrificed to their gods. (1 Kgs 11:7–8)

The high places that Solomon built were used by a majority of subsequent kings of Judah to worship foreign gods. Their existence also encouraged the people of Israel to use them for non-YHWH worship. It was for this reason that although Kings Asa, Jehoshaphat, Jehoash, Amaziah, Azariah, and Jotham were assessed as doing right in the eyes of YHWH, they were blamed for entertaining idolatry in Judah because they failed to remove the high places and thus stop their use (1 Kgs 15:3; 22:43; 2 Kgs 12:3; 15:4; 15:35). Although King Hezekiah removed the high places (2 Kgs 18:4), King Manasseh rebuilt them (2 Kgs 21:3). King Josiah (2 Kgs 23:13, 19) eventually destroyed them all. In "Israel" King Jeroboam, like King Solomon, also made high places – which remained in use for worship of foreign gods throughout the life of "Israel." King Manasseh even appointed priests for them (1 Kgs 12:32).

Altars, which were artificially elevated sites for sacrifices, were also built by Israel's kings for non-YHWH cultic worship. Ahab, who was the wickedest king of "Israel" according to 1 Kings, "erected an altar for Baal in the house of Baal, which he built in Samaria" (1 Kgs 16:32). Manasseh, the worst king of Judah, erected altars for Baal in the temple of YHWH (2 Kgs 21:5). King Ahaz of Judah commanded the priest Uriah to build a bronze altar modelled on the one he saw in Damascus (2 Kgs 16:10) for his exclusive cultic use in the temple (2 Kgs 16:15). This was a sure sign that he worshipped the gods of the Assyrians in the temple.

In regard to asherim, or images of the goddess Asherah (a deity within the Canaanite pantheon),[1] King Ahab of Israel "made an Asherah" (1 Kgs 16:33 RSV) manifesting his worship of the same. The Asherah seems to have remained in Samaria until its destruction (2 Kgs 13:6). King Manasseh of Judah rebuilt an Asherah (2 Kgs 21:3) to worship the goddess in YHWH's house (2 Kgs 21:7) after the earlier one had been cut done by King Asa (1 Kgs 15:13). The kings of "Israel" also had or made idols beside the Asherah. King Jeroboam "made two calves of gold" (1 Kgs 12:28), which he placed in Bethel and Dan, and identified them as the gods of "Israel": "Here are your gods, O Israel, who brought you out of the land of Egypt" (1 Kgs 12:28). By building two idols and proclaiming them as the gods of "Israel," King Jeroboam led "Israel" into idolatry: "And this thing became a sin, for the people went to worship before the one at Bethel and before the other one as far as Dan" (1 Kgs 12:30). All the kings of Israel maintained the worship of these golden calves for they walked in the same sin of King Jeroboam by "which he made Israel to sin" (1 Kgs 15:26; 15:34; 16:26 etc.).

The kings of Israel and Judah also had pillars (*matsebhah*) for idols. According to Graesser's study,[2] pillars were used for memorial, legal, commemorative, and cultic purposes. In regard to cultic purposes, Graesser points out that pillars were used to mark the presence of a deity. To these cultic purposes we may add that pillars were revered as abodes of deities. This particular cultic purpose is seen in Jacob's vow to God to make the pillar he had used in Bethel his abode (Gen 28:20–22; 35:13–14). Graesser points out too that it was the pillars' cultic use that led to their idolatrous usage by the kings and people of Israel.[3] They were destroyed by Kings Hezekiah and Josiah (2 Kgs 18:4; 23:14), both of whom did not entertain any form of idolatry in Israel.

We turn now to the worship of Baal as another element in the idolatry of the kings of Israel. The wickedest kings in "Israel" and Judah (Ahab and Manasseh respectively) were devotees of Baal. King Ahab "served Baal and worshipped him" (1 Kgs 16:31). In addition, he built a house and an altar for Baal: "he erected an altar for Baal in the house of Baal, which he built in Samaria (1 Kgs 16:32). Manasseh did the same and worse. Not only did he erect altars for Baal (2 Kgs 21:3), but he erected some of them in the temple's outer court and inner room (2 Kgs 21:5).

---

1. See for a helpful reading Elana Newberger, "Asherah: The Israelite Goddess and the Cultic Object," *J. Theta Alpha Kappa* 29.1 (2005).

2. For more see Carl F. Graesser, "Standing Stones in Ancient Palestine," *BA* 35.2 (1972).

3. Graesser, "Standing Stones in Ancient Palestine," 37.

As for child sacrifices as an element in the idolatry of Israel's kings, King Ahaz of "Israel" and King Manasseh of Judah sacrificed their children as burnt offerings. They both made their sons "pass through the fire" (2 Kgs 16:3; 21:6) or, more directly, burned their sons "as an offering" (2 Kgs 16:3; 21:6 RSV). The motivation behind the sacrifice of one's child, as reflected in the Talmud, was "the desire to present the god with the most precious possible offering."[4] The sacrifice of one's son was the ultimate sacrifice, offering a deity one's most precious possession. Such a sacrifice would, therefore, have demonstrated one's utter devotion, gratitude, or loyalty to a deity. Such loyalty is seen in the obedience of Abraham in taking his son up to the altar as a sacrifice to YHWH (Gen 22:1–14) who had ordered him so to do (Gen 22:2). There is also evidence from biblical literature that child sacrifices were also offered apparently to secure the salvation of a city or a nation: Japheth's child sacrifice saved Israel (Judg 11:29–40), while that of King Mesha saved Moab (2 Kgs 3:24–27).[5]

Although it is not mentioned to whom Ahaz and Manasseh offered their child sacrifices, they were most likely offered to Molech. Molech was the Canaanite deity most associated with child sacrifice: "You shall not give any of your offspring to sacrifice them to Molech" (Lev 18:21). He is also the deity specifically mentioned as the one the Israelites offered their child sacrifices to (2 Kgs 23:10). Regardless of to whom the kings offered their child sacrifices, the sacrifices were idolatrous because they were not to YHWH who had forbidden them: "No one shall be found among you who makes a son or daughter pass through fire" (Deut 18:10). The sacrifices pointed to Kings Ahaz and Manasseh's utter devotion to the gods they offered them, and not to YHWH.

Consultation of mediums and soothsayers was another element of the idolatrous ways of Israel's kings. King Manasseh "used fortune telling (*ʿānan*) and omens (*nāḥaš*), and dealt with mediums (*ʾôb*) and necromancers (*yiddᵉʿōnî*)" (2 Kgs 21:6 ESV), which were idolatrous means of getting knowledge or information which was beyond human capacity to acquire. They were idolatrous because they were a replacement (thus a rejection) of YHWH, from whom such knowledge was to be sought. *ʿānan* ("fortune-telling") was given by soothsayers or their equivalent. *ʾôb* and *yiddᵉʿōnî* ("necromancers") were mediums, and *nāḥaš* ("omens") were signs believed to be from the gods and interpreted by mediums and soothsayers alike. More specifically, mediums

---

4. Jon D. Levenson, *The Death and Resurrection of the Beloved Son: The Transformation of Child Sacrifice in Judaism and Christianity* (Yale: Yale University Press, 1993), 21–22.

5. For more see, Omri Boehm, "Child Sacrifice, Ethical Responsibility and the Existence of the People of Israel," *VT* 54.2 (2004).

sought concealed knowledge from the dead or their ghosts by conjuring up the dead, hence the term "necromancers." King Saul sought a medium for divine knowledge when YHWH would not speak to him (see 1 Sam 28:3–24; Isa 29:4). Soothsayers or fortune-tellers, on the other hand, used a variety of means such as dreams, reading of animal parts, the stars, the moon, certain objects and lots to acquire such knowledge and to interpret omens. The king of Babylon used such means for concealed information (Ezek 21:21; see also Isa 47:13; Hos 4:12) and the Egyptians would turn to it to no avail (Isa 19:3). YHWH had forbidden all these kinds of divination: "you shall not practice augury" (Lev 19:26; also Deut 18:10–18) as an abomination which indicated their idolatrous nature (we shall revisit this later). Knowledge beyond human capacity to acquire was to be sought from YHWH directly, or through his priests and prophets.

The consequence of idolatrous ways of the kings of Israel was not limited to them. It also affected the people of Israel. This is made clear by the narrator of the books of Kings who places blame of "Israel"'s idolatry on the kings: the Israelites walked "in the customs that the kings of Israel had introduced" (2 Kgs 17:8). We pointed out above that Jeroboam, the first king of "Israel," made "Israel" sin by leading them into the worship of the two golden calf images he had made (1 Kgs 12:30); so did kings after him because they followed his ways (1 Kgs 15:26; 15:34; 16:19; 22:52 etc.). For this reason the idolatrous ways of the people of "Israel" were identical to that of their kings:

> They rejected all the commandments of the LORD their God and made for themselves cast images of two calves; they made a sacred pole, worshipped all the hosts of heaven, and served Baal. They made their sons and their daughters pass through the fire; they used divination and augury. (2 Kgs 17:16–17)

The kings of Judah also led the people into the sin of idolatry. Under Rehoboam who did evil in YHWH's sight, for example, the people of Judah "built for themselves high places, and pillars, and sacred poles on every high hill, and under every green tree; and there were also male temple prostitutes in the land" (1 Kgs 14:23). Under the influence of the Davidic kings the idolatrous ways of Judah were just as those of "Israel." However, the description of Judah's idolatry gives us more information on the extent of idolatry in all Israel. The people practised idolatry in every hospitable place: on high hills as residences of gods, and under every green tree for their shade which ensured their idolatrous activities proceeded without the discomfort of the elements (Hos 4:13; Ezek 20:28). The people of Judah also had sacred male prostitutes (*qādēš*) who were a part of the flourishing fertility cults of Israel's neighbours. Sacred prostitutes were found in, amongst other places, houses of the deities to whom they were devoted. Their function was to engender fertility of humans, animals, and land by means of sexual intercourse with people.

> A characteristic of fertility cult ideology has been the belief that the propagation of human life, under certain conditions supposed to be controlled by the gods, will bring greater productivity of fields and flocks and hence prosperity to the social group. Persons dedicated to the gods who were officials of the cult were sought, especially at festivals, by laity who sincerely believed that intercourse with these persons would cure sterility of human beings, of animals and of the land, and that by actual union with the human representatives of the deity one could assist the gods in bringing prosperity to mankind.[6]

This understanding is alluded to in Hosea where YHWH says that Israel's prostitution will not give them fertility: "they shall play the whore, but not multiply" (Hos 4:10). All this took place despite YHWH forbidding Israel from the practice: "None of the daughters of Israel shall be a temple prostitute; none of the sons of Israel shall be a temple prostitute" (Deut 23:17).

The foregoing discussion brings us to a crucial question about the disobedience of the kings of Israel which we must seek to answer: why an inordinate focus on idolatry as the disobedience of the kings of Israel and the people of Israel whom they influenced? The focus on idolatry is meant to forcefully show that the kings and people of Israel rejected or forsook YHWH and, therefore, broke the covenant he had with them. We explain this conclusion below.

The first and second commandment stipulated the following:

> I am the LORD your God who brought you out of the land of Egypt, out of the house of slavery; you shall have no other gods before me. You shall not make for yourself an idol, whether in form of anything that is in heaven above, or that is on the earth beneath, or that is in the water under the earth. You shall not bow down to them or worship them. (Exod 20:1–5)

The importance of these two commandments lies in God's reaction if they were broken and in the term used to signify their disobedience. Possessing

---

6. Beatrice A. Brooks, "Fertility Cult Functionaries in the Old Testament," *JBL* 60.3 (1941): 243.

other gods and having idols would provoke YHWH to jealousy out of which he would punish those concerned: "for I . . . am a jealous God, punishing children for the iniquity of parents, to the third and fourth generation of those who reject me" (Exod 20:5). The marital metaphor throws into sharp relief the significance of YHWH's jealousy. It is exclusively through this metaphor that the two commandments are appreciated. Israel was like YHWH's wife from whom he expected absolute faithfulness. Just as a rejected husband who was left by his wife in favour of someone else, or betrayed by her, YHWH would be filled with jealousy and anger if Israel turned to other gods. It is only Israel's affection for and service of other gods and idols other than YHWH that would arouse his wrathful and punitive nature.

God would be displeased, for example, if one did not keep the Sabbath, or if one would covet his neighbour's property, but those sins, unlike idolatry, would not make him jealous. Those committing such sins would not necessarily be rejecting YHWH for another god. YHWH's provocation to jealousy with Israel's idolatry is then an indication that idolatry was unfaithfulness to him, his outright rejection, or abandonment. Indeed, it is the marital metaphor – the language of adultery and unfaithfulness – that YHWH uses to describe his rejection or abandonment by Israel by virtue of their idolatry, as the quote from Hosea suffices to demonstrate:

> My people consult a piece of wood
> and their divining rod gives them oracles.
> For a spirit of whoredom has led them astray,
> and they have played the whore,
> forsaking their God. (Hos 4:12)

There was, therefore, no sin as grievous to YHWH as idolatry. The grievousness of Saul's sin was clearly demonstrated when God equated it to idolatry; it was, like idolatry, a rebellion against (i.e. a rejection of) YHWH:

> For rebellion is no less a sin than divination,
> and stubbornness is like iniquity and idolatry.
> Because you have rejected the word of the LORD,
> he has also rejected you from being king. (1 Sam 15:23)

Since YHWH's dealings with Israel and her kings was based on his covenant with them, his demonstrable rejection through idolatry would have a deeper implication. It would mean that the kings and people of Israel had rejected his covenant on which the laws, and promises, he gave them stood. Forsaking YHWH would nullify the vocation of Israel as royal priests and invalidate the role of the Davidic kings as rulers of God's kingdom (Israel) regardless of whether they were in practice living by God's other laws or not. In other words, the first and second commandment, unlike the others, were foundational to YHWH's relationship with Israel. Breaking them, even when still keeping the other commandments, would make Israel cease to be his *sᵉgūllâ* and royal priests, and the Davidic kings cease to be his *māšiaḥ*. For this reason, these two commandments were meant to be inviolable with the consequence that the sin committed in breaking them was viewed as an "abomination" (*tô ʿēbah*); an extremely grievous sin.

A *tô ʿēbah*, or any of its equivalents such as *šiqqûṣ*, was an abhorrent or detestable thing.[7] It was an attempt to convey an extreme hatefulness towards something; the objectionableness of the thing to the extent that it became an anathema or a taboo. Revulsion was then, naturally, the overwhelming emotional reaction when an abomination was committed. Idolatry was an abomination as is clearly seen in instances where abomination is substituted for idols (see Jer 7:30) and foreign gods (see 1 Kgs 11:7; Jer 16:18), and their worship (see Jer 6:15; Ezek 8:9; 16:2; 33:26). Since idolatry was as an abomination to YHWH, it was a sin he profoundly loathed (for reasons we have just examined). Those paying attention ought to have noted then that the first and second commandment were meant to be inviolable, and that idolatry was a taboo. We should note here that abominations were not limited to making and having idols but included the following forms: divination (Deut 18:12), child sacrifice as an offering and one offered to a foreign god (Deut 12:31), and cultic prostitution (Deut 23:18).

The Davidic kings, therefore, committed grievous sins and also led Israel into committing them. Their abominations made them fail in their monarchical roles as God's *māšiaḥ*, and made the Israelites fail in their priestly vocation on the land. More specifically, the Davidic kings, in the first instance, failed directly in their priest-king role. Rather than being priests of YHWH and leading Israel accordingly, they ended up being priests of foreign gods and leading Israel into idolatrous worship. This is epitomized in King Ahaz who had an altar built for an Assyrian god in the house of YHWH and commanded Uriah, the priest, to use it to offer sacrifices (2 Kgs 16:15). By their idolatrous ways within the house of YHWH and outside, the Davidic kings subverted their role as priest-kings to bless the people of Israel, to preside over sacrifices and offer sacrifices to God,

---

7. See E. Gerstenberger, "בעת," in E. Jenni and C. Westermann (eds.), *Theological Lexicon of the Old Testament*, Vol. 3, trans. M. E. Biddle (Peabody: Hendrickson, 2004).

and to give God's word to the people. Their function as mediators between YHWH and his people was compromised by their idolatry.

Second, idolatry as a rejection of YHWH also meant that the kings of Israel failed in their warrior-king role. Peace and security were not secured in Israel by the Davidic kings through YHWH's help, as was intended. There were wars between "Israel" and Judah, God's people against each other. King Rehoboam of Judah fought ceaselessly with King Jeroboam of "Israel" (1 Kgs 14:30). King Abijah of Judah fought too with King Jeroboam (1 Kgs 15:7). King Asa of Judah fought with King Baasha of "Israel" (1 Kgs 15:16), and King Amaziah/Uzziah of Judah fought with King Jehoash of "Israel" (2 Kgs 14:8–14).

Internationally the Davidic kings as God's *māšîaḥ* were not extending Israel's reign (as the kingdom of God) abroad by subjugating resistant nations and bringing them under God's rule. To the contrary, after Kings David and Solomon, "Israel" and Judah were variously under the powers of Syria, Egypt, Assyria, or Babylon until their exile. For example, under King Rehoboam, Judah was attacked and pillaged by Shishak the king of Egypt (1 Kgs 14:25–28). Jehoash the king of Judah paid off Hazael the king of Syria to stop his intention to subjugate Judah (2 Kgs 12:17–18). "Israel" under King Baasha, and then Judah under King Asa, were vassals of Syria (1 Kgs 15:17–20). King Ahaz of Judah entreated King Tiglath-Pileser of Assyria with silver and gold and vassalage to rescue Judah from being overrun by Rezin the king of Syria (2 Kgs 16:5–9). The people of "Israel" from then on became a vassal of Assyria (2 Kgs 15:19–20) until the Assyrians themselves destroyed them (2 Kgs 17:4–5). Although YHWH delivered Judah under King Hezekiah from the Assyrians, he soon after showed willingness to be a vassal of Babylon (2 Kgs 20:12–15). Under King Jehoahaz, Judah was a vassal of Egypt (2 Kgs 23:31–35). A few years later Judah under King Jehoiakim became a vassal of Babylon (2 Kgs 24:1) and was eventually destroyed when King Jehoiakim tried to rebel.

Lastly, idolatry as a rejection of YHWH meant the kings of Israel failed in their judicial kingly role. Having rejected YHWH, their reign would not be informed by social justice according to YHWH's laws. YHWH, according to pre-exilic prophetic literature, which we shall look at below, had much to say about this failure. We have evidence of this in the reign of King Ahab who unjustly acquired Naboth's piece of land (1 Kgs 21:5–16), and King Manasseh who shed innocent blood (2 Kgs 21:16). King Rehoboam split the kingdom of Israel as a result of a lack of justice (1 Kgs 12:12–20).

In the unfolding story of the Bible, the rejection of YHWH by the Davidic kings, on the one hand, led to their failure to execute their judicial, warrior and priest-kingly roles, and thus to their failure to rule Israel as God's kingdom and extend the kingdom to the rest of the world. On the other hand, the rejection of YHWH by the people of Israel meant that they ceased to be a royal priesthood representing God to the nations through abundant life. Not having the blessings of abundant life, Israel did not attract other nations to Zion where God dwelled, to lead to their knowledge of God and submission to his laws. The nations could not, therefore, become a part of God's kingdom and experience thereby the blessings of abundant life. In short, God's kingdom and dwelling were not restored in the world through Israel and the Davidic kings (Abraham's offspring) as intended.

Failure of Israel in Pre-exilic Prophets

The assessment of the kings and people of Israel as idolatrous in the Bible's historical narratives and therefore their subsequent judgement by YHWH is mirrored in pre-exilic prophetic literature (Amos, Hosea, Micah, Habakkuk, Zephaniah, Joel, Isaiah 1–39, Jeremiah, and Ezekiel). Through the pre-exilic prophets, YHWH charged Israel with committing idolatry. Specifically, for example, the people of Israel were charged by YHWH of making idols: "With their silver and gold they made idols" (Hos 8:4; 13:2; see also Jer 8:19; 16:18). They were also charged with worshipping idols and foreign gods (Hos 11:2; Jer 5:19; 9:14; 13:10) and of worshipping Baal (Hos 2:8; 13:1; Jer 32:29). The more they increased in population and wealth the more they built altars and stronger pillars (Hos 10:1) to the extent that in Judah every city had a god the people of Israel worshipped: "For your gods have become as many as your towns, O Judah" (Jer 11:13). They worshipped these gods on altars they built (Jer 17:2), and on high places, hills, and under green trees (Hos 4:13; Jer 11:13; 17:2–3; 19:5; Ezek 6:13; 20:28). Their idolatrous ways were also evident in their sacrifice of children (Jer 7:31; 32:35; Ezek 16:20; 23:37). YHWH also charged the people of Israel with not seeking from him information that was beyond human natural ability to grasp or know but instead seeking it in idolatrous ways, through mediums and fortune tellers (Isa 8:19; Hos 4:12; Jer 27:9) and through Baal.

> In the prophets of Samaria
> I saw a disgusting thing:
> they prophesied by Baal
> and led my people Israel astray. (Jer 23:13)

We pointed out that YHWH used a marital metaphor to communicate the nature of idolatry as a great sin because those committing it were rejecting him. This point is explicit in YHWH's messages through the prophets. YHWH described the idolatry he charged the Israelites with as unfaithfulness and/or harlotry (adultery). Ezekiel 16 and 23 epitomize such descriptions with YHWH's extended marital metaphor message to describe Israel's unfaithfulness, her idolatry. Shorter messages using a marital metaphor to communicate the implication of Israel's idolatry, particularly from Hosea, where Israel is allegorized as YHWH's wife (Hos 2:19–20):

> My people consult a piece of wood,
> and their divining rod gives them oracles.
> For a spirit of whoredom has led them astray,
> and they have played the whore,
> forsaking their God. (Hos 4:12; see also Hos 1:2; 2:1–5; 3:1; 5:3–4; 9:1–2)
>
> You have played the whore with many lovers;
> and would you return to me?
> Says the LORD
> Look at the bare heights and see!
> Where have you not been lain with?
> By the waysides you have sat waiting for lovers. (Jer 3:1–2; see also Jer 2:20–28; 3:20; 5:7–9)

We should note, however, that at other times, YHWH did not use the marital metaphor to signify his rejection by Israel, but directly charged them in plain language with rejecting or rebelling against him (Isa 1:2–6; 5:8–10; Jer 2:29–32; 4:17; 6:19; Zeph 3:1–2; Ezek 3:9; 12:1–3), or rejecting his laws (Amos 2:4; Jer 6:19). We also pointed out that all forms of idolatry were classified as *tôʿēbah* (abomination), to highlight their grievous nature. In line with this, YHWH labelled the various forms of Israel's idolatry as abominations. More specifically, YHWH referred to their idols (Jer 7:30; 16:18; 32:34; Ezek 11:18, 21) and their non-YHWH cultic worship (Jer 6:15; 32:35; Ezek 16:47; 16:50–52) as abominations to show their grievous nature.

Unlike the historical narratives, pre-exilic prophetic literature reveals another area of Israel's disobedience besides idolatry, which helps us to advance our understanding of how Israel fared in the land. Specifically, there is a focus on Israel's sins of social injustice. In the last chapter we mentioned that social justice was concerned with the downtrodden, to uplift them from their wretched plight, or to ameliorate it. In biblical literature, YHWH's social justice laws protected the poor from the oppression of the powerful and prescribed the responsibility and help to be given to orphans, widows, and outsiders

(Exod 22:21–24; 23:9–11; Lev 19:9–10; Deut 15:4–11; 23:25–26; 24:19–22). The Jubilee and Sabbath year laws were the most detailed social justice laws. They contained elaborate commandments from YHWH on wealth redistribution and on restraining the excesses and greed of the powerful (Lev 25:8–55).

In the unfolding story of the Bible, we are made aware that the people of Israel did not keep the prescribed social justice laws. YHWH charged the powerful Israelites with enriching themselves at the expense of the weak and poor whom they did not care about:

> Listen, you heads of Jacob and rulers of the house of Israel!
>   Should you know justice? –
> you who hate the good and love the evil,
>   who tear the skin off my people,
> and the flesh off their bones;
>   who eat the flesh of my people,
> flay their skin off them,
>   break their bones in pieces,
> and chop them like meat in a kettle,
>   like flesh in a caldron. (Mic 3:1–3)

> They sell the righteous for silver,
>   and the needy for a pair of sandals –
> they who trample the head of the poor into the dust of the earth,
>   and push the afflicted out of the way. (Amos 2:6–8; see also Amos 8:4–6; Jer 34:8–17; Ezek 22:27)

The powerful also enriched themselves by defrauding people (Mic 6:10–12; Hos 12:7–8; Jer 6:13; Ezek 22:27). Moreover, rather than use their power to uplift and grant justice to the weak and poor, YHWH charged Israel's leaders of using their power to destroy them:

> The LORD enters into judgement
>   with the elders and the princes of his people;
> It is you who have devoured the vineyard;
>   the spoils of the poor in your houses.
> What do you mean by crushing my people,
>   by grinding the face of the poor? says the LORD God of hosts. (Isa 3:14–15; see also Isa 29:21; 10:1–2; Mic 2:1–2; Ezek 22:29)

The greed of the powerful in Israel had no bounds; weak and poor people were driven into destitution and slavery (Isa 5:8). What is more, rulers and even priests and prophets would not come to their aid or help but, to the contrary, were party to their marginalisation by giving their services to those who could pay for them:

> Its rulers give judgement for a bribe,
> > its priests teach for a price,
> its prophets give oracles for money. (Mic 3:11; see also Isa 1:23)

Why, alongside idolatry, would social injustice as a disobedience of the Israelites be especially in focus? We discussed in our last chapter that social justice was the foundation of God's throne; that YHWH loved social justice and social justice was in the interest of his rule. Social injustice bred slavery, poverty, insecurity, anger and resentment, pain, and sorrow (which were a far cry from the blessings of abundant life), while social justice directly bred peace which was a crucial blessing in the blessings of abundant life. No other factor has a greater direct impact on societal joy, abundance and life than the presence of social justice. This justice dividend is captured in YHWH's words through the prophet Isaiah:

> Then justice will dwell in the wilderness,
> > and righteousness abide in the fruitful field.
> The effect of righteousness will be peace,
> > and the result of righteousness, quietness and trust
> > > forever. (Isa 32:16–17)

This is why God had a premium on justice as the foundation of his reign. Its keeping would then be of greater concern to him than, perhaps, the neglect of other laws (with the exception of idolatry). YHWH's charge of social injustice against Israel was therefore a very serious one. In neglecting it Israel was doing away with laws that provided conditions for the blessings of abundant life on the land. It is on this account that social injustice is in focus (alongside idolatry) despite the presence of other sins mentioned in the prophets such as deceit (Jer 8:5; 9:3–6; Hos 7:13; Amos 2:4; Isa 28:13), violence and murder (Amos 3:10; 6:3; Hos 6:8–9; 12:1; Isa 1:21; 3:13–15; Mic 3:10; 6:12; Jer 2:34; 7:8–11; Ezek 6:11; 22:1–6), and insincere worship (Amos 4:4–5; 5:21–23; Isa 1:12–17; 29:13; Jer 5:1–2; 6:8–20).

In pre-exilic prophetic literature the implication of Israel's disobedience was, just as in the books of Kings, the invalidation of their vocation in the land. This implication is communicated through covenant logic. Since Israel had broken the covenant with YHWH (Jer 11:10; 31:31–32; Ezek 17:18–19; Hos 8:1), it would therefore not become God's *sᵉgullâ* and would be unable to become a blessing to all nations. Not having the blessings of abundant life, Israel would not attract other nations to YHWH and his kingdom so that those nations could in turn experience the same blessings as a part of God's kingdom. The curses foretold by YHWH would befall them as a judgement from YHWH, and rather than being an attraction to other nations, they would be derided and mocked. This observation is clarified in YHWH's warning to idolatrous and socially unjust Israel of his impending, if not imminent judgement. Two examples of judgement on disobedient Israel (with more in the section below) will suffice to illustrate this observation:

> Do not rejoice O Israel!
> > Do not exult as other nations do;
> for you have played the whore,
> > departing from your God.
> You have loved a prostitute's pay
> > on all the threshing floors.
> Threshing floor and wine vat shall not feed them,
> > and the new wine shall fail them.
> They shall not remain in the land of the LORD;
> > but Ephraim shall return to Egypt,
> and in Assyria they shall eat unclean food. (Hos 9:1–3)

> Hear this, you rulers of the house of Jacob
> > and chiefs of the house of Israel,
> who abhor justice
> > and pervert all equity . . .
> Therefore because of you
> > Zion shall be plowed as a field;
> Jerusalem shall become a heap of ruins,
> > and the mountain of the house a wooded height. (Mic 3:9–12)

Judgement of Israel and the Davidic Kingship

The unfolding story of the Bible tells us repeatedly then that Israel failed to fulfil its vocation in the land, and the Davidic kings did not live up to their monarchical roles. For this reason, according to the books of Kings' narrative, YHWH punished the people of Israel by a foreign nation, according to the curses he had forewarned through Moses would befall them if they disobeyed him. In the words of the narrator of the books of Kings concerning "Israel":

> In the ninth year of Hoshea, the king of Assyria captured Samaria; he carried the Israelites away to Assyria... This occurred because the people of Israel had sinned against the LORD their God, who brought them up out of the land of Egypt from under the hand of Pharoah king of Egypt. They worshipped other gods and walked in the customs of the nations whom the LORD drove out before the people of Israel, and in the customs that the kings of Israel had introduced. (2 Kgs 17:6–8)

As for Judah, YHWH's punishment through the Babylonians was decided in the reign of Manasseh and came swiftly in the reign of King Jehoiachin. Despite the faithfulness of Josiah:

> Still the LORD did not turn from the fierceness of his great wrath, by which his anger was kindled against Judah, because of all the provocations with which Manasseh had provoked him. The LORD said "I will remove Judah also out of my sight, as I removed Israel; and I will reject this city that I have chosen, Jerusalem, and the house of which I said, My name shall be there." (2 Kgs 23:26–27)

The same message is communicated in pre-exilic prophetic literature, albeit as prophecy. Because of the failure of the Israelites to obey God on the land, "Israel" would fall by the sword and be taken captive to Egypt and Assyria:

> They shall return to the land of Egypt
>   and Assyria shall be their kingdom
> because they have refused to return to me. (Hos 11:5; see also
>   Hos 9:3; Amos 4:2–3; 5:27)

Judah, too, would fall by the sword and be taken captive to Babylon: "And I will give all Judah into the hand of the king of Babylon; he shall carry them captive to Babylon, and shall kill them with the sword" (Jer 20:4; also Jer 32:21; 7:30; Mic 4:10). This was to take place because Assyrian and Babylonian kings and armies were YHWH's chosen instruments of judgement against Israel (Isa 5:26–30; Jer 15:5–9; 33:5; Ezek 23:22–29, 46–49).

Unlike the biblical narratives, in the prophets, "Israel" and Judah's fall by the Assyrians and Babylonians is also articulated in the context of the day of the Lord (the day of YHWH). We mentioned in our fourth chapter that YHWH as a warrior-king used war as one way to punish nations and to destroy his enemies or subdue them, in order to impose his kingship. The day of YHWH was a day when YHWH would wage on his enemy (or enemies) in judgement, thus destroying it (or them) and in consequence manifesting his kingship. That day would be cataclysmic with YHWH's cosmic epiphany particularly terrifying. The earth would tremble or be shaken, the hills and mountains quake, and darkness would ensue. The sky would be black; sun, moon, and stars would not bear their light, and the moon would be turned to blood. Depending on the context of the day of YHWH, the outcome was, or would be, the salvation of his people Israel (for whom YHWH's enemies was theirs too). Through the prophetic literature, we read that YHWH proclaimed that his judgement on "Israel" and Judah would be the day of YHWH, which would accordingly be a dreadful day of their destruction (Isa 2:5–22; Zeph 1:7–18; Ezek 7:14–27), and a day of their defeat respectively at the hands of the armies of the Assyrian and Babylonians (see, for instance, Isa 13:13–22; Joel 2:1–13). For this reason the day of YHWH was also called "the day of his wrath/anger/ vengeance" (Isa 13:13; Zeph 1:18; Lam 2:22) or "the great and dreadful day of the YHWH" (Joel 2:31; Mal 4:5).

There is more about Israel's punishment in pre-exilic prophetic literature that is not revealed in biblical narratives of Israel. Pre-exilic prophetic literature gives us a fuller picture of Israel's judgement, and thereby demonstrates the imminent fulfilment of the curses YHWH promised would fall upon disobedient Israel. As mentioned in our third chapter, the curses God promised would fall on the Israelites if they disobeyed him included the curses of insecurity, diseases, low yields, famine, slavery, subjugation, loss of the land and exile (Lev 18:28; 20:22; 26:14–39; Deut 28:15–68). The fuller picture of Israel's judgement which we get from pre-exilic prophetic literature demonstrates the imminent fulfilment of these curses in the way which we discuss below.

Many of the people of Israel would die by the sword, at the hands of the Assyrians and Babylonians as articulated in YHWH's words through Amos: "their corpses shall be many, cast out in every place" (Amos 8:3; see also Amos 8:9–10; Isa 5:25; Jer 21:7; Ezek 6:4, 13). The Israelites, as captives, would be servants of their enemies (Jer 12:7; 15:14; 17:4) and the subject of their scorn and mockery (Mic 6:16; Jer 24:9; Ezek 5:14–15; 22:4). Those who would be left in the land, having escaped the sword and captivity, would die of famine or pestilence (Jer 21:9; 24:10; Ezek 4:16–17; 5:16–17). Jerusalem and other cities, houses, idols, altars, high places would be destroyed by the invading army (Hos 10:1–8; Jer 3:5–9; 5:17; Mic 1:6–7; 3:12; Ezek 6:4–7). Ultimately, the land would become desolate, forsaken and unproductive (Isa 1:7–9; 5:9–10; 6:11–13; Jer 4:23–26; 9:11; Ezek 6:14). The temple would be destroyed (because of the abominations and hypocritical worship in there):

> Go now to my place that was in Shiloh, where I made my name dwell at first, and see what I did to it for the wickedness of my people Israel. And now, because you have done all these things, says the LORD, and when I spoke to you persistently, you did not listen . . . therefore I will do to this house that is called by my name, in which you trust, and to the place that I gave to you and your ancestors, just what I did to Shiloh. (Jer 7:12–14; see also Mic 3:12)

The kings of "Israel" would be dethroned (Hos 10:7; 13:9–11), while the rule of the Davidic kings would be cut short (Jer 13:18; Hos 10:7). The people of Israel would be forsaken by YHWH just as they had abandoned him, and would no longer be, an object of his love but of his wrath:

> I have forsaken my house
> > I have abandoned my heritage;
> I have given the beloved of my heart
> > into the hands of my enemies. (Jer 12:7; see also Jer 7:29; 11:15, 17; Hos 1:9; 4:6)

A critical look at this fuller picture makes it clear that Israel's judgements revolved around the loss of the land which God gave them. As we mentioned earlier, the land was the site on which the Israelites, being Abraham's offspring, were meant, as a royal priesthood, to represent God to the nations and thus become a blessing to all nations. If Israel lived in obedience, the land would have the blessings of abundant life as God's kingdom. The blessings of abundant life would attract the nations to YHWH, in Zion where he lived, leading them to know him and obey his laws (just as Israel did). If the Israelites would not fulfil their priestly vocation by obeying God in the land, they would be expelled from it, so that, rather than being an attraction to other nations as a royal priesthood, they would be an object of scorn. This is exactly what the judgement prophecies we have examined pointed to. Since the Israelites were continually disobedient, they were going to be expelled from the land through death by the sword, through famine and pestilence in the land, and through captivity by foreign armies. They would also, in consequence, be mocked and scorned by other nations.

Israel's expulsion from the land through the sword, captivity, famine, and pestilence would mean the end of Israel. Israel's end was in line with the curses God promise would befall them if they disobeyed: "All these curses shall come upon you, pursuing you and overtaking you until you are destroyed, because you did not obey the LORD your God" (Deut 28:45). Israel's covenant with YHWH would no longer be in effect. They would have failed to become God's people (his *sᵉgullâ*), blessing the nations. So, instead of God dwelling with them in his temple in Jerusalem and on the land, their land would be desolate, Jerusalem would be in ruins and the temple would be destroyed. Instead of the Davidic kings as God's *māšiaḥ* ruling Israel as God's kingdom, there would be no heir of David on the throne ruling Israel. What would remain of Israel would be the memories held by captives (or by those in exile). They would have memories of Zion, for example:

> By the rivers of Babylon –
> > there we sat down and there we wept
> when we remembered Zion. (Ps 137:1)

They would have memories of YHWH's covenant with David because of which they cried to YHWH:

> You have renounced the covenant with your servant;
> > you have defiled his crown in dust. (Ps 89:39)

Some would have memories of YHWH's fallen purpose for the Davidic kingship, and pray that YHWH would revive it:

> But let your right hand be upon the one at your right hand,
> > the one whom you made strong for yourself. (Ps 80:17)

Some would also have memories of their Abrahamic heritage of being delivered by YHWH from Egyptian bondage, and would pray that he might restore them, like a vine planted in the land:

> Turn again, O God of hosts;
> > look down from heaven, and see;
> have regard for this vine,
> > the stock that your right hand planted. (Ps 80:14)

6

An Interlude: The Promises and Delay of Israel's Restoration

We continue our study of the unfolding story of the Bible in this chapter by examining the promises of God to restore Israel and David's kingship, and thus God's faithfulness to the promise he gave Abraham to be a blessing to all nations. We shall subsequently conclude this chapter by observing that the story of the Bible in the Old Testament ends with the Israelites still waiting for the fulfilment of YHWH's promises to restore them, despite being back on their land and having rebuilt the temple and Jerusalem. During this waiting period, we shall point out, Israel's worldview underwent a significant shift that would prepare the way for comprehending the spiritual nature of their restoration, which took place typologically in Jesus, according to the writings of the New Testament.

Restoration of Israel in the Prophets

If Israel ended, it would mean that God was not faithful to his promise to Abraham that all nations would be blessed through him. It would mean that the restoration of his dwelling and kingdom in the world through Abraham would not be fulfilled as promised. Such a scenario would compromise the story of the Bible and make YHWH, contrary to the witness of biblical literature, to be unfaithful to his promises. Yet God would never withdraw from his promises to Abraham. This is why the unfolding story of the Bible clarifies that Israel's end would not be final. YHWH himself made it known through the same prophets that the end of Israel would not be absolute: "But even in those days, says the LORD, I will not make a full end of you" (Jer 5:18; also Amos 9:8; Jer 4:27; 5:10; 30:11). The preservation of Israel, despite its punishment, was guaranteed by the power of YHWH, in the same way as his power guaranteed the order of creation (Jer 31:35–37); thus a remnant would be preserved:

> On that day the remnant of Israel and the survivors of the house of Jacob will no more lean on the one who struck them, but will lean on the LORD, the Holy One of Israel, in truth. A remnant will return, the remnant of Jacob, to the mighty God. For though your people Israel were like the sand of the sea, only a remnant will return. Destruction is decreed, overflowing with righteousness. (Isa 10:20–23; also Isa 11:11; 37:31–32; Jer 23:3; 50:20; Ezek 6:8–10; Mic 7:18–20)

Indeed, through the prophets YHWH promised that he would restore Israel. We have numerous messages from YHWH concerning the return of the remnant of the people of Israel to the land. To give a series of examples, according to the oracle of Isaiah, YHWH promised that he would gather Israel from all the places they would be taken to, and return them to the land where they would worship him in Jerusalem:

> On that day the LORD will thresh from the channel of the Euphrates to the Wadi of Egypt, and you will be gathered one by one, O people of Israel. And on that day a great trumpet will be blown, and those who were lost in the land of Assyria and those who were driven out of the land of Egypt will come and worship the LORD on the holy mountain at Jerusalem. (Isa 27:12–13)

Through the prophet Jeremiah, YHWH promised the Israelites an exodus from their lands of captivity back to the promised land. That exodus would be, in remembrance, equivalent to their exodus from Egypt:

> Therefore, the days are surely coming, says the LORD when it shall no longer be said, "As the LORD lives who brought the people of Israel up out of the land of Egypt," but "As the LORD lives who brought the people of Israel up out of the land of the north and out of all the lands where he had driven them. For I will bring them back to their own land that I gave to their ancestors. (Jer 16:14–15; see also 23:7–8; 30:1–3)

Through the same prophet YHWH promised a return to the land after a period of seventy years in exile (Jer 25:11–12; 29:10). Through the prophet Ezekiel, YHWH promised to give the land back to the remnants of Israel: "Thus says the LORD God: I will gather you from the peoples, and assemble you out of the countries where you have been scattered, and I will give you the land of

Israel" (Ezek 11:17). Through the prophet Hosea YHWH promised to return the Israelites like droves of birds to their homes:

> They shall come trembling like birds from Egypt,
>   and like doves from the land of Assyria;
> and I will return them to their homes, says the LORD.
>   (Hos 11:11; see also Isa 14:1; 31:8; Mic 2:12)

YHWH's promissory messages to return Israel to the land were combined with promises of the recovery of their population, which would be decimated by YHWH's impending punishment. YHWH promised the Israelites that on return to their land they would "be like the sand of the sea, which can neither be measured nor numbered (Hos 1:10; see also Jer 33:22). Elsewhere YHWH promised them that he would make them many (Jer 30:19), and that their population would be multiplied (Ezek 36:10; 37:26) so that the land and cities will be filled with the Israelites (Isa 27:6).

YHWH's promises of Israel's return to the land were also mixed with his promises of peace and security when they returned to it. For instance, YHWH through the prophet Hosea said:

> I will make for you a covenant on that day with the wild animals, the birds of the air, and the creeping things of the ground, and I will abolish the bow, the sword, and war from the land; and I will make you lie down in safety. (Hos 2:18)

We find more promises of peace and security to Israel when they return to the land through the prophets Isaiah (Isa 33:20), Jeremiah (for example, Jer 30:10; 32:37; 46:27), Ezekiel (for example, Ezek 28:26; 34:25; 37:26), and Zephaniah (Zeph 3:13).

YHWH's promises of Israel's return to the land were also combined with his promises that there would be abundance and prosperity on the land when they returned to it. There would be abundant fruit and grain, green pastures, large flocks and herds, overflowing streams, showers in season, and a lack of famine (Amos 9:13–15; Isa 33:21; Jer 33:6–9; Ezek 36:11; 34:26–27; 36:29). There would be extraordinary transformation of the land that would contribute towards this abundance and prosperity. The wilderness and desert would be transformed into rich abundant land flowing with streams of water and dotted with springs (Isa 35:1–2; 35:6–7). There would even be a life-giving stream bubbling from the house of YHWH in Jerusalem (Ezek 47:1–12; see also Joel 3:18). As a result of this transformation, the land would become like the garden of Eden (Isa 51:3; Ezek 36:35).

Jerusalem as YHWH's city (for he would dwell there) had a special focus in YHWH's promises of Israel's return to the land. The city that was once in ruins, YHWH promised, would be rebuilt (for example, Isa 44:26–28; Jer 30:18; 31:38–40; Joel 3:1; Ezek 48:15–20; 48:30–35). Once rebuilt, it would experience similar fortunes of abundance, peace and security prevailing on the land (Isa 33:20; 54:11–17).

It is important to keep in mind here that these conditions that the people of Israel would go back to in the land – peace, security, abundance, prosperity, fruitfulness of humans, animals, produce, and vine, and lack of famine – were none other than the blessings of abundant life. As we earlier discussed, YHWH had promised these blessings if the Israelites would be obedient to him (Lev 26:3–13; Deut 28:1–14). To obey YHWH would be to choose life, and to disobey him would be choosing death. These conditions on the land, therefore, presuppose that Israel would be obedient when it returned to the land (a subject we shall revisit a little later below).

Alongside YHWH's promises of Israel's return to the land were also his promises that the Israelites would once again be his people, his $s^e g\bar{u}ll\hat{a}$, and he would be their God (for example, Hos 2:23; Jer 24:7; 30:22; 32:38; Ezek 11:20; 34:30–31; 36:28; Isa 44:1–5; 51:16). Israel would even once again be God's son and YHWH his father (Jer 31:9). YHWH also promised that Israel would be his people as one nation, and not separately as "Israel" and Judah: "In those days the house of Judah shall join the house of Israel, and together they shall come from the land of the north to the land that I gave your ancestors for a heritage" (Jer 3:18; see also Hos 1:11; Isa 11:12–13; Ezek 37:23).

The promise that Israel would once again be God's people and, correspondingly, YHWH would be their God when they returned to the land, implied that YHWH's promises of Israel's return to the land were combined with the remaking of a covenant with them. As we earlier discussed, Israel became God's subjects, his people, and YHWH became their God (their king, their great *suzerain*) by means of a covenant. When they broke their covenant with YHWH, they rejected him and ceased to be his people as we witnessed in some of the judgement messages (for example, Hos 1:9; 4:6; 9:17; Isa 2:6; Jer 7:28, 29). Worse still, they became his enemies and thus objects of his wrath and destruction on the day of YHWH (for example, Jer 4:23–28; Zeph 1:7–18; Ezek 7:14–27). A return to the land as God's people necessitated the renewing of the covenant, or making a new one altogether. YHWH promised the latter, as was most explicit through the prophet Jeremiah:

The days are surely coming says the LORD, when I will make a new covenant with the house of Israel and the house of Judah. It will not be like the covenant that I made with their ancestors when I took them by the hand to bring them out of the land of Egypt – a covenant that they broke, though I was their husband, says the LORD. But this is the covenant that I will make with the house of Israel after those days, says the LORD: I will put my law within them and I will write it on their hearts, and I will be their God, and they shall be my people. No longer shall they teach one another, or say to each other, "Know the LORD," for they shall all know me, from the least of them to the greatest, says the LORD; for I will forgive their iniquity and remember their sin no more. (Jer 31:31–34; see also Jer 32:40; Ezek 16:59–63)

We may recall the elements of suzerainty treaties we discussed in our third chapter. The third element in the structure of these covenants was "stipulations." They detailed the obligations imposed on a *vassal* in order for the *suzerain* to secure his interests. Unlike the old covenant, YHWH's interests in the new covenant would be secured by a guarantee that Israelites would carry out their obligations of keeping the law without the possibility of failure. The guarantee was by means of YHWH putting his laws in their hearts and making them know him without the use of teachers. "I will give them a heart to know that I am YHWH" (Jer 24:7). Such a heart would help them to recognize YHWH as the holy God on account of what he had done for them both in bringing them back to the land and in the joyous and prosperous conditions they would return to (for example, Jer 16:21; Ezek 28:25–26; 34:30; 36:11; 39:28; Joel 3:17). It would also help them to know YHWH through their recognition that he was the author of what had befallen them – sword, captivity, famine and pestilence – because of their disobedience.

We should note the importance of knowing YHWH in guaranteeing Israel's obedience. The first matter of importance is that knowledge of YHWH is tied to obeying the cardinal first and second commandments of the laws YHWH gave to Israel when he made a covenant with them. We pointed out that these two commandments were of significance since their breaking was a rejection of YHWH. For this reason to have other gods and idols was taboo and a grievous sin where it occurred. In this new covenant there would be no idolatry because the Israelites would know YHWH as their God, and thus never reject him in favour of other gods or idols. Understanding that the knowledge of YHWH pre-empts his rejection through idolatry is well supported by the charge YHWH had against the people of Judah. He accused them of rejecting him because they did not know him:

> Sons have I reared and brought up,
> > but they have rebelled against me.
> The ox knows its owner,
> > and the ass its master's crib;
> but Israel does not know,
> > my people does not understand. (Isa 1:2–3 RSV)

This same outlook is also suggested when YHWH related, metaphorically, Israel as his wife to their knowledge of him as their husband. YHWH would take Israel as his wife and the Israelites would reciprocate, by knowing YHWH as their (only) God: "I will take you for my wife in faithfulness; and you shall know the LORD" (Hos 2:20).

The second reason for the importance of knowing YHWH (which is related to the first) is its direct relationship with keeping God's commandments. As we discussed in our third chapter, knowing YHWH results in obeying his laws and viceversa (Hos 4:1–3; Joel 2:26–27; Jer 4:22; 9:1–6). Thus Israel's knowledge of YHWH as guaranteed in the new covenant meant that they would obey YHWH without the possibility of failure. Through other prophets we learn of additional means by which YHWH would guarantee that Israel will follow his commandments. YHWH would give the people of Israel a new heart (or spirit), or a heart of flesh, in order for them to obey him (for example, Ezek 11:19–20; 36:26–27), and to fear him (Jer 32:39–40). YHWH would also weed out the haughty as well as the unrepentant and rebellious Israelites, leaving only the humble and repentant ones who will obey him in the land (Zeph 3:11–13; Ezek 14:6–11; 20:33–38).

YHWH would also ensure that Israel kept the covenant by pouring his Spirit on them (Ezek 36:27; 39:29; Isa 44:3–4). Wind (*ruach*) must have been experienced in ancient society to be a powerful but mysterious force which brought good or unleashed evil. In biblical literature of the Old Testament YHWH created the wind (Amos 4:13) as demonstrated by its coming from YHWH's storehouses (Ps 135:7; Jer 10:13). He used it by gathering it in his fist (Prov 30:4), directing it for his purposes (Num 11:31; Job 28:25; Pss 78:26; 135:7), blowing it over the earth (Gen 8:1), hurling it to cause a great tempest in the sea (Jonah 1:4), and so on. YHWH's Spirit (*rûaḥ*) was a more powerful force than the wind he created and made use of. Thus YHWH used his Spirit to create the world and to give and sustain life (Gen 2:7; 6:3; Job 26:13; 27:3; 34:14–15; Ps 33:6; 104:29–30; Isa 32:15). The power of YHWH's Spirit was seen not only in God using it for creation and sustenance of life, it was also evident when YHWH used it to enable people such as judges (Judg 3:10; 6:34; 11:29), kings (1 Sam 10:10; 16:13; Isa 11:1–3; 61:1–3), and even workmen (Exod 31:1–3) to do his will. The power of YHWH's Spirit was also demonstrated as it was used to give prophets the power to discern the message of YHWH (Num 11:25; 11:29; 24:2–3; 1 Sam 10:6; 19:20; 19:23; Mic 3:8; Joel 2:28).

Since YHWH's Spirit was associated with his power generally (and with the power of divination specifically), the pouring of his Spirit on the Israelites would in consequence empower them to obey him. This view is intimated in YHWH's promise through Ezekiel to the Israelites when they returned to the land: "I will put my spirit (*rûḥî*) within you, and make you follow my statutes and be careful to observe my ordinances" (Ezek 36:27). Furthermore, due to the pouring out of the Spirit upon their return to the land, the people of Israel would be empowered to observe justice and peace (Isa 32:12–30). These guarantees of obedience may explain why the rebuilt city of Jerusalem would not become once again a harlot (Isa 1:21) and an oppressive city (Zeph 3:1), but would be exalted as a city of social justice (Isa 1:24–27; 28:16–17) and a holy city (Joel 3:17).

Moreover, due to the pouring out of God's Spirit the people of Israel would not commit idolatry by consulting mediums, fortune tellers, or foreign gods for knowledge beyond human ability to acquire. There would be no need for that because through YHWH's Spirit such knowledge would be widely available to them. Not only would it be found amongst his priests and prophets but also among Israel's youth who would prophesy and see visions, and among Israel's elderly who would dream dreams:

> I will pour out my spirit on all flesh;
> > your sons and your daughters shall prophesy,
> your old men shall dream dreams,
> > and your young men shall see visions. (Joel 2:28)

Further still, YHWH's promises of Israel's return to the land were also combined with the day of YHWH. Their return would coincide with the day of YHWH. We mentioned that the day of YHWH would be a day of judgement that YHWH meted on his enemies by a spectacularly devastating war, thus destroying them and saving his people. Through the prophet Joel, YHWH promised that his restoration of the people of Israel's fortunes (Joel 3:1) and their return to the land of abundance and prosperity (Joel 3:18) and to a thriving population forever (Joel 3:20), would go hand in hand with "the great and terrible day of the LORD" (Joel 2:31). In that day he would judge and punish Israel's capturers (Joel 3:2–8; 3:19; 3:21) by means of war (Joel 3:12) and save his people (Joel 2:32; 3:16). YHWH promised the same through Habakkuk (and possibly Isa 25:6–12). He would wage war against the wicked nations, those who captured, mistreated and oppressed Israel (Hab 3:12; 3:16), and destroy them (Hab 3:3–14; 3:16), while saving his people Israel (Hab 3:13a).

We turn now to YHWH's promises through the pre-exilic prophets to restore the Davidic kingship, which would happen when they returned to the land as part of the promises of the restoration of Israel. YHWH gave the promises of the restoration of the Davidic kingship directly, and also through the metaphors of a booth/house, a stump, and a shepherd. Through the prophet Amos, YHWH promised the restoration of the Davidic kingship through the metaphor of a booth, that he would "raise up the booth of David that is fallen" (Amos 9:11). Through the prophet Isaiah YHWH promised, in a direct way, to establish the throne of David (Isa 9:6–7; 16:5). Through the same prophet YHWH promised, by metaphor, the restoration of the fallen Davidic kingship, by the promise to grow a branch (*nēṣer*) from Jesse's stump:

> A shoot shall come out from the stock (stump) of Jesse,
>> and a branch shall grow out of his roots. (Isa 11:1; see also
>> Isa 4:2)

Through the prophet Jeremiah YHWH promised the restoration of the kingship using the same metaphor as well, by promising to grow a "righteous branch" (*ṣemaḥ ṣaddîq*) from Jesse's stump ("raise up for David a righteous branch" [Jer 23:5; 33:15]). Through the same prophet YHWH promised, in a direct way, a time when Israel would serve their king David whom he would have raised up (Jer 30:9). Through the prophet Ezekiel, YHWH also promised through the metaphor of shepherd that Israel would have his servant David as their shepherd. As a good shepherd, he would take care of them and lead them (Ezek 34:23; 37:24).

All of YHWH's promises of restoring the Davidic kingship envisaged the restoration of the Davidic kingship through an individual offspring, and not through lineal descendants of David. This individual figure was referred to as "a branch" (Isa 11:1) or "a righteous branch" (Jer 23:5; 33:15), or simply as David: "my servant David" (Ezek 34:23; 37:24). We will from here on refer to this individual offspring as the new David or the promised Davidic king.

There were also indications in YHWH's promises of the restoration of the Davidic kingship that the new David would be divine. His divine identity is most clear in Isaiah through whom YHWH said the new David would be called, amongst other names, "the might of God" or "mighty God" (*'ēl gibbôr*,

Isa 9:6). We have no details from this prophecy of what "mighty God" means, but the most logical interpretation was that the new David would be a divine figure. In Micah the divinity of the new David is demonstrated by reference to his non-human divine origin. Unlike other Davidic kings, his identity would not be defined solely as belonging to the clan of Judah or Jesse's family. He would come from the house of Jesse but would transcend that identity because, YHWH declared, he would originate from a very long, unquantifiable, distant past (*mîmê ʿôlām*, translated "from ancient of days," but literally "from days of eternity"). Thus he would be a person from a very distant past; virtually from eternity. Given eternity's associations with God, which we discussed in our fourth chapter, this declaration implied at the very least that the new David, although from the clan of Judah, would be in some sense divine:

> But from you, O Bethlehem of Ephrathah . . .
> 	from you shall come forth for me
> one who is to rule Israel,
> 	whose origin is from old,
> from ancient days. (Mic 5:2)

Our conclusion that the promised new David would be divine on account of his ancient origins is further supported by the book of Daniel. In Daniel's vision, God appeared anthropomorphically in the form of one who had been in existence for a very long time, the "ancient/aged of days" (rendered *ʿattîq yômîn* in Aramaic – Dan 7:9, 13, 22). This view of God captured his immortality, for YHWH alone, we pointed out, is eternal in biblical literature. If our interpretation is here correct, then the new David's origin from ancient days pointed to his divine origins, or, at the very least, his divine associations. The new David was, therefore, going to be more than a human offspring of David.

We have mentioned that YHWH's interests in the new covenant would be secured by his guarantee that Israel would carry out its law obligations without the possibility of failure. In regard to the new David, YHWH guaranteed his obedience too, albeit implicitly, through promises of his success which revealed he would be unfailingly obedient. As his *māšiah*, YHWH's king was designed to rule Israel as YHWH's kingdom; he would fulfil without failure his judicial and warrior-king roles thus enforcing social justice and securing peace and safety in Israel. For this reason, he would be the ideal Davidic king. We consider below some examples of YHWH's promises concerning the success of the new David which imply YHWH's guarantee of his unfailing obedience.

Through the prophet Isaiah, YHWH promised that the new David would uphold social justice forever:

> for the throne of David and his kingdom
> He will establish and uphold it
> > with justice and with righteousness
> from this time onward and forevermore. (Isa 9:7)

Through the same prophet YHWH promised too that the new David would judge the poor and lowly fairly, in the interests of social justice (Isa 11:3–4). The enforcement of social justice by the new David is also promised in YHWH's metaphorical reference to him as the righteous branch (Jer 23:5). A righteous Davidic king would be one who would rule in the interest of social justice and enforce social justice because justice and righteousness, as we earlier discussed, are synonyms. This understanding is perfectly clear in YHWH's own words through Jeremiah: "In those days and at that time I will cause a righteous Branch to spring up for David, and he shall execute justice and righteousness in the land" (Jer 33:15; also 23:5).

In regard to peace, YHWH promised that the new David would bring peace as the name by which he would be called, "prince of peace" (śar-šālôm), indicated (Isa 9:6). This peace would be endless:

> For a child has been born for us
> > a son given to us;
> authority rests upon his shoulders;
> > and he is named
> Wonderful Counsellor, Mighty God,
> > Everlasting Father, Prince of Peace.
> His authority shall grow continually,
> > and there shall be endless peace. (Isa 9:6–7; also Isa 42:1–4)

The peace would also be extraordinary by encompassing nature to the extent that there would be peace between herbivores and carnivores, and between humans and animals (Isa 11:6–8).

The new David would also defeat the enemies of YHWH, who would be the enemies of Israel and thus make Israel dwell in safety:

> He shall strike the earth with the rod of his mouth,
> > and with the breath of his lips he shall kill the wicked. (Isa 11:4; also Mic 5:9)

Through the prophet Micah, YHWH also promised that the new David would bring peace and safety (Mic 5:4–5) by in part prevailing over his enemies (Mic 5:9). In Ezekiel, YHWH's promise of the new David's enforcement of social justice as well as bringing peace and security is given against the background of the erstwhile failure of the Davidic kings. The former kings, metaphorically called shepherds of Israel, neglected the feeding, strengthening, and protecting of the sheep because of their own selfish interests (Ezek 34:1–10). They also did not judge between the flock to ensure justice (Ezek 34:17–19). The new David would be the opposite of these kings thus taking care of the flock (Ezek 34:23). We may surmise that the divine identity of the new David was the means by which YHWH guaranteed the success of the new David. The erstwhile kings being only the human descendants of David could and did fail, but one from the line of David, also simultaneously a divine figure from YHWH, could not and would not fail.

The general scenario we get from the foregoing prophetic literature on Israel's restoration is the following. The Israelites under the new David and under a new covenant would be gathered back in the land by YHWH. The new covenant would make them once again YHWH's people, his sᵉgūllâ, but this time as a nation especially enabled to live in obedience to YHWH's laws. They would therefore never break their new covenant with YHWH. The new David would unfailingly enforce social justice. He would also secure their peace and safety by defeating their enemies or subjugating and incorporating them into the kingdom of Israel which he would expand to all the world. Consequently, Jerusalem would be holy as a city of justice, and the Israelites would dwell in the land in peace and safety, and they would increase greatly in numbers. The Israelites would also be prosperous and joyous, living in abundance of flocks and herds, grain and fruit.

The scenario means that the Israelites would have received the blessings of abundant life on their return to the land and become truly a royal priesthood representing God to the nation through those blessings. Their blessings would attract nations to YHWH in Zion (because he would dwell there), making them know him and obey his laws, thus experiencing abundant life as a part of God's kingdom. Alongside this, the new David would expand Israel as God's kingdom into a universal one by subjugating nations and incorporating them into Israel.

To put it a little bit differently, this scenario implied that when the Israelites under the new David would be gathered back in the land, they would fulfil their vocation of royal priesthood in the land (as Abraham's offspring and recipients with him of the land promise) to be a blessing to all nations. As a royal priesthood the people of Israel would represent God to the nations through the blessings of abundant life. Those blessings would draw the nations to YHWH in Zion, where he would be dwelling, because they would desire what they would have seen him do for Israel. This would lead them into the knowledge of YHWH and submission to his laws (like Israel). As a result, these nations would have submitted to God's rule and received too the blessings of abundant life as a part of God's kingdom. The blessings to all nations would also be through the new David bringing under his dominion the kingdoms of the world, thereby having them experience abundant life as a part of YHWH's kingdom, which he would be ruling as YHWH's *māšiah*. This way, God's dwelling and kingdom would gradually be restored in the world through Israel and David's dynasty as intended in the blessings-to-all-nations promise given to Abraham.

This scenario we have summarized above, together with its significance, is found in prophetic literature. We have glimpses, in YHWH's messages, of Israel's return to the land under the new David bringing blessings to the nations. In those messages, blessings through Israel are manifest in nations going to Zion (or enjoining themselves to Israel), in their knowing of YHWH, and in their subjugation and thus incorporation into the kingdom of Israel as the kingdom of God. We first look at YHWH's messages of restoration where the blessings-to-all-nations promise through Israel comes about by the nations' attraction to YHWH, who dwells in Zion, because they notice the blessings of abundant life he gives Israel.

In YHWH's messages through Isaiah and Micah, days would come after the restoration when nations would come to Mount Zion (the temple, God's dwelling), in order to learn about YHWH's laws and consequently walk in his ways:

> In days to come
> the mountain of the LORD's house
>   shall be established as the highest of mountains,
> and shall be raised above the hills;
>   all nations shall stream to it.
> Many peoples shall come and say
>   "Come, let us go to the mountain of the LORD,
> to the house of the God of Jacob;
>   that he may teach us his ways
>   and that we may walk in his paths."
> For out of Zion shall go forth instruction,
>   and the word of the LORD from Jerusalem. (Isa 2:2–3; Mic 4:1–2)

Many nations would flock to Zion because they took notice of Israel's blessings of abundant life in the land, and the one responsible for them. Desiring for themselves the same blessings, they would then be attracted to Zion, the source of the blessings: to YHWH, the God of Jacob, who would be dwelling in Zion. In going to Mount Zion the nations would know YHWH and obey his laws. Doing so would bring them into God's kingdom, and they would experience the blessings of abundant life. In these messages, the blessings of abundant life experienced by the nations flocking to Mount Zion would be peace and safety (Isa 2:4; Mic 4:3–4). The same sequence of events leading to nations becoming a part of God's kingdom is intimated in YHWH's messages of restoration, where nations would bring their gifts to him in his house in Zion (Isa 18:7; also Isa 19:16–24), and where they would gather to worship him (Jer 3:17).

Moreover in messages that manifested Israel's blessing to all nations through their attraction to Zion, YHWH promised that he would be glorified in Israel (Isa 44:23). YHWH's glorification in Israel would naturally attract other nations to Zion (where he would be dwelling) yearning to have a share of the same. In another message, it is clear that when YHWH returned to be with his people in Zion (Isa 40:3–11) "all flesh would see it together" (Isa 40:5) and as a consequence be attracted to Zion. In other such like messages through Isaiah, YHWH reminded the Israelites of their priestly vocation to the nations when they returned to the land in terms of attracting the nations to Zion by their blessings of abundant life. Israel, for example, would be a light for the benefit of the nations (Isa 42:6): "I will give you as a light to the nations, that my salvation may reach to the ends of the world" (Isa 49:6; see also Isa 42:6).

In other similar messages, Israel would be attractive to the nations due to their blessings of abundant life so that "aliens will join them and attach themselves to the house of Jacob" (Isa 14:1). To become joined with Israel would mean that they too would come to be YHWH's subjects, thus experiencing abundant life as a part of his kingdom. Elsewhere, YHWH said that Israel ("the root of Jesse," meaning lineage of Jesse)[1] will be a signal or banner to the nations, and that they would seek after this post-exilic Israel (Isa 11:10). As a signal, the Israelites would be highly visible or very loud (see on signal, Isa 18:3; 62:10; Jer 50:2) in order to rally the nations to Zion. Such a visibility could only be from their blessings of abundant life in the land which, as something extraordinary, would thus be highly noticeable to, and desired by, the nations. A blessing of abundant life that would act as a banner to the nations mentioned here is the wealth (*kābôd*) of Israel – translated in RSV as "glorious": "On that day the root of Jesse shall stand as a signal to the peoples; the nations shall

---

1. See J. Renz, "שׁלשׁ," *Theologisches Wörterbuch zum Alten Testament*, Vol. 8, eds. G. J. Botterweck and H. Ringgren (Stuttgart: Kohlhammer, 1973), 485.

inquire of him, and his dwelling shall be glorious" (Isa 11:10). YHWH himself made it clear that blessings on the people of Israel will lead to nations wanting to become a part of them:

> See, you shall call nations that you do not know,
> and nations that do not know you shall run to you,
> because of the LORD your God, the Holy One of Israel,
> for he has glorified you. (Isa 55:5)

Such messages are another manifestation of the blessings-to-all-nations promise through Israel. Through Ezekiel, YHWH said that nations would know that he is YHWH when through Israel he would display his holiness to them:

> I will sanctify my great name, which has been profaned among the nations, and which you have profaned among them; and nations shall know that I am the LORD, says the LORD God, when through you I display my holiness (*biqādšī*) before their eyes. (Ezek 36:23; see also Ezek 39:27)

The root meaning from which the Hebrew word for holiness (*qōdes*) is derived has to do with "otherness" (being separate, different, unadulterated, cut off, on its own). YHWH's holiness in these messages, as their content demonstrates, would be the display of his sovereign power. Consequently, he would be exclusive, not be numbered among the gods (for example), nor confused with any of them. This is clear in YHWH's message from which the verse we have quoted above comes. YHWH's holiness would be manifest to the nations through his unparalleled power: cleansing of the people of Israel, miraculously delivering them from their captives in foreign lands and returning them home, empowering them there to obey him, and granting them the extraordinary blessings of abundant life in the land (Ezek 36:24–31). The same is echoed in YHWH's message through Jeremiah. YHWH's acts in Israel and for Israel, their exile from the land, subsequent return and blessings of abundant life in it, would make the nations know YHWH and revere him (as the holy God):

> And this city shall be a name of joy, a praise and a glory before all the nations or the earth who shall hear of all the good that I do for them; they shall fear and tremble because of all the good and all the prosperity I provide for it. (Jer 33:9; see also Isa 49:22–23; 52:9–10; Mic 7:15–17)

This outlook is encapsulated in the prayers of psalmists who implore YHWH to deliver and restore them for his name's sake lest the nations continue to discount who he is and question his praise (Ps 74:10; 79:8–10). According to YHWH's messages then, Israel's return to the land and their blessings of abundance will make nations reckon that he is YHWH. By extension, these nations will obey his laws (as Israel will be doing), thus becoming a part of God's kingdom and thereby experiencing the blessings of abundant life. We say "by extension," because to know YHWH, as we mentioned, results in the rejection of idols and other gods, and obeying him.

We turn now to the manifestation of blessings-to-all-nations through their incorporation into the kingdom of Israel. We already pointed out that there is an implicit guarantee given by YHWH that the new David would fulfil his judicial and warrior-king roles with unfailing obedience, thus enforcing social justice in, and ensuring the peace and safety of, Israel. As such, he would rule Israel as the kingdom of YHWH, which it was under the covenant. This role is in keeping with our discussion in the previous chapter, that the kingship of David was intimately linked to YHWH's by being designed to rule for God's pleasure and not independently of his rule. The Davidic kings were meant to be kings of Israel as God's servants because God was Israel's ultimate king, the great king. Some of YHWH's messages on the restoration of Israel demonstrate this role by showing that the reign of the new David would be close to YHWH's kingship, or under his kingship. The most forthright of these messages is through the prophet Micah. YHWH promised that when the Israelites return to their land they will be under the new David with YHWH as their head:

> Their king will pass on before them,
>   the LORD at their head. (Mic 2:13)

Other messages of YHWH imply his ultimate kingship through the Davidic kingship, because the new David would subject himself to God's kingship. YHWH promised that Jerusalem would be recognized as his throne and so called the throne of YHWH (Jer 3:17). In another message, YHWH promised that he would be sought in Zion from where he would judge and bring peace to the nations (Isa 2:3–4; also Isa 51:4–5). We should link this message to YHWH's messages promising his return to dwell in Zion once again with his people (Isa 40:9–11; Jer 31:6; Joel 3:17). Since, as earlier discussed, God's dwelling and throne are inseparable, if he was dwelling in Zion, then his throne would be there as well, and the new David (by virtue of his unfailing obedience) would be subject to it, recognising YHWH as the ultimate king. What is more, the announcement to the Israelites that YHWH reigned was tied to his return to take abode in Jerusalem:

> How beautiful upon the mountains
> > are the feet of the messenger who announces peace,
> who brings good news,
> > who announces salvation
> > who says to Zion, "Your God reigns."
> Listen! Your sentinels lift up their voices,
> > together they sing for joy;
> for in plain sight they see
> > the return of the LORD to Zion. (Isa 52:7–8)

Consequently, the wars of the new David to subjugate hostile or wicked nations would inevitably be, as earlier mentioned, kingdom wars – wars to extend the kingdom of God by incorporating subjugated nations into Israel. In other words, subjugated nations would become subjects of YHWH's king and therefore abide by YHWH's laws, invariably thereby becoming a part of the kingdom of YHWH. They would then, like Israel, experience the blessings of abundant life. Some of YHWH's messages on the restoration of Israel make clear this universal reign of the new David by which other nations become incorporated into Israel, and thus blessed as part of the kingdom of God. Through Micah, YHWH promised that the restored Israel (under the new David) would be a blessing to many peoples, like dew from YHWH on the grass, by ruling over them:

> The remnant of Jacob,
> > surrounded by many peoples,
> shall be like dew from the LORD,
> > like showers on the grass,
> which do not depend upon people,
> > or wait for any mortal.
> And among the nations the remnant of Jacob,
> > surrounded by many peoples,
> shall be like a lion among the animals of the forest,
> > like a young lion among the flocks of sheep,
> which, when it goes through, treads down
> > and tears in pieces, with no one to deliver. (Mic 5:7–8)

YHWH's promise of blessings through the new David to the nations is even clearer through the prophet Isaiah. Because of the universal reign of the new David, nations will all know YHWH and thus be obedient to him, resulting in the world becoming a part of God's kingdom (Isa 11:1–9):

> They shall not hurt or destroy
>   on all my holy mountain;
> for the earth will be full of the knowledge of the LORD
>   as the waters cover the sea. (Isa 11:9)

In some messages the universal reign of the new David is equated to the nations that King David ruled over when he was the king: the Ammonites, the Moabites, the Edomites, the Philistines, Geshur, Aram and Hamath. In YHWH's message through Amos, the restoration of the Davidic kingship is in the interest of the new David's universal reign:

> On that day I will raise up
>   the booth of David that is fallen . . .
> in order that they may possess the remnant of Edom
>   and all the nations who are called by my name,
> says the LORD who does this. (Amos 9:11–12; also Isa 9:1–7; 11:14)

Although only Edom is mentioned directly among the nations that will come under the new David's reign, reference to the nations who are "called by my name" is actually reference to the nations in the erstwhile kingdom under David: the Edomites, the Ammonites, the Moabites, the Philistines, and the northern empires of Geshur, Aram and Hamath. In his study of this oracle, Mauchline pointed out that the Hebrew here speaks of "the nations over whom my name has been called,"[2] thus fixing the reference of the nation to events in the past. The nations "over whom my name has been called" could, therefore, only have been the ones that were once a part of the kingdom of Israel under Kings David and Solomon. This is the case because a nation "could have been called by Yahweh's name only when they were part of the community of his people."[3] Moreover, it is the nations that were once under the Davidic kingship that are in focus in the prophecies of Amos (Amos 1–2). We should note here, though, that the equating of the new David's universal reign with the territory under King David could have been symbolic of the new David's universal reign because Israel's maps/territory were not just geographical but a microcosm of the world itself.[4]

---

2. John Mauchline, "Implicit Signs of a Persistent Belief in the Davidic Empire," *VT* 20.3 (1970), 292.
3. Mauchline, "Implicit Signs," 292.
4. See Rachel Havrelock, "The Two Maps of Israel's Land," *JBL* 126.4 (2007): 656–58.

In some of the messages on the universal reign of the new David, YHWH promised the same without giving an indication of its goal:

> See, I made him a witness to the peoples,
> a leader and commander for the peoples. (Isa 55:4; also Mic 4:11; 7:11–12)

The new David's universal reign, existing so that other nations can become a part of God's kingdom, should be presumed to be the goal of these messages. They should not be divorced from the family of messages about the new David's reign, which are explicit about the universality of that reign.

Israel's Wait for Restoration

According to the word of YHWH through the pre-exilic prophets, about the year 721 BC Samaria fell to the Assyrians and the people of "Israel" were taken captive and deported to Assyria (2 Kgs 17:6–8).[5] At around 597 BC, Jerusalem fell into the hands of Nebuchadnezzar the Babylonian king, and the king of Judah, Jehoiachin, together with leading members of the kingdom, were taken into exile. Subsequently, in 586 BC the Babylonians sacked Jerusalem and razed the temple to the ground, and deported more Judeans to Babylon (2 Kgs 25:8–17; Jer 39:1–10; 52:3–30).[6] The people of Israel started to return to their land in 539 BC soon after Cyrus the king of Persia conquered Babylon and allowed the exiles to go back home (Ezra 1:2–4; 2 Chr 36:23).[7] YHWH had singled out this Cyrus as his shepherd so that the Israelites could return home and rebuild Jerusalem and the temple (Isa 44:28; 45:13).

The return of the Israelites back to their land (42,360 Israelites according to Nehemiah [Neh 7:66]) was a sign of the fulfilment of the promises of restoration (2 Chr 36:21–23; Zech 1:12–17). However it did not lead to the fulfilment of accompanying restoration promises given by YHWH through the pre-exilic prophets: it was a partial and not a full restoration. Although the Israelites were back in the land, the promises of YHWH of a burgeoning population, of abundance and prosperity, and of peace and security in the land under the new David did not accompany their return. Jerusalem was depopulated, the people poor and insecure, and living in poverty under foreign rule. Moreover the city

---

5. Hershel Shanks, ed., *Ancient Israel: From Abraham to the Roman Destruction of the Temple*, 3rd ed. (Washington, DC: Biblical Archaeological Society, 2011), 178–180.

6. Shanks, *Ancient Israel*, 201–203.

7. Shanks, *Ancient Israel*, 218.

and temple were still in ruins. The Israelites rebuilt the temple in 515 BC (Ezra 3:1–5:1; 6:13–22).[8] They also rebuilt the walls of Jerusalem (Neh 7:1–4) and attempted to repopulate the city (Neh 11:1). Under the guidance of Ezra the scribe, the Israelites pledged their commitment to keep the covenant which they had started to break on return to the land (Neh 9:1–10:39; Ezra 9).

However, despite the rebuilding of the temple and the walls of Jerusalem, together with the renewal of the covenant, the promises of YHWH to Israel when they returned to the land were delayed. Israel therefore could not be a kingdom of priests representing God to the nations through the blessings of abundant life. There was nothing spectacular in Israel for nations to take notice of and be attracted to Zion. The restoration of God's kingdom and his dwelling in the world through Abraham and his offspring, and through the Davidic kingship, was thus delayed too, although the people of Israel were back in the land. It is in this situation (coupled with the questions and disappointments it brought on those who believed the prophecies of the pre-exilic prophets) that YHWH repeated anew his promises to restore Israel through the post-exilic prophets (Isa 55–66, Zechariah, and Malachi) as follows.

The promise of return to the land was renewed. There would in fact be a second wave of returnees for YHWH would bring still even more Israelites back to the land:

> Thus says the LORD God,
> > who gathers the outcasts of Israel,
> I will gather others to them
> > besides those already gathered. (Isa 56:8)

YHWH renewed his promise of abundance by reassuring the people of Israel that they would be prosperous (Isa 66:12). There would be an abundance of food (Zech 8:12) which would be supported by living waters flowing from Jerusalem throughout the year (Zech 14:8). Israel would have a big population on the land. YHWH renewed this promise directly by telling the Israelites that even the weakest and smallest among them would have many offspring (Isa 60:22). Indirectly, YHWH renewed this promise by assuring the Israelites that they would enjoy their buildings and agricultural labours (Isa 65:22–23), and live to their old age without exception (Isa 65:20, 23). These promised realities meant that their population in the land would dramatically increase.

YHWH also renewed his promise of peace in the land. Israel would dwell secure, never to be overrun by enemies (Isa 62:6–9; Zech 14:11), nor would

---

8. Shanks, *Ancient Israel*, 221–222.

there be violence within her borders (Isa 60:18). We noted that social justice led to peace; this was imminent. The prophet declared that YHWH had empowered him specially to declare the year of Jubilee, the grand year of social justice to the poor, downtrodden, and oppressed (Isa 61:1–2). YHWH renewed, too, the promise of extraordinary peace in the land that would encompass nature to the extent that "the wolf and the lamb shall feed together" (Isa 65:25). Similar to this extraordinary peace, YHWH promised an extraordinary transformation of the world that would result in "a new heaven and earth" (Isa 65:17). Given the association of light in biblical literature with God's presence (Ps 104:2), life (Job 17:12–13), salvation (Ps 18:28; Isa 9:2; Mic 7:8), and wisdom (Eccl 2:13), the new cosmos would have all these eternally, for YHWH would become its everlasting light (Isa 60:19–20; also Zech 14:8). Darkness in biblical literature symbolized death (Ps 88:13; Job 10:21), judgement on the day of YHWH (Joel 2:1–2; 3:15; Amos 5:18, 20; Isa 13:9–10), YHWH's terrifying theophanies (Deut 4:11; 2 Sam 22:10–12), ignorance (Ps 82:5), captivity and exile (Ps 107:10–11; Lam 3:1–2), and precreation hostile to life (Gen 1:1); these would thus not exist in the new cosmos.

YHWH also promised anew that his restoration of Israel would coincide with the day of YHWH. In keeping with the day of YHWH, Israel's restoration would also be the day when YHWH would judge and punish his (and also Israel's) enemies by a spectacularly devastating war (Isa 66:15–16; Mal 3:18–4:1; Zech 14:12–15). To this end Isaiah had been empowered by YHWH to declare the imminent arrival of this day (Isa 61:2). Furthermore, through the prophet Malachi YHWH gave more detail about the day of YHWH by revealing that he would send his messenger, Elijah the prophet, before that day, so that Israel would not be the subject of his wrath (we shall revert to this below):

> Lo, I will send you the prophet Elijah before the great and terrible day of the LORD comes. He will turn the hearts of the parents to their children and the hearts of children to their parents, so that I will not come and strike the land with a curse. (Mal 4:5–6)

To complete our look at the renewal of the promises to restore Israel in post-exilic prophets, YHWH renewed his promise to Israel to restore the kingship of David. He called on the people of Israel to rejoice, for the new David would in victory humbly march into Jerusalem riding on a donkey (Zech 9:9). We should note here that this promise through Zechariah was unparalleled, because YHWH not only renewed his promise to restore the Davidic kingship, but promised very specifically the way the new David would enter Jerusalem when the restoration took place. This new David would extend his rule to all the nations as well as bring peace to them:

> Rejoice greatly, O daughter Zion!
>   Shout aloud, O daughter Jerusalem!
> Lo, your king comes to you;
>   triumphant and victorious is he,
> humble and riding on a donkey,
>   on a colt, the foal of a donkey. (Zech 9:9)

These renewed promises of restoration implied that the people of Israel and the new David would be obedient and thus fulfil their vocation in the land as Abraham's offspring. They would thus be a royal priesthood under the new David, blessing all nations. As a royal priesthood the people of Israel would represent God to the nations through the blessings of abundant life. Those blessings would draw the nations to YHWH in Zion, where he would be dwelling, because the nations would desire what they saw him doing for Israel, thus leading them into the knowledge of YHWH and submission to his laws. Consequently, these nations would receive, too, the blessings of abundant life as a part of God's kingdom. The blessing to all nations would also be through the new David incorporating the nations into Israel, thereby having them experience abundant life as a part of YHWH's kingdom, which David would be ruling as YHWH's *māšiah*. This way, God's dwelling and kingdom would gradually be restored in the world through Israel and David's dynasty as intended in the blessings-to-all-nations promise given to Abraham.

Some of YHWH's messages through the post-exilic prophets confirm the implication we have just explained. YHWH promised that Israel would be a delight (Isa 65:18) and a blessing to the nations (Zech 2:11; 8:13; 8:23). Nations would take notice of the blessings of the Israelites (Isa 61:9). For this very reason YHWH pointed out that the nations would recognize that the Israelites are priests of YHWH (Isa 61:5–7), and would then call them a "holy people," and "redeemed of YHWH" (Isa 62:12). In addition, they would also call Jerusalem the "city of the LORD," the "Zion of the Holy one of Israel" (Isa 60:14–15) because YHWH, who would have bestowed on them the blessings of abundant life, would be dwelling there. For this reason too, all nations would be attracted to Zion:

> Many peoples and strong nations shall come to seek the LORD of hosts in Jerusalem, and to entreat the favour of the LORD. Thus says the LORD of hosts: In those days ten men from the nations of every language shall take hold of a Jew, grasping his garment

and saying, "Let us go with you, for we have heard that God is with you." (Zech 8:22–23)

By virtue of the blessings of abundant life, Zion would be a light to the nations who would thus flock to the city (Isa 60:1–6). Israel would appropriately be called "sought out" (Isa 62:12). The survivors of the day of YHWH would come to worship YHWH in Zion (Zech 14:16–19). For these reasons, God's house in Zion would become a house of prayer for all nations (Isa 56:7) and God would pick some from the nations to be priests and Levites (Isa 66:18–21).

Concerning the new David and the subjugation of the nations in order to incorporate them into Israel as God's kingdom, YHWH through the postexilic prophets revealed that the new David would not only rule Israel but would subdue the nations in all the world "from the rivers to the ends of the world" (Zech 9:10b). Peace was singled out by YHWH as one of the blessings of abundant life that the nations enjoined to Israel would have as a part of God's kingdom:

> He will cut off the chariot from Ephraim
> and the war-horse from Jerusalem;
> and the battle bow shall be cut off,
> and he shall command peace to the nations;
> his dominion shall be from sea to sea,
> and from the River to the ends of the earth. (Zech 9:10)

Mixed with YHWH's renewed promises of restoration through the postexilic prophets were his messages about obedience. YHWH still lamented Israel's disobedience, with a focus, again, on idolatry and social justice (Isa 56:9–12; 57:1–10; 59:1–5; Mal 1:6–10; 2:1–17). YHWH required Israel's obedience pending their full restoration (Isa 56:1–2; Zech 8:14–18). For this reason, he warned Israel against disobedience. They were not to be like their ancestors who refused to repent (Zech 1:1–6). They were to follow all of God's commands (Mal 4:4). In some cases, YHWH warned the people of Israel that their obedience was a precondition for their full restoration (Isa 58:1–8; Mal 3:6–10). Furthermore, only the obedient Israelites would be beneficiaries of the full restoration. They would be YHWH's people, his $s^e g\bar{u}ll\hat{a}$(Mal 3:16–18; see also Isa 66:1–2), but not the disobedient ones. Differently stated, it would be those who took refuge in YHWH (his servants) who would inherit the land and the imminent blessings of abundant life to be bestowed on it (Isa 57:13; 65:8–16). It is to the Israelites that would turn away from their transgressions that YHWH would appear in Zion as redeemer (Isa 59:20).

Moreover, the day of YHWH (which, as we pointed out, would coincide with the full restoration of Israel) would be the day that YHWH would separate the obedient Israelites from the disobedient ones. The disobedient Israelites together with all of YHWH's enemies would be the objects of his wrath on that day (Isa 59:15–19; Isa 66:15–17; Mal 3:5; 4:1). To pre-empt this, YHWH specifically pointed out through the prophet Malachi that he would send the prophet Elijah to make Israel obedient. The obedience singled out in this instance centred on families:

> Lo, I will send you the prophet Elijah before the great and terrible day of the LORD comes. He will turn the hearts of parents to their children and the hearts of children to their parents, so that I will not come and strike the land with a curse. (Mal 4:5–6)

From YHWH's commandments, we know that children (sons and daughters) were to honour their parents (Exod 20:12; 21:15, 17; Lev 20:9; Deut 21:18–21; Prov 20:20; 30:17). The significance of this commandment was in its guarantee of some of the blessings of abundant life – the promise of length of days in the land (Exod 20:12). This promise meant being blessed with good health, daily bread, as well as protection from enemies, ill fortune and adversity – without which one would not live a long life. To honour parents thus very directly meant the blessings of abundant life, and to dishonour them meant curses. If enough of the people of Israel kept this commandment, the blessings of abundant life would ensue in the land, and curses if they did not.

There is more to the significance of the fifth commandment in the foreground in Malachi: the blessing of peace. The blessings of peace and security were in part founded on good inter-generational family relationships. God's message through the prophet Micah already pointed this out. The outcome of many in Israel dishonouring their parents included hostilities and enmity from within one's own household (Mic 7:5–6). If we use Proverbs to shed light on this matter, one who did not honour his parents was a scoffer (Prov 13:1), a fool (Prov 15:5), a destroyer (Prov 28:24) and would bring them shame and sorrow (Prov 10:1; 17:21; 19:26). The dishonouring of parents then was to some extent symptomatic of their children's lack of care for them. A lack of care from children was likely to force parents to withdraw from their lives, resulting in children's loss of parental advice and instructions, goodwill, support and care, with all the consequences of such a loss (Prov 13:24; 19:18; 23:13–14). The end result would be a lack of peace and safety in Israel, even in the absence of external aggressors.

Obedience to the fifth commandment was therefore as important as the observing of social justice, since the blessing of peace and security was not only engendered by social justice, but also by proper inter-generational family relationships. Those disobeying this commandment were no different from those not observing justice since both were important factors in ensuring peace and safety in the land. This is why social injustice and dishonouring of parents went together in YHWH's promise, poetically expressed, of punishing Israel's disobedience:

> The people will be oppressed,
> > everyone by another
> and everyone by a neighbour;
> > the youth will be insolent to the elder. (Isa 3:5)

The Israelites, therefore, would be denied peace in the land by their oppression of each other and their children's insolence to their parents. Observing the fifth commandment brought peace and directly contributed to the blessings of abundant life in the land. Keeping it was, then, as with social justice, of a greater concern to YHWH than the neglect of other laws (with the exception of idolatry). For this reason God singled it out as a commandment of cardinal importance which the Israelites needed to obey. He would send Elijah to help the people of Israel to obey it.

Israel's Further Wait for Restoration and Apocalypse

Prophetic literature in the Old Testament ended with the post-exilic prophets. From the third century BC, apocalyptic and the reuse and interpretation of biblical texts (apocalyptic literature and pseudepigrapha respectively) took the place of prophecy as the avenues of divine-to-human communication in Israel.[9] Some of the features of apocalyptic literature (a number of which may be found in any given apocalyptic literature) include the following. They contain a revelation ("apocalypse") or revelations – visual and/or auditory – of the beyond or the future; they are orientated to end-times; they periodize history; have highly symbolic and mythological language; talk of the day of YHWH as the final punishment of God's enemies; and have otherworldly beings.[10] In biblical literature the book of Daniel belongs to apocalyptic literature (other

---

9. A good and referential summary on this shift in divine communication can be found in Benjamin D. Sommer, "Did Prophecy Cease? Evaluating a Reevaluation," *JBL* 115.1 (1996).

10. See John J. Collins, *The Apocalyptic Imagination: An Introduction to Jewish Apocalyptic Literature*, 2nd ed. (Grand Rapids: Eerdmans, 1998), 1–42.

apocalyptic literature books are in the Apocrypha/deuterocanonical books). We therefore examine the apocalypse of Daniel to follow the unfolding story of the Bible.

The promises of the full restoration of Israel which YHWH gave through the post-exilic prophets were not coming to pass. After the renewal of the restoration promises through the post-exilic prophets, the people of Israel suffered more than two centuries of the continued delay of their full restoration. Against this backdrop, the apocalypse of Daniel revealed the renewal, for a second time, of God's promise to restore Israel. In Daniel's vision (Dan 7:2–14), four different beasts arose in succession from the sea with varying degrees of attributes and powers. However, the fourth beast was singled out as "terrifying and dreadful, and exceedingly strong" (Dan 7:7). Thrones were set up, with an Ancient of Days taking his throne in the court of judgement where books were opened. Consequently the fourth beast was killed and its body burned while the other beasts had their dominion taken away but their lives spared for a while. One like "a son of man" (Dan 7:13 RSV) came with the clouds and was presented to the Ancient of Days and given an everlasting and universal kingdom:

> To him was given dominion
> and glory and kingship,
> that all peoples, nations, and languages
> should serve him.
> His dominion is an everlasting dominion
> that shall not pass away,
> and his kingship is one
> that shall never be destroyed. (Dan 7:14)

The four beasts were interpreted (Dan 7:19–27) as four kingdoms that would arise from the earth. The fourth of these kingdoms would have a king with a vast domain which would include the "holy ones" (*qaddîšê*). In the end God would judge and destroy him, and give the kingdom to the holy ones.

Daniel's historical context was the period of Israelite's extreme oppression and persecution under Antiochus IV Epiphanes. The apocalypse's content substantially revolved around him as the terminus of worldly rule, and the oppressor of Israel, in chapters 2, 7, 8, 9, 11 and 12. Since the first of the four kingdoms was identified in the apocalypse as Babylon under King Nebuchadnezzar (Dan 2:39–40), the second was Media, the third Persia, and the fourth Macedonia. It was Antiochus IV Epiphanes of Macedonia who in 167 BC unleashed a variety of measures meant to humiliate, punish and crush the Israelites. He forced them to build houses and altars for other deities and tried to force them to worship idols.[11] Worse still, he set up an altar "upon the altar of the burnt offering in the temple court, and solemnly dedicated (it) to the worship of the Olympian Zeus" (Dan 8:12).[12] Besides this, he forbade the Israelites "to observe a wide range of commandments, from performing circumcisions, studying Torah, possessing a Torah scroll and observing the Sabbath and holidays, to offering sacrifices, meal offerings and libations at the Temple"[13] (Dan 7:25; 8:9–13; 11:21–39). Subsequently, the apocalypse of Daniel pointed to his destruction and the subsequent granting of an everlasting dominion to the "son of man." When read in relationship with the story of the Bible so far, the son of man was the promised new David who would then sit on the throne of David as God's *māšiah*, ruling the kingdom in the interests of YHWH, the ultimate king. According to this apocalypse, the identity of the new David was also – just as had been alluded to in YHWH's promises through the pre-exilic prophets – more than human, for he would come with clouds from above, pointing to his divine origins. He would therefore not fail in executing his role.

We should note here that "kingdom" in biblical literature is both the king's (so kingdom of David [Isa 9:7], or of Jehoshaphat [2 Chr 20:30]), as well as the nation he rules (so the kingdom of Israel [Hos 1:4], or the kingdom of Judah [Isa 37:31]). It should therefore not be a surprise that in Daniel's apocalypse the everlasting kingdom is also given to the people of Israel who are referred to as the "holy ones" (a term also used to refer to faithful Israelites in the Psalms [Ps 34:9]):

> As for these four great beasts, four kings shall arise out of the earth. But the holy ones of the Most High shall receive the kingdom and possess the kingdom forever – forever and ever. (Dan 7:17–18; see also 7:22, 27)

Since, as we pointed out, the kingdom of Israel through the covenant with YHWH was his kingdom, the Israelites' reception of the kingdom would have also meant that they would become the kingdom of God, and thereby receive the blessings of abundant life (as promised when they returned to the land). The apocalypse of Daniel itself pointed explicitly to this outcome by revealing

---

11. Shanks, *Ancient Israel*, 247.

12. F. F. Bruce, *Israel and the Nations: The History of Israel from the Exodus to the Fall of the Second Temple*, rev. David Payne (Downers Grove: InterVarsity Press 1983), 142.

13. Shanks, *Ancient Israel*, 247.

that God himself would set up his everlasting kingdom after destroying the fourth kingdom (Dan 2:36–45), thus identifying the kingdom that the new David and Israel would receive as God's. God's kingdom would therefore be restored to all the world through Israel and the Davidic kingship because all kingdoms of the world would be incorporated into Israel under the new David (Dan 7:14, 27).

The apocalypse of Daniel also revealed, in line with YHWH's earlier messages, that the Israelite's disobedience was the cause for the continued delay of the restoration of Israel. In Daniel chapter 9, Daniel sought God by prayer and fasting in regard to the delay of the restoration which ought to have come to pass after seventy years "according to the word of the LORD to the prophet Jeremiah" (Dan 9:2). Daniel's confessions revealed that he was convinced that it was the disobedience and the continued rebellion of Israel that had delayed their full restoration (Dan 9:7–14). His conviction was affirmed by God's messenger, Gabriel, who came and spoke to him in response to his prayers. In his message, the reason for the delay of their restoration was their disobedience which had to be done away with first to give way to the restoration.

Accordingly, it would take "seven sevens" (*šābū 'îm šib 'îm*) – seventy sabbatical cycles of Jubilees = 490 years[14] – for the Israelite's disobedience to be dealt with: "Seven times seventy years is the length of time God has set for freeing your people and your holy city from sin and evil" (Dan 9:24 GNB). The seven sabbatical years would span from the time of the word "to restore and rebuild Jerusalem" (Dan 9:25) to that of the "the abomination that desolates, until the decreed end is poured out upon the desolater" (Dan 9:27). The end of this time, when considered in the light of the rest of the apocalypse is when God would sit in judgement and destroy the king of the fourth kingdom and give dominion to the new David and Israel. The length of time was therefore an interpretation of Jeremiah's prophecy of when the punishment of Israel would end (Jer 25:11–12; 29:10) whereby a year was interpreted to be a sabbatical cycle of seven years: six years plus one sabbatical year (Lev 25:1–4). Seven of these sabbatical cycles would themselves be a sabbatical cycle of Jubilee (49 years). Seventy of these sabbatical cycles of Jubilees, alluded to in Daniel's apocalypse, would then amount to 490 years.

---

14. For more on sabbaticals as the basis of Daniel's times see Ben Zion Wacholder, "Chronomessianism: The Timing of Messianic Movements and the Calendar of Sabbatical Cycles," *HUCA* 46 (1975); and Paul L. Reddit, "Daniel 9: Its Structure and Meaning," *Catholic Biblical Quarterly* 6.2 (2000).

Further still the apocalypse of Daniel, in line with YHWH's message through the post-exilic prophets, revealed that the restoration would be a preserve of the obedient Israelites. We could conclude that this was alluded to already by referring to the Israelites as the "holy ones." More directly, the apocalypse revealed that it was those Israelites whose names were "found written in the book" (Dan 12:1), the purified ones (Dan 12:10), who would be delivered and receive the kingdom. From other references in the apocalypse, these would be the ones who would not "violate the covenant" (disobey God) because they would know YHWH their God, preventing them from rejecting him for other gods or idols. For this reason, they would be the ones who would be loyal and stand firm (Dan 11:32). These obedient Israelites were referred to in the apocalypse as wise (*maśkilîm*). They are the ones who would understand the times and lead others (Dan 12:10). Because of their wisdom, they would lead others away from disobedience by helping them understand the times and be faithful (Dan 11:33), thus leading many Israelites to righteousness (Dan 12:3).

Pointers to a Spiritual Restoration

With the apocalypse of Daniel, the story of the Bible in the Old Testament ends with the people of Israel still awaiting their full restoration according to YHWH's promises. This also means that the story ends with the restoration of God's dwelling and kingdom in the world pending. We will pick up the continuation of the story in the New Testament where we shall see that both the restoration of Israel and, therefore, of God's dwelling and kingdom in the world took place spiritually (but typologically) in Jesus Christ. We conclude this chapter with some brief comments on this spiritual restoration in order to prepare for the second half of the story of the Bible which we shall begin to look at from the next chapter.

The result of a concrete biblical theological reading of the story of the Bible, such as ours, is the view that God's dwelling and kingdom would be in the earthly sphere. That is, God's dwelling and kingdom would be in this physical world, where people live in definite historical, cultural, socio-economic and political contexts. Israel by its covenant with YHWH would be a theocratic kingdom on earth, from where it would be restored to the whole world through both a gradual religious conversion of the nation to the knowledge of YHWH and through imperial expansion. YHWH would dwell with Israel his people as his *sᵉgullâ*, in Zion. He would reign over them through his kings, the heirs of David, who would then ultimately rule the whole world according to

YHWH's pleasure. The Davidic kings would establish their universal reign through, on the one hand, subjugating (with YHWH's help) hostile nations, and on the other, through obedient Israel's blessings of abundant life (as God's kingdom). Israel's blessings would attract nations to Zion, where YHWH would be dwelling, because they, too, would desire his blessings of abundant life. In Zion they would know YHWH and his ways, submit to his rule through his *māšiah*, and thereby receive too the blessings of abundant life as a part of God's kingdom. Ultimately the whole world would be restored to God's kingdom with his throne and dwelling in Zion. Unfortunately, the Israelites and the Davidic kings failed in the first instance to be the centre of God's kingdom and its subsequent expansion. They now awaited a second chance to be a theocratic kingdom, the kingdom of YHWH, through their full restoration.

However, as we shall see in the New Testament, there is an alteration in the sphere within which their restoration would take place. This correspondingly also means there is a change in the nature of God's dwelling and kingdom, and thus the sphere within which their restoration in the world takes place. The restoration of Israel would not be fulfilled concretely in the earthly sphere, but spiritually (in a way that transcends the physical world) resulting in the radical transformation of Israel, God's dwelling, the Davidic kingship, land, and even God and Israel's enemies, in the following way. The Davidic kingship would be restored in Jesus Christ, the new David who would not just be of David's lineage but also both Lord and son of God. In addition, his house and throne would not be in Jerusalem but in heaven. Israel would be restored as the people of God, his *sᵉgūllâ*, in those with faith in God and his son, the Lord Jesus Christ. Believing Jews and gentiles in all the world across generations would become God's *sᵉgūllâ*; not simply the living descendants of Jacob. The promise of God's dwelling once again with Israel in Zion would be fulfilled by his dwelling in some mystical way with believing Jews and gentiles on Mount Zion above, the heavenly Jerusalem, with his people. He would also dwell within his people as his temple. In line with this manner of fulfilment, the promised land, as a site for Israel's vocation, would be transformed to become the whole world wherever God's people are.

Consequently, although Israel, the Davidic kingship, the promised land, Jerusalem and the temple remained the centre of God's kingdom and its restoration, the spiritual nature of their restored state would mean that God's dwelling and kingdom would also be heavenly in nature. God's kingdom, for example, would not simply be the earthly theocratic kingdom of Israel in Zion in the promised land. It would be both earthly and heavenly. Its subjects would not just be the generation of those alive who would believe in God and his son, the Lord Jesus, but believing Jews and gentiles from myriad past generations who will all be together when the dead in Christ are resurrected. The kingdom of God would expand not by the nations' attraction to Zion on account of Israel's blessings of abundant life, but through believers proclaiming the good news, and anyone believing it and repenting entering the kingdom. The enemies of God and his kingdom would no longer be the primordial cosmic sea or hostile (or evil/proud/idolatrous) nations, subject to subjugation or destruction, but Satan, demons (or evil spirits), the flesh, the world, and even death. Therefore, God's *māšîaḥ* would subjugate or destroy God's enemies by non-human weapons – God's Spirit, and angels.

Although the spiritual restoration of Israel and the corresponding heavenly nature of God's dwelling and kingdom is revealed by, and manifest in, Jesus Christ and his apostles, there are traces of it in the Old Testament. YHWH's promises to restore the kingship of David point to the spiritual identity of the new David. Unlike past Davidic kings, the promised new David's identity would be human as well as divine. In regard to the enemies of God's kingdom, there are also indications in the Old Testament that they transcended the nations to include non-human beings and powers. The serpent who tempted the first humans to rebel against God was certainly a non-human enemy of YHWH. "The Satan" (*śāṭān*), the sinister "accuser" or "prosecutor" in God's court (Job 1:6–12) or, as a recent study has shown, "YHWH's executioner,"[15] also identified directly as Satan (*śāṭān* 1 Chr 21:1; Zech 3:1–2), was a non-human enemy of YHWH in a non-human realm, the heavenly/spiritual realm. We also have non-human enemies of God in the apocalypse of Daniel. God's heavenly army led by his messenger (*malēk*) Gabriel, assisted by Michael, the protector of God's people (Dan 12:1), fought in the heavenly realm with God's enemies the "prince of Persia" and "prince of Greece" (Dan 10:13–21). Likewise the weapons by which such wars are fought are non-human. Thus, one of the weapons by which the new David would fight his enemies, would not be an arrow nor a spear, but his word and breath. His battle armour would be justice and faithfulness:

> He shall strike the earth with the rod of his mouth,
>   and with the breath of his lips he shall kill the wicked.
> Righteousness shall be the belt around his waist,
>   and faithfulness the belt around his loins. (Isa 11:4–5)

---

15. Ryan E. Stokes, "Satan, YHWH's Executioner," *JBL* 133.2 (2014).

Traces of the spiritual restoration of Israel and the corresponding heavenly nature of God's dwelling and kingdom are also found in the existence of non-human enemies of YHWH in obscure powers used over people and aspects of nature through sorcery (witchcraft/magic). Such powers were not in line with God's ways, and so the use of sorcerers was an abomination, forbidden by YHWH. In addition, we also have the existence of evil spirits in the Old Testament taken for granted. King Saul was tormented by such a spirit (1 Sam 16:14–23). Even foreign gods, to the extent that they are not viewed as non-existent, are indirectly depicted as hostile to God. We also see this depiction in the apocalypse of Daniel where the king from the fourth kingdom is helped to defeat "the strongest fortresses by the help of a foreign god" (Dan 11:39). This is why the Israelites could not have another god alongside YHWH.

A last trace in the Old Testament of spiritual aspects of Israel's restoration and the nature of God's kingdom is found in the resurrection. YHWH demonstrated his power to raise people from the dead through the prophets Elijah (1 Kgs 17:17–24) and Elisha (2 Kgs 4:32–37). The resurrection of the Israelites is given as a mighty act YHWH would perform in order to restore the Israelites back to the land:

> Thus says the LORD God: I am going to open your graves, and bring you up from your graves, O my people; and I will bring you back to the land of Israel. And you shall know that I am the LORD, when I open your graves and bring you up from your graves, O my people. (Ezek 37:12–13)

In the apocalypse of Daniel, those who were going to become a part of the restoration and thereby receive the kingdom would not just be the faithful living Israelites. Through resurrection the obedient Israelites who had died would be a part of the kingdom too forever (Dan 12:2). By the same resurrection disobedient Jews would be judged and punished by an everlasting shame and contempt.

Traceable aspects of the spiritual restoration of Israel, and corresponding heavenly nature of God's dwelling and kingdom and their restoration, became fully blown in the Second Temple period. During that period there was a paradigm shift in the worldview of the Israelites under Greek and Persian influence. There was a drastic increase of emphasis on two dimensions in the Israelites' tripartite cosmology (which we shall return to later) – on the earthly world and the heavenly (or spiritual) world – but with more elaboration on the latter. The invisible heavenly world's spiritual realities and beings (some human-like and some not) were now in the foreground of the beliefs of the

Israelites. A case in point is in the elaboration of God's non-human enemies as found in the LXX, in apocalyptic and pseudepigraphical literature (such as in *Tobit*, 4 *Maccabees*, *Jubilees*, *1 Enoch*, *Testament of Solomon*, and *Martyrdom of Isaiah*) and in the Qumran scrolls. For this reason, the new David in this literature would destroy his enemies not by human weapons but by the word of his mouth. He also would bring peace and safety and bring judgement by the power of his mouth.[16]

In this literature too Satan (or Devil, Azazel, Belial, Masatema, Beelzebul) is "the adversary" of God and identified with the serpent of Eden who led humans astray. He is understood to have been an archangel who exalted himself and rebelled against God, from two biblical poetic messages of YHWH against his enemies – Babylon (Isa 14:12–20) and Tyre (Ezek 28:11–19). These enemies are addressed symbolically as the fallen angel whose judgement, like theirs, was inevitable.[17] The fallen angel was referred to as a star ("Day Star"), which in some cases refers to angels in biblical literature (Judg 5:20; Job 38:7) and Jewish Second Temple devout literature.

> How you are fallen from heaven,
>   O Day Star, son of Dawn! . . .
> You said in your heart,
>   "I will ascend to heaven;
> I will raise my throne
>   above the stars of God;
> I will sit on the mount of assembly
>   on the heights of Zaphon." (Isa 14:12–13)
>
> You were the signet of perfection,
>   full of wisdom and perfect in beauty,
> You were in Eden, the Garden of God;
>   every precious stone was your covering . . .
> With an anointed cherub as guardian I placed you;
>   you were on the holy mountain of God;
> You walked among the stones of fire.
>   You were blameless in your ways
> from the day that you were created,
>   until iniquity was found in you. (Ezek 28:12–15)

---

16. For specific references see Cornelis Bennema, "The Sword of the Messiah and the Concept of Liberation in the Fourth Gospel," *Bib* 86.1 (2005).

17. For specific references see Neil Forsythe, *The Old Enemy: Satan and the Combat Myth* (Princeton: Princeton University Press, 1987), 107–146.

In the same literature demons (*daimōn, daimonion*) are understood to be foreign gods (or the gods of the nations – Deut 32:17; Pss 105:37; 96:5 in LXX). Although some view evil spirits as having originated from demons, they are viewed here as demons which lead people astray and cause misfortune, maladies, and death. They are also understood to be fallen angels who too, like Satan, rebelled against God. Accordingly, Satan is their leader (the arch-demon or "prince of demons") leading God's non-human enemies in the heavenly realm.[18] On the other side are angels (*angeloi*) who are seen as a specific class of heavenly beings who serve God, intercede for God's people and deliver his messages to them. They are also perceived as hierarchically ordered, with principal or archangels having names, having a command of angels under them, fighting God's non-human enemies, protecting God's people, and even executing God's judgements.[19]

The Israelites of the Second Temple period, then, naturally believed in and/or could make sense of their prospective spiritual restoration. They could also make sense of the non-earthly nature of God's dwelling and kingdom and its restoration in ways that those before them would not have been able to. The worldview at the time provided a hospitable environment for elaborate beliefs in spiritual restorations of Israel and the corresponding heavenly restoration (and nature) of God's dwelling and kingdom. An awareness of this worldview helps contemporary readers of the Bible in following the story of the Bible in the New Testament, by relating it to the story of the Old Testament, and appreciating its further development and conclusion in the New Testament by means of typology.

A typology is the temporal relationship between two entities such as persons, peoples, events, activities, places, objects, and phenomena. In this relationship, the first entity in time (usually called a "type") resembles or is repeated in the subsequent entity (its "antitype"). For this reason, the type can be understood as an image, prefigurement, foreshadow, or pointing forward to the anti-type. However, the similarities between a type and its anti-type are never absolute. There is usually some degree of difference in nature, identity, location, meaning, function or efficacy between a type and its antitype.

---

18. For specific references see, Dale Basil Martin, "When Did Angels Become Demons?" *JBL* 129.4 (2010); Henrike Frey-Anthes, "Concept of 'Demons' in Ancient Israel," *Die Welt des Orients* 38 (2008).

19. For specific references see Charles A. Gieschen, *Angelomorphic Christology: Antecedents and Early Evidence*, Reprint Edition, Library of Early Christology (Waco: Baylor University Press, 2017), and Saul M. Olyan, *A Thousand Thousand Served Him: Exegesis and the Naming of Angels in Ancient Judaism,* TSAJ Series, no. 36 (Tubingen: Mohr Siebeck, 1993).

When this understanding of typology is applied to the story of the Bible, the spiritual restoration of Israel (and the corresponding heavenly restoration of God's dwelling and kingdom in the world) means that the Old Testament entities – Israel, the Davidic kingship, land, Jerusalem, temple (Mount Zion) and others – are the earthly types, that prefigure respectively the church, Jesus, inheritance of God's people, the new Jerusalem and Mount Zion above, which are their spiritual anti-types in the New Testament. In addition, although the Old Testament types are similar to their subsequent New Testament anti-types, the former are, generally speaking, in the physical earthly sphere and less effective, while the latter are spiritual and efficacious. As we shall see in the chapters that follow, it is in this typological way that the story of the Bible in the Old Testament continues in the New, and ends with the expectation of the full heavenly restoration of God's dwelling and kingdom in the world.

7

The Restoration of God's Kingdom via Jesus

YHWH's renewal of his promises, through the post-exilic prophets and the apocalypse of Daniel, to restore Israel, concluded our examination of the story of the Bible in the Old Testament. The Davidic kingship would be restored, and the promised new David (from now on the promised Davidic king) would not only rule Israel but would subdue the nations and rule universally. The Israelites would return to the land where they would dwell with a big population, in peace and abundance of grain, fruit, herds and flocks. By virtue of the blessings of abundant life, Zion would be a light to the nations and God's house would be a house of prayers for all nations. The restoration of Israel would coincide with the Day of YHWH, which would be preceded by YHWH's messenger, Elijah, in order to prepare Israel for YHWH's blessing. In the New Testament, the story of the Bible further unfolds by demonstrating that the restoration of Israel took place through Jesus. To this we turn by first looking at the way the New Testament shows that the fulfilment of the restoration of the Davidic kingship took place in Jesus, and consequently shows how he reigns to advance and restore God's kingdom in the world.

Gospel Narratives and Restoration of Davidic Kingship in Jesus

The first place we begin to examine the way the restoration of the Davidic kingship is understood to have been fulfilled in New Testament literature is in the settings of the Gospels. Settings in narratives give the background against which stories are made sense of. Such background information includes the place where the events in a story take place, as well as the time they occur. They could also include prior events that are related to events in a story. Background information offers readers a perspective with which to view a story and make sense of it. It also helps readers of a story identify its concerns and isolate its purpose. The role of settings is crucial in the opening sections of stories where readers are supposed to pick up the right perspective to the story, become aware of its concerns, and know its purpose.

Part of the setting of the introduction of Matthew's Gospel is given by means of Jesus's genealogy. The genealogy pointed to Jesus as the fulfilment of the restoration of the Davidic kingship. Jesus's Davidic ancestry was laid out to show that he was the promised Davidic king: "An account of the genealogy of Jesus the Messiah the son of David, the son of Abraham" (Matt 1:1). Furthermore, the genealogy revealed that Jesus's birth into the world brought to an end an epoch characterized by the prolonged dethronement of the Davidic kingship, from the time of "Jechoniah and his brothers, at the time of his deportation to Babylon" (Matt 1:11) to that of "Joseph the husband of Mary, of whom Jesus was born" (Matt 1:16). This epoch coincided with the period the people of Israel were waiting for their restoration. This setting clearly indicates, therefore, that the concern of Matthew's Gospel was with the fulfilment of YHWH's promise to restore the Davidic kingship in Jesus, and to demonstrate the ways in which Jesus executed the kingship.

The setting of the introduction to Mark's Gospel – which is found as well in the introduction to Luke's Gospel (Luke 3:21–22) – also shows its concern with the restoration of the Davidic kingship in Jesus. At his baptism by John the Baptist Jesus was declared by God to be his son: "And a voice came from heaven, 'You are my son, the Beloved; with you I am well pleased'" (Mark 1:11). A cursory glance could lead one to conclude that in this event God was affirming the divine identity of Jesus. However, against the background of the identity of the Davidic kingship, the pronouncement was a confirmation that Jesus was the promised Davidic king. In our earlier discussion on the Davidic kingship, we noted its divine-sonship which came into being during the coronation of a Davidic king. When an heir to the throne of David ascended his throne, YHWH proclaimed to him that he was from that day on his son: "He said to me, 'You are my son; today I have begotten you'" (Ps 2:7). Against this background, the voice from heaven, alluding to this psalm, pointed to the enthronement of Jesus on that day as the promised Davidic king. The coming of the Spirit upon him was, therefore, not incidental. God had also used his Spirit in the Old Testament to enable kings (1 Sam 10:1; 16:13). For this reason, the Spirit had come upon Jesus to enable him to execute his divinely mandated role. The rest of the Gospel then proceeds to demonstrate his reign.

The setting of the introduction to Luke's Gospel also shows that the concern of the Gospel was with the restoration of the Davidic kingship, and its purpose consequently to demonstrate that restoration of the Davidic kingship took place in Jesus. This setting is first provided by an angel's message. The angel Gabriel was sent to Mary to let her know that the child she would soon carry in her womb would be enthroned by YHWH on the throne of his ancestor David and rule forever:

> The angel said to her, "Do not be afraid, Mary, for you have found favour with God. And you will conceive in your womb and bear a son, and you will name him Jesus. He will be great, and will be called the Son of the Most High, and the Lord God will give him the throne of his ancestor David. He will reign over the house of Jacob forever, and of his kingdom there shall be no end."Luke 1:30–33)

Jesus was thus the promised Davidic king. In him, God fulfilled his promise given in the Old Testament's story to restore the Davidic kingship. The content of the Gospel, as we shall later discuss, would subsequently demonstrate that fulfilment.

The setting showing Luke's concern with the restoration of the Davidic kingship in Jesus is also provided by the prophetic hymn of Zechariah. According to Luke's Gospel, when John the Baptist was born, Zechariah his father prophesied about the restoration of the Davidic kingship in line with YHWH's promises through the prophets. In accordance with our discussion on the warrior role the Davidic kings would play, Zechariah prophesied that the Davidic king would, in his capacity as a warrior-king, secure the peace and security of Israel:

> Blessed be the Lord God of Israel,
>   for he has looked favourably on his people and redeemed them.
> He has raised up a mighty saviour for us
>   in the house of his servant David,
> as he spoke through the mouth of his holy prophets from of old,
>   that we would be saved from our enemies
> and from the hand of all who hate us. (Luke 1:68–71)

In his prophecy, it is his child who would prepare the way for this promised Davidic king whom the Gospel points out was Jesus:

> And you, child, will be called the prophet of the Most High;
>   for you shall go before the Lord to prepare his ways.
>   (Luke 1:76–77)

Another part of the setting showing Luke's concern to demonstrate that the restoration of the Davidic kingship took place in Jesus is provided by the narrator's comments about God's revelation to Simeon. Luke commented that God had revealed to Simeon that "he would not see death before he had seen the Lord's Messiah" (Luke 2:26), the Lord's king. In asking the Lord to let him depart in peace as he held the child Jesus in his arms (Luke 2:29), Simeon identified the child to be the Lord's king. In addition he spoke prophetically about the role the promised Davidic king would play in the world, namely, salvation for Israel and a light to the nations:

> For my eyes have seen your salvation,
> > which you have prepared in the presence of all peoples,
> a light for revelation to the gentiles
> > and for the glory to your people Israel. (Luke 2:30–32)

Still another aspect of the setting to Luke's Gospel, which showed the concern of the Gospel to demonstrate the restoration of the Davidic kingship in Jesus, is given by the prophetic words of Anna. Anna, whom the narrator identified as a prophetess (Luke 2:36), spoke prophetically about the child Jesus as the fulfilment of the restoration of Davidic kingship. She gave her prophecy at exactly the same time that Simeon held the child Jesus in his arms in the same temple and identified him as the promised Davidic king:

> She never left the temple but worshipped with fasting and prayer night and day. At that moment she came, and began to praise God and to speak about the child to all who were looking for the redemption of Jerusalem. (Luke 2:37–38)

The last part of the setting to Luke's Gospel, which shows its concern with the restoration of the Davidic kingship in Jesus, is provided by Jesus's own proclamation in the synagogue that YHWH's words in Isaiah 61 were now fulfilled in him:

> The Spirit of the Lord is upon me,
> because he has anointed me
> to bring good news to the poor.
> He has sent me to proclaim release to the captives
> and recovery of sight to the blind,
> to let the oppressed go free,
> to proclaim the year of the Lord's favour.

> And he rolled up the scroll, gave it back to the attendant, and sat down ... Then he began to say to them, "today this scripture has been fulfilled in your hearing. Luke 4:18–21)

Jesus's proclamation of this fulfilment came immediately after he was empowered by the Holy Spirit (Luke 4:14) and at the onset of his ministry. The timing of his proclamation was therefore significant because it highlighted the work that would characterize his ministry, for which he had just been empowered by the Holy Spirit. That work included the three functions designated to the Davidic kingship as we discussed earlier: warrior, judge, and priest. As the promised Davidic king, Jesus was going to be a judicial king, executing justice for the weak and downtrodden.

Common, then, to all the synoptic Gospels are settings to their introduction that make readers aware that they are concerned with the restoration of the Davidic kingship in Jesus. Their purpose therefore was to demonstrate that the promised restoration of the Davidic kingship was fulfilled in Christ. Indeed, this demonstration occupies the rest of the content of the Gospels and thereby advances the story of the Bible. Before we discuss how the Gospels demonstrate the restoration of the Davidic kingship in Jesus, it is important that we further underline the Gospels' concern with the fulfilment of God's promise to restore the Davidic kingship. We do so by examining the way Jesus was referred to, his own self-disclosure, and the significance of his spectacular entry into Jerusalem.

Messiah, Son of Man, Triumphal Entry, and Restoration of Davidic Kingship

Jesus was referred to as the Messiah. Although "Christ," "Jesus Christ," or "Christ Jesus" later, as seen in the epistles (and in some part of John's Gospel), became Jesus's proper name and title, he was mostly referred to as the Christ (*Christos*) in the Gospels. In Matthew's Gospel, for example, Peter identified Jesus as the Christ when his identity was the subject of conversation: "You are the Christ" (*ho Christos*, Matt 16:16 ESV). Moreover, there are numerous places in Matthew's Gospel where Jesus was referred to as the Christ (Matt 1:1; 1:16; 2:4; 11:2; 16:20; 27:17; 27:22). This is also the case in Mark's Gospel (Mark 1:1; 8:29; 9:41), in Luke's Gospel (Luke 2:11; 2:26; 4:41; 9:20; 20:41; 23:2; 24:26) and in John's Gospel (John 1:41; 11:27; 20:31).

Christos in the Gospels is the Greek equivalent of the Hebrew "anointed" (*māšiah*). As mentioned earlier, David or an heir of his who sat on the throne was referred to as YHWH's, "his king" (1 Sam 2:10; Pss 2:6; 18:50). He was also referred to synonymously as his *māšîaḥ* (2 Sam 23:1; Pss 2:2; 20:6; 132:10; 132:17; Lam 4:20). As we mentioned, it was an alternative way to refer to a king because kings were anointed. This understanding applied to Jesus when he was referred to as *Christos* in the Gospels. For example, the Gospels refer to Jesus as the Lord's Messiah (*Chrison Kuriou*, Luke 2:26) or God's Messiah (*ton Christon tou Theou*, Luke 9:20).

Beyond referring to Jesus as God's Messiah, the Messiah is substituted for the king in the Gospels. For example, when King Herod was threatened by the news of the birth of the king of the Jews (*Basileus tōn Ioudaiōn*, Matt 2:2), the narrator of Matthew's Gospel let it be known that he made inquiries about where the Messiah (*ho Christos*) would be born (Matt 2:4). For another example, the political context of the accusation against Jesus, "forbidding us to pay taxes to the emperor, and saying that he himself is the Messiah, a king" (Luke 23:2) only makes sense if "Messiah" meant king. To put it differently, they were accusing Jesus of claiming to be king (Messiah) of the Jews, and as such taking their taxes in the place of the emperor. A similar clarification of the Messiah as a reference to the king is when Jesus was mocked by the chief priests and scribes thus: "Let the Messiah, the King of Israel, come down from the cross now that we may believe" (Mark 15:32).

We turn now to Jesus's self-disclosure as the Son of Man. As we earlier discussed, God renewed his promise in the revelation contained in the apocalypse of Daniel. We mentioned that in Daniel's vision (Dan 7:2–14), four different beasts arose in succession from the sea with varying degrees of attributes and powers. The fourth beast was singled out as "terrifying and dreadful, and exceedingly strong" (Dan 7:7). He was destroyed while dominion was taken away from the other beasts. Subsequently, one like "a son of man" (Dan 7:13 RSV) came with the clouds and was presented to the Ancient of Days and given an everlasting and universal dominion:

> To him was given dominion and glory and kingship,
>   that all peoples, nations, and languages should serve him.
> His dominion is an everlasting dominion that shall not pass away,
>   and his kingship is one that shall never be destroyed.
>   (Dan 7:14)

We pointed out that given Daniel's historical context, the fourth kingdom represented Antiochus IV Epiphanes under whom the Israelites were extremely oppressed. The apocalypse of Daniel pointed to his destruction and the subsequent granting of an everlasting dominion to one like "a son of man"..

The everlasting nature of his dominion meant that the "son of man" was a Davidic king. As we argued, the eternal nature of David's throne signalled its association with God's throne via the Davidic kings ruling Israel as the kingdom of God: ruling it according to God's pleasure. That God himself would set up his everlasting kingdom after destroying the fourth kingdom (Dan 2:36–45), was confirmation that, unlike the previous kingdoms, the kingdom which one like "a son of man" would receive was God's. The one like "a son of man" being given God's kingdom to rule according to his pleasure was then a Davidic king. Thus, in the apocalypse of Daniel, YHWH renewed his promise to restore the Davidic kingship in the one like "a son of man."

In the Gospels, Jesus pointed to himself as the fulfilment of this promise in Daniel when he referred to himself as the "Son of Man" (see for e.g., Mark 2:28; 8:31; Matt 17:22; 20:18; Luke 5:24; 18:31; 21:36). It is difficult to miss this message at his trial in the Gospel according to Mark. The high priest, Caiaphas, wanted to know from Jesus whether he was the promised King or not: "Are you the Christ, the Son of the Blessed One?" (Mark 14:61). Jesus's response was an allusion to the renewal of God's promise in Daniel to restore the Davidic kingship. In other words, he told Caiaphas that he was the promised Davidic king, but in the language and vision of the apocalypse of Daniel. He was the "son of man" whom Daniel saw coming down with the clouds:

> Jesus said, "I am; and
>   'you will see the Son of Man
>   seated at the right hand of the Power,'
>   and 'coming with the clouds of heaven.'" (Mark 14:62)

In Matthew's Gospel, Jesus also alluded to the promise of God in Daniel to restore the Davidic kingship, in discourse to the disciples concerning his return to the world. He prophesied to them that when he returned to the world, all would see him "coming on the clouds of heaven" (Matt 24:30), just as Daniel saw one like "a son of man" coming down from the clouds. By alluding to the vision of Daniel, Jesus was saying that he was the promised Davidic king promised in the apocalypse.

Concerning the triumphal entry, we pointed out in chapter six that although the people of Israel began to return to the promised land, the promises of YHWH concerning what would take place upon their return and of the restoration of the Davidic kingship were not forthcoming. In the context of this delay, YHWH renewed his promises through the post-exilic prophets to restore Israel and the Davidic kingship. We mentioned that in one such renewed promise YHWH called on the people of Israel to rejoice because of the very specific way the promised David king would enter Jerusalem riding humbly and victoriously on a donkey:

> Rejoice greatly, O daughter Zion!
> Shout aloud, O daughter Jerusalem!
> Lo, your king comes to you;
> triumphant and victorious is he,
> humble and riding on a donkey,
> on a colt, the foal of a donkey. (Zech 9:9)

In the Gospels, the triumphal entry of Jesus into Jerusalem at the Passover festival just before his death was spectacular. As it was the Passover, the city would have been teaming with more people than usual because of the presence of Jews/Israelites (used interchangeably from here on)[1] who had travelled from "the country," and the Jews in diaspora who would have travelled far and wide to get to Jerusalem. Jesus rode into the city on a donkey. The term for donkey (*pōlos* or *ovos* [Matt 21:2] or *onarion* [John 12:14]) may mean a hybrid donkey, or a hybrid donkey but from a jenny, or a young hybrid donkey,[2] but in any case Mark tells us that it had never been ridden before (Mark 11:2). Jesus was welcomed into the city by many people, some of whom spread clothes and palm tree branches (Luke 19:36; John 11:12) on the road for him to ride his donkey on. The spreading of cloaks on the road was indicative of Jesus's royal status since such practice was reserved for kings (see 2 Kgs 9:12–13), as was the spreading of palm tree branches, as had happened when the city welcomed Simon Maccabeus as a king upon his recapture of Jerusalem (1 Macc 13:51). The shouts of praise from the multitude escorting Jesus was a recognition that he was the promised Davidic king in whom the Davidic kingship was being restored:

> Hosanna!
> Blessed is the one who comes in the name of the Lord!
> Blessed is the coming Kingdom of our ancestor David!
> Hosanna in the highest heaven! (Mark 11:9–10; see also Matt 21:1–11; Luke 19:29–44; John 12:12–19)

---

1. We use "Jews" alongside and/or in the place of "Israel" or "the Israelites" following the New Testament which uses the two interchangeably (Jewish literature from the second half of the Second Temple period also uses the two terms interchangeably; see David Goodblatt, "From Judeans to Israel: Names of Jewish States in Antiquity," *JSJ* 29.1 [1998]). However, the term "Jew" could also signify Israelite religion (Judaism) or a Judean as opposed to, say, a Samaritan.

2. For nuances in the range of meanings of "donkey" in Hebrew with which Greek translations of Zech 9:9 grapple see Kenneth C. Way, "Donkey Domain: Zechariah 9:9 and Lexical Semantics," *JBL* 129.1 (2010).

The triumphal entry according to the Gospels was the fulfilment of YHWH's promise through Zechariah, of the way the promised Davidic king would enter Jerusalem when he restored the Davidic kingship. The Gospel of Matthew and John were very clear that this event was indeed Zecharian fulfilment:

> This took place to fulfil what had been spoken through the
> prophet, saying,
> "Tell the daughter of Zion,
> Look, your king is coming to you
> humble, and mounted on a donkey
> and on a colt, the foal of a donkey." (Matt 21:4–5; also
> John 12:14–15)

Moreover, this Zecharian fulfilment (the entry of the Messiah into Jerusalem riding on a donkey) was focused upon by the extraordinary way the donkey was secured and its reservation for use by the Messiah. First, Jesus directed the disciples to the place to go to get the donkey, and informed them of the state they would find it in: "Go into the village ahead of you, and immediately as you enter it, you will find tied there a donkey that has never been ridden; untie it and bring it" (Mark 11:2). Second, the disciples were told what to say if anyone objected to their untying of the donkey: "If anyone says to you, 'Why are you doing this?' just say this, 'The Lord needs it and will send it back immediately'" (Mark 11:3). Upon following the instructions of Jesus, the disciples found the donkey just as they had been told, and when a bystander objected to their untying the donkey they responded as instructed and were allowed to take it (Mark 11:4–5).

With respect to the donkey's reservation for Jesus's use, only animals which had never been sat on were used for sacred duty (see Num 19:2; Deut 21:3; 1 Sam 6:7). The fact, therefore, that the donkey had never been ridden hitherto (Mark 11:2), was a sign that it was specially reserved to be used by the promised Davidic king in his entry to Jerusalem, in fulfilment of the promise God gave through Zechariah. Perhaps responding that the "Lord has need for it" would have made sense to those who questioned the disciples' actions, because they would have understood it, by virtue of its lack of use, to be dedicated for religious purposes. "Lord" would then have been referring to God.

The triumphal entry of Jesus into Jerusalem according to the Gospels, therefore, demonstrated conspicuously that Jesus was the promised Davidic king in whom the Davidic kingship was being restored. It was of such importance that the disciples reckoned with it after Jesus's resurrection: "His disciples did not understand these things at first; but when Jesus was glorified, then they remembered that these things had been written and had been done to him" (John 12:16).

Jesus did not ascend to the throne in Jerusalem or a throne anywhere in the world; rather, he subsequently sat on the throne which was at God's right hand. As we noted earlier, the significance of the psalmist's vision of a Davidic king sitting at YHWH's right hand (Ps 110:1) was in YHWH enabling the king to rule as *his* king. YHWH would enable the Davidic king to defeat his enemies. Since Davidic kings were to rule according to God's will, his enemies would be God's enemies. As such, God would either defeat them, or subdue and bring them under the rule of the Davidic kings. God's kingdom would then advance to the whole world through the kingship of David. In the Gospels and other New Testament literature, we indeed encounter such an advance of God's kingdom through Jesus's defeat, as the promised Davidic king, of God's enemies.

However, unlike the Davidic kings who metaphorically sat at God's right hand, Jesus was seated spiritually, at a non-material, invisible place beyond the earthly physical realm, at his right hand. More specifically, he sat at God's right hand in heaven where he ascended: "So then the Lord Jesus, after he had spoken to them, was taken up into heaven and sat down at the right hand of God" (Mark 16:19; see also 1 Pet 3:22). Elsewhere in New Testament literature, he is seated at God's right hand "in the heavenlies" (*en tois epouraniois*). God put his power to work with Christ when he raised him from the dead and seated him at his right hand in the heavenly places (Eph 1:20; see also Heb 8:1). Jesus is also revealed to be seated at God's right hand "on high" (*en upsēlois*): "When he made purification for sins, he sat down at the right hand of the Majesty on high" (Heb 1:3); or simply understood to be seated at God's right hand "above" (*ta anō*): "seek the things which are above, where Christ is, seated at the right hand of God" (Col 3:1).

In this heavenly location of the throne of Jesus at God's right hand, we encounter the spiritual restoration of the Davidic kingship we mentioned in our sixth chapter. In the Gospels as well as in other New Testament literature, we see correspondingly the spiritual nature of the reign of the promised Davidic king as warrior, judge, and priest as he advanced, and began to restore, God's kingdom in the world. We turn now to Jesus's warrior, judicial, and priestly kingship in the light of the Gospels and relevant New Testament literature.

Restoration of God's Kingdom via Jesus's Kingship

In our fourth chapter, we pointed out that Davidic kings were meant to be warriors, judges, and priests in the service of advancing God's kingdom. We now look at how Jesus, according to the Gospels and other New Testament literature, performed these roles and thereby advanced God's kingdom. We begin by examining Jesus as a warrior-king.

If we may recapitulate our discussion in chapter 4, Davidic kings were meant to advance God's kingdom in Israel by securing the peace and safety of Israel in the midst of her enemies (who would also be enemies of YHWH). Peace and safety were two of the blessings of abundant life resident in obedient Israel as God's kingdom. On the basis of their obedience, the Davidic kings were also meant to advance God's kingdom by subjugating their enemies (through YHWH's support) and bringing them under their rule. In becoming a part of Israel, the nations would know YHWH, submit to his laws and thus become a part of his kingdom, experiencing the blessings of abundant life in the same way as Israel. Thus, through the Davidic kings, God's kingdom would advance and be restored in the world.

In the New Testament, however, the reign of Jesus, and thus the advance of God's kingdom, was chiefly seen in the subjugation of Satan and demons/unclean spirits who were the forces behind the suffering and disobedience of Israel. As we pointed out in our sixth chapter, the Second Temple period witnessed a major shift in worldview, resulting in the view of God and Israel's enemies as primarily spiritual. Although God had non-human enemies all along, the focus of the forces with which God fought changed from the nations to spiritual entities: Satan, and demons or evil spirits. Satan was understood as the arch-demon or "prince of Demons," leading God's non-human enemies in the heavenly realm. Non-human enemies of God were influencing humans and the nations to disobedience and leading them astray. They also caused sicknesses and all manner of maladies in human beings. Thus in the New Testament, and the Gospels in particular, the forces which God empowered his promised Davidic king to defeat were spiritual entities: Satan, demons or unclean spirits (*ta pneumata ta akatharta*), and death.

In the Gospels Jesus cast out demons and unclean spirits (demons from hereon) from people (Mark 1:23–26; 9:20–25; Luke 8:26–39; 9:42–43; Matt 9:32–33). The casting out of demons from people characterized the work of Jesus (see Mark 1:32–34; 3:7–11; Matt 4:24; 8:16; Luke 13:32). Jesus told his disciples that exorcisms were one of the reasons he came (Mark 1:38–39). He also told Herod as much:

> He said to them, "Go and tell that fox for me, 'Listen, I am casting out demons and performing cures today and tomorrow, and on the third day I finish my work.'" (Luke 13:32)

In casting out demons, Jesus was waging a victorious war against Satan, and thus fulfilling his Davidic warrior-king role with the goal of advancing the kingdom of God. Jesus himself pointed this out when he said: "But if it is by the Spirit of God that I cast out demons, then the kingdom of God has come to you" (Matt 12:28). Since the Spirit of God was his power (hence "finger of God" in Luke 11:20 as seen in God's mighty works in Egypt through Moses [Exod 8:19]), Jesus had been empowered by God himself as his king, to defeat his enemies, Satan and demons, in order to restore his kingdom in the world.

The context of Jesus's defence against the Pharisees reveals even more. The Pharisees had accused Jesus of casting out demons by the prince of demons (Matt 12:24), to which Jesus had replied that Satan's kingdom could not stand if that was the case (Matt 12:26). Contrary to the thoughts of the Pharisees, his work was indeed an all-out assault on Satan. Satan was the strong man whom, by the power of God, Jesus had bound. He was then proceeding to plunder his kingdom thus delivering the people of Israel from it, and thereby expanding God's kingdom in the world.

The binding of Satan by Jesus is manifested by certain events in the life of Jesus. He had already come up against Satan in the wilderness where he defeated him, and victoriously departed in the power of God's Spirit (Luke 4:14). Consequently, Jesus started announcing the good news of the kingdom (Mark 1:12–15). The archenemy of Israel and God could no longer stand in the way. Jesus's sighting of the devil falling down from heaven (Luke 10:18) confirmed his defeat. It was this humiliation of the devil that allowed the plundering of his kingdom via the exorcism of Jesus's disciples, for which they rejoiced (Luke 10:17).

Having bound Satan, Jesus was able to cast out demons from people at will. It is no wonder that demons recognized Jesus's power over them: "What have you to do with us, Jesus of Nazareth? Have you come to destroy us?" (Mark 1:24; see also Mark 3:11; 5:7; Matt 8:29; Luke 8:28). Since Jesus had bound the strong man, his disciples as well as those in God's kingdom were also able to cast out demons in his name. Moreover, Jesus's binding up of Satan (the strong man) is what made the scale of his exorcisms incomparable to that of his Jewish contemporaries (Matt 12:27). The Pharisees, therefore, needed to take heed of his advice by switching to his side, thereby becoming a part of

God's kingdom rather than remain on the side of Satan (in whose power they accused him of casting out demons):

> How can one enter a strong man's house and plunder his property, without first tying up the strong man? Then indeed the house can be plundered. Whoever is not with me is against me, and whoever does not gather with me scatters. (Matt 12:29–30)

> John said to him, "Teacher, we saw someone casting out demons in your name, and we tried to stop him, because he was not following us." But Jesus said, "Do not stop him; for no one who does a deed of power in my name will soon afterward be able to speak evil of me. Whoever is not against us is for us. (Mark 9:38–40)

In casting out demons Jesus, the promised Davidic king, was freeing God's people from the oppression and influence of the devil and demons, triumphing over God's enemies, and thereby advancing God's kingdom. This view is thrown into sharp relief in the Gospels by the link between Satan and demons on the one hand, and human bondage, misery and sinfulness on the other. The Gospels and other New Testament literature are very clear that Satan, being against God's purposes, was tempting God's people and/or driving their disobedience. The devil was against God's purposes by sowing tares in the field (Matt 13:39), snatching the good news from people's hearts (Mark 4:15), and tempting God's people (Matt 6:13) and Peter the disciple (Luke 22:31). He also incited people against Jesus, the promised Davidic king (John 8:42–44) and was responsible for Judas' betrayal of Jesus (John 13:2). His work was to steal from, slaughter and destroy God's people (John 10:10). Moreover, as a prince of this world (John 12:31–32) he had many people under his power, deceiving them and leading them away from God. He also made people unreceptive to the good news of God's kingdom (1 Cor 4:4). As van Oudtshoorn puts it:

> The devil, as the father of lies, is primarily at work to undermine people's trust in Jesus and the message from God that he represents with his very being. Unbelief ultimately leads to the realm of the devil, the realm of death, the very realm from which Jesus came to save the world.[3]

The Gospels, and other New Testament literature, are also clear that Satan was oppressing God's people. We have a direct reference to Satan as the cause

---

3. André van Oudtshoorn, "Where Have All the Demons Gone?: The Role and Place of the Devil in the Gospel of John," *Neot* 51.1 (2017): 76.

of the misery of God's people in Luke's Gospel. The woman with a curved spine whom Jesus healed on the sabbath was a hostage of Satan: "And ought not this woman, a daughter of Abraham whom Satan had bound for eighteen long years, be set free from this bondage on the sabbath day?" (Luke 13:16). In the extension of Luke's Gospel, Jesus's work was described as delivering of people from Satan's oppression through their healing:

> You know the message he sent to the people of Israel, preaching peace by Jesus – he is Lord of all. That message spread throughout Judea, beginning in Galilee after the baptism that John announced: how God anointed Jesus of Nazareth with the Holy Spirit and with power; how he went about doing good and healing all who were oppressed by the devil, for God was with him. (Acts 10:36–38)

The Gospels are clear as well that demons were oppressing God's people through sickness and disabilities. Casting out demons therefore resulted in their healing. The epileptic boy who had suffered greatly was healed immediately when Jesus cast a demon from him: "And Jesus rebuked the demon and it came out of him and the boy was cured instantly" (Matt 17:18; also Luke 9:42). The daughter of the Syrophoenician woman who was possessed by a demon was healed when Jesus remotely cast out the demon (Matt 15:21–28; see also Mark 7:24–30). Seven women, including Mary Magdalene, had been healed by Jesus when he cast demons out of them (Luke 8:1–2). Those troubled by unclean spirits were said to have been cured by Jesus through exorcism (Luke 6:18; 7:21). Indeed, demoniacs were classified among the sick who were brought to Jesus and healed:

> So his fame spread throughout all Syria, and they brought to him all the sick, those who were afflicted with various diseases, and pains, demoniacs, epileptics, and paralytics, and he cured them. (Matt 4:24; see also Luke 7:21)

Demons were even responsible for causing blindness and deafness in people. The blind and deaf demoniac was healed and was able to see and talk after Jesus cast out the demon possessing him (Matt 12:22). There were other ways that demons oppressed people. The man possessed by a legion of demons, for example, had been oppressed by them variously with self-mortification and isolation from human habitation to live alone among the tombs (Mark 5:1–13; see also Matt 8:28–34; Luke 8:26–39). He was freed from self-harm and transformed into a gentle hospitable person when Jesus cast out the demons from him (Mark 5:15).

Besides Jesus's own explanation that the significance of his exorcisms lay in advancing God's kingdom, the narratives of the synoptic Gospels give a similar significance by emphasizing Galilee as the site of Jesus's exorcisms. One of the promises of the restoration of Israel and the Davidic kingship which God gave through Isaiah the prophet mentioned Galilee:

> But there will be no gloom for those who were in anguish. In the former time he brought into contempt the land of Zebulun and the land of Naphtali, but in the latter time he will make glorious the way of the sea, the land beyond the Jordan, Galilee of the nations.
>
> The people who walked in darkness have seen a great light;
> > those who lived in a land of deep darkness – on them
> > > light has shined.
>
> You have multiplied the nation, you have increased its joy;
> > they rejoice before you . . .
>
> For the yoke of their burden, and the bar across their shoulders,
> > the rod of their oppressor, you have broken as on the day
> > > of Midian . . .
>
> For a child has been born for us,
> > a son given to us;
>
> authority rests upon his shoulders;
> > and he is named
>
> Wonderful counsellor . . .
>
> His authority shall grow continually, and there shall be endless
> > peace
> > > for the throne of David and his kingdom,
>
> He shall establish and uphold it with justice. (Isa 9:1–7)

As we earlier pointed out in our sixth chapter, this was one of the promises in which the universal reign of the promised Davidic king was equated to the recapture of the nations that King David ruled over when he was the king. What we did not point out was that in the case of this particular promise, the territory that was once under the rule of King David was singled out specifically as Galilee.

Galilee was occupied by the tribes of Asher, Issachar, Naphtali, and Zebulun, and was occasionally known by their names as, for example, the land of Issachar or Zebulun. When YHWH judged Israel (2 Kgs 17:4–5), it was Galilee that first came under the dominion of the Assyrians in 733 BC and was subsequently divided into three Assyrian provinces of Megiddo, Dur, and

Gilead.[4] The descriptive references to this region in the prophecy correspond to these provinces thus: "the way of the sea corresponds to Dor (*dō'r*) the land beyond the Jordan to Gilead (*gil'ād*) and Galilee of the nations to Megiddo (*mᵉgiddô*)."[5] Galilee was thus the first territory in Israel to be humiliated and experience oppression from the hand of Israel's enemy.

According to God's promise, this state of the people of Israel would change from darkness to light (Isa 9:2). Specifically, the Israelites would be delivered from their oppressor by the promised Davidic king (Isa 9:6–7) and live in joy, peace and justice. As we pointed out earlier, darkness in biblical literature symbolized death (Ps 88:12; Job 10:21), captivity and exile (Ps 107:10–11; Lam 3:1–2). In contrast, light was associated with, amongst other things, life (Job 17:12–13) and deliverance or salvation (Ps 18:28; Isa 9:2; Mic 7:8). Given that their situation, darkness, was specified as that of oppression by their enemy (Isa 9:4), the promise to the people of Galilee that great light would shine upon them, was salvation, peace and security under the promised Davidic king (Isa 9:7). Deliverance from the oppressor would be akin to that of their forbears under Gideon (Judg 6:2–6) from the Midians (Isa 9:4). The burning of the boots and soiled garments of their oppressor's warriors referred to (Isa 9:5), "portrays the end of Holy War against the enemy when the war-boots and military uniforms had to be burned."[6] In a nutshell, the people in the territory that was the first in Israel to experience God's judgement were singled out to be the first recipients of the kingdom of God under the promised Davidic king. The Galileans would in consequence have peace and security, the blessings of abundant life which characterize God's kingdom.

In the synoptic Gospels, Galilee was the home of Jesus (Matt 2:22; 3:13; Mark 1:9; 14, 39; Luke 1:26; 23:5; see also John 7:41). It was the place where Jesus executed his kingship which was characterized by exorcism; indeed nearly all his exorcisms are carried out in Galilee. Mark's Gospel summarizes quite forthrightly that the site of Jesus's work was Galilee:

> They said to him, "Everyone is searching for you." He answered, "Let us go on to the neighbouring towns, so that I may proclaim the message there also; for that is what I came out to do." And he went throughout Galilee, proclaiming the message in the

---

4. Bruce, *Israel and the Nations*, 54.
5. Ronald E. Clement, *Isaiah 1–39*, NCB (Grand Rapids: Eerdmans, 1981), 106.
6. John D. W. Watts, *Isaiah 1–33*, WBC Vol. 24 (Waco: Word Books, 1985), 134.

synagogues and casting out demons. (Mark 1:37–39; see also Matt 4:23–25; Luke 4:14; Luke 4:31–42)

In Matthew's Gospel the onset of Jesus's work, which was in Galilee, was tied to both his defeat of Satan in the wilderness and the arrest (and subsequent death) of John the Baptist. It was after the arrest of John that Jesus went to Galilee (Matt 4:12) because the time for God to fulfil the promise he gave to the people of Galilee through the prophet Isaiah had come. In the words of Matthew:

> Now when Jesus heard that John had been arrested, he withdrew to Galilee. He left Nazareth and made his home in Capernaum by the sea, in the territory of Zebulun and Naphtali, so that what had been spoken through the prophet Isaiah might be fulfilled:
>
> "land of Zebulun, land of Naphtali,
> on the road by the sea, across the Jordan, Galilee of the gentiles –
> the people who sat in darkness
> have seen a great light,
> and those who sat in the region and shadow of death
> light had dawned." (Matt 4:12–16)

As we have just discussed, the promise given to the people of Galilee signified the restoration of the Davidic kingdom. The promised Davidic king as a warrior-king would succeed in advancing God's kingdom by defeating the enemies of Israel. The people of Israel would then enjoy peace and security, the blessings of abundant life which characterize God's kingdom, which would have come upon them. In this case, however, the enemies who were oppressing the people of Galilee were not the Assyrians but Satan and demons, whom Jesus defeated and from whom he delivered the Galileans. Their individual circumstances were accordingly transformed from darkness to light.

The significance of the exorcisms of Jesus in Galilee, therefore, lay in his advancement of the kingdom of God as the promised Davidic king. The synoptic Gospel narratives were saying in unison that Jesus, the promised Davidic king, was advancing the kingdom of God in Galilee as foretold. The people of Galilee were thus delivered from the bondage and oppression of Satan and demons, and into the freedom of peace and joy, the blessings of abundant life, characteristic of God's kingdom which Jesus had brought upon them. It is for this reason that the onset of Jesus's proclamation of the good news that the kingdom of God had arrived was linked by the Gospel narrators to his arrival and residence in Galilee:

> Now when Jesus heard that John had been arrested, he withdrew to Galilee. . . . From that time Jesus began to proclaim, "Repent for the kingdom of heaven has come near." (Matt 4:12, 17; see also Mark 1:14)

From the Gospels' perspective, we can now understand that Jesus the Davidic warrior-king had waged an all-out war on the devil and demons in order to deliver Israel and advance God's kingdom in the process of fully restoring it in the world.

The defeat of Satan and demons was not the only way that Jesus fulfilled his Davidic warrior-king role of advancing God's kingdom, nor was his deliverance of people from Satan and demons the only manifestation of the blessings of abundant life amongst those upon whom God's kingdom had dawned. The blessings of abundant life were also manifest in health and wholeness, life, abundance, and security which accompanied Jesus wherever he went. In all these cases he was the Davidic warrior-king vanquishing the enemies of God and his people and advancing God's kingdom. We examine below these other blessings in the Gospels' narratives.

In numerous instances the Gospels narrate Jesus healing the sick. He healed Peter's mother-in-law (Mark 1:30–31), the haemorrhaging woman (Matt 9:18–26), the bed-ridden servant of the centurion (Matt 8:5–13), the Syrophoenician girl (Mark 7:24–30), the man with dropsy (Luke 14:1–6), and the son of the nobleman (John 4:46–54). Jesus brought healing to the people wherever he went (Matt 14:14, 36; 15:30; 19:2; 21:14; Mark 1:34; Luke 4:40; 9:11). Because of his fame in Galilee, the people also flocked to him to be healed (Matt 12:15; 21:14). Jesus also made people whole. He restored the sight of the blind (Mark 8:22–26; Matt 9:27–31; Luke 18:35–43; John 9:1–41), restored withered hands (Matt 12:9–14), opened the ears and tongue of a deaf-mute (Mark 7:31–37), and enabled the crippled and paralysed to walk (John 5:1–18; Mark 2:1–12; Luke 13:10–17).

The Gospels also give accounts of Jesus giving life to people by raising the dead. The most dramatic was the raising of Lazarus from the dead (John 11:38–44). In addition, Jesus raised the daughter of Jairus from the dead, as well as the son of the widow of Nain (Luke 7:11–16). The blessings of life as a manifestation of the kingdom of God are also seen symbolically in Jesus's cleansing of lepers. Leprosy was associated with death. The social exclusion required of lepers (Lev 13:45–46) would have made life extremely difficult, if not impossible for them, while the categorisation of leprosy as something unclean (Lev 13:1–40) thus polluting even of clothing and garments (Lev 13:47–59) made it to be considered as a form of death, "a living death."[7] The view of leprosy as death is confirmed in the cry of Aaron to God not to make Miriam as good as dead when he struck her with leprosy: "Let her not be as one dead, of whom the flesh is consumed when he comes out of his mother's womb" (Num 12:12 RSV). For this reason, a leper who had recovered could not simply walk back into society. He would have had to be examined by a priest to confirm his recovery and through elaborate ritual, which included various offerings, be cleansed before reintegration into the community (Lev 14:1–32). Jesus therefore brought life by healing/cleansing lepers. The Gospels narrate one such incident: a man with leprosy near Gennesaret approached Jesus and beseeched his cleansing. Jesus cleansed him, and in keeping with the law on leprosy, asked him to go show himself to the priest for examination and subsequent rituals (Mark 1:40–45).

Healing of the sick, making of people whole, cleansing of lepers and raising people from the dead were some of the blessings of abundant life which characterized God's kingdom. This is the reason why, when John the Baptist wanted a confirmation as to whether Jesus was the promised Christ, Jesus responded thus:

> And he answered, go and tell John what you have seen and heard: the blind receive their sight, the lame walk, the lepers are cleansed, the deaf hear, the dead are raised up, the poor have the good news brought to them. (Luke 7:22)

This was to let John know without a doubt that Jesus was the promised Davidic king, and was duly fulfilling the role of the Davidic kingship by subduing God's enemies, thereby advancing God's kingdom. The kingdom of God was evident in the health and wholeness, and in life: that is, in the blessings of abundant life, which he was bringing to the people.

Food abundance and wealth were also blessings of abundant life which manifested the advancement of God's kingdom through Jesus as the Davidic warrior-king. Jesus turned water into wine (John 2:1–11), provided tax money from fish (Matt 17:24–27), and enabled the disciples to have a huge catch of fish in two instances (Luke 5:1–11; John 21:1–14). When the people who had come out to listen to the good news which Jesus was proclaiming had no food to eat, he provided more than enough food for over five thousand (Matt 14:15–21), and for over four thousand (Matt 15:32–38).

---

7. Gilbert Lewis, "A Lesson from Leviticus: Leprosy," *Man* 22.4 (1987), 602.

Peace and security were also blessings of abundant life which manifested the advancement of God's kingdom through Jesus. These blessings are seen in relationship to water. We mentioned in our second chapter that the sea in the ancient Near Eastern worldview was seen as a force for chaos and therefore a threat to life and order. YHWH imposed (and continued to impose) his kingship upon it. For example:

> You silence the roaring of the seas,
>   the roaring of their waves. (Ps 65:7; also Ps 93:3–4)

The sea then became symbolic both of God and Israel's enemy. For example, the enemies of Davidic kings (and God's), the nations, were symbolized as the chaotic forces of the waters:

> I will set his hand on the sea
>   and his right hand on the rivers (Ps 89:25; cf. Isa 17:12–13; Hab 3:15)

In the Gospels, Jesus ruled the waters. When his disciples' lives were threatened by the sea, Jesus commanded it to be calm:

> He woke up and rebuked the wind, and said to the sea. "Peace! Be Still!" Then the wind ceased, and there was a dead calm. (Mark 4:39; see also Matt 8:23; Luke 8:22–25)

In this encounter, the sea, being a force of death and symbolic of God's enemy, was defeated by Jesus as the Davidic warrior-king advancing God's kingdom. He thereby brought the blessings of peace and security to his disciples on whom the kingdom of God had come upon through him. In addition, Jesus's walking on water (Mark 6:48–49) communicated his defeat of chaos and death as God's enemies in his advancement of God's kingdom in the world, thus bringing the blessings of peace and security. As pointed out by Malbon, "By his deed Jesus treats the sea as if it were land; he walks on the sea (6:48); for him chaos is made order."[8] Our view is supported by Mark's Gospel. The narrator of the Gospel draws our attention to the relationship between Jesus's provision of food (abundance) as one of the blessings of abundant life, and Jesus walking on water (peace and security) as another blessing of abundant life:

> But when they saw him walking on water, they thought it was a ghost and cried out; for they all saw him and they were terrified. But immediately he spoke to them and said, "Take heart, it is I;

---

8. Elizabeth Struthers Malbon, "Galilee and Jerusalem: History and Literature in Marcan Interpretation," *CBQ* 44.2 (1982), 251.

do not be afraid." Then he got into the boat with them and the wind ceased. And they were utterly astounded, for they did not understand about the loaves, but their hearts were hardened. (Mark 6:49–52)

Both abundance and security were, as blessings of abundant life, manifestations of the kingdom of God which Jesus, the Davidic warrior-king, was advancing in the world. Unfortunately, the disciples did not understand this, hence their shock at his walking on water: Jesus was bringing peace and security where there was chaos and destruction of life.

We turn to look at Jesus's judicial role as a Davidic king. In John's Gospel Jesus proclaimed his judicial role in relation to his Davidic kingship:

For just as the Father has life in himself, so he has granted the Son also to have life in himself; and he has given him authority to execute judgement, because he is the Son of Man. (John 5:26–27; see also Acts 10:42)

We mentioned that the Son of Man in the apocalypse of Daniel is the promised Davidic king through whom the Davidic kingship and kingdom of Israel would be restored. In the words of Jesus himself, the reason God gave him authority to judge is because he was the Son of Man, the promised Davidic king. The authority granted to him was in keeping with the roles YHWH gave the Davidic kingship. It was therefore incumbent upon Jesus to enforce justice in accordance with the will of God, and thereby advance God's kingdom in the world.

From some writings of the New Testament, it seems that Jesus's Davidic kingship's judicial role would take place at the end of time. The following examples clarify this. When Jesus proclaimed that he had been given authority to judge, he pointed to the resurrection as the time he would exercise it: "for the hour is coming when all will hear his voice, and will come out – those who have done good, to the resurrection of life, and those who have done evil, to the resurrection of condemnation" (John 5:27–28). The apostle Peter proclaimed that Jesus will judge both the living and the dead (Acts 10:42); the same is mentioned in the pastoral epistles (2 Tim 4:1). In the Gospels reference is made to the "day of judgement" (Matt 10:15; 11:22, 24; 12:36), "the judgement" (Luke 10:14; 11:31–32) or simply "that day" (Luke 10:12) as an event in the future where judgement will be executed. There is also mention of the vindication of those who cry out to God for justice at the return of Jesus (Luke 18:6–8). In other New Testament literature Paul mentioned Christ's judgement seat before which all shall appear in the future (2 Cor 5:10; see also Rom 14:10–11), and of a day designated for this judgement (Acts 17:31).

However, the Gospels linked Jesus's exorcisms and healings, as the promised Davidic king, to his delivery of justice in their times, the here-and-now. The link between healing and justice is made explicitly in Matthew's Gospel:

> Many crowds followed him, and he cured all of them, and he ordered them not to make him known. This was to fulfil what had been spoken through the prophet Isaiah:
>
> Here is my servant, whom I have chosen,
> > my beloved, with whom my soul is well pleased.
> I will put my Spirit upon him,
> > and he will proclaim justice to the gentiles.
> He will not wrangle or cry aloud,
> > nor will anyone hear his voice in the streets.
> He will not break a bruised reed
> > or quench a smouldering wick
> until he brings justice to victory.
> > And in his name gentiles will hope. (Matt 12:15–21)

God's promise through Isaiah of the restoration of the Davidic kingship through his servant, the promised Davidic king, was in view. The successful execution of social justice as the Davidic kingship's judicial role was contained and assured in the promise. The narrator of Matthew therefore perceived Jesus's healings in some sense as the beginning of the fulfilment of that promise.

Matthew's perspective should not surprise us. We discussed at length in chapter 4 that the judicial role of the Davidic kings was primarily the execution of social justice. Social justice was binary in nature. It entailed on the one hand justice – rescue or deliverance of the suffering, weak and lowly – and on the other punishment of the culpable high and mighty in society. When Jesus healed people, he delivered them from the pain and misery caused by the sicknesses. Since Satan and demons caused sicknesses, those who were healed were thus also delivered from the oppression and captivity of the devil and demons. In other words, Jesus, the Davidic judicial king, gave the sick justice through healing and delivering them from their tormentors.

The link between healing and justice in the ministry of Jesus is also evident in the cries of those who begged for his mercy. As Kleinig clarifies,[9] there are two kinds of mercy that arise, because they obtain from two different

---

9. John Kleinig, "Mercy and Justice," *PPR* 44.170 (1969).

contexts. One comes from a context of wrongdoing and punishment where mercy is the less-than-deserved punishment an offender receives or, we may add, the suspension of a deserving punishment from the offender altogether. The other context is "treating with benevolence those who are in need, distress, debt or under threat of some sort"[10] (who in the case of social justice are the down-trodden). In this sense mercy is shown to the poor, to the widow or the orphan, but never to the rich, powerful or strong. This kind of mercy is in keeping with social justice that Davidic kings were to uphold. Understanding mercy in this way makes comprehensible requests to Jesus to have mercy on the blind (Matt 9:27; 20:30; Mark 10:47; Luke 18:37), on one possessed by demons (Matt 15:22) and on an epileptic boy (Matt 17:15). The requests for mercy were not for a lesser punishment nor suspension of punishment (for they had committed no sin or offense) but, rather, for rescue from their miserable states. The association of their cries for mercy to Jesus's Davidic ancestry presumed the recognition of Jesus as the promised Davidic king upon whom they could therefore plead for justice:

> They then came to Jericho. As he and his disciples and a large crowd were leaving Jericho, Bartimaeus son of Timaeus, a blind beggar, was sitting by the roadside. When he heard that it was Jesus of Nazareth, he began to shout out and say "Jesus, Son of David, have mercy on me!" (Mark 10:46–47)

> As Jesus went on from there, two blind men followed him, crying loudly, "Have mercy on us, Son of David!" (Matt 9:27)

Justice so executed by the promised Davidic king in the healing of the sick and in the transformation of the miserable states of the downtrodden resulted in their experience of the blessings of health, peace and joy. These blessings were characteristic of God's kingdom which had dawned on them through the promised Davidic king.

As the Davidic judicial king, Jesus also enforced in the here-and-now the other side of social justice: punishment of those victimizing the weak and poor. His banishment of demons as a punishment for oppressing the people of God seems suggested in the rhetorical question they asked him about their impending banishment: "What have you to do with us, Jesus of Nazareth? Have you come to destroy us?" (Mark 1:24; Luke 4:34). Jesus alluded as well to the judgement of the devil (John 16:11) as something that had taken place,

---

10. Kleinig, "Mercy and Justice," 341.

and whose effects were ongoing, which was in the freeing of people from Satan's hold.

Jesus, then, as the promised Davidic king, fulfilled his Davidic kingship's judicial role for the sake of God's kingdom through his exorcisms and healings, and making people whole. He also did so by banishing demons that were oppressing God's people through various illnesses and physical conditions. Moreover, this Davidic king's judicial role transcended his present activities to include a time in the future when he will judge all people alive and dead.

Finally, we discuss Jesus's priesthood role as a Davidic king according to the Gospels and other New Testament literature. According to the book of Hebrews, Jesus was appointed by God as a priest in the order of Melchizedek. The Hebrews' writer quotes Psalm 110:4 directly to shed light on Jesus's appointment as a royal priest:

> Every high priest chosen from among mortals is put in charge of things pertaining to God on their behalf, to offer gifts and sacrifices for their sins . . . And one does not presume to take this honour, but takes it only when called by God, just as Aaron was. So also Christ did not glorify himself in becoming a high priest, but was appointed by the one who said to him,
> "You are my Son
>   today I have begotten you"
> as he says also in another place,
> "You are a priest forever,
>   according to the order of Melchizedek." (Heb 5:1–6)

When discussing the roles of Davidic kings in our fourth chapter, we pointed out that this psalm applied to Davidic kings and revealed their role as priest-kings. Jesus being the promised Davidic king was, and still is, accordingly a royal priest.

In the same discussion, we pointed out that mediation between God and humans was the work of priests. This was seen in virtue of priests attending to God in his house, but particularly in their offering of sacrifices, in their intercessions, and in their giving of God's word. According to the writer of Hebrews these functions (except the giving of God's word – see below) are all carried out by Jesus as a royal priest. Concerning priests as servants of God in his house, the writer of Hebrews points out that Jesus serves in God's house. However, unlike the Aaronic high priest who served on earth in a sanctuary made by hands and "a sketch and shadow of what is in heaven" (Heb 8:5; see also 9:1–10, 23), Jesus serves God in his spiritual house, in heaven, in the "true tent that the Lord, and not any mortal, has set up" (Heb 8:2; also 9:11, 24).

Concerning priests and sacrifices, the writer of Hebrews points out that Jesus offered only one single sacrifice to God to atone for the sins of the world. This single sacrifice was himself. As a high priest, "he entered once for all into the Holy Place, not with blood of goats and calves, but with his own blood, thus obtaining eternal redemption" (Heb 9:12; also 10:10). It was the eternal effectiveness of Jesus's sacrifice that rendered his continual offering of sacrifices as a royal priest unnecessary:

> And every priest stands day after day at his service, offering again and again the same sacrifices that can never take away sins. But when Christ had offered for all time a single sacrifice for sins, "he sat down as the right hand of God," and since then has been waiting "until his enemies would be made a footstool for his feet." For by a single offering he has perfected for all time those who are sanctified. (Heb 10:11–14)

With regards to intercessions, the Hebrews' writer points out the eternal nature of Jesus's royal priestly intercessions. As an eternal priest Jesus is able to make intercession ceaselessly for "those who approach God through him" (Heb 7:23–25). These intercessions, according to Hebrews, are at the throne of grace in heaven where Jesus has gone, having passed through the heavens (Heb 4:14) and sat at God's right hand (Heb 1:3; 8:1; 12:2), in God's very presence for God's people (Heb 9:24). For these reasons Jesus's prayers are heard. Other New Testament literature also mentions Jesus's effective intercession for God's people. Paul directly points out that Jesus intercedes for God's people:

> Who will bring any charge against God's elect? It is God who justifies. Who is to condemn? It is Christ Jesus who died, yes, who was raised, who is at the right hand of God, who indeed intercedes for us. (Rom 8:33–34)

In John's epistle, Jesus is pointed out as an advocate of God's people before God: "But if anyone does sin, we have an advocate with the Father, Jesus Christ the righteous" (1 John 2:1).

By virtue of his royal priesthood Jesus advances God's kingdom in enabling those in God's kingdom to approach God, and thus to abide in his kingdom which they have received (Heb 12:27), through forgiveness, acceptance by God, and through the acquisition of God's help and power. Hebrews makes clear that approaching God is enabled by Jesus. It is made possible by the sympathetic priesthood (Heb 4:14–15) Jesus offers God's people. It is made possible by his blood which atones for the failures and weaknesses of God's people (Heb 10:19). It is also made possible by Jesus's presence with God (Heb 9:24). In addition, in view of Jesus's royal priesthood (Heb 4:14–15), those in God's kingdom can approach the throne of grace with confidence to receive mercy and grace to help them in their moments of need (Heb 4:16).

We have mentioned that Hebrews does not touch on Jesus's royal priesthood concerning the giving of God's word. This aspect of Jesus's royal priesthood, however, is implied in the Gospels. In Matthew, the crowds recognized the authority by which Jesus taught (Matt 7:28; also Mark 1:22; Luke 4:32). That recognition came after Jesus had taught the crowds. The comparison of his teaching with that of the scribes confirms that the content of his teaching was the word of God. Scribes seemed to have taken over from the priests, although the two seemed to be one as seen in Ezra (Neh 8:9) in the study and teaching of the law. They were "the originators of the synagogue service . . . After AD 70 the importance of scribes was enhanced. They preserved in written the oral law and faithfully handed down the Heb. Scriptures."[11] It was because scribes taught the law that they were referred to as "teachers of the law" (for example, Matt 12:38; 15:1; Mark 2:6; 3:22; Luke 5:21; 9:22). According to the crowds, then, Jesus taught the law better than the scribes. However, it is in John's Gospel that Jesus's giving of the word of God is clearest since Jesus taught what was the Father's: "My teaching is not mine but his who sent me" (John 7:16–17; also 3:34; 8:28; 12:49; 17:8).

Giving of the word of God was an activity that Jesus was continually involved with (Matt 11:1; 13:53; 26:1; Mark 6:2). In Jesus's teaching people received the word of God authoritatively. In this regard, we could argue that by virtue of his royal priesthood, Jesus advanced God's kingdom. He did so by enabling those on whom God's kingdom had dawned to know and follow the will of God. He taught them the law and the prophets, for example (Matt 7:12), and the "secrets of the kingdom" (Mark 4:11) that those not in God's kingdom were blind to, in order for them to know and follow God's will. This function of Jesus's royal priesthood would not stop at his death, nor even at his ascension to God's right hand. He had promised his disciples that the Spirit would teach them what he would have taught them and would remind them all that he had taught them: "But the Helper, the Holy Spirit, whom the Father will send in my name, he will teach you all things, and bring to your remembrance all that I have said to you" (John 14:26 ESV).

---

11. C. L. Feinberg, "Scribes," *New Bible Dictionary* 1:1079.

From the foregoing, we encounter in our reading of New Testament literature the further unfolding of the story in the Bible which is the restoration of the Davidic kingship through Jesus the promised Davidic king. The literature reveals that as the promised Davidic king, Jesus advanced the kingdom of God as a warrior, judge, and priest-king. However, Jesus exercised his reign spiritually as epitomized in the heavenly location of his throne, which is at God's right hand.

Newness in Jesus's Restoration of God's Kingdom

In our concluding sections of this chapter, we look at new understandings of God's kingdom, and the new ways of God's working to restore his kingdom through Jesus. Knowledge of this newness will further help us appreciate the nature of God's kingdom as demonstrated and revealed by Jesus, and the ways it is being restored in the world. Jesus talked of newness in the context of the offense caused to the scribes and Pharisees by the non-fasting of his disciples. The disciples were feasting in contrast to the fasting of the disciples of John the Baptist:

> He also told them a parable: "No one tears a piece from a new garment and sews it on an old garment; otherwise the new will be torn, and the piece from the new will not match the old. And no one puts new wine into old wineskins; otherwise the new wine will burst the skins and will be spilled, and the skins will be destroyed. But new wine must be put into fresh wineskins. And no one after drinking old wine desires new wine, but says, 'The old is good.'" (Luke 5:36–39; also Mark 2:20–22; Matt 9:14–17)

Though not spelled out, the talk of new wine hinted at differences between what was there before and what was current with the coming of Jesus the promised Davidic king. This change, the newness of things, is what the scribes and Pharisees seemed to have struggled to accept because they were used to the old.

We have already accounted for the restoration of the kingdom of God through Jesus's kingship on the basis of a spiritual restoration. Jesus the promised Davidic king sat on the throne of David, but at God's right hand on high and not in the king's palace in Jerusalem. He advanced the kingdom of God by fighting and defeating God's non-material enemies holding his people captive, and by delivering social justice via banishing non-human actors victimising God's people. He also advanced God's kingdom in the world by helping those who had come to abide in God's kingdom through his royal priesthood, on account of which he gave God's word, and also opened access to God and to his help and power. This spiritual restoration of God's kingdom resulted in significant changes in the nature of God's kingdom, away from the concrete geophysical nature encountered in the kingdom of Israel in the Old Testament.

We must reckon with new things about God's kingdom besides its heavenly restoration. Jesus himself drew attention to new perceptions of the kingdom of God when he enlightened his disciples about its nature (Matt 13:1–50):

> "Have you understood all this?" They answered "yes." And he said to them, "Therefore every scribe who has been trained for the kingdom of heaven is like a master of a household who brings out of his treasure what is new and what is old." (Matt 13:52)

Jesus's words pointed out that the scriptures had old as well as new content which his coming as the promised Davidic king was revealing. While the scribes of the time were limited to bringing out only the old from scriptures, scribes on whom God's kingdom had dawned (his disciples) had the ability to bring out of it both the old and new. As Hagner explains:

> Jesus refers to a new kind of scribe, one instructed (*mathēteutheis*, lit. "having been made a disciple") *tē basileia tōn houranōn*, "in the kingdom of heaven," i.e. concerning the nature of the kingdom as it has been elucidated through the parables. He thus has in mind the disciples whom he has been teaching.[12]

There are at least three new things which Jesus taught about the kingdom of God. The first was about the nature of God's kingdom in regard to its establishment. Rather than the promised Davidic king dramatically advancing the kingdom of God in the world by subjugating the enemies of God and Israel, Jesus taught that the kingdom of God began small but would in time be the biggest kingdom and universal in scope (Matt 13:31–32; Mark 4:30–32; Luke 13:18–19; also Matt 13:33; Luke 13:20–21). We mentioned in our fifth chapter that according to the promise of God through Malachi, the restoration of the Davidic kingship and Israel would coincide with the Day of YHWH which would not occur before the coming of Elijah, the messenger of God (Mal 4:5–6). In line with the new understanding about the nature of the advance of God's kingdom, Jesus taught that the kingdom of God had come but its full restoration in the world, and thus the judgement of evil doers, would take

---

12. Donald A. Hagner, *Matthew 1–13*, WBC, Vol. 33A (Dallas: Word Publishers, 1993), 401.

place in the future. For this reason, the kingdom of God would co-exist with the kingdom of Satan (Matt 13:24) and the righteous with the wicked (Matt 13:47–50) until the end of the age, when God's kingdom is fully restored in all the world. For this reason, too, Jesus taught his disciples to pray for the full restoration of God's kingdom in the world whenever they pray:

> Your kingdom come,
> Your will be done,
> on earth as it is in heaven. (Matt 6:10)

In line with the inconspicuous advance of the kingdom of God, Jesus also taught that its growth was mysterious. Like the sprouting and growing of a seed to maturity, the way the kingdom of God would grow was beyond human comprehension (Mark 4:26–29).

Jesus's new teaching about the advancement of God's kingdom and its full restoration is indirectly seen elsewhere in New Testament literature where God's kingdom is perceived as an inheritance of believers. In Paul's letter to the believers in Corinth, he revealed to them that the unjust (*adikoi*) would not inherit the kingdom of God (1 Cor 6:9; also Eph 5:5). This was in contrast to believers (1 Cor 6:1) who as the saints (*tōn agion*) and not the unjust (1 Cor 6:1) would inherit it. Furthermore, Paul also revealed in his letter to the Galatians that believers who walked in the Spirit would inherit God's kingdom (Gal 5:21). Since the Greek word *klēronomeō* ("to inherit") has the sense of a good gift for which one must wait, the kingdom was a future prospect related to the complete full restoration of the kingdom of God in the fullness of time (see Acts 20:32; Eph 1:13–14; 1 Pet 1:4).

The second new thing Jesus taught about God's kingdom concerned the means by which people entered it. For the people of Israel, belonging to God's kingdom (the kingdom of David) was through Abrahamic ancestry, and was to be actualized by their obedience. For the nations, entry would be through becoming a part of Israel, and consequently knowing YHWH and obeying his laws. However, Jesus taught that entry into God's kingdom was through belief and repentance. Jesus's initial proclamation to the Jews foregrounded repentance and belief as the requirements to enter God's kingdom: "The time is fulfilled, and the kingdom of God has drawn near; repent, and believe in the good news" (Mark 1:15; see also Matt 4:17).

Jesus thus taught that entry into God's kingdom was to those born anew (John 3:3), which would occur when one believed (John 3:14–18). Some have suggested that in John's Gospel "life" has been used for "kingdom of God."[13] We must take seriously this suggestion given that life, as we pointed out in our second chapter, is the epitome of the blessings of abundant life which characterize God's kingdom. This conclusion is supported by the question posed by the rich man who asked Jesus how to attain eternal life. Jesus's answer directly associated eternal life with God's kingdom:

> And as he was setting out on a journey, a man ran up and knelt before him, and asked him, "Good teacher, what must I do to inherit eternal life? . . . Then Jesus looked around and said to his disciples, "How hard it will be for those who have wealth to enter the kingdom of God!" (Mark 10:17-23)

If we take it that life in John's Gospel stands for the kingdom of God, then it becomes even clearer that belief in Jesus and his words is a prerequisite to entry into God's kingdom. Whoever believes in Jesus has life (enters God's kingdom): "This is indeed the will of my Father, that all who see the Son and believe in him may have eternal life; and I will raise them up on the last day" (John 6:40; see also 3:16; 8:24; 11:26; 20:30-31 amongst others). We should note here too that belief as the gateway to God's kingdom is the reason why the spread of God's kingdom in the population was based on their belief in the good news and in their persistence in it (Matt 13:18-23; Mark 4:13-20; Luke 8:11-15).

Belief as the avenue of entry into God's kingdom was demonstrated by those on whom the blessings of abundant life came. In particular, the blessings of health and wholeness were received by those who believed, as demonstrated in the following examples. The paralytic man was made whole because he and his companions believed (Matt 9:2; Mark 2:5; Luke 5:20); the haemorrhaging woman was healed because she believed (Mark 5:34; Matt 9:22; Luke 8:48); the blind beggar, Bartimaeus, received his sight because he believed (Mark 10:52; Luke 18:42); and the Syrophoenician woman had her daughter healed because of her great faith (Matt 15:28). God's kingdom had come to all these individuals because they believed the Messiah and his message of the good news. In contrast, since unbelief was a stumbling block to receiving God's kingdom, unbelievers did not receive the blessings of abundance (that is, miracles): "And he did not do many deeds of power there, because of their unbelief" (Matt 13:58; also Mark 6:5-6).

---

13. See Andreas J. Köstenberger, *A Theology of John's Gospel and Letters: The Word of Christ, the Son of God* (Grand Rapids: Zondervan, 2015), 285-286.

As for repentance as an entry point to God's kingdom, Jesus was unhappy with those who did not repent at his message and deeds of power. Jesus proclaimed that they were doomed to judgement (Matt 11:20–24; Luke 10:12–15). He even warned them about not repenting by giving past examples of God's judgement on the unrepentant (Luke 13:3–5). Repentance was therefore precious. Those who repented following Jesus's preaching and miracles brought joy in heaven because they entered God's kingdom where, according to God's original intentions, they belonged (Luke 15:8–10, 11–32; Matt 15:3–7; 18:12–14). We should bear in mind as we finish our discussion on belief and repentance as entry points to God's kingdom that the two, given the contexts in which they appear in the Gospels, are not separate. Belief presupposed repentance, and repentance presumed belief.

The third new thing which Jesus taught about the kingdom of God concerned humility as a cardinal virtue in the kingdom. As we discussed in our fourth and fifth chapter, social justice and the worship of YHWH were the laws emphasized in the Old Testament. In contrast, Jesus emphasized humility as a key virtue in the kingdom of God. He taught that the greatest in the kingdom of God was the least, and he who wanted to be first in God's kingdom would have to practice being last (Matt 18:1–4; Mark 9:33–35; Luke 9:46–48). The significance of this virtue in the kingdom of God was also underlined by Jesus's parable of the marriage feast (Luke 14:7–11). Jesus instructed his disciples that when they were invited to such feasts they were to avoid the seats of honour, unless asked to occupy them by their host. The parable was meant to inculcate an attitude of humility amongst them. The greatest in God's kingdom was one who would be a servant to all (Mark 10:35–45; Matt 20:20–28) which was in itself an exercise in humility as demonstrated by Jesus's washing of his disciples' feet (John 13:5–15).

Not only was the emphasis on humility as a cardinal virtue in God's kingdom new, but this sense of humility was altogether new. As demonstrated in Dickson and Rosners' survey of the Old Testament, "'humility,' understood as the virtue of lowering oneself before an equal (*or one of a lower status*), is simply not present in the scriptures of Israel" (emphasis added).[14] The humility that was known in the Old Testament was that of lowering oneself before one of a greater rank.

We turn now to new ways of God's working to restore his kingdom through Jesus, the promised Davidic king. The first we look at is the death

---

14. John P. Dickson and Brian S. Rosner, "Humility as a Social Virtue in the Hebrew Bible," *VT* 54.4 (2004): 479.

and resurrection of the promised Davidic king. In the Gospels, Jesus on more than one occasion made it clear to his disciples that he, as the promised Davidic king, would be killed and rise after three days:

> He was teaching his disciples saying to them, "the Son of Man is to be betrayed into human hands, and they will kill him, and three days after being killed, he will rise again." But they did not understand what he was saying and were afraid to ask him. (Mark 9:31–32; also Matt 17:22–23; Luke 9:43–45)

The disciples did not understand what he meant, because the death of the promised Davidic king and his subsequent resurrection was not part of the promises concerning the promised Davidic king in the Old Testament. It was an extraordinary new revelation about the promised Davidic king. This accounts for Peter's misguided objection to Jesus's revelation (Mark 8:31–32; Matt 16:21–28).

The death of the promised Davidic king was instrumental in dealing with sin, by securing forgiveness as prescribed by God in the Old Testament. Jesus alluded to his sacrificial death when he said, as the promised Davidic king, that he came to give his life as a ransom for many: "For the Son of Man came not to be served but to serve, and to give his life a ransom for many" (Mark 10:45; also Matt 20:28). Caiaphas, the high priest who presided over the Sanhedrin before which Jesus was charged, prophesied that Jesus would die for the people:

> But one of them, Caiaphas, who was the high priest that year said to them, "You know nothing at all! You do not understand that it is better for you to have one man die for the people than to have the whole nation destroyed." He did not say this on his own, but being high priest that year he prophesied that Jesus was about to die for the nation. (John 11:49–51)

John the Baptist recognized that Jesus would play this role when he referred to him as a sacrificial animal: "Look, here is the lamb of God!" (John 1:36). The promised Davidic king's name, "Jesus" (Heb. *yeshua* – salvation), according to Matthew (Matt 1:21), indicated that he would save God's people from their sins.

The events on the cross clarified that Jesus took on the sins of the world and was punished for it by God as a sacrificial lamb who bore the sins of the one who offered it. The darkness which accompanied Jesus's crucifixion (Matt 27:45; Mark 15:33; Luke 23:44) symbolized God's punishment. As we noted earlier, the day of YHWH was a day of judgement for evil doers. On that day, the stars, moon and sun would stop giving out their light (Amos 8:9; Deut 28:29; Isa

13:9–10; Jer 4:28; Joel 2:10; Zeph 1:15). The three-hour darkness confirmed that Jesus, the sacrificial lamb, was dying as a result of God's judgement for the sake of humanity. On that cross Jesus took upon himself the sins of the world: "He himself bore our sins in his body on the cross" (1 Pet 2:24). That day God put Jesus "forward as a sacrifice of atonement by his blood" (Rom 3:25).

Jesus's death was clearly viewed in Hebrews, as already mentioned, as a self-sacrifice he offered to God to atone for the sins of the world. His sacrificial death was therefore similar to the sacrifice offered by the high priest on the day of atonement for the sins of the whole nation and not merely an individual. Jesus's sacrificial death was a single non-repetitive sacrifice he offered to God, that secured humanity's continual atonement for the sake of their entry into God's presence and thus kingdom. This is why at the death of Jesus on the cross, the temple curtain was split open, signifying that access to God's house was from that moment effected (Mark 15:38). Sin, which denied human beings access to God and being a part of his kingdom, had been cast aside. Those who repented and believed could now approach God and be a part of his kingdom.

Mention of the cross as a tree underlines Jesus's sacrificial death for the sake of human beings. In other New Testament literature, the cross where Jesus suffered death is referred to as a tree: "They put him to death by hanging him on a tree (*xulou* – Acts 10:39; also Acts 5:30; 13:29; 1 Pet 2:24). The labelling of the cross as a tree was to communicate the sacrificial nature of Jesus death. In the context of the Old Testament, being hung on a tree was a punishment reserved for crimes punishable only by death (Deut 21:23). One so punished was therefore accursed by God. This understanding was applied to Jesus's crucifixion to make sense of the significance of his death: "Cursed be everyone who hangs on a tree" (Gal 3:13). Accordingly, he suffered punishment by death for the sins of humanity, and was therefore hung on a tree, enduring the curse of God. With sin out of the way, the door for people who repented and believed to enter God's kingdom was opened.

There is even more to the promised Davidic king's death and resurrection in advancing God's kingdom. The cross is also presented as "the place where the devil, as the cosmological representative of all evil, is finally, and exhaustively defeated."[15] This is alluded to in the Gospel of John when Jesus said the following (in the context of his imminent death on the cross [John 12:20–26]): "Now is the judgement of this world; now the ruler of this world will be driven out" (John 12:31). Jesus's sacrificial death and subsequent resurrection exorcized the devil, denying him global influence as the ruler of the world. By his death

---

15. Oudtshoorn, "Where Have all the Demons Gone?," 67.

therefore Jesus opened the way for humans to come to him and enter God's kingdom: "And I, when I am lifted up from the earth, will draw all people to myself" (John 12:32).

Victory over Satan through the cross is also mentioned in Hebrews:

> Since, therefore, the children share flesh and blood, he himself likewise shared the same things, so that through death he might destroy the one who has the power of death, that is, the devil, and free those who all their lives were held in slavery by the fear of death. (Heb 2:14–15)

Through his sacrificial death and his subsequent resurrection by God's power, Jesus defeated Satan in whose hands the power of death lay. Consequently, Satan no longer has that power over those who through faith and repentance have received God's kingdom. For them, in ways similar to the audience of Hebrews, life has been secured by the victory of the promised Davidic king over Satan through the cross. Those in God's kingdom are thus freed from living in the fear of death.

The second new way of God's working to restore his kingdom through Jesus is in the divine sonship of Jesus. The Davidic kings whom God elected to use to restore his kingdom in the world were all human descendants of David. As we discussed earlier, their special role brought them into a close relationship with God to the extent that a Davidic king was, during his enthronement, designated as God's son (Ps 2:7). In Jesus, God started to restore his kingdom through his very own son. Although, as discussed in our fifth chapter, there were allusions to the divinity of the promised Davidic king (Isa 9:6; Mic 5:2), they did not indicate divine sonship; this revelation was completely new. In the Gospels, Jesus's virgin conception revealed his divine origins: "And the angel said to her, 'The Holy Spirit will come upon you, and the power of the Most High will overshadow you; therefore the child to be born will be holy; he will be called Son of God'" (Luke 1:35; see also Matt 1:20–23). For this reason, the promised Davidic king shared in the divinity of God and was thereby one with God. This was an extraordinary revelation for the Jews to fathom or accept. They therefore accused Jesus of blasphemy since calling himself the son of God made him equal with, or like, God (John 5:18; 10:33).

God's working to restore his kingdom through his own son becoming the promised Davidic king resulted in Jesus's effectiveness in restoring God's kingdom. For example, as God's son, Jesus, the royal priest, delivered to God's people God's very words. This is clear in Jesus's own words about speaking only what came from God: "My teaching is not mine but his who sent me" (John

7:16–17; also John 8:28; 17:8). Indeed, according to the Gospels God told the disciples to listen to Jesus because he was his son: "This is my Son, the Beloved; listen to him!" (Mark 9:7; Matt 17:5; Luke 9:35). Further still, as God's son, Jesus made known God's will perfectly by his divinatory interpretation of God's laws because, unlike the scribes and Pharisees, he knew the laws' intent and spirit: "In everything do to others as you would have them do to you; for this is the law and the prophets" (Matt 7:12; also Matt 22:36–40; Mark 10:17–21).

A second example of the effectiveness of God's son as the promised Davidic king, was Jesus's ruling in line with God's will. Jesus did not do anything according to his wishes but only what his father wanted (John 5:36), or what he saw God himself do (John 5:19–21). A third and last example of the effectiveness of God's son as the promised Davidic king in restoring God's kingdom concerns its eternity. The reign of Jesus did not end with his physical death. Being eternal in nature as God's son, Jesus's death was only temporary. He was resurrected and continued to rule as the promised Davidic king seated at God's right hand. This is why he is able to continue executing his role as a royal priesthood: "but he holds his priesthood permanently, because he continues forever" (Heb 7:24). Because he lives forever, he will continue to rule until he restores God's kingdom in the world. In the language of the apostle Paul, "he must reign until he has put all his enemies under his feet" (1 Cor 15:25). Ultimately, because he is God's son who became man and ascended the throne of David, "all beings in heaven, on earth, and in the world below will fall on their knees, and will openly proclaim that Jesus Christ is Lord, to the glory of God the Father" (Phil 2:10–11 GNB).

Since the promised Davidic king was God's own son, this new way of God working to restore his kingdom guaranteed the restoration of his kingdom. In Jesus, God would not fail to restore his kingdom in Israel and in the world, because Jesus's divine sonship insulated him from the failures which characterized the erstwhile Davidic kings.

8

Israel's Restoration and the Restoration of God's Kingdom

In our last chapter, we looked further at the unfolding story of the Bible. We did so by discussing the ways in which the New Testament demonstrated that the promised restoration of the Davidic kingship took place in Jesus, and consequently also showed the manner in which his kingship was advancing and restoring God's kingdom in the world. In this chapter, we continue to look at the unfolding story of the Bible by examining the ways in which the promised restoration of Israel was understood to have taken place in New Testament literature. We shall also examine the ways in which the restored people of Israel played their role, as Abraham's offspring, to be a blessing to all nations by bringing people into the kingdom of God.

John the Baptist and Israel's Restoration

It is revealed in the Gospels that John the Baptist is Elijah, the messenger whom God promised would come before the restoration of Israel as God's chosen people and the Davidic kingship:

> He will turn many of the people of Israel to the Lord their God. With the spirit and power of Elijah he will go before him, to turn the hearts of parents to their children, and the disobedient to the wisdom of the righteous, to make ready a people prepared for the Lord. (Luke 1:16-17)

> For all the prophets and the law prophesied until John came; and if you are willing to accept it, he is Elijah who is to come. (Matt 11:13-14)

We mentioned in our fifth chapter, concerning Elijah and the restoration of Israel, that in the Second Temple period, YHWH repeated anew his promises to restore Israel. However, YHWH specifically promised that Israel's restoration would coincide with the day of YHWH. In keeping with the day of YHWH, Israel's restoration would, therefore, also be the day when YHWH would judge and punish his enemies by a spectacularly devastating war (Isa 66:13–16; Mal 3:18–4:1; Zech 14:12–15). We pointed out that through the prophet Malachi, YHWH gave more details about the day of YHWH by revealing that he would send his messenger, Elijah the prophet, before that day so that Israel would not be the subject of his wrath but rather of his salvation as his chosen people:

> Lo, I will send you the prophet Elijah before the great and terrible day of the LORD comes. He will turn the hearts of the parents to their children and the hearts of children to their parents, so that I will not come and strike the land with a curse. (Mal 4:5–6)

On that day, YHWH would separate the obedient Israelites from the disobedient ones. The disobedient Israelites together with all of YHWH's enemies would be the objects of his wrath (Isa 59:15–19; Isa 66:15–17; Mal 3:5; 4:1). Elijah would help Israel avoid God's wrath on the Day of YHWH by making the people obedient, thereby be restored and become a part of God's kingdom under the promised Davidic kingship.

We mentioned that obedience to social justice laws was fundamentally about upholding peace, and for that reason, YHWH singled out the Israelites' disobedience as a key reason for judging Israel. In this regard, YHWH's emphasis on peace was only second to his emphasis on loyalty; not forsaking him for other gods, and so not practicing idolatry. Elijah would help Israel avoid God's wrath by inspiring them to uphold peace through their obedience to the fifth commandment because, as we argued, proper inter-generational relationship, like social justice, engendered peace. The Israelites who would avoid God's wrath by upholding peace would then be the ones restored.

In line with God's promise, John the Baptist as the promised Elijah came before the restoration of Israel. His work preceded the appearing of Jesus, the promised Davidic king, through whom Israel would be restored. This is clear in the Gospel narratives, which by the sequence of the events related inform us that John the Baptist appeared from the wilderness and began preaching and baptising the Israelites before Jesus sat on the throne of David. In Luke's Gospel, the coming of Elijah before the promised Davidic king is realized in the birth of John the Baptist, which takes place a few months before the birth of Jesus (Luke 1:39–45). In Mark's Gospel the dual role of John the Baptist as the promised Elijah and the voice in the wilderness who prepares the way for the Lord is emphasized in the passage below, which conflates God's promise through Malachi with the one through Isaiah:

> The beginning of the good news of Jesus Christ, the Son of God.
> As it is written in the prophet Isaiah,
>> "See, I am sending my messenger ahead of you,
>> who will prepare the way;
>> the voice of one crying out in the wilderness:
>> 'Prepare the way of the Lord,
>> make his paths straight'"
>
> John the baptizer appeared in the wilderness, proclaiming a baptism of repentance for the forgiveness of sins. (Mark 1:1–3)

Furthermore, according to the Gospels' account of John the Baptist's messages, by proclaiming repentance John the Baptist prepared the people of Israel to be God's restored people, and be saved rather than suffer God's wrath on the day of YHWH. We see this most directly in Matthew's Gospel, where John the Baptist's call to repentance was directly related to Israel's restoration under the promised Davidic king whose coming was near: "Repent, for the kingdom of heaven has come near" (Matt 3:2). We see the same in Mark's and Luke's Gospels where the Baptist proclaimed "a baptism of repentance" (Luke 3:3; see also Mark 1:5). He called for repentance as the way for the people of Israel to save themselves from God's impending wrath:

> But when he saw many Pharisees and Sadducees coming for baptism, he said to them. "You brood of vipers! Who warned you to flee from the wrath to come? Bear fruit worthy of repentance. Do not presume to say to yourselves, "We have Abraham as our ancestor"; for I tell you, God is able from these stones to raise up children to Abraham. Even now the axe is lying at the root of the trees; every tree therefore that does not bear fruit is cut down and thrown into the fire. (Matt 3:7–10; also Luke 3:7–9)

In line with the promise of Elijah to help Israel uphold peace by keeping the fifth commandment and thus receive salvation from God's wrath, John the Baptist helped the repentant Israelites to uphold peace by observing social justice. When they asked him specifically what they were to do to avoid God's wrath he exhorted those in positions of power or privilege to uphold social justice in ways specific to their positions:

> And the crowds asked him, "What shall we do?" In reply he said to them, "Whoever has two coats must share with anyone who has none; and whoever has food must do likewise." Even tax collectors came to be baptized, and they asked him, "Teacher, what should we do?" He said to them "Collect no more than the amount prescribed for you." Soldiers also asked him, "And we, what should we do?" He said to them, "Do not extort money from anyone by threats or false accusation, and be satisfied with your wages." (Luke 3:10–14)

John the Baptist's preaching was highly successful in preparing the people of Israel for their restoration:

> And people from the whole Judean countryside and all the people of Jerusalem were going out to him, and were baptized by him in the river Jordan, confessing their sins. (Mark 1:5; see also Luke 3:10–15)

However the success of John's preaching was not absolute. There were those who treated his message with contempt. Thus Jesus could say, "They did to him whatever they pleased" (Mark 9:13). As a result, those who repented at his proclamation were prepared to be part of the restored Israel, while those who did not repent were excluded and subject to God's wrath. We arrive at this conclusion because for the repentant Israelites John pointed to the imminent arrival of one who was greater than him (Matt 3:11; Mark 1:7; Luke 3:16): Jesus the promised Davidic king. The repentant ones would have believed John the Baptist, because it was on account of his preaching that they had, in the first place, turned to God.

The relationship of belief or unbelief in John's message with belief or unbelief in Jesus and his message, is present in the Gospels. Jesus himself pointed out that those who rejected John the Baptist, calling him a demon, were also the same ones rejecting the promised Davidic king, labelling him "a glutton, and a drunkard, a friend of tax collectors and sinners!" (Matt 11:18–19). He also pointed out that prostitutes and tax collectors were entering the kingdom of God because they had believed John the Baptist (and thereby believed Jesus), while the chief priests and elders were not because they disbelieved John and thus disbelieved Jesus:

> For John came to you in the way of righteousness and you did not believe him, but tax collectors and the prostitutes believed him;

and even after you saw it, you did not change your minds and believe him. (Matt 21:32; also Luke 7:29–30)

It is this belief in John, leading to belief in Jesus, that accounts for some of the disciples of John abandoning him to follow Jesus (John 1:35–37). We therefore turn now to the way the restoration of Israel took place in Jesus which, though unstated, must have been predominantly among the repentant whom John the Baptist had prepared according to the Lord's promise.

The Twelve and Israel's Restoration

In the Gospels Jesus called twelve individuals to follow him (Mark 3:14; Luke 6:13) who were referred to as the twelve (for example, Matt 26:14; Mark 4:10; 6:7; 9:35; 10:32; Luke 8:1; 9:1, 12; John 6:67, 71; 20:24). On a few occasions they were referred to as the twelve disciples (Matt 10:1; 11:1), or the twelve apostles (Matt 10:2; Mark 6:30). This number of disciples is related in various ways to Israel. By understanding the number's use, therefore, in the Old Testament generally and in the Gospel and Acts specifically, we shall uncover the way the restoration of Israel was fulfilled in Jesus.

In his study of the number twelve as a biblical number, Buch demonstrated on the evidence of the ancient Middle Eastern socio-economic context the significance of numbers six and twelve (and their multiples), that "the number is meant to express a totality."[1] There was evidence of its use in numerous parts of the Old Testament. He pointed out for example that Genesis 4:

> . . . mentions only 12 of Adam's male descendants, although there were other progeny besides them: Cain, Abel, Enoch, Irad, Mehujael, Methusael, Lamech, Jabal, Jubal, Tubal-Cain, Seth and Enosh. In fact, the Hebrew root meaning "to give birth" appears exactly 12 times in this chapter. Seth and his male descendants were also 12, as Genesis 5 tells us: Seth, Enosh, Kenan, Mahalalel, Jared, Enoch, Methuselah, Lamech, Noah, Shem, Ham and Japheth. In two generations following Noah, sons and grandsons are named from among numerous siblings to add up to 12 or 24 each for Shem, Ham, and Japheth. It is of great significance that,

---

1. Joshua Buch, "The Biblical Number 12 and the Formation of the Ancient Nation of Israel," *JBQ* 22.1 (1999), 49.

while repeating some names and being inconsistent with their sequences, both chapters state exactly 12 names.[2]

To this he added that Jacob and Esau had twelve sons each. On this basis he concluded that "the number 12, as represented in the 12 tribes, is meant to express the totality of Israel."[3] It is for this reason, he points out, that Israel became a nation only after the 12 sons of Jacob evolved into 12 tribes.[4] Thus although the list of the twelve tribes found in the Old Testament had some differences arising from the omission or inclusion of the tribes of Joseph, Ephraim, Manasseh, Levi, and Simeon, they were always twelve (with the exception of ten in Judges 5). As Buch puts it: "Since it was considered to be the perfect number, the Nation, the perfect social and political order that was promised to Abraham had to be built on the base of 12."[5]

With twelve as the fixed number of the tribes of Israel also came the association of that number with Israel, resulting in its use to symbolize or represent Israel. In relationship to physical objects, there were, for example, twelve pillars (Exod 24:4), twelve breastplate stones (Exod 39:14), twelve bowls (Num 7:84), twelve bulls, rams, lambs, goats (Num 7:87), and twelve staffs (Num 17:2).

We should also note that the number twelve was used in the socio–political and economic ordering of Israel. So, for example, there were twelve leaders of the people of Israel under Moses and the Davidic kings (Num 1:4–16; 1:44; 7:2; 1 Chr 23:2). The promised land was divided up into twelve tribes (Josh 13–19) and named after the twelve as we mentioned, for example, in regard to the land of Naphtali and Zebulun. There were even twelve cities for Benjamin (18:21–24), twelve cities for Zebulun (19:15), and twelve cities for the Merarites (21:7).

The institution of twelve leaders in the polity of Israel started even before they settled on the land. By YHWH's command, Moses chose twelve men from each of the twelve tribes to assist him and Aaron to number the people of Israel:

> You and Aaron shall enrol them, company by company. A man from each tribe shall be with you, each man the head of his ancestral house. (Num 1:4)

---

2. Buch, "The Biblical Number 12," 50.
3. Buch, "The Biblical Number 12," 49.
4. Buch, "The Biblical Number 12," 51.
5. Buch, "The Biblical Number 12," 57.

These twelve men who helped with the census became the leaders of the tribes and were referred to that way: "These are those who were enrolled, whom Moses and Aaron enrolled with the help of the leaders of Israel, twelve men, each representing his ancestral house" (Num 1:44; see also 7:2; 10:4; 21:18; 27:2; 32:2). The rule of Israel with the help of twelve leaders continued into Israel's monarchical period. From the books of Chronicles we learn that twelve leaders helped King David to rule Israel (1 Chr 23:1–2; 29:6). King Solomon as well ruled with twelve leaders. They were by his side when he oversaw the carrying of the ark of the covenant into the temple:

> Then Solomon assembled the elders of Israel and all the heads of the tribes, the leaders of the ancestral houses of the Israelites, before King Solomon in Jerusalem, to bring up the ark of the covenant of the LORD out of the city of David, which is Zion. (1 Kgs 8:1)

The twelve, translated as "princes" or "officials" (*śarim*), are also said to have led Israel under King Hezekiah (2 Chr 30:2; 30:12). In one of YHWH's promises of the restoration of Israel, the twelve leaders are mentioned against the background of their oppression of God's people. God promised through Ezekiel the prophet that the twelve leaders of Israel shall cease to oppress the people:

> And my princes shall no longer oppress my people; but they shall let the house of Israel have the land according to their tribes ... Enough, O princes of Israel! Put away violence and oppression, and do what is just and right. Cease your evictions of my people, says the LORD God. (Ezek 45:9–10)

Jesus's choice of the twelve was, therefore, an indication that he had chosen them to be the leaders of Israel, and as such to be instrumental in their restoration. It is confirmed in the replacement of Judas Iscariot by Matthias to keep their number to twelve, to continue to show that they were the chosen leaders of Israel. The twelve as Israel's chosen leaders is also confirmed by the role which Jesus promised they would have in the future; a role which the twelve leaders of Israel historically played, namely, judging the tribes of Israel:

> Jesus said to them, "Truly I tell you, at the renewal of all things, when the Son of Man is seated on the throne of his glory, you who have followed me will also sit on twelve thrones, judging the twelve tribes of Israel." (Matt 19:28; see also Luke 22:28–29)

As the leaders of Israel, Jesus gave the twelve the responsibility to seek the Israelites and bring them into the kingdom of God. Their leadership in

Israel's restoration was carried out through this mission (see Matt 10:1–15; Mark 6:7–13; Luke 9:1–6), and through their role as his witnesses (Acts 1:8). It is worthwhile, then, to examine how the disciples exercised their leadership in Israel's restoration through both these ways. We begin by looking at how they carried out their leadership in the mission Jesus gave them: through the content of their preaching, the authority they were given, and the places they were asked to go.

The twelve were to proclaim to the people of Israel that God's kingdom had drawn near (Matt 10:7), or simply proclaim the kingdom of God in their midst (Luke 9:2). This was because Jesus, the promised Davidic king, had proclaimed its arrival and demonstrated that he was advancing it. The twelve, being intimate witnesses of this demonstration, would therefore have proclaimed the kingdom with confidence and enthusiasm to the Israelites and told them "that all should repent" (Mark 6:12). Those who repented and believed would be included in the restored community and enter the kingdom of God. Thus through their preaching as commissioned by Jesus, the twelve carried out their leadership role in Israel's restoration by precipitating repentance and belief, and thus entry into God's kingdom.

In addition, those restored would have experienced the blessings of abundant life in God's kingdom, because they had entered it. Their experience of the blessings of health, wholeness, peace, and security from Satan's oppression was made possible by God's power at work in the twelve to exorcize demons, and to heal (Jesus, the promised Davidic king had, by God's power, thus defeated the enemies of God and his people). For this reason the Israelites who believed the twelve received blessings, while the unbelievers faced the prospect of judgement:

> As you enter the house, greet it. If the house is worthy, let your peace be upon it, but if it is not worthy, let your peace return to you. If anyone will not welcome you or listen to your words, shake off the dust from your feet as you leave the house or the town. Truly I tell you it will be more tolerable for the land of Sodom and Gomorrah in the day of judgement than for that town. (Matt 10:14–15; see also Mark 6:11; Luke 9:5)

Thus the twelve carried out their leadership role in Israel's restoration by using the authority Jesus gave them to cast out demons and heal the sick, thereby advancing God's kingdom concretely amongst those who had repented.

The twelve's leadership role in Israel's restoration was evident as well by virtue of the places they went to preach, cast out demons, and heal. The twelve were sent to the towns and villages, to all the places where the Israelites lived, to seek "the lost sheep of the house of Israel" (Matt 10:6). Going to these places enabled them to preach repentance so that these "lost sheep" could be included amongst the community of God's people, and enter God's kingdom.

It was because the twelve were leaders of Israel that Jesus assigned them the responsibility to be his witnesses. Jesus stated to the twelve that they would receive God's power to enable them to be his witnesses:

> But you shall receive power when the Holy Spirit has come upon you; and you will be my witnesses in Jerusalem, in all Judea and Samaria, and to the ends of the earth. (Acts 1:8)

To be Jesus's witnesses in Jerusalem, Judea and Samaria and then to the ends of the earth indicated that the priority of their witness would first be to all Israel. Jerusalem, Judea, and Samaria were all territories of the people of Israel. The twelve as their leaders would first bear witness to them before they could proceed to the ends of the world. The narrative of Luke-Acts demonstrates this priority. The twelve therefore started their witness in Jerusalem (Acts 2:1–8:3) then moved to Judea and Samaria (Acts 8:4–12:25). Where there is mention of their witness in non-Jewish areas, such as Damascus (Acts 9:1–22), and Phoenicia, Cyprus and Antioch (Acts 11:19–27), their witness was exclusively to Jews: "and they spoke the word to no one except Jews" (Acts 11:19). It was only after Judea and Samaria that they bore witness to non-Israelites.

The prioritisation of Israel is also seen in Peter's concern exclusively for Jews in his preaching: "You that are Israelites . . ." (Acts 2:22), "Fellow Israelites . . ." (Acts 2:29), "Therefore let the entire house of Israel know" (Acts 2:36), and "let it be known to all of you, and to all the people of Israel" (Acts 4:10). Through their prioritisation of Israel they were able to carry out their leadership in the restoration of the Israelites and their entry into God's kingdom. As witnesses preaching to Israel the good news would have given the Israelites the opportunity to be restored and enter God's kingdom, if they believed. It is therefore important that we shed light below on the relationship between the disciples' witness and their preaching which led to the restoration of Israel according to Acts.

Jesus pointed out that the twelve had been witnesses of his suffering, death and resurrection (Luke 24:44–48). They were also witnesses of his exorcisms and deeds of power, and witnesses of significant events in his life, which included the transfiguration, and the meaning he gave to his last meal with them. In Peter's words, the twelve were witnesses to all that Jesus had done: "We are witnesses to all that he did both in Judea and in Jerusalem" (Acts

10:39–41). Consequently, the twelve were to go and preach to all the house of Israel based on their witness of Jesus's words, deeds, suffering and resurrection. This is why the person who was elected to replace Judas Iscariot was required to come from among those who witnessed Jesus's messages, deeds, suffering, and resurrection (Acts 1:21–23). Without this witness, the content of a disciple's preaching would fall short of being about what Jesus did and said, and would therefore be insufficient to bring about the restoration of the people of Israel and their entry into God's kingdom.

Our understanding that "witnessing" meant preaching whose content was based on Jesus words and deeds is seen in the encounter between the twelve and the Jewish authorities. When the authorities twice sought to stop the twelve from preaching to the people of Israel, the disciples responded in a manner that showed their preaching was based on what Jesus did and said: "for we cannot keep from speaking about what we have seen and heard" (Acts 4:20; see also 5:27–32). It was this manner of preaching to Israel that the twelve were empowered to carry out as Jesus's witnesses from the day of Pentecost. Indeed, the events on that day also clarify our understanding that being a witness of Jesus meant preaching based on the disciples witness of Jesus's words and deeds.

When the Holy Spirit came upon the twelve, they were empowered to preach to all the people of Israel who were within earshot by speaking in the languages of all the places they had come from (Acts 2:5–18). The preaching was about the great things which God had done in Jesus, as the context suggests (Acts 2:11). God had enabled the twelve through his power to be witnesses of Jesus which, as we are arguing, was to preach his messages and deeds.

Through their preaching to Israel, therefore, the twelve carried out their leadership role in Israel's restorations. Their preaching on the day of Pentecost led to the repentance of 3,000 of the people of Israel, who thereby were added to the numbers of the community of the restored Israelites and gathered into God's kingdom. Thereafter the narrative of Luke-Acts makes it clear that through their preaching, there were considerable numbers added to the restored community, thus being gathered into God's kingdom under the promised Davidic king whom the twelve made clear had been exalted as Lord (Acts 2:36; 5:31). We have for example 5,000 men in Acts 4:4, "multitudes" (*plēthē*) in Acts 5:14, and all the inhabitants of Lydda and Sharon in Acts 9:35.

Those added to the number of the restored community and entering into God's kingdom thereby experienced the blessings of abundant life (the state of affairs in God's kingdom) such as health and wholeness, peace and security, and even life. This is because the twelve continued to be used by God as the leaders of Israel's restoration in advancing God's kingdom through exorcisms, healings, deeds of power, and raising the dead (which all signalled their deliverance from the captivity and oppression of Satan). Peter, for example, prayed for the lame man and he was able to walk (Acts 3:1–9). He also raised Tabitha from the dead (Acts 9:36–40). Those who had believed brought many who were "sick and those tormented by unclean spirits" (Acts 5:16) to the twelve and they were healed. Philip, the evangelist appointed by the twelve, exorcized demons and healed many who were infirm (Acts 8:4–7). Luke-Acts described God's power that was at work in the twelve to advance his kingdom succinctly: "many signs and wonders were done among the people through the apostles" (Acts 5:12; see also Acts 2:43).

To sum up: John the Baptist prepared the way for the restoration of Israel. As a result, when Jesus began his work in Galilee, many Galileans and other Israelites welcomed him as the promised Davidic king and believed his words, leading to their restoration and entry into the kingdom of God. Moreover, Jesus chose the twelve, as leaders in Israel's restoration, to work with him before and after his death and subsequent ascension. The twelve consequently played a significant role in the restoration of Israel, particularly from the day of Pentecost onwards. Thus after the ascension of Jesus, the number of Israelites who were added to the restored community and entered into the kingdom of God, due to their witness, increased dramatically. In consequence, the community of the restored Israel was firmly established in the kingdom of God under their leadership as seen in their devotion to their instructions (Acts 2:42) and deference to their authority (Acts 8:14; 11:22). According to the Gospels and Acts, God had fulfilled his promise to restore repentant Israel as his people in his kingdom under the reign of the promised Davidic king, Jesus.

Restoration of God's Kingdom via Restored Israel

We pointed out in our third chapter that Israel, as God's *sᵉgullâ*, was of great value to him. If the people of Israel obeyed God, they would be royal priests representing God to the nations. By keeping God's laws, Israel would experience the blessings of abundant life, having become a part of God's kingdom. The blessings of abundant life would be the means by which Israel would act as God's representative to other nations, and influence them to know YHWH and submit to his rule. Submitting to God's rule would make these nations become a part of his kingdom. Putting this in the biblical language of blessings, Israel would be the first nation to be blessed, and thereafter, as a royal priesthood, used by God to have other nations blessed. God would have used Israel to fulfil his promise to Abraham to have all nations blessed through him.

God did not revoke his choice of Israel as Abraham's offspring to restore the world to his kingdom when he punished them for their disobedience. As we observed in our sixth chapter, God promised to restore Israel as his people, his sᵉgullâ (for example in Hos 2:23; Jer 24:7; 30:22; 32:38; Ezek 11:20; 34:30–31; 36:28; Isa 44:1–5; 51:16). They would return to their land to blessings of abundant life, to be a part of God's kingdom. The conditions they would return to implied that they would be restored as God's people to fulfil their destiny as the people instrumental to the restoration of God's kingdom in the world.

Having just looked at the fulfilment of God's promise to restore Israel according to New Testament literature, we turn now to look at how God used restored Israel to advance his kingdom in the world. In the Acts of the Apostles, Peter, in his second preaching to the people of Israel after the day of Pentecost, touched on Israel's vocation to advance God's kingdom in the world:

> You are the descendants of the prophets and of the covenant that God gave to your ancestors, saying to Abraham, "And in your descendants all families of the earth shall be blessed. When God raised up his servant, he sent him first to you, to bless you by turning each of you from your wicked ways. (Acts 3:25–26)

God had sent his servant, Jesus, to the Israelites so that they could be the first to receive his blessings. The narratives of the Gospels demonstrate this in the following ways. The Gospels show that Jesus preached and advanced God's kingdom only amongst the people of Israel. Luke's Gospel shows Jesus emphasizing the recipients of his work to be the children of Abraham: "a daughter of Abraham" being delivered from Satan's oppression (Luke 13:16) and "a son of Abraham" receiving salvation from God's wrath and entry into the kingdom of God (Luke 19:9). The only encounter Jesus had with a non-Israelite in the Gospels is the Syrophoenician woman (Mark 7:24–30; Matt 15:21–28). Jesus was reluctant to extend his deeds of power to her daughter, for his priority was Israel: "Let the children be fed first, for it is not fair to take the children's food and throw it to the dogs" (Mark 7:27). It is on account of Jerusalem that Jesus was vexed (Matt 23:37; Luke 13:34–35). Lastly, in John's Gospel, Jesus did not reach out to the Greeks who inquired about Jesus, but rather took that as a sign that his sacrificial death was imminent (John 12:20–24).

We must understand the blessings mentioned here, as we have done in this study, to imply the presence of God's kingdom, because they describe the quality of life, the state of affairs, in God's kingdom. On this understanding, we can conclude that God, therefore, sent Jesus to the people of Israel first so that they would be the first people to enter into his kingdom under the promised

Davidic king. The fact that Peter talked about Jesus as God's servant, sent to bless them by turning each one of them from their sins, supports our view that blessings here mean their entry into God's kingdom, thus experiencing the kingdom's state of affairs. This is because, as we mentioned, the gateway into God's kingdom was through repentance. That gate to the kingdom was open to the Israelites on account of their repentance, which was inspired by Jesus.

Peter's preaching also pointed to the reason why the people of Israel were designated to be the first to enter the kingdom of God, namely, they were the offspring of Abraham. As such, God would use them to fulfil the blessings-to-all-nations promise he gave Abraham. Israel as Abraham's offspring would become the nation through which all other nations would be blessed, by being instrumental in the nations' entry to God's kingdom. In order for God to use them this way, the Israelites had to first themselves become a part of God's kingdom. This was precisely the point of Peter's preaching. God's plan had therefore not changed, and his promise to Abraham still stood. The restoration of God's kingdom in the world was designed to begin with Israel, and then consequently the nations of the world.

The restoration of God's kingdom beginning with Israel and then advancing to the rest of the nations is underlined in the deliberations of the Jerusalem council in Acts 15. When some in the restored community of Israel opposed gentile inclusion in the community and kingdom, James invoked God's promise through Amos to justify it. The promise to restore Israel was not merely for Israel's own sake but in view of Israel's vocation as Abraham's offspring, to be a blessing to all nations:

> After this I will return,
>   and I will rebuild the dwelling of David,
> which has fallen;
>   from its ruins I will rebuild it,
> and I will set it up,
>   so that all other peoples may seek the Lord –
> even the gentiles over whom my name has been called.
> Thus says the Lord, who has been making these things known
>   from long ago. (Acts 15:16–17)

Other peoples, therefore, were also meant to be included in the kingdom which they could enter through repentance and belief, as was happening. Although the Jews were destined to be the ones through whom they would enter God's kingdom, gentiles did not have to become Jews in order to enter it. This understanding must have been the reason why Paul talked of the good news going to the Jew first; "For I am not ashamed of the gospel; it is the power of God for salvation to everyone who has faith, to the Jew first but also to the Greek" (Rom 1:16).

We see God's choice of Israel to bring other peoples into his kingdom at play in the Luke-Acts narrative, which tells us that gentiles entered the kingdom of God due to the witness of the Israelites, which precipitated gentile repentance and belief. With enough numbers of the Israelites having entered God's kingdom, it seemed the time was ripe for them to fulfil their vocation by going to other nations to preach the good news. This is exactly what happened first when Peter went to preach to Cornelius and his household. Under God's very specific guidance, Peter went to the house of Cornelius to preach to him (Acts 10). In a vision, God had prepared Peter for this mission by removing the barriers that made Jews generally to separate themselves from other nations whom they considered unclean: "You yourselves know that it is unlawful for a Jew to associate with or to visit a gentile; but God has shown me that I should not call anyone profane or unclean" (Acts 10:28–29).

While Peter was preaching to Cornelius and his household by recapitulating the content of his preaching to fellow Jews (Acts 10:34–42), they were filled with the Holy Spirit. Their filling with the Holy Spirit was a sign that they too, like the twelve and the Israelites, had received the blessings of God:

> While Peter was still speaking, the Holy Spirit fell upon all who heard the word. The circumcised believers who had come with Peter were astonished that the gift of the Holy Spirit had been poured out even on the gentiles, for they had them speaking in tongues and extolling God. (Acts 10:44–45)

Indeed, this significance of their reception of the Holy Spirit was noted by Peter. It was a sign to him that, just like them, they too had believed in Jesus.

> And as I began to speak, the Holy Spirit fell upon them just as it had upon us in the beginning. And I remembered the word of the Lord, how he said, "John baptized with water, but you will be baptized with the Holy Spirit." If then God gave them the same gift that he gave us when we believed in the Lord Jesus Christ, who was I that I hinder God?" (Acts 11:15–17)

Because they believed, Cornelius and his people had, just like the Israelites, entered into God's kingdom. They had done so thanks to the people of Israel, by the preaching of Israelites. In the wider scheme of things, God had prepared Cornelius for this through a vision Cornelius had (Acts 10:1–7) as seen in

Cornelius' words to Peter: "So now all of us are here in the presence of God to listen to all that the Lord has commanded you to say" (Acts 10:33). It seems that this first episode of the fulfilment of Israel's vocation to bless other nations was providential and extraordinary, in order to serve as a lesson to restored Israel, as well as to leave no doubt of their vocation as Abraham's offspring.

However, it is in Paul's mission and missionary journeys in Luke-Acts that we encounter comprehensively the fulfilment of Israel's vocation to advance God's kingdom to other nations. Paul repented and believed when he met Jesus in a blinding light on the road to Damascus (Acts 9:1–9). At that moment, in ways similar to the repentant Israelites, he was blessed, included in the restored community of Israel and brought into God's kingdom under the promised Davidic king. Subsequent to his repentance was his commission which made him instrumental in Israel's vocation to restore God's kingdom among the nations. Concerning him, Jesus said to Ananias: "Go, for he is an instrument whom I have chosen to bring my name *before the gentiles* and kings and before the people of Israel" (Acts 9:15, emphasis added).

Paul was then the first Israelite to be specially commissioned to preach the good news to the gentiles. In some cases, he was actually led by God to preach the good news to the gentiles (Acts 16:9–10). The national vocation of Israel coincided with the individual vocation of Paul. We therefore see Paul as narrated in Luke-Acts taking the good news to the Cyprians (Acts 13:4–5), the Pamphylians (Acts 13:13), the Pisidians (Acts 13:48–49), the Lycaonians (Acts 14:1–8), the Phrygians and Galatians (Acts 16:6), the Macedonians (Acts 16:11–12; 17:1–15), the Greeks (Acts 17:16–34), the Achaians (Acts 18:1), and the Asians (Acts 19:10). His preaching led to many gentiles believing and entering the kingdom of God. To give some examples, many Pisidians in Pergia and Antioch believed (Acts 13:48) as well as a large number of Greeks in Iconium believed (Acts 14:1). Gentile individuals are also mentioned as believing on account of Paul's preaching. The Macedonian prison guard and his household in Philippi believed (Acts 16:30–34), and the Greek Dionysius the Areopagite and Damaris both in Athens believed (Acts 17:34). It is clear that through Paul's preaching, the good news of Jesus and the kingdom of God went forth from the Israelites to other nations, and the many who believed entered into God's kingdom. We see, therefore, in Luke-Acts the fulfilment of the vocation of Israel as Abraham's offspring: as the nation through whom other nations are blessed, and enter into God's kingdom through Israel's proclamation.

Restoration of God's Kingdom via New Israel

Just as with the kingdom of God, there is newness with respect to Israel in the New Testament, and consequently the way God was restoring his kingdom through Israel in the world. In New Testament literature, we learn in the unfolding story of the Bible that the identity of the people of God underwent a transformation from the elected nation of Israel (historical Israel) into believing Jews and gentiles. The seeds of this transformation were laid in God's promises to restore Israel. In those promises, as we pointed out in our sixth chapter, God warned that only obedient Israelites would become part of the restored nation. According to our discussion above, the New Testament revealed that these promises to restore Israel were fulfilled in repentant and believing Israelites; they are the ones who became a part of the restored Israel. It was, therefore, from this restored Israel, and not simply historical Israel, that the kingdom of God then advanced among the gentiles. We thus see, in the fulfilment of the promises to restore Israel, the first step in the transformation of the identity of Israel.

The transformation of Israel is revealed in the teaching of unity in Ephesians, in the mention of the spiritual descendants of Abraham in the writings of Paul, and in the reference to believers in the first epistle of Peter with words that parallel YHWH's in Exodus concerning Israel. Starting with Ephesians, we will examine each of these revelations.

In Ephesians 2:11–22, we have a pastoral admonition that is based on the experience of gentile believers and aimed at the unity of believers thus:

> So then, remember that at one time you gentiles by birth, called "the uncircumcision" by those who are called "the circumcision" – a physical circumcision made in the flesh by human hands – remember that you were at that time without Christ, being aliens from the commonwealth (*politeias*) of Israel, and strangers to the covenants of promise, having no hope and without God in the world. But now in Christ Jesus you who once were afar off have been brought near by the blood of Christ. For he is our peace; in his flesh he has made both groups into one and has broken down the dividing wall, that is, the hostility between us. He has abolished the law with its commandments and ordinances, that he might create in himself one new humanity (*ana kainon anthrōpon*) in place of the two, thus making peace, and might reconcile both groups to God in one body through the cross, thus putting to death that hostility through it. So he came and proclaimed peace

to you who were far off and peace to those who were near; for through him both of us have access in one Spirit to the Father. So then you are no longer strangers and aliens, but you are citizens (*sumpoliteia*) with the saints (*tōn agiōn*) and also members of the household of God. (Eph 2:11-19)

Divisions and hostility between Jewish and gentile believers, to whom the letter is addressed, is the context of this admonition. From a factual point of view, it was historical Israel and not the gentiles who had YHWH, the true living God, as their God. Accordingly, YHWH had made covenants with them. As our previous discussions showed, YHWH's covenant with Abraham their ancestor (the Abrahamic covenant) was foundational, the basis on which God made a covenant with Israel at Sinai (the Sinaitic covenant), and a covenant with David (the Davidic covenant). Promises were integral to these three covenants, hence "covenants of promise" (*tōn diathikōn tēs epangelias*). Since gentiles did not have citizenship (*politeias*) in historical Israel, they were not a part of these covenants. Knowing this, the Israelites had a negative sense of their holiness and a feeling of superiority as was indicated in references to themselves as "the circumcised" and to gentiles as "the uncircumcised." It is certainly the case that there was tension between Jews and gentiles.

From the deuterocanonicals and Jewish pseudepigraphical writings, we know that the Israelites actively sought, for the sake of their purity, to keep away from gentiles, whom they considered unclean. They endeavoured not to marry them, buy from them, keep their company or stay close to them, or eat with them:

> Now you, my son Jacob, remember and keep the commandments of your father Abraham. Separate from the nations and do not eat with them. Do not act as they do, and do not become their companion. (*Jubilees* 22:16, see also *Jubilees* 30, *Tob* 1:10)

Jewish resolve to remain separate from gentiles is evident in the Gospels which narrate Jesus's clash with the Pharisees and scribes because his disciples ate without washing hands (Mark 7:1-5; Matt 15:1-20). His disciples' trip to Jerusalem would have brought them into contact with gentiles and to handle gentile goods in the marketplaces, thereby making their hands unclean. Handwashing was then required to cleanse their hands to pre-empt the pollution of the food that they would eat using their hands. The same Jewish resolve to separate from gentiles accounts also for the tensions in Acts 15 where it was reported that some Jews did not accept gentile believers unless they became Jews, and were "circumcised according to the custom of Moses" (Acts 15:1).

It was not just one side that was solely responsible for the divisions between the two. From relevant literature,[6] we know that gentiles scorned Jews for their religious beliefs and practices. They considered monotheism foolish and abstinence from eating pork something of a mockery. Keeping of the Sabbath was looked down upon as time wasting, while circumcision was derided as a mutilation of the flesh.[7] Each side, then, negatively viewed the other's religious practices, as summarized in the words of Tacitas the Roman historian: "They regard as profane everything that we hold as sacred – and vice versa."[8] We have knowledge of hostility towards Jews because the Romans gave Jews some measure of privilege by allowing them to practice their religion.[9] Divisions and hostilities between Jews and gentiles would therefore have affected the relations between the Jews and gentiles who had believed in Jesus.

Against this background, the message of Ephesians was that there was a new reality for believing Jews and gentiles to reckon with. This new reality made their unity real by nullifying the past and making nonsense of the divisions and tensions it spawned. Essentially, the new reality was that the two groups – believing Jews and believing gentiles – were one people in Jesus Christ. He had created "in himself one new humanity in place of the two" (Eph 2:15). Since the new humanity, literally "one new man" (*ana kainon anthrōpon*), was in contrast to two groups of people (*ta hamphotera*), we should understand *ana kainon anthrōpon* to mean that Jesus created in himself a new people of God. He did so out of believers from both historical Israel and gentiles, who became the one people of God in Christ. The two peoples, historical Israel and the nations, continued to exist, but the new people of God whom Jesus created from them transcended both.

Because of the new reality that had been brought about by Jesus Christ, believing gentiles were no longer strangers to God's covenants. Rather, on account of their common citizenship with believing Israel, they had become together with them its recipient: "but you are fellow citizens (*sumpoliteia*) with the saints (*believing Jews*) and also members of the household of God

---

6. Eric S. Gruen, *The Construct of Identity in Hellenistic Judaism: Essays on Jewish History and Literature* (Berlin: De Guyter, 2016).

7. Gruen, *The Construct of Identity*, 67–268.

8. Gruen, *The Construct of Identity*, 264.

9. Christopher D. Stanley, "'Neither Jew nor Greek': Ethnic Conflict in Graeco-Roman Society," *JSNT* 19.64 (1997).

(Eph 2:19 ESV). Although in the New Testament saints, literally "holy ones" (*tōn agiōn*), means believers (see Eph 1:1; 4:12; 5:3; 6:18) we have taken it here to refer to believing Jews based on the argument we give below. One of the points belaboured in the epistle is that the erstwhile status of gentiles was one without Jesus and of exclusion from Israel's citizenship: "excluded from the citizenship (*politeia*) in Israel, and foreigners to the covenants of promise" (Eph 2:12 NIV). In a discussion on the meaning of *politeia* in antiquity, Cuchet and Doherty pointed out that citizenship was more than statutory. They concluded from empirical evidence that citizenship was defined by participation in the affairs of a city by virtue of belonging there: to participate (*metechein*) "is almost always used when it is a question of describing citizenship in concrete terms, and is so used by Aristotle."[10] This participation was broad, including religious, deliberative, judicial, administrative, and governmental participation.

Only a person who belonged was entitled or granted such participation. Belonging was by virtue of a permanent residence in a place, usually a city so that one belonged to the *polis* (city). Belonging could also be on account of the residence of one's ancestors in that particular city, or even by way of honour for what one had done for a city. Habitation and filiation were the predominant bases for citizenship. Paul, for example, could say that he was a Roman citizen by filiation since he was either born in Rome or belonged to a family that lived in Rome (Acts 22:28). On this understanding, the point the epistle is making was that formerly gentiles could not participate in Israel's affairs (or covenants) because they were not Israelites. As interpreted aptly in Today's English Version, gentiles "did not belong to God's chosen people" (Eph 2:12 GNB).

However, due to their belief in Jesus, the status of these gentiles had changed to that of fellow citizenship (*sumpoliteia*) with believing Israelites. This common citizenship was by virtue of their common membership in God's family, "members of the household of God" (*oikeioi tou theou*, Eph 2:19). They had not only become one people, the "new humanity" Jesus created, but also belonged to the *polis* of the new Jerusalem, which is the dwelling of God and thus the kingdom of God (more on this in our next chapter). They belonged to the *polis* of new Jerusalem on account of their membership in God's family, which made them belong to it through filiation as opposed to residency. Although not touched on in this epistle, their membership in God's family through Jesus Christ was on very intimate terms. In Christ, believing

---

10. Sebillote Cuchet and Lillian Doherty, "Female Citizens Reconfiguring the Political," *Clio. Women, Gender, History* no. 43, (2016), 199.

Jews and gentiles were children of God; "for in Christ Jesus you are all children of God through faith" (Gal 3:26; also Rom 8:16). Thus their *politeia* together with that of believing Jews was in the new Jerusalem. Elsewhere, Paul directly pointed to believers' citizenship in the heavenly Jerusalem when he wrote to the Philippians: "But our citizenship (*politeia*) is in heaven" (Phil 3:20).

The gentiles' former status, which was cast in relationship to Israel's citizenship (*politeia*) in verse 12, was contrasted to their new status as gentile believers, cast in relationship to their common *politeia* (*sumpoliteia*) with the saints in verse 19. In other words, the contrast of gentiles' status is with the *politeia* of Israel, from which they were excluded in the past but presently included, thanks to Jesus. This contrast was thus based on the identity between Israel in verse 12 and the saints in verse 19 being the same; it would break down if the two were not the same, because it would mean a lack of correspondence between the citizenship gentiles were excluded from formerly but included in currently. We have upheld this contrast in our interpretation by taking "the saints" to refer to "believing Israelites" since "believing Israel" is a subset of Israel and therefore the same as "Israel." Understanding believing Jews as a subset of Israel should not surprise us here for it has an Old Testament precedent. As we pointed out in our sixth chapter, the term was used in the Psalms to refer to "faithful Israel" as a subset of Israel.

In the letters of Paul to the Galatians and to the Romans, there is a revelation that believing Jews and gentiles are the new people of God by virtue of being the descendants of Abraham. In his epistle to the Galatians, Paul was writing to a group of people constituting "the churches of Galatia," (Gal 1:2) who believed in Jesus through his proclamation (Gal 3:1–5; 4:13–15). This group was composed of believing gentiles. Paul was unhappy with them (Gal 1:6; 3:1–5) because they were being convinced by some believing Jews (Gal 6:12) to become Jews through circumcision (Gal 5:1) and by observing the law (Gal 3:2, 10; 4:8–11, 21). The gentiles seemed to have been under the impression that through Judaism they would acquire righteousness (Gal 2:12–21), receive God's blessings (Gal 3:1–14), inherit God's promises (Gal 3:19–22; 4:28–31), and even know God more (Gal 4:8–11). Paul thus wrote to seek to reverse their conversion. Two of the reasons which Paul gave to dissuade them from Judaism concerned their new status in Christ. The two reasons revealed an extraordinary new reality in Jesus: believing Jews and gentiles were in fact Abraham's descendants.

One of the two reasons was anchored in parent-child likeness by means of which Paul revealed to the Galatians their shared Abrahamic ancestry with believing Jews. When talking about Israel as a son in our third chapter, we alluded to the view that a son (or child) was a mirror of his father's attributes. Thus, for example, since the Israelites as YHWH's son/children were to act in ways reflective of him, YHWH pointed out their betrayal for failing to act as his children (Deut 32:4–6). To add another example, we have in Genesis this parent-child likeness when the narrator mentioned that Seth was the likeness of his father, Adam (Gen 5:3). It is apparent that this outlook was revered by Paul's first-century audience. Paul therefore used it to let the Galatians know that believing Jews and gentiles were the children of Abraham because their believing exhibited Abraham's trait: "Just as Abraham 'believed God, and it was reckoned to him as righteousness, so, you see, those who believe are descendants of Abraham" (Gal 3:6–7). Paul's revelation was in harmony with Jesus's words when, according to the Gospel of John, he stated that the Jews listening to him were not children of Abraham because their actions did not match up with his:

> They answered him, "Abraham is our father." Jesus said to them, "If you were Abraham's children, you would be doing what Abraham did." (John 8:39)

The Galatians then did not need to become circumcised and follow the law to receive God's blessings, for they were already children of Abraham together with believing Jews, and therefore recipients of God's blessings (Gal 3:8–9). They also did not need circumcision and observance of the law for righteousness, since like their father, Abraham, they had been justified through faith (Gal 3:2–22).

The other reason was based on faith in Christ, by means of which Paul revealed to the Galatians that they shared Abrahamic progeny with believing Jews. Paul let them know that in Christ they were God's children. Others who, like them, had faith in Jesus were also members with them of God's family. Intimate membership into God's family made all of them one regardless of whether they were Jews or of gentile ethnicity, and even regardless of their station in life or of their gender. Belonging to Jesus, having faith in him, had made them all children of Abraham:

> But now that faith has come, we are no longer subject to a disciplinarian, for in Christ Jesus you are all children of God through faith. As many of you as were baptized into Christ have clothed yourselves with Christ. There is no longer Jew or Greek, there is no longer slave or free, there is no longer male or female, for you are all one in Christ Jesus. And if you belong to Christ,

then you are Abraham's offspring, heirs according to the promise. (Gal 3:25–29)

Gentiles' unity with believing Jews was thus secured both through their membership in God's family, and through Abraham their common ancestor. In the first century Graeco-Roman world, an *ethnos* (nation), or *genos* (race), or *phylon* (tribe) or *laos* (people) – since these terms all designated an ethnic group[11] – was based on having common blood which signified "collective descent, lineage, ancestry, kingship.[12] Common blood also signified a common history and a common geographical territory although some people were transregional.[13] Having Abraham as their father meant that believing Jews and those from any of the gentile ethnicities (Greeks, Romans, Galatians, Cretans, Phrygians, Cappadocians, Arabians etc), were now one *ethnos*, albeit spiritually and not biologically. It therefore would make no sense for the Galatians to want to be circumcised and follow the law of Moses in order to become like believing Jews; they were already one people, having, through Christ, become descendants of Abraham.

Paul repeated the revelation of the Abrahamic progeny of believing Jews and gentiles to Christians in Rome, but with a focus on the way Abraham was made the father of both groups. In his letter to the Romans, Paul made clear that Abraham's righteousness on account of faith came before his circumcision (Rom 4:11), which followed later to seal it. The purpose of this sequence of events was to make Abraham the father of both the circumcised and uncircumcised believers, the father of both believing Jews and gentiles:

> We say, "Faith was reckoned to Abraham as righteousness." How was it reckoned to him? . . . It was not after, but before his circumcision. He received the sign of circumcision as a seal of the righteousness that he had by faith while he was still uncircumcised. The purpose was to make him the ancestor of all who believe without being circumcised and who thus have righteousness reckoned to them, and likewise the ancestor of the circumcised but who also follow the example of the faith that our ancestor Abraham had before he was circumcised. (Rom 4:9–12)

---

11. See Erich Gruen, "Did Ancient Identity Depend on Ethnicity? A Preliminary Probe," *Phoenix* 67.1 (2013).

12. Gruen, "Did Ancient Identity Depend on Ethnicity?," 2.

13. Kostas Vlassopoulos, "Ethnicity and Greek History: Reexamining our Assumptions," *BICS* 58.2 (2015).

Paul's revelation about Abrahamic ancestry of both believing Jews and gentiles was an extraordinary one. The children of Abraham in the era of the reign of the promised Davidic king metamorphosed from his physical descendants, historical Israel, to believing Jews and gentiles, the new Israel. In the unfolding story of the Bible, we now had a new Israel made up of non-hereditary descendants of Abraham, whom Paul seemed to have addressed as such in his benediction to the Galatians: "peace be upon them, and mercy, and *upon the Israel of God*" (Gal 6:16, emphasis added). Believing Jews and gentiles were now one people, spiritually, as children of Abraham.

The new people of God were one despite the continued existence of the circumcised and uncircumcised, male and female, slave and free. Their oneness as a spiritual *ethnos* was more fundamental than their other identities, if it had not surpassed them. Paul's extraordinary revelation was in keeping with God's power implied in the words of John the Baptist to the Israelites when he warned the people of Israel that God had the ability to create, out of stones, descendants for Abraham; "Do not presume to say to yourselves, 'We have Abraham as our ancestor': for I tell you, God is able from these stones to raise up children for Abraham" (Matt 3:9).

The extraordinary revelation of a new Israel in the unfolding story of the Bible is substantiated in Peter's first epistle. Peter wrote his epistle to those he termed "exiles" or "sojourners" (*parepidēmoi*, 1 Pet 1:1; 2:11) scattered in different areas south of the Black Sea and north of the Taurus mountains in Asia Minor, which is modern day Turkey (1 Pet 1:1). They were exiles metaphorically in the sense that their present residences were not their true home, any more than Babylon was the "home" of exiled Israelites. For this reason, they were to live as exiles by following God's ways and not the ways of the places they lived (1 Pet 1:17; 2:11). Due to references to their past ignorance (1 Pet 1:14), the futile ways they inherited from their ancestors (1 Pet 1:18), and to past behaviour they had done away with (1 Pet 4:4-3), it can be inferred that these exiles were gentiles, since such references fitted the general description in New Testament literature of gentile believers' past (see for example 1 Cor 12:2; Eph 2:11-12; 4:17-19; Gal 4:8; 1 Thess 4:5).

On account of their belief in Jesus, "to you then who believe" (1 Pet 2:7), Peter revealed to the gentile exiles their special status as the new people of God. He did so with words that matched YHWH's words to the people of Israel at the foot of Mount Sinai thus:

> But you are *a chosen race, a royal priesthood, a holy nation, a people of his own possession*, that you may proclaim the excellencies of

him who called you out of darkness into his marvellous light.
(1 Pet 2:9 ESV, emphasis added)

Now therefore, if you will indeed obey my voice and keep my covenant,
you shall be *my treasured possession among all peoples*,
for all the earth is mine;
and you shall be to me *a kingdom of priests, and a holy nation*.
(Exod 19:5–6, emphasis added)

In discussing YHWH's words in Exodus 19:4–5 to Israel in our third chapter, we pointed out that Israel's royal priesthood and holiness as a nation were the consequences of being God's "most prized possession" (*sᵉgūllâ*). This was because the clause (Exod 19:6) "and you shall be to me a kingdom of priests, and a holy nation," was parallel to the one which preceded it (Exod 19:5): "you shall be my treasured possession among all peoples." In keeping with Hebrew poetry's synthetic parallelism, the second clause advanced the thought of the first one by further defining it. Thus God's plain message was: "you will become my *sᵉgūllâ* and therefore a royal priesthood and a holy nation."

Our interpretation of YHWH's words to Israel is mirrored in the content of Peter's revelation in the following way. Their status as a "chosen race" (*genos eklekton*) corresponded with Israel's as God's *sᵉgūllâ*. Just as the Israelites were chosen to be God's *sᵉgūllâ* out of the nations which all belong to God, believing Jews and gentiles were now God's chosen people, "a people of his own possession" (*laos eis peripoiēsin*) out of the nations which all belong to God. Just as the Israelites were destined to be a royal priesthood because they were God's *sᵉgūllâ*, believers were also a royal priesthood because they were *laos eis peripoiēsin*. Finally, just as Israel as God's *sᵉgūllâ* was a holy nation, believing Jews and gentiles were also, as God's own possession, a holy nation (*ethnos hagion*).

On the basis of our analysis, the implication of Peter's revelation is put into sharp relief. He was revealing to the gentile exiles that they were, as believers, exactly the same as what YHWH told the Israelites they would be if they obeyed him. In other words, believing Jews and gentiles were what historical Israel was meant to be; they were the new Israel, the people of God (*laos theou*). Peter restated this revelation immediately and more directly saying that they were *loas theou* in contrast to their former nondescript gentile ethnicities:

Once you were not a people,
but now you are God's people. (1 Pet 2:10)

The correspondence between the new Israel and what historical Israel was meant to be is accordingly seen in the purpose of their royal priesthood. We pointed out in our third chapter that the purpose of Israel's priesthood, of their representation of God to the nations, was to have other nations blessed in fulfilment of their destiny as Abraham's offspring. If Israel lived in obedience, the land would have the blessings of abundant life because it would become a part of God's kingdom. The blessings of abundant life would attract the nations to YHWH, in Zion where he lived, desiring for themselves the same blessings. In going to Zion, nations would know God and obey his laws (just as Israel did). Doing so would bring them into God's kingdom and have them thereby experience the blessings of abundant life. This purpose of historical Israel's royal priesthood corresponded exactly with that of new Israel's, as we demonstrate below.

The purpose of new Israel's royal priesthood was to proclaim God's mighty acts; "that you may proclaim (*exangeilēte*) the mighty acts of him who called you out of darkness into his marvellous light" (1 Pet 2:9). This specific purpose, as with historical Israel's, had to do with advancing the kingdom of God to the world, thus blessing the nations. The NRSV has translated the Greek word *aretas* as God's "mighty acts" (*tas aretas*) whose proclamation is the purpose of the royal priesthood of the new Israel; but *aretas* is also translated as God's "praise" (NIV), "wonderful acts" (GNB), "triumphs" or "his excellencies" (ESV) because it has no straight-forward meaning. As pointed out by Feldemeier, the range of meanings covered by this Greek word is broad: it "actually means 'ability,' 'mastery,' any good quality at all, then also moral qualities such as virtue, courage, magnanimity, philanthropy, and the like."[14]

We take the view that *aretas* translated as God's "mighty acts" in NRSV best captures the meaning of the word when it is determined by its literary context. The subordinate clause of the sentence in verse 9 reads: "who called you from darkness into his marvellous light." This clause requires us to relate God's mighty acts to the exiles' experience of God's power. Logically, this subordinate clause would have made the gentile exiles think of the mighty acts of God they were to declare in relationship to that of their calling from darkness into light. Consequently, their declaration of the mighty acts of God would be out of their own personal experience of his powerful act of calling them from darkness into light. As we demonstrated in the biblical literature of the Old Testament, darkness connotes death, judgement, ignorance, and captivity,

---

14. Henry G. Liddel and Robert Scott, *A Greek-English Lexicon*, rev. and aug. H. S. Jones with R. McKenzie (Oxford: Oxford University Press, 1996), 238.

while light symbolizes God's presence, life, salvation, and wisdom. The same is also the case in the New Testament where darkness and/or light is used to describe the experience of believers before and after their belief in Jesus, so for example: "He has rescued us from the power of darkness and transferred us into the kingdom of his beloved Son, in whom we have redemption, the forgiveness of sins" (Col 1:13–14; also Acts 26:18; Eph 5:8; 2 Cor 4:6; 6:14–15).

In line with this symbolism, darkness and light were related to the circumstances of the gentile exiles before and after they received the good news of God's kingdom (1 Pet 1:12). The content of this good news was Jesus (1 Pet 1:25), who was advancing God's kingdom because he was the promised Davidic king (1 Pet 3:21–22; 4:4–5). Through their belief in the good news, the exiles had, on the one hand, experienced God's power by their deliverance from Satan's bondage, of which Peter mentions ignorance (1 Pet 1:14). On the other hand, upon their belief in Jesus, they experienced God's mighty acts through their entry into God's kingdom referred to as "his eternal glory in Christ" (1 Pet 5:10) whose fullness, in line with Jesus's teaching, they would see at the end (1 Pet 1:5, 13; 2:12). Being in God's kingdom, the exiles had experienced the blessings of abundant life such as eternal life (1 Pet 1:4; 3:7), salvation (security) (1 Pet 1:5, 9–10) and health (1 Pet 2:24). Their declaration of the mighty acts of God would, therefore, be based on their personal experience of dramatic changes in their circumstances from darkness to light on account of their faith in Jesus.

Consequently, the purpose of their proclamation was to represent God to the nations. Since, as we discussed in our second chapter, the role of priests was mediatorial, to represent God to the people and viceversa, they were, as royal priests, representing God to the nations in their proclamation of his mighty acts. We say this because proclamation of God's mighty works would not constitute representing humans before God, but rather God to human beings. In other words, God's mighty acts were to be declared to human beings even if it was in the context of God's house. The use of the verb "to proclaim" (*exangellō*) elsewhere in biblical literature clarifies this (see for example in the Septuagint Ps 71:15 [Ps 70:15 in LXX], Ps 73:28 [Ps 72:28 in LXX] and Ps 107:22 [Ps 106:22 in LXX], and the shorter ending of Mark).

Representing God to the people by proclaiming his mighty acts, based on their personal experience, made the exiles witnesses of his power. They were to proclaim the gospel to the world's nations that people would come to believe in Jesus and enter into God's kingdom, because they had experienced it – they had tasted "that the Lord is good" (1 Pet 2:3). Thus, as was destined for historical

Israel, God's kingdom would be restored in the world through this new Israel. In the language of blessings, the world would now be blessed through the new Israel. Historical Israel related, then, to the new Israel typologically. This is the reason we said in our seventh chapter that the restoration of Israel is fulfilled typologically: historical Israel is a type of new Israel, which is its antitype.

The implication of Peter's revelation on the purpose of new Israel's royal priesthood that we have drawn out, was the culmination of the fulfilment of the restoration of the Israelites and their vocation. As we discussed earlier, following a period of preparation by John the Baptist, the restoration of Israel began through Jesus and his twelve disciples. Those who believed their proclamation of the good news of God's kingdom became a part of the restored community and of God's kingdom under Jesus, the promised Davidic king. Having been restored, the people of Israel could then fulfil their vocation and have all nations blessed through them. We saw how this fulfilment took place in the unfolding story of the Bible in the New Testament. According to the preaching of the apostle Peter, the Israelites were restored and the first to enter God's kingdom, in order that they might be used, as Abraham's offspring, to advance God's kingdom to other nations. This vocation of historical Israel was demonstrated in Peter's preaching to Cornelius, and in Paul's preaching to various gentile peoples. As should be clear, restored Israel was not entirely identical to historical Israel because non-believing Israelites, who were legitimately Abraham's descendants, were not a part of it.

As the story of the Bible in the New Testament unfolds, we learn that the identity of restored Israel did not remain static but shifted to transcend it and include believing gentiles. Believing Jews and gentiles became the new people of God. The revelation of the inclusion of believing gentiles in the people of God is seen in the Jerusalem Council in Acts 15. In response to Peter's preaching to Cornelius and his house and what happened consequently, James specifically mentioned that God had taken from among them some to be his people: "Simeon has related how God first looked favourably on the gentiles, to take from among them a people for his name" (Acts 15:14). Before this revelation, God had prepared Peter to accept gentiles as God's people alongside the Israelites. Against the concerns of Jewish purity as a holy nation which we mentioned in our earlier section, God had told Peter that what he had made clean, no human could call unclean (Acts 10:15), thereby freeing him to mingle with Cornelius and his family, preach to them, and accept them emphatically as God's people too. The latter was particularly clear to Peter when Cornelius and his family received the promise of the Holy Spirit, which was a promise for

God's people, thereby qualifying them as God's people too. The profundity of this event was not lost to the believing Jews. That is the reason why they were shocked, or jolted "out of their senses" (*exestēsav*),[15] for nothing had prepared them for this new thing which God had just done: "The circumcised believers who had come with Peter were astounded (*exestēsav*) that the gift of the Holy Spirit had been poured out even on the gentiles" (Acts 10:45).

A transformation of the identity of God's people invariably meant that the vocation of restored Israel to bring other nations under the kingdom of God, through the proclamation of the good news, was now on the shoulders of the new people of God. This transformation, and the consequential transfer of the vocation of Israel to the new people of God, is what the revelation of Peter to the gentile exiles most clearly and directly articulated. Peter's revelation confirmed that the restoration of Israel that began with believing Israel, from whom the gentiles received the gospel, had ended with the people of God constituting both believing Jews and gentiles.

The unfolding story of the Bible is, therefore, very clear. Israel was restored, but spiritually, resulting in a new Israel made up of believing Jews and gentiles who, by an act of God, had also become Abraham's offspring. For this reason, the restoration of God's kingdom in the world was taking place through the new Israel, in fulfilment of God's blessings-to-all-nations promise to Abraham. Since Jesus's parable of the wicked tenant suggested this scenario, we conclude this chapter by examining it.

A parable communicates by way of analogies between its elements and corresponding elements drawn from elsewhere. When analogies between elements of a parable and corresponding ones are not obvious, the parable lends itself to a variety of interpretation. This is the case with the parable of the wicked tenants, resulting in over sixteen different interpretations in New Testament scholarship.[16] Our reading of the parable will be one more

---

15. With respect to the context we are elaborating, we view the verb *existēmi* (parsed *exestēsan*) here to have the sense of shock or of being confounded. It communicates the effect that gentile inclusion (alongside believing Jews) into God's people had on the Jewish believers more accurately than its other meanings: "astonished" (GNB, NIV) or "amazed" (RSV, ESV). NRSV's translation, "astound," is ambiguous for it could mean shock as well as amazement. See G. Abott-Smith, *A Manual Greek Lexicon of the New Testament*, 3rd ed. (Edinburgh: T&T Clark, 2001), 160–161.

16. Surveys can be found in Klyne R. Snodgrass, "Recent Research on the Parable of the Wicked Tenants: An Assessment," *BBR* 8 (1998), and Kelly R. Iverson, "Jews, Gentiles, and the Kingdom of God: The Parable of the Wicked Tenants in Narrative Perspective (Mark 12:1–12)," *BibInt* 20.3 (2012).

addition to these diverse interpretations. Reading the parable our way, which is in the light of the story of the Bible we have looked at, is not only called for by our biblical-theological study, but crucially justified by our interpreting the futuristic element in the parable (the "other" to whom the vineyard is given in Mark 12:9) through a corresponding analogy we have drawn from subsequent content of the story of the Bible in the book of Acts.

The six main elements in the parable of the wicked tenants are: the vineyard, the owner of the vineyard, his tenants, his servants, his son, and "others." The elements with the most obvious correspondence are the owner of the vineyard, the tenants, and the servants. We say so because it is to the people of Israel that God sent his servants, the prophets, whom the Israelites mistreated, and whose messages they rejected. More precisely, the tenants were unbelieving Israelites. Jesus singled them out as the culprits rejecting God's servants, mistreating and even killing them when he said that they were the ones (but metaphorically as the city of Jerusalem) who "kill the prophets and stones those who are sent to it!" (Matt 23:37; Luke 13:34–35). These unbelieving Israelites would not see him again until the day they would believe in him (Matt 23:39). The vineyard owner was God, the tenants were unbelieving Israelites, and the slaves/servants were the prophets. The actions of the tenants were, therefore, the actions of unbelieving Israelites, and so God's indictment was on them and not on all of Israel.

Following these three elements, in the order of the ease of identifying their corresponding analogies, is the son of the vineyard owner. Being the heir to the vineyard, he represents Jesus the Son of God. It is therefore the unbelieving Israelites, in our interpretation, who condemned and killed Jesus. A key charge brought against Jesus at his trial was that he was the Christ, the promised Davidic king, which the unbelieving Israelites led by their religious leaders rejected in unbelief.

It is instructive to note here that after Jesus gave this parable, the Jewish religious leaders knew that it was given against them (Mark 12:12). In other words, they understood the parable well enough to identify themselves as the tenants Jesus was talking about. Accordingly, they were the builders, in Jesus's conclusion to the parable, who rejected the stone that became the cornerstone (Mark 12:10). If we follow Peter's revelation of the stone's rejection (1 Pet 2:6–7) and his sermon to disbelieving Jews in Acts (Acts 4:11), we understand clearly that the rejected stone that became the cornerstone was Jesus whom they rejected through their unbelief:

> For it stands in scripture:
> "See, I am laying in Zion a stone,
> > a cornerstone chosen and precious;
>
> and whoever believes in him will not be put to shame."
> *To you then who believe, he is precious; but for those who do not believe,*
> "The stone that the builders rejected
> > has become the very head of the corner." (1 Pet 2:6–7, emphasis added)
>
> This Jesus is
> "the stone that was rejected by you, the builders;
> > it has become the cornerstone." (Acts 4:11)

The elements in the parable to which it is difficult to assign corresponding analogies are the vineyard and its produce, and the "others" to whom it was given. It seems to me that the vineyard and its produce must be related to the stewardship (or the privilege) of Israel. Since the vineyard was given to be taken care of, and its produce given to the owner, the tenants must have been its stewards. In the story of the Bible in the Old Testament, we pointed out that the Israelites, as Abraham's offspring, were given the promised land as a site for their vocation to represent God to the nations through obeying him. Their representation of God would lead to the nations being blessed through them. The produce represents Israel's vocation. They were to lead the nations into God's kingdom, but they failed because of their disobedience and unbelief.

Moreover, at their hour of restoration which was the last chance they had to fulfil their vocation, they had killed John the Baptist and were going to kill Jesus himself, the Son of God (which corresponds to the sending of the vineyard owners' son to the tenants – the ultimate person the owner could send them, thinking that they would hand over the produce out of respect for him as his son). The unbelieving Israelites could not, therefore, lead the nations to God's kingdom as intended. For this reason, God judged the unbelieving Israelites, took away their vocation and gave it "to others" (*allois* – Mark 12:9). These *allois* were, according to the story of the Bible in the New Testament we have examined, believing Jews and gentiles, the new Israel. They were now the ones with the vocation to lead nations to God's kingdom through their proclamation of the good news. God was now using them as the (spiritual) offspring of Abraham to restore his kingdom in the world in fulfilment of his blessings-to-all-nations promise to Abraham.

We mentioned in our third chapter that the promised land was the site for Israel's vocation. The land was therefore inextricably tied to the vocation of historical Israel. But with the spiritual transformation of historical Israel into the new Israel, the promised land, as the exclusive site for Israel's vocation as a kingdom of priests, was detached from God's people. The world took the place of the land as the site of the vocation of the new Israel. This substitution was revealed by Paul in his epistle to the Romans. In the context of believing Jews and gentiles as the descendants of Abraham, Paul mentioned the world, instead of the land, as what God promised Abraham: "For the promise that he would inherit the world did not come to Abraham or to his descendants through the law but through the righteousness of faith" (Rom 4:13; see also Eph 6:3). The logic of this substitution should be clear to us: everywhere and anywhere, believers became the site of their vocation to lead others into God's kingdom. The whole world now became the site of the mission of the new Israel as alluded to in the commission to the twelve: "you will be my witnesses . . . to the ends of the earth" (Acts 1:8). Having lost its significance for Israel's vocation on account of the spiritual restoration of Israel, the demonstration of the restoration of Israel to the land and to conditions therein of the blessings of abundant life under the promised Davidic king is absent in New Testament literature.

9

Restoration of God's Dwelling via Jesus

To recapitulate our discussion in chapter 3 concerning the restoration of God's dwelling with humans in the world, this restoration (just as with his kingdom) was to start with Israel in the promised land. God was to reside with the Israelites in the temple, and thereby live with them in Jerusalem and in the land. In fact, YHWH's presence amongst the Israelites in the land could not be taken for granted, as it was dependent on their obedience. Without obedience, God would not dwell with the people of Israel: "if you walk in my statutes, obey my commandments by walking in them, then . . . I will dwell among the children of Israel" (1 Kgs 6:12–13). We noted that if the Israelites obeyed God, they would become his kingdom, thereby having the blessings of abundant life. These blessings would attract other nations to Zion and have them know him, follow his laws, and come under his kingdom. Since, as we pointed out, kingdom and dwelling were interrelated, the lands that the nations returned to would then also become God's dwelling, experiencing the same blessings of abundant life. In the end the world would once again be God's dwelling with human beings.

According to the story of the Bible in the Old Testament, Israel failed to obey God and thus failed to become his dwelling. For this reason, God had Jerusalem and the temple destroyed. God promised through the prophets that he would restore Israel and his dwelling with them, after which the nations would flock to Zion. In the unfolding story of the Bible in the New Testament, we are informed about the way God spiritually restored his dwelling with Israel (the new Israel), and of its expansion until the world once again becomes his dwelling with human beings. This restoration and the ultimate dwelling of God in all the world is the subject of this chapter. We begin where the restoration of God's dwelling began, in Jesus the promised Davidic king.

Second Temple and Restoration of God's Dwelling

The destroyed temple was rebuilt by the people of Israel when they returned to the land. However, there are indications in biblical literature that this rebuilt temple was not the promised restored temple. In our sixth chapter, we pointed out that the blessings of abundant life were the conditions that the people of Israel would go back to in the land as part of their restoration. What we did not mention were the promises that YHWH gave Israel that life would emanate from the restored temple because God would dwell there. In the vision God gave Ezekiel, the prophet saw water flowing out of the temple:

> Then he brought me back to the entrance of the temple; there, water was flowing from below the threshold of the temple toward the east (for the temple faced east); and the water was flowing down below the south end of the threshold of the temple, south of the altar. Then he brought me out of the way of the north gate, and led me around on the outside to the outer gate that faces toward the east; and the water was coming out on the south side. (Ezek 47:1–2)

This temple water flowed out southwards becoming a river that flowed to the Arabah, the southern region of the Dead Sea, and eventually into the sea. It would give life to creatures which swam in it (Ezek 47:9) and make fresh the Dead Sea water (Ezek 47:8). Furthermore, on the banks of this river would grow trees that would produce fruit for food throughout the year and possess healing leaves:

> Their leaves will not wither nor their fruit fail, but they will bear fresh fruit every month, because the water from them flows from the sanctuary. Their fruit will be for food, and their leaves for healing. (Ezek 47:12)

YHWH's promises of the restoration of Israel through the prophet Joel also contained the promise that a fountain would flow out of his house when he restored Israel: "a fountain shall come forth from the house of the LORD" (Joel 3:18). We also find the mention of life-giving water flowing from the temple in Jerusalem, in YHWH's renewal of his restoration promises to Israel through the prophet Zechariah: "On that day living waters shall flow out from

Jerusalem, half of them to the eastern sea and half of them to the western sea; it shall continue in the summer as in winter" (Zech 14:8).

The temple as a source of life because YHWH resided in it is not exclusively seen in YHWH's promises of its restoration. Glimpses of the temple as a source of life can also be found in two instances in the psalms. The first was the psalmist's praise of God because the river of his delights (*naḥal 'ădānêkā*) in his house was the fountain of life:

> How precious is your steadfast love, O God!
>   All people may take refuge in the shadow of your wings.
> They feast on the abundance of your house,
>   and you give them drink from the river of your delights.
> For with you is the fountain of life;
>   in your light we see light. (Ps 36:7–9)

The second was in a psalmist's vision of Jerusalem, the possibility that never was, as a city enlivened by streams from the temple:

> There is a river whose streams make glad the city of God,
>   the holy habitation of the Most High. (Ps 46:4)

The temple as God's dwelling, then, was associated with the most fundamental blessings of abundant life, and of life itself. The Israelites' reception of life from God's house, this extraordinary phenomenon symbolized by life-giving water, would have been a reality if they had obeyed him. Now God promised through the prophets that life would emanate from his restored temple to the benefit of restored Israel with whom he would dwell. Since there is no evidence in biblical literature suggesting that the Second Temple was a source of life, it is logical to conclude that it was not the promised restored temple.

Our conclusion has crucial support from Jesus's prophecy of the Second Temple's destruction. According to the Gospels, Jesus prophesied the destruction of the Second Temple when one of his disciples admired its magnificence:

> As they came out of the temple, one of his disciples said to him, "Look, Teacher, what large stones and what large buildings!" Then Jesus asked him "Do you see these great buildings? Not one stone will be left here upon another; all will be thrown down." (Mark 13:1–2; also Matt 24:1; Luke 21:5–6)

This was an astonishing prophecy and difficult for the disciples to fathom because the temple was God's house. Jesus himself had gone to the temple in their company because it was God's house. Moreover, prior to his prophecy he had pointed to it as God's house. In the context of the temple abuse by traders, Jesus highlighted its function, by use of Jeremiah's prophecy, as a house of prayer because it was God's house: "my house shall be called a house of prayer for all nations" (Mark 11:17). It is no wonder that the disciples sought reassurances through some sign that its destruction as Jesus had prophesied would come to pass (Mark 13:4).

If the Second Temple was overlooked as the restored temple, where was God's dwelling with his people, and how was it to be extended to the rest of the world? In New Testament literature, it is revealed that in Jesus God had restored his temple, his dwelling with human beings.

Restoration of God's Dwelling in Jesus and Israel

The most direct revelation comes from John's Gospel where Jesus referred to himself as God's temple. According to John's account, the Jews must have taken offense at Jesus's driving out of traders from the temple and overturning the tables of trade. They, therefore, asked him for a sign to show his authority to regulate temple practice. Jesus responded thus: "Destroy this temple and in three days I will raise it up" (John 2:19; see also Matt 26:61; Mark 14:58). They disbelieved him because what he was saying he could do was incredible. Unknown to them and Jesus's disciples at that time was that Jesus was referring to himself as God's temple. Understanding of Jesus's body as God's temple would dawn on Jesus's disciples only after his resurrection:

> The Jews then said, "This temple has been under construction for forty-six years, and will you raise it up in three days?" But he was speaking of the temple of his body. After he was raised from the dead, his disciples remembered that he had said this; and they believed the scripture and the word that Jesus had spoken. (John 2:20–22)

God restoring his dwelling in the body of Jesus, the promised Davidic king, was mind-boggling. An exchange of body for a building or house would not have been anticipated. The prophecies of the restoration of the temple would not have prepared the people to accommodate this manner of fulfilment; but this kind of fulfilment was in keeping with the wider scheme of the spiritual restoration of the Davidic kingship and Israel as discussed in our previous chapters.

Alongside this direct revelation in the Gospel according to John are four indirect revelations of Jesus as God's temple. These indirect revelations centre on Jesus as: (1) the one through whom God is to be approached (John 4:23–24); (2) the life-giving water (John 4:10–14; 7:37–39); (3) the one in whom God's glory was seen (John 1:14); and (4) the ladder on whom angels ascended to heaven and descended on earth (John 1:51). We discuss each of these indirect revelations below.

The first indirect revelation of Jesus as God's temple which we look at is in the conversation that Jesus had with the Samaritan woman in John 4. In her encounter with Jesus, the Samaritan woman brought up the topic of access to God: "Our ancestor worshipped (*prosekunēsan*) on this mountain, but you say the place where people must worship (*proskunein*) is in Jerusalem" (John 4:20). This Greek word in the LXX (*proskunein*) that is translated "worship" literally means "to bow down." It signifies submission to the one a person bows down to, or an acknowledgment of his superiority. In Old Testament literature, bowing down was predominantly before a deity or an idol (see for example Exod 20:5; Lev 26:1; Num 22:31; Deut 4:19; Josh 23:7; 1 Kgs 19:18) at a place where deity was believed to be accessible – usually a house or a high place. Consequently, *proskunein* in Old Testament biblical literature chiefly implied accessing God in the temple and thereby offering him prayers.[1] The issue then which the woman confronted Jesus with was about the right place to go to access God because God lived there; whether this place was in Mount Gerizim or in Zion.

Jesus's response to the Samaritan woman's remarks was astonishing. His remarks pointed to the fact that the second temple in Jerusalem was not the restored temple, and that one could access God apart from any physical location because Jesus was the restored temple of God:

> But the hour is coming, and is now here, when true worshippers will worship the Father in spirit and truth, for the Father seeks such as these to worship him. God is spirit, and those who worship him must worship him in spirit and truth. (John 4:23–24)

Samaritans previously accessed God in Gerizim, while the Judeans were still approaching God in Jerusalem, thanks to the Second Temple. Jesus overlooked both as locations to access God and pointed to "spirit and truth" (*pneumati kai alētheia*) as the new locus of accessing God. Jesus's coming into the world marked the beginning of the time when those who truly accessed (*hoi alēthinoi proskunētai*) the Father (Jesus's way of referring to God), did it in spirit and truth, which indirectly pointed to Jesus as the new location of accessing God.

---

1. For more on this word and its cultic context see J. M. Scholer, *Proleptic Priests: Priesthood in the Epistle to the Hebrews*, JSNTSS 49 (Sheffield: JSOT Press, 1991), 91–95.

This made the Second Temple and Gerizim obsolete. We explain how this was the case below.

Truth, according to its usage in the Gospel of John, has its common sense ("reality"/"genuineness"), as well as a moral sense ("acting uprightly"/"righteous acts"), and a revelatory sense ("disclose"/"make known").[2] It was personified to express its moral or revelatory effects. In all these usages, truth in John's Gospel indirectly referred to Jesus by being centred on him. Jesus was the truth (John 14:6); truth came through him (John 1:17); he came to give testimony to the truth; he told the truth (John 8:45) which he heard from God (John 8:40); and he who heard Jesus's voice heard the truth (John 18:37). Thus, those who believed in Jesus, his followers, met the truth, heard the truth, were set free by the truth (John 8:32), were led into truth, and, for our purposes, would thus approach God in truth. This then reveals that accessing God "in truth" was in essence doing so in or through Jesus.

Concerning spirit (*pneuma*), we know that it generally refers to the Holy Spirit in John except when it is specifically used to refer to Jesus's spirit, his non-material being. For example, spirit could refer to Jesus's emotional distress: "When Jesus saw her weeping . . . he was greatly disturbed in spirit and deeply moved" (John 11:33; also 13:21). It could also refer to Jesus's life:

> He said, "It is finished." Then he bowed his head and gave up his spirit. (John 19:30)

Mention of approaching God in the Holy Spirit is an indirect reference to Jesus, because the Holy Spirit is inextricably associated with Jesus. The Spirit descended upon him (John 1:32) before he began to fulfil his destiny. As the Spirit of truth (John 14:17; 15:26; 16:13) who would take over after Jesus's physical departure, as "another companion" (*allon paraklēton*, John 14:16), he would guide the disciples into the truth (John 16:13), revealing to them Jesus's and the Father's truth (John 16:14–15). Jesus would also baptize believers with the Spirit (John 1:33) which would also be given to them (John 7:39). This then reveals that approaching God "in spirit" was essentially doing so in or through Jesus.

In effect, Jesus revealed that he was the restored temple of God. As such, he enabled those who believed in him to access God at any place in the world so that approaching God in Gerizim or in the temple was no longer necessary. Through Jesus, believers could access God anywhere, for Jesus would be present everywhere by the Spirit who was promised to all those who believed in him.

---

2. See Dennis R. Lindsay, "What is Truth? Ἀλήθεια in the Gospel of John," *RQ* 35.3 (1993).

To put it differently, in Jesus, believers would have the Spirit, by virtue of which they would approach God wherever they were. This interpretation is well portrayed in GNB's rendering of the Greek text thus: "God is Spirit, and only by the power of his Spirit can people worship him as he really is" (John 4:24 GNB). Our understanding of accessing God in Jesus as a result of Jesus coming into the world, which thereby displaces accessing him in Gerizim or Jerusalem, sheds light on some of Jesus's instruction to his disciples. These instructions were concerned specifically with approaching God in, or through, him thus:

> On that day you will ask nothing of me. Very truly I tell you if you ask anything of the Father in my name, he will give it to you. Until now you have not asked for anything in my name. Ask and you will receive so that your joy may be complete. (John 16:23–24)

> On that day you will ask in my name. I do not say to you that I will ask the Father on your behalf. (John 16:26)

> If you abide in me, and my words abide in you, ask whatever you wish, and it will be done to you. (John 15:7)

> You did not choose me but I chose you. And I appointed you to go and bear fruit, fruit that will last, so that the Father will give you whatever you ask in my name. (John 15:16)

The second indirect revelation of Jesus as God's temple has to do with Jesus as the source of life-giving water. In the first instance, we encounter this revelation in John's Gospel, in Jesus's offer of life-giving water to the Samaritan woman and then to pilgrims in Jerusalem. We saw earlier that there would be a life-giving river from the restored temple. Thus Jesus as the restored temple offered life-giving water in the narrative of the Gospel of John. In the first instance, in conversation with the Samaritan woman, Jesus had already alluded to himself as God's temple before he revealed to her that accessing God would therefore henceforth take place in him. Next to Jacob's well, Jesus told the woman that had she known God's gift and who was asking her for water, she would have asked to be given living water:

> If you knew the gift of God and who it is that is saying to you "Give me a drink," you would have asked him, and he would have given you living water. The woman said to him, "Sir, you have no bucket, and the well is deep, Where do you get that living water? Are you greater than our ancestor Jacob, who gave us the well, and with his sons and his flocks drank from it?" Jesus said to her, "Everyone who drinks of this water will be thirsty again, but those

who drink of the water that I will give them will never be thirsty. The water that I will give will become in them a spring of water gushing up to eternal life." (John 4:10–14)

From the conversation, God's gift of water through Jesus was greater than the gift of water from Jacob's well because Jesus's water would give everlasting life. For this reason, Jesus was greater than Jacob; he was God's restored temple and as such, life-giving water would flow from him and be received (as the context indicates) by those who would believe in him (John 4:39–42).

In the second instance of this indirect revelation in John's Gospel, Jesus invited the pilgrims in Jerusalem to drink life-giving water from him. He gave this invitation in the context of the feast of the Tabernacles (John 7:2), also known as Sukkot (meaning "booths" in Hebrew). The feast of Tabernacles was celebrated for eight days, in tents overlaid with branches and flowers, in the month of Tishri (Tishri [September-October] would have been the first month of the calendar of ancient Israel but changed to the seventh following the Babylonian calendar).[3] The feast was both a harvest festival, the ingathering of grapes and olives, as well as a feast of remembrance of the Israelites' wandering in the wilderness (Lev 23:39–44; Num 29:2–38; Deut 16:13–17). The common motif between the festival and the memorial was water. On the one hand, as glimpsed through rabbinic sources on the observance of Sukkot close to Jesus's context,[4] water from the Siloam river in the form of libation was poured out from golden bowls onto the base of the altar daily during the celebration to petition YHWH for rain. This was significant because Tishri marked the beginning of the autumn rains whose coming would ensure a good harvest and, in consequence, life. On the other hand, the water reminded them of water that had miraculously come out of the rock when the wandering Israelites desperately needed water.

The revelation that Jesus would give of himself as God's temple from whom, therefore, living waters flowed, comes from the remembrance part of the festival, for this pointed to the temple. The rock in the wilderness out of which life-giving water flowed, in some Jewish traditions, related to the temple.[5] The foundation rock on which the temple was built was believed to

---

3. John C. Reeves, "The Feast of the First Fruits of Wine and the Ancient Canaanite Calendar," *VT* 42.3 (1992), 361.

4. See *m. Sukk.* 4:9–10.

5. See *m. Yoma.* 2, and W. D. Davies and Dale C. Allison, *A Critical and Exegetical Commentary on the Gospel according to Saint Matthew*, 3 Vols. (ICC; Edinburgh: T&T Clark, 1997), 2:626–628.

symbolize it. Life-giving water would come from the foundation rock to the base around the altar; this was expected and constituted part of the promises of restoration which God gave Israel concerning the restored temple. Jesus would then declare to the pilgrims that he was the temple of God from whom living water would flow thus:

> On the last and greatest day of the festival Jesus stood and cried out aloud, 'If anyone is thirsty let him come to me; whoever believes in me, let him drink.' As scripture says, 'Streams of living water shall flow out *of his belly (ek tēs koilas autou)*.' He was speaking of the Spirit which believers in him would receive later; for the Spirit had not yet been given, because Jesus had not yet been glorified. (John 7:37–39 NEB, my own translation in italics)

Here Jesus revealed that he was God's temple, and that those who believed in him would drink from him and have life. Jesus even referred to Scripture's reference to the temple and life, to reinforce his invitation to the pilgrims to believe in him and have life. The Old Testament reference could have been Isaiah 12:3 where YHWH's message of drawing from the wells of salvation was associated with the feast of Tabernacles, the Spirit, and the belly in rabbinic interpretations, and read as a restoration promise.[6] More likely it was a reference to Ps 105:41, which was one of the psalms sung during the libations[7] where mention was made of the rock (read temple) being opened and water gushing out. This expectation was now fulfilled in Jesus. Since, as we have just pointed out, the rock in the wilderness from which water gushed out was symbolized in the rock on which the temple was founded, then Paul's reference to Jesus as the rock (1 Cor 10:4) implicitly confirms that Jesus is the restored temple of God from whom living waters flow.

The third indirect revelation of Jesus as the temple of God is in the terminologies that the narrator of John's Gospel used to describe Jesus's (the Word's) coming into the world. The terminologies came from the Old Testament where they were used with reference to the tabernacle and the temple and the activities which took place there, thus intimating that Jesus was God's temple. The Word was not simply talked of as having come into the world. Rather the incarnated Word was described as a residence, as having "tabernacled" amongst us: "the Word became flesh and *tabernacled (eskēnōsen)*

---

6. *b. Sukk.* 48b; 50b; *y. Sukk.* 5:1. Also, see the short discussion of Joel Marcus, "Rivers of Living Water from Jesus's Belly (John 7:38)," *JBL* 117.2 (1998).

7. See F. J. Badcock, "The Feast of Tabernacles," *JTS* 24.94 (1923), 172.

among us" (John 1:14a, my translation in italics). In view of the Word having been pitched, John immediately talked of beholding his glory (*doxa*, the Greek for Hebrew *kābôd*), which was God's glory: "and we have seen his glory, the glory as of a father's only son" (John 1:14b). Beholding God's glory in the Word that tabernacled among us parallels as God's house the glory (*kābôd*) of God – the physical manifestation of YHWH we discussed in our third chapter – which filled both the tabernacle and temple when they were dedicated as God's houses. The narrator's description of Jesus is then designed to make it known that Jesus is the temple of God in whom God was now dwelling with his people.

The fourth and last indirect revelation of Jesus as the restored temple which we look at in John's Gospel is in Jesus's words to Nathanael:

> And he said to him, "Very truly, I tell you, you will see heaven opened and the angels of God ascending and descending upon the Son of Man. (John 1:51)

We already discussed in our seventh chapter that Jesus was the Son of Man because he was the promised Davidic king. Reference then to angels ascending and descending upon the Son of Man had to do with him. However, the biblical context that sheds light on these words is in Genesis. In the relevant narrative, Jacob had a dream in a place somewhere between Beersheba and Haran. In the dream was a ladder set up connecting God, in heaven, and human beings on earth. Because of this he was able to be visited by YHWH, who repeated to him the promises he had given Abraham. Upon waking up, Jacob was able to tell that the place he spent the night was a place where God could be accessed; it was his house indeed:

> And he dreamed that there was a ladder set up on the earth, the top of it reaching to heaven; and the angels of God were ascending and descending on it. And the LORD stood beside him and said, "I am the LORD, the God of Abraham your father" . . . Then Jacob woke from his sleep and said, "Surely the LORD is in this place – and I did not know it!" And he was afraid, and said, "How awesome is this place! This is none other than the house of God, and this is the gate of heaven." (Gen 28:12–17)

Against this background, Jesus's words to Nathanael of angels ascending and descending upon him, was therefore a revelation that Jesus was the house of God. And in the sweep of the unfolding story of the Bible, he was thus the restored temple.

We mentioned that according to the Gospel of John, Jesus's most direct reference to himself as God's temple was in his words to the Jews: "Destroy this temple and in three days I will raise it up" (John 2:19) by which he meant his body (John 2:21–22). These words meant that Jesus's body was not only the restored temple prior to his crucifixion and death, but was also after his resurrection. His post-Easter body was as much God's restored temple as was his physical body before his death. In one instance of its kind in the New Testament, Jesus's risen body is revealed to be God's temple. In his epistle to the Colossian believers, Paul revealed that Jesus's body was God's temple: "For in him the whole fullness (*plerōma*) of deity dwells bodily" (Col 2:9; see also Col 1:19). Within the context of the Old Testament, the Greek words for fullness, *plerōma* and *plērōtis* (LXX translations of Heb. *mālē'*), was used to communicate God's immanence, his dwelling in every corner of the world. For example: ". . . may his glory fill the whole world" (Ps 72:19), and "The LORD said '. . . as I live, and as all the earth shall be filled with the glory of the LORD'" (Num 14:21; see also Isa 6:3; 11:9; Hab 2:14). When Paul's revelation is read against this Old Testament background, it becomes clear that he was revealing that the risen Lord was God's dwelling.

Moreover, Paul also revealed to the Colossian believers the manner of the dwelling of God's fullness in Christ through the use of the adverb "bodily" (*sōmatikōs*). In so doing, Paul underlined the corporeal nature of the dwelling of God in Jesus. In Jesus, God's fullness dwells in the body of a person: God dwells in Jesus's body. This understanding is highlighted in the translation of the NIV: "in Christ the fullness of the Deity lives in bodily form." Since this was a current reality and not a reference to Jesus's life on earth before his death, as some may suppose, the body referred to was not physical but spiritual. For the above reason, as the story of the Bible in the New Testament unfolds, we learn of the evolution of the restored temple of God to include believers, the new Israel. Having been incorporated into Jesus's body, believers too became with him God's dwelling place. Paul indeed, shortly after revealing that the risen Lord was God's dwelling bodily, informs the Colossian believers that they have been incorporated into his body by exhorting them to hold fast to Jesus who was the head of their body. Some of them had been swayed to the teachings and practices we mentioned and had thus been unfastened from the head, and thus ceased to be part of Jesus's body:

> Therefore do not let anyone condemn you in matters of food and drink or of observing festivals, new moons, or sabbaths. These are only a shadow of what is to come, but the substance belongs

to Christ. Do not let anyone disqualify you, insisting on self-abasement and worship of angels, dwelling on visions, puffed up without cause by human way of thinking, and *not holding fast to the head*, from whom the whole body, nourished and held together by its ligaments and sinews, grows with a growth that is from God. (Col 2:16–19, emphasis added)

In Ephesians, the church (believers, those assembled [*ekklēsia*] by God through Christ) is identified as the body of the risen Lord: "And he has put all things under his feet and made him the head over all things for the church, which is his body" (Eph 1:22–23). For this reason, as is clear in other New Testament literature, believers are the dwelling place of God. In his pastoral instructions to the believers in Corinth to shun sexual immorality, Paul revealed to them in clear terms that their bodies were members of Christ's body:

Do you not know that your bodies are members of Christ? Should I therefore take the members of Christ and make them members of a prostitute? Never! (1 Cor 6:15)

Parallel to the way a believer's body became one body with a prostitute through sexual intercourse, Paul revealed to believers in Colossae that their bodies became one with the Lord's body by being united with him (through faith):

Do you not know that whoever is united with a prostitute becomes one body with her? For it is said, "The two shall be one flesh." But anyone united to the Lord becomes one spirit with him. (1 Cor 6:16–17)

Since believers were Jesus's spiritual body with him as its head, God dwelt in their bodies by the Holy Spirit: "Or do you not know that your body is a temple of the Holy Spirit within you, which you have from God, and that you are not your own?" (1 Cor 6:19). In this sense, we could say that the coming of the Holy Spirit upon Jesus's disciples in Jerusalem according to Acts 2 marked the incorporation of believers into the body of the risen Lord, because they started to be the dwelling place of God by virtue of being members of Christ's body.

In our understanding of a body, the head is its centre, coordinating and directing its actions to achieve certain ends, and ensuring the proper functioning of all its parts including its nourishment, growth, and repair. The head therefore is the leader of the body. In the body of Jesus, he is the head through whom believers are incorporated into his body. Accordingly, he coordinates and directs all the members of his body, as well as ensuring their nourishment and growth as his body. This was precisely the force of Paul's revelation to the Colossian believers. Believers were a part of Jesus's spiritual body only in relationship to him. Their faith in Jesus was the basis of their incorporation. Believers were therefore directly exhorted to grow up in Jesus, the head of the body they belong to, by growing in the truth, which is the knowledge of Jesus, the Son of God (Eph 4:13):

> But speaking the truth in love, we must grow up in every way into him who is the head, into Christ, from whom the whole body, joined up and knitted together by every ligament with which it is equipped, as each part is working properly, promotes the body's growth in building itself in love. (Eph 4:15–16)

For this reason, the Colossians who had ceased to have faith in Jesus had consequently ceased to be part of Jesus's body, no longer "nourished and held together" by the head. In line with Paul's revelation to believers in Corinth as we have discussed, they were no longer united with Jesus and thus one spirit (body) with him.

This belief (that believers are the dwelling place of God) is elsewhere expressed metaphorically in New Testament literature. We come across this metaphorical expression in the epistle to the Ephesians (Eph 2:20–22) and in Peter's first epistle (1 Pet 2:4–5). Believers are the stones which make up the dwelling of God. However, they are stones constructed into a dwelling for God only in relationship to Jesus because he is the "foundational cornerstone." They were God's holy temple in Jesus Christ because they were all set as stones into the building with reference to Jesus who was the cornerstone (*akrogōniaios*): "built upon the foundation laid by the apostles and prophets, and Christ Jesus himself as the foundation-stone (*akrogōniaiou*)" (Eph 2:20 NEB).

Due to little by way of literary or archaeological evidence the precise meaning of *akrogōniaios*, which literally means an "angle stone"[8] is debatable as witnessed in English translations of the Greek text – for example, "chief cornerstone" (NIV), cornerstone (NRSV), and (our preferred) "foundational stone" (NEB). Its significance is not lost because the context of its usage here points to its presence as integral to the construction of the building. In other words, a building cannot stand without the *akrogōniaios*. This is the reason why we have understood this particular stone to be the one upon which all the other stones have been set. In this sense, this particular stone is the foundation-stone. The revelation of this stone as "chosen (*eklekton*) and precious (*entimon*)" to God in the first epistle to Peter (1 Pet 2:4), is indicative of its function to secure

---

8. G. Abbott-Smith, *A Manual Greek Lexicon*, 18.

the integrity of the building that is God's house. The point is clear that believers' building up into a spiritual house of God (1 Pet 2:5) is based on Jesus, the living stone (1 Pet 2:4). What is implied in Ephesians 2:20 and Peter's first epistle is made explicit in Ephesians 2:21–22 where it is revealed in plain language that in Jesus Christ the house of God has been constructed:

> In him the whole building is bonded together and grows into a holy temple in the Lord. In him you too are being built with all the rest into a spiritual dwelling for God. (Eph 2:21–22 NEB)

In conclusion, we should note that in New Testament literature the fact that believers are the promised restored temple is exclusively clarified within the context of God's promises of restoration (in the second epistle of Paul to the Corinthians). This is a crucial observation, because in clarifying believers as God's temple within the context of God's restoration promises, Paul's revelation links this phenomenon directly to the story of the Bible in the Old Testament. As we discussed in chapter 5, it was against the background of the impending destruction of Jerusalem and the temple that God promised the people of Israel that he would restore Israel and the Davidic kingship. Concerning the details of the restoration, God promised in various ways that he would restore his dwelling with the people of Israel at their restoration and that of the Davidic kingship. In one specific instance, God promised Israel, through the prophet Ezekiel, that he would restore his dwelling and once again become their God: "My dwelling place shall be with them; and I will be their God, and they shall be my people" (Ezek 37:27). It was this promise which Paul had revealed to believers in Corinth that had now been fulfilled. According to God's past promise, he told them, they had become God's temple:

> For we are the temple of the living God; as *God said*,
> "I will make my dwelling among them and walk among them,
> and I will be their God,
> and they shall be my people". (2 Cor 6:16 ESV, emphasis added)

In other words, Paul's words revealed that the promise of God to restore the destroyed temple was in fact fulfilled in believers of the promised Davidic king. They were the restored temple of God according to God's promise, "as God said (*eipen ho Theos*)."

What we see, then, revealed in plain language, and metaphorically in the unfolding story of the Bible in the New Testament, is that the restored dwelling of God was initially the body of the promised Davidic king, Jesus. After his ascension, the restored dwelling of God evolved to include believing Jews and gentiles as part of the body of Christ. The dwelling of God was thus enlarged as the number of those who repented and believed the good news of the kingdom increased. By receiving the good news and believing in Jesus, men, women and children became part of the body of Christ and thus the dwelling of God. The dwelling of God would grow to accommodate others who believed in the gospel, and keep doing so in that way until its full restoration in the world.

This spiritual manner of the restoration of God's dwelling is in parallel with the restoration of God's kingdom. Jews and gentiles who believed entered God's kingdom with no geographical location or centre. They also became his non-brick and mortar dwelling. Since God's kingdom was being restored spiritually, so was his dwelling and vice versa. Such a scenario is anticipated in the inseparability of God's house from his throne which we discussed in our second chapter. Through believers, God's dwelling will continue to grow until it is overtaken by God's extraordinary act resulting in every inch of the world becoming his dwelling and a part of his kingdom. In the unfolding story of the Bible in the New Testament, this extraordinary act will take place when God brings down from heaven the new Jerusalem. To this phenomenon we turn now.

Restoration of God's Dwelling in the New Jerusalem

Although God's house was his residence, the temple was not the only place he dwelt. We have just alluded to Jerusalem as the city of God's dwelling. In our third chapter, we pointed out that because Jerusalem was the city where God's house was, it was also his dwelling. In YHWH's own words: "So you shall know that I, the LORD your God, dwell in Zion, my holy mountain" (Joel 3:17). In the words of a psalmist who mentioned Jerusalem as God's holy habitation (*miškān*):

> There is a river whose streams make glad the city of God,
> > the holy habitation of the Most High. (Ps 46:4; also Ps 135:21)

Consequently God's house (the temple, Mount Zion) was not the only place where he dwelt. The city (Zion) was also God's dwelling. Just as God had promised the people of Israel the restoration of his house, the temple, he had also promised the restoration of the city of his dwelling, Jerusalem.

Once rebuilt, Jerusalem would experience the abundance, peace and security prevailing in the land (Isa 33:20; 54:11–17), the blessings of abundant life, because YHWH would dwell there and the city would thereby become the centre of his kingdom. This is why, as we pointed out, the announcement to the Israelites that YHWH reigned was tied to his return to take up his abode in Jerusalem:

> How beautiful upon the mountains
> > are the feet of the messenger who announces peace,
> who brings good news,
> > who announces salvation,
> who says to Zion, "Your God reigns."
> Listen! Your sentinels lift up their voices,
> > together they sing for joy;
> for in plain sight they see
> > the return of the LORD to Zion. (Isa 52:7–8)

Jerusalem would be recognized as his throne (Jer 3:17) and a holy city (Joel 3:17). In Zion YHWH would judge and bring peace to the nations (Isa 2:3–4; also Isa 51:4–5).

The overall picture we have of Jerusalem's restoration is a city where YHWH would dwell and rule. As such it would experience the blessings of abundant life. After its destruction, Jerusalem was rebuilt but without the blessings of abundant life. It was not even under the reign of the promised Davidic king. Under these circumstances, God renewed his promises to restore it. Coming to the unfolding story of the Bible in the New Testament, Jesus did not reign from the earthly Jerusalem, but ruled instead spiritually at God's right hand. In line with this, God did not dwell in the city of Jerusalem but in the heavenly one. The promises of a rebuilt Jerusalem with the blessings of abundant life ensuing because it was the centre of God's kingdom were not, therefore, fulfilled in the rebuilt Jerusalem that was in Judea.

However, Jerusalem in Judea not being the restored city did not mean that God had yet to fulfil his promises and thereby implement his plans to restore the world to his dwelling and kingdom. According to New Testament literature, the restored city was, like the throne of the promised Davidic king, spiritual. Although believers on earth belonged to it, it was not located on earth, and its manifestation would occur simultaneously with the full restoration of God's dwelling in the world. To make sense of this revelation and thus the manner of Jerusalem's restoration, we must first understand the cosmology portrayed in the Old Testament and in particular with respect to the world above the physical land and sea.

We mentioned in passing in our sixth chapter that the Israelites had a tripartite cosmology. Indeed, we have in the Old Testament a tripartite spatial view of the world. We have *sheol* which was believed to be the world beneath the sea and dry land (the earth [*'ereṣ*]). It was essentially the underworld:

> For the wise the path of life leads upward,
>   in order to avoid Sheol below. (Prov 15:24; see also
> Isa 57:9; Amos 9:2)

For this reason, *sheol* was described in terms of depth (Deut 32:22; Job 11:8; Isa 7:11), or descent (Job 17:16; Isa 14:15; 57:9), or simply as "the Pit" (*bôr* or *šāhat* – Ps 16:10; 28:1; Ezek 26:20). It was the abode of the dead (Gen 37:35; 1 Kgs 2:6; Ps 6:5; Isa 5:14; 38:18), and referred to as a vast graveyard (Isa 14:20; Ezek 32:18–32; Prov 7:27). In some cases, *sheol* was referred to as death itself (Isa 38:18) and known as a place of darkness (Job 10:21–22; Lam 3:6). It also symbolized threats to life (2 Sam 22:6; Ps 116:3; Jonah 2:2–3).

Above the earth were the "heaven(s)" (*šāmayim*) – always in the dual form in Old Testament literature. Thus it was referred to as something above; "He calls to the heavens above" (Ps 50:4), or "high above the earth" (Ps 103:11). Even descriptions of things or activities relative to the heavens were in the language of ascent. God's love was described as higher than the heavens (Ps 108:4). One could also go up to the heavens (Deut 30:12; Ps 139:8; Prov 30:4). The heavens were also referred to as "high places" or "heights" (*mārôm*, Pss 68:18; 93:4), and were higher than the earth (Ps 103:11; Isa 55:9).

"The heavens" was also rendered in Old Testament literature as the "expanse" (*rāqîaʿ*) as is aptly captured in the synonymous parallelism of one psalmist:

> The heavens are telling the glory of God;
>   and the firmament (*rāqîaʿ*) proclaims his handiwork. (Ps 19:1)

šāmayim and *rāqîaʿ* were used interchangeably; what could be said of *rāqîaʿ* could apply to *šāmayim* and viceversa. The *šāmayim* was filled with what we see during the day and at night: clouds, sun, moon, and stars (Deut 4:19; Ps 8:3; Ezek 32:8; Joel 2:10):

> When I look at your heavens, the work of your fingers,
>   the moon and the stars that you have established. (Ps 8:3)

The heavens' occupants were also referred to as hosts (*ṣābā'*) (Deut 17:3; Jer 8:2). The wind too was part of the heavens (1 Kgs 18:45; Ps 78:26) and so was thunder (Ps 77:17). It is in the heavens that the birds of the air flew (Gen 1:20).

There is yet more to the world above the earth in the cosmology of the Old Testament. In some places in Old Testament literature, the heavens were viewed to have a *rāqîaʿ* which was a sort of solid plate-like hemispherical structure that enveloped the heavens, effectively becoming its ceiling. This perception is what accounts for the translation of *rāqîaʿ* as "the sky" or a "vault" and not as the "heavens" in English translations of the Bible (for example, Job 37:21; Ps 78:23). References to God creating the world imply that the heavens had some solid ceiling. So, for example, God spread the *rāqîaʿ* like a tent over the earth (Ps 104:2; Isa 44:24), or like a gauze (Isa 40:22), or like a molten mirror (Job 37:18). The *rāqîaʿ* could also be rolled back like a scroll (Isa 34:4). Moreover, as a solid hemispherical structure, God fixed the sun, moon and stars in the *rāqîaʿ*:

> And God said, "Let there be lights in the dome (*rāqîaʿ*) of the sky (*šāmayim*) to separate the day from the night; and let them be for signs and for seasons and for days and years, and let them be lights in the dome (*rāqîaʿ*) of the sky (*šāmayim*) to give light upon the earth. (Gen 1:14–19)

As a ceiling of the heavens, birds of the air could only fly under (across) the *rāqîaʿ* but not above or in it: "And God said '. . . let birds fly above the earth across the expanse (*rāqîaʿ*) of the heavens'" (Gen 1:20 ESV).

In the context of this understanding of *rāqîaʿ*, God dwelt above or on top of it. His glory – the physical manifestation of God's presence to human beings we talked about – therefore, was above the heavens and not within it:

> The LORD is high above all nations,
>   and his glory above the heavens. (Ps 113:4; see also
>   Ps 148:13)

YHWH could also be said to sit on the *rāqîaʿ* enveloping the earth:

> It is he who sits above the circle (*ḥûg*) of the earth. (Isa 40:22)

Elsewhere, YHWH was described as the one who walks on the circle of heaven (Job 22:14). We see this cosmological perception of God's dwelling above the *rāqîaʿ* vividly in the two visions of God captured in Exodus and in Ezekiel. In Ezekiel's vision, YHWH's glory was upon what looked like a throne above the crystal-like shining firmament (Ezek 1:22):

> And above the dome (*rāqîaʿ*) over their heads there was something like a throne, in appearance like sapphire; and seated above the likeness of a throne was something that seemed like a human form. Upwards from what appeared like the loins I saw something like gleaming amber, something that looked like fire enclosed all round . . . This was the appearance of the likeness of the glory of the LORD. (Ezek 1:26–28)

In Exodus, when Moses, Aaron, Nadab, Abihu, and the seventy elders of Israel went up the mountain, they are said to have had a vision of God where they saw his feet on top of a crystal-clear pavement:

> Then Moses and Aaron, Nadab and Abihu, and the seventy of the elders of Israel went up, and they saw the God of Israel. Under his feet there was something like a pavement of sapphire stone, like the very heavens for clearness. (Exod 24:9–10)

The description of the pavement echoes the *rāqîaʿ* above which YHWH dwelt. It seems the pavement was the *rāqîaʿ*, which separated them from YHWH when they beheld him up the mountain. In other words, they were not on the earth but in the heavens just below the *rāqîaʿ* where the God of Israel dwelt when they beheld him standing on it.

It is in the context of this cosmology of the heavens that we understand expressions such as God bending (*nāṭâ*) the heavens when he came down to the earth (2 Sam 22:10; Ps 18:9). This bending applies only if *rāqîaʿ* was a barrier that had to be bent for YHWH to pass through and come down. There were thus wishes for YHWH to bow the heavens and descend to the earth:

> Bow your heavens, O LORD, and come down. (Ps 144:5)

This applies as well to understanding the wish of the prophet in Isaiah that YHWH would tear (*qāraʿ*) the heaven and come down; "O that you would tear open the heavens and come down" (Isa 64:1). Without the *rāqîaʿ* as a thin solid cover, there would be nothing to tear apart were YHWH to come down.

From his dwelling in Heaven (we use capital "H" to distinguish it here and in what follows from the heavens generally) which was above the *rāqîaʿ* capped heavens, God was described as looking down upon the heavens and the earth (Pss 14:2; 113:6; Lam 3:50) or looking down from heaven (Deut 26:15; Isa 63:15; Ps 80:14). He could thunder from heaven (1 Sam 2:10; 2 Sam 22:14), hear from heaven (1 Kgs 8:30–39), send fire down from heaven (2 Kgs 1:10), and sit in heaven (Pss 2:4; 123:1; Isa 66:1). God could call Abraham from heaven (Gen 22:11, 15), speak from heaven (Exod 20:22; Deut 4:36; Ps 76:8), and the city's outcry would go up to him in heaven (1 Sam 5:12). In reaching out to God, people would spread out their hands towards heaven (1 Kgs 8:22), and their prayers would reach heaven (2 Chr 30:27) for that was where God was living (2 Chr 20:6; Job 16:19; Eccl 5:2; Ps 115:3).

Old Testament literature, then, locates the dwelling of God within this tripartite cosmology to be above the earth. God's was in Heaven, above the heavens whose ceiling was the *rāqîaʿ*, or simply in the heavens when the *rāqîaʿ*

was not mentioned or in view. However, as we mentioned in our sixth chapter, consciousness of the world above intensified in the Second Temple period leading to elaborate beliefs on non-material beings (some human-like and some not) inhabiting it.

This tripartite cosmology is evident in New Testament literature with respect to the world above the earth. We come across this cosmology in some events in the life of Jesus. When the angel of God, who appeared to the shepherds soon after Jesus's birth, finished giving them the message, there appeared many more praising God who was in the highest heaven: "Glory to God in the highest heaven" (Luke 2:14). Seemingly recalling the *rāqîaʿ*-capped heavens, John is said to have seen the heavens "being torn" (*skizomenous*) for the Spirit of God from God's dwelling in Heaven to pass through when he descended on Jesus: "And just as he was coming out of the water, he saw the heavens torn apart (*skizomenous*) and the Spirit descending like a dove on him (Mark 1:10; see also Matt 3:16; Luke 3:21). It is from heaven that God's voice was heard by the disciples (Mark 1:11). Furthermore, when Jesus prayed he looked up to heaven (Mark 7:34; John 17:1). During Jesus's triumphal entry into Jerusalem, the one whom the crowds prayed to (in the language of Psalm 118:25) was in Heaven: "Hosanna in the highest heaven (Mark 11:10; Matt 21:9). In the mentioned Psalm, "hosanna" meant "save us now." In the context of the triumphal entry, it was a prayer the crowd uttered in joyous anticipation of their salvation coming through God's *christos*: "save us now in the highest heaven." Rather than mentioning God directly, the crowd addressed him by referring to where he resided: in the highest heaven, in Heaven above the *rāqîaʿ*.

Furthermore, according to New Testament literature, Jesus ascended to Heaven (Luke 24:51; Acts 1:9–11; Mark 16:19) where he is seated there at God's right hand:

> He raised him up from the dead and seated him at his right hand in the heavenly places. (Eph 1:20)

> We have such a high priest, one who is seated at the right hand of the throne of the Majesty in the heaven. (Heb 8:1 RSV; see also Heb 1:3)

From Heaven Jesus will appear when he returns to the world: "For the Lord himself, with a cry of command, with the archangel's call and with the sound of God's trumpet, will descend from heaven" (1 Thess 4:16). We should note here that it is in Heaven, when the *rāqîaʿ* was opened, that Stephen is said to have seen Jesus standing at God's right hand: "Look . . . I see the heavens opened and the Son of Man standing at the right hand of God" (Acts 7:56; also Acts 10:11).

We also come across the tripartite cosmology in which God resides in Heaven in Jesus's teachings. Jesus referred to God as "my heavenly Father (Matt 15:13; 18:35), as "our Father in Heaven" (Matt 6:9), as "your Father who is in heaven" (Matt 6:1), as "your heavenly Father" (Matt 5:48; 6:26; Luke 11:13). He taught about laying up treasures in Heaven for there they could not be destroyed or stolen (Matt 6:19–20). It was in Heaven that God's will was done; the disciples needed to pray that the same would take place on the earth (Matt 6:10). Jesus also pointed to Heaven as God's dwelling, by virtue of having his throne (Matt 5:34), and according to Matthew's Gospel, Jesus referred to the kingdom of God as the kingdom of Heaven (Matt 13:24, 45).

Having established the cosmological background to the New Testament, we are now in a position to make sense of the spiritual restoration of Jerusalem we alluded to. The first revelation about restored Jerusalem which we examine comes within the context of Paul's exhortation to the Galatian believers not to aspire to be Jews. As we mentioned in our eighth chapter, Paul was unhappy with the gentile Galatian believers (Gal 1:6; 3:1–5) because they were being convinced by some believing Jews (Gal 6:12) to become Jews. One of the various ways Paul dissuaded them from Judaism was by letting them know by means of an allegory in Galatians 4:28 that those under the law were in slavery, while those who believed were free. The slavery of those under the law corresponded to the rebuilt Jerusalem in Judea, while the believing who were free belonged to the Jerusalem above:

> Now this is an allegory: these women are two covenants. One woman, in fact, is Hagar, from Mount Sinai, bearing children for slavery. Now Hagar is Mount Sinai in Arabia and corresponds to the present Jerusalem, for she is in slavery with her children. But the other woman corresponds to the Jerusalem above; she is free, and she is our mother. (Gal 4:24–25)

To have Jerusalem as one's mother was to say, following the LXX's rendering of Ps 87:5 (Ps 86:5 in LXX), that one was born in that city.[9] Since, as discussed in our eighth chapter, one way of being a citizen of a city was by filiation, Paul's reference to the city above as "our mother" was an indirect way of saying that believers belonged to the city above.

---

9. See Christl M. Maier, "Psalm 87 as a Reappraisal of the Zion Tradition and its Reception in Gal 4:26," *CBQ* 69.9 (2007).

In referring to the Jerusalem above as the city believers belonged to, Paul was revealing that the city in Judea was not the restored Jerusalem YHWH promised to return to dwell in with his people. To the contrary, he was revealing that the destroyed city had been restored at a different site (above), where God was dwelling with his people. Given the cosmology of the time, this site was, quite astonishingly, in Heaven, for it was the one above the earth. Our interpretation of "above" (*anō*) as meaning in Heaven is confirmed by Paul's linkage of the word precisely with Heaven above as the dwelling of God where Jesus was:

> Seek the things above (*ta anō*), where Christ is, seated at the right hand of God. Set your minds on things that are above, not on things on earth. (Col 3:1–2)

Paul then revealed that God did not restore the destroyed city of Jerusalem here on earth, as would have been expected, but had done so, extraordinarily, in Heaven where he dwells. It was to this Jerusalem that believers, as the new Israel, belonged, and not the one on earth.

The city of Jerusalem in heaven as the promised restored city is further clarified in Hebrews. The Hebrews' writer reveals to his audience of Jewish believers that they had not come to an earthly place, "to something that can be touched, a blazing fire and darkness, and gloom, and a tempest" (Heb 12:18). This is what took place at the foot of Mount Sinai, an earthly site, when their forefathers met YHWH (Exod 19:12–22). On the contrary, but in ways akin to the journeys the Israelites were making to rebuilt Jerusalem in Judea while on pilgrimage, the Jewish believers had come to Jerusalem that was in Heaven above: "But you have come to Mount Zion and to the city of the living God, the heavenly Jerusalem" (Heb 12:22). Within this perspective, believers were in some sense with God in Jerusalem (possibly in their experience of the blessings of abundant life), the heavenly city he had built as a restoration of the one which was destroyed when the Israelites broke the covenant. Believing Jews and gentiles belonged to the city (Gal 4:26), and their life was in it (Col 3:2–3). As citizens of the heavenly city (Phil 3:20), the state of affairs, concerns, and activities of the city were theirs.

However, the fact that believers were living on the earth below meant that they were not fully dwelling with God in the heavenly city, nor fully participating in it. In the unfolding story of the Bible in the New Testament, a complete dwelling with God in Jerusalem and a full participation in the state of affairs of the heavenly city would take place sometime in the future. In a sweeping vision, John saw the heavenly Jerusalem come down from heaven to the earth below. When that took place, the distinction between Heaven and the world was erased because the earth became Heaven, thus becoming entirely God's dwelling. At that point the restoration of the world as God's dwelling with human beings would be absolutely achieved. The whole world will then be full of God's glory (or his knowledge).

Given the inextricable link between God's dwelling and throne, the world will at that point also be fully restored to God's kingdom, experiencing absolutely the blessings of abundant life, the state of affairs in God's kingdom:

> And I saw the holy city, the new Jerusalem, coming down out of heaven from God, prepared as a bride adorned for her husband.
> And I heard a loud voice from the throne saying:
> "See, the home of God is among mortals.
> > He will dwell with them;
> they will be his peoples,
> > and God himself will be with them;
> he will wipe away every tear from their eyes.
> Death will be no more;
> > mourning and crying and pain will be no more.
> > (Rev 21:2–4; see also Rev 3:12)

10

Conclusion

Our whole-Bible study examining the narrative of Old and New Testament literature has been in two distinct but related parts. In the first part of our study, our reading of the story and its implications from Abraham onward was quite concrete and earthly. The story was within the geographical, socio-economic, and political set-up of Israel, and made perfect sense within it. We recapitulate the first part of our study below.

When Adam and Eve rebelled against God's rule, the world ceased to be God's dwelling with humans and a part of his kingdom. In calling Abraham and giving him the blessings-to-all-nations promise, YHWH intended to restore his dwelling and kingdom by beginning first with Israel, in the promised land. By way of a covenant with YHWH, the Israelites became his *sᵉgullâ* and royal priests. As such, Israel would be God's kingdom under the rule of the Davidic kings whom God had chosen to rule on his behalf. With his house in Jerusalem, YHWH would also dwell with the people of Israel on the land. Israel would be God's kingdom and the nation he dwelt with on condition that the Israelites obeyed God, and the Davidic kings ruled in justice.

Obedience by the Israelites would result in their experience of the blessings of abundant life in the promised land, because Israel would have become God's kingdom indeed, and Jerusalem the centre of his dwelling. The blessings of abundant life in the land would attract nations to Zion where YHWH dwelt. By going to Zion, the nations would know YHWH and submit to his laws. They would thereby come under God's kingdom which would then spread to their lands and kingdoms. The just rule of the Davidic kings would also result in their defeating God's enemies, subjugating rebellious nations, and incorporating them into Israel, the kingdom of God. By means of obedience and just ruling, the kingdom of God in Israel would spread to its neighbours, and ultimately to the ends of the world. God's glory would spread in tandem with his kingdom and thus also ultimately fill the whole world, because God would dwell with all nations that would have come under his kingdom.

Unfortunately, due to Israel's disobedience and failure of the Davidic kings to rule in justice and righteousness, Israel did not become God's kingdom, nor did God's glory abide in the land. After departing from his dwelling amongst them in Jerusalem, God had Jerusalem and the temple destroyed, and Israel's population decimated except for a remnant who went into slavery in exile. The Israelites also ceased to occupy the land, and the Davidic kingship was dethroned.

Due to God's promises to Abraham, God offered the Israelites and the Davidic kingship a second chance to fulfil their destiny. He promised the restoration of Israel and the Davidic kingship in the land, and his return to dwell with them in Zion. God's promises of restoration indicated that there would be no failure the second time round. Consequently, restored Israel would be God's kingdom experiencing the blessings of abundant life under a certain Davidic king whom God had promised. Through Israel, then, God's kingdom would be advanced to the rest of the nations. Also, the promised Davidic king would rule in justice and defeat all of God's enemies, thereby advancing God's kingdom to the rest of the world.

In the second part of our study, the continuation of the story in the fulfilment of God's promises of the restoration was spiritual. Our reading was that Israel and the Davidic kingship (together with elements associated with both) were restored in a non-material manner: in a manner not readily relatable to ordinary human life, and to Israel's own concrete realities. In consequence, although Israel, the Davidic kingship, land, Jerusalem, and the temple were the subjects of restoration, their restoration transcended their earthly nature, resulting in their extraordinary transformation. We recapitulate below this reading of the second part of the narrative of the Bible.

The restoration of the Davidic kingship was through Jesus, the promised Davidic king; but instead of reigning from Jerusalem in Judea, as would be expected of a Davidic king, he died, was raised from the dead, and ascended to Heaven to sit at God's right hand and rule from there. In addition, the promised Davidic king was no ordinary descendant of David. Although he was God's son as an enthroned Davidic king, he was truly God's Son in fact. His kingship would not therefore be succeeded by an heir of David, but he would sit on the throne until he fully restored God's kingdom. Moreover, in line with his throne in Heaven, God's kingdom under his reign was not located territorially in Israel where it would spread to the rest of the world. Rather, the kingdom of God became a spiritual reality ("not of this world") divorced thus from any particular territory; but which people, regardless of their physical location, could enter through faith and repentance and receive the blessings of abundant life. The enemies of God and his people whom Jesus defeated to advance God's kingdom were Satan and demons, and not hostile nations. When he finishes defeating all of God's enemies, the kingdom of God will be fully restored in the world.

With respect to the restoration of Israel, starting with the twelve disciples, Israel was not restored simply by the regathering of the twelve tribes on the land under the promised Davidic king. Rather, Israel was restored spiritually, through believing Jews and gentiles, persons who had submitted to the rule of the promised Davidic king. The new Israel was not divorced from Abraham and was therefore a party to the promise of blessings-to-all-nations which God gave him. Just as in historical Israel, believing Jews and gentiles had Abraham as their ancestor on account of sharing his believing attributes. As Abraham's offspring, this new Israel, instead of historical Israel, became God's *sᵉgūllâ* and royal priesthood thus bringing the nations to God's kingdom. They had no particular place to fulfil their vocation but could carry it out wherever they were by proclaiming the gospel through which others, upon belief and repentance, could enter God's kingdom. Blessings to all nations was thus still through Abraham and his descendants and would continue to be so in this way until God's kingdom was fully restored in the world.

The restoration of God's dwelling with his people took place, but not through brick and mortar, that is, not through the rebuilt temple in Jerusalem, but spiritually. Through the resurrected Lord, Jesus Christ, believers together with him were the temple of God. God now dwelt in people who were under the rule of his *christos*. Likewise, the restoration of God's dwelling with his people in Jerusalem was heavenly. The city was rebuilt by God, but in Heaven above. It was in the new Jerusalem that, in some sense, God's people were dwelling with him. This status quo will prevail until God brings the new Jerusalem into the world to dwell fully with his people. When this happens, the whole world will have become God's dwelling once again: every inch of it will be filled with God's glory.

Our two-part reading of the whole Bible thus strongly linked the Old Testament to the New Testament, and vice versa. The story of the Bible we read in the Old Testament revolved around Abraham and his descendants, his promised monarchy, the promised land, Jerusalem, and the temple, with the goal of restoring God's dwelling and kingdom in the world. The story of the Bible in the New Testament continued to revolve around the same people and kingship, land, city and temple, albeit spiritually, still with the goal of restoring God's dwelling and kingdom in the world. The story in earthly terms and settings in the Old Testament, and its continuation in spiritual terms and settings in the New Testament, is what anchors the typological relationship we mentioned in our sixth chapter between the two parts of the story. The Davidic kingship, Israel, the land, Jerusalem, and the temple in the Old Testament prefigure respectively Jesus, the new Israel, the world, new Jerusalem, and believers as God's living temple in the New Testament. Although typology is based primarily in similarities between the type and antitype, the New Testament antitypes had some contrasts and discontinuations from their preceding Old Testament types as we saw in our comprehensive reading of the story of the Bible.

Our concluding comments on our two-parts reading of the story of the Bible bring us to some closing reflections. The nature of the New Testament as a continuation of the first part of the story of the Bible, demonstrates that the faith, experiences, and hope of the first Christians were deeply embedded in the concrete realities and experiences of historical Israel and expressed in Israel-centric terms. Their Lord Jesus was Israel's Davidic king, the son of David; their self-identity was Israel (the new Israel); the temple was themselves in Christ; and Jerusalem was their city – the heavenly Jerusalem whose entry into the world they awaited.

The rooting of faith, experiences, and hopes in the realities and experiences of historical Israel cannot be a preserve of the first Christians. It is a necessity for all Christians because, as was the case with the first Christians, the Old Testament writings and the light they shined on Jesus should equally inform their faith and experiences, and the understanding of both. Moreover, taking the New Testament writings seriously as scriptures (as Christians ought to) precipitates this rooting of faith in the realities of historical Israel because the New Testament, on nearly every page, takes its readers to the Old Testament. It is actual knowledge of the content of the Old Testament itself, of the Old Testament leading into the New Testament, and of the New Testament content harking back to the Old, that can foster the rooting of Christian faith and experiences in the realities of historical Israel. As such, biblical-theological studies are of fundamental importance in the study of the Bible. On these terms, biblical theologians are critical in leading the way because they can open up the content of the whole Bible to God's flock and help them make sense of their faith and experiences in its light as God's special revelation. For this reason, we cannot overemphasize the priority that should be given to forming those training for pastoral ministry into biblical theologians. We can only hope that this biblical-theological study and others like it will be put to use towards that end.

Bibliography

Abbott-Smith, G. *A Manual Greek Lexicon of the New Testament*. 3rd Edition. Edinburgh: T&T Clark, 2001.

Allison, Dale C. and W. D. Davies. *A Critical and Exegetical Commentary on the Gospel according to Saint Matthew*. 3 Vols. ICC. Edinburgh: T&T Clark, 1997.

Altman, Amnon. "The Role of the 'Historical Prologue' in the Hittite Vassal Treaties: An Early Experiment in Securing Treaty Compliance." *J. Hist. Int. Law* 6.1 (2004): 43–63.

Angel, Hayyim, "The Eternal Davidic Covenant in II Samuel Chapter 7 and its Later Manifestations in the Bible." *JBQ* 44.2 (2016): 83–90.

Badcock, F. J. "The Feast of Tabernacles." *JTS* 24.94 (1923): 169–174.

Bahrani, Zainab. *The Graven Image: Representation in Babylonia and Assyria*. Philadelphia: University of Pennsylvania, 2003.

Beale, G. K and Benjamin L. Gladd. *Hidden But Now Revealed: A Biblical Theology of Mystery*. London: SPCK, 2014.

Beale, G. K. and Mitchell Kim. *God Dwells Among Us: Expanding Eden to the End of the Earth*. Nottingham: Inter-Varsity Press, 2014.

Beentjes, Pancratius C. "'Holy People': The Biblical Evidence," in *A Holy People: Jewish and Christian Perspectives on Religious Communal Identity*. Edited by M. Poorthius and J. Schwartz. Leiden: Brill, 2006.

Bennema, Cornelis. "The Sword of the Messiah and the Concept of Liberation in the Fourth Gospel." *Bib* 86.1 (2005): 35–58.

Blomberg, Craig L. *Christians in an Age of Wealth: A Biblical Theology of Stewardship*. Biblical Theology for Life. Grand Rapids: Zondervan, 2013.

Boehm, Omri. "Child Sacrifice, Ethical Responsibility and the Existence of the People of Israel." *VT* 54.2 (2004): 145–56.

Brooks, Beatrice A. "Fertility Cult Functionaries in the Old Testament." *JBL* 60.3 (1941): 227–53.

Bruce, F. F. *Israel and the Nations: The History of Israel from the Exodus to the Fall of the Second Temple*. Revised by David Payne. Downers Grove: InterVarsity Press 1983.

Buch, Joshua. "The Biblical Number 12 and the Formation of the Ancient Nation of Israel." *JBQ* 22.1 (1999): 49–57.

Clement, Ronald E. *Isaiah 1–39*. NCB. Grand Rapids: Eerdmans, 1981.

Clifford, Richard, J., S.J. "Creation Ex Nihilo in the Old Testament/Hebrew Bible." Pages 55–76 in *Creation "ex nihilo": Origin, Developments, Contemporary Challenges*, edited by Gary A. Anderson and Markus Bockmuehl. Notre Dame: University of Notre Dame Press, 2017.

———. *The Cosmic Mountain in Canaan and the Old Testament*. Cambridge: Harvard University Press, 1972.

Cohn, Robert L. "The Mountains and Mount Zion." *Judaism* 26 (1977): 97–115.

Collins, John J. *The Apocalyptic Imagination: An Introduction to Jewish Apocalyptic Literature*. 2nd ed. Grand Rapids: Eerdmans, 1998.

Connery, Christopher. "There Was No More Sea: The Supersession of the Ocean, from the Bible to Cyberspace." *J. Hist. Geogr.* 32.3 (2006): 494–511.

Cuchet, Sebillote and Lillian Doherty. "Female Citizens Reconfiguring the Political." *Clio. Women, Gender, History*. no. 43 (2016): 186–216.

Dempster, Stephen G. *Dominion and Dynasty: A Theology of the Hebrew Bible*. NSBT. Downers Grove: InterVarsity Press 2003.

Denio, F. B. "The Kingdom of God in the Old Testament." *The Old Testament Student* 6.1 (1886): 71–76.

De Vaux, Roland. *Ancient Israel: Its Life and Institutions*. Translated by John McHigh. London: Darton, Longman & Todd, 1961.

Dickson, John P. and Brian S. Rosner. "Humility as a Social Virtue in the Hebrew Bible." *VT* 54.4 (2004): 459–79.

Dunn, James D. G. *New Testament Theology: An Introduction*. Library of Biblical Theology, Nashville: Abingdon Press, 2009.

Durham, John I. *Exodus*. WBC 3. Nashville: Thomas Nelson, 1987.

Duvall, J. Scott and G. Marvin Pate, J. Scott Duvall et al. *The Story of Israel: A Biblical Theology*. Downers Grove: InterVarsity Press 2004.

Eldredge, Laurence and John Sandys-Wunsch. "J. B. Gabler and the Distinction Between Biblical and Dogmatic Theology: Translation, Commentary, and the Discussion of His Originality." *SJT* 33 (1980): 133–58.

Eliade, Mircea. *Patterns in Comparative Religion*. Cleveland: Meridan, 1958.

Feinberg, C. L. "Scribes." *New Bible Dictionary*. Edited by J. D. Douglas. 2nd ed. Leicester: Inter-Varsity Press, 1982; Repr. 1990: 1079.

Fletcher-Louis, Crispin H. T. "God's Image, His Cosmic Temple and the High Priest." Pages 81–99 in *Heaven on Earth: The Temple in Biblical Theology*, edited by T. Desmond Alexander and Simon Gathercole. Carlisle: Paternoster, 2004.

Forsythe, Neil. *The Old Enemy: Satan and the Combat Myth* (Princeton: Princeton University Press, 1987).

Frey-Athens, Henrike. "Concept of 'Demons' in Ancient Israel." *Die Welt des Orients* 38 (2008): 38–52.

Gerstenberger, E. "בעת." In *Theological Lexicon of the Old Testament*, edited by E. Jenni and C. Westermann. Vol. 3. Translated by M. E. Biddle. Peabody: Hendrickson, 2004.

Gieschen, Charles A. *Angelomorphic Christology: Antecedents and Early Evidence*. Reprint Edition. Library of Early Christology. Waco: Baylor University Press, 2017.

Gilmore, David D. *Monsters: Evil Beings, Mystical Beasts, and All Manner of Imaginary Terrors*. Philadelphia: University of Pennsylvania Press, 2003.

Goldingay, John. *Old Testament Theology: Israel's Gospel*. Vol. 1. Downers Grove: InterVarsity Press 2003.

———. *Old Testament Theology: Israel's Faith*. Vol. 2. Downers Grove: InterVarsity Press 2006.

———. *Old Testament Theology: Israel's Life*. Vol. 3. Downers Grove: InterVarsity Press 2009.

Good, Robert M. "The Just War in Israel." *JBL* 104.3 (1985): 385–400.

Goodblat, David. "From Judeans to Israel: Names of Jewish States in Antiquity." *JSJ* 29.1 (1998): 1–36.

Graesser, Carl F. "Standing Stones in Ancient Palestine." *BA* 35.2 (1972): 33–63.

Gruen, Erich S. *The Construct of Identity in Hellenistic Judaism: Essays on Jewish History and Literature*. Berlin: De Guyter, 2016.

———. "Did Ancient Identity Depend on Ethnicity? A Preliminary Probe." *Phoenix* 67.1 (2013): 1–22.

Hagner, Donald A. *Matthew 1–13*. WBC. Vol. 33A. Dallas: Word Publishers, 1993.

Hahn, Scott W. *Kinship By Covenant: A Canonical Fulfilmemt of God's Saving Promises*. The Anchor Yale Bible Reference Library. Yale: Yale University Press, 2019.

Hamilton, Victor P. *The Book of Genesis Chap. 1–17*. NICOT. Grand Rapids: Eerdmans, 1990.

———. *Exodus: An Exegetical Commentary*. Grand Rapids: Baker Academics, 2011.

Haran, M. "Priests and Priesthood" in *Encyclopedia of Judaism*, edited by Alan J. Avery-Peck, Jacob Neusner, and William S. Green. Leiden: Brill Academic, 1999.

Havrelock, Rachel Havrelock. "The Two Maps of Israel's Land." *JBL* 126.4 (2007): 656–58.

Hays, J. Daniel. *From Every People and Nation: A Biblical Theology of Race*. NSBT. Downers Grove, IL: InterVarsity Press 2003.

Herring, Stephen. *Divine Substitution: Humanity as the Manifestation of Deity in the Hebrew Bible and the Ancient Near East*. FRLANT 247. Gottingen: Vandenhoeck & Ruprecht, 2013.

Hurtado, Larry. *God in the New Testament*. Library of Biblical Theology. Nashville: Abingdon Press, 2010.

Irwin, Brian P. "Not Just Any King: Abimelech, the Northern Monarchy, and the Final Form of Judges." *JBL* 131.3 (2012): 443–54.

Iverson, Kelly R. "Jews, Gentiles, and the Kingdom of God: The Parable of the Wicked Tenants in Narrative Perspective (Mark 12:1–12)." *BibInt* 20.3 (2012): 305–35.

Janzen, Waldemar. "War in the Old Testament." *MQR* 46.2 (1972): 155–66.

Kaminsky, Joel S. *Yet I loved Jacob: Reclaiming the Biblical Concept of Election*. Nashville: Abingdon Press, 2007.

Kleinig, John. "Mercy and Justice." *PPR* 44.170 (1969): 341–42.

Köstenberger, Andreas J. *A Theology of John's Gospel and Letters: The Word of Christ, the Son of God*. Grand Rapids: Zondervan, 2015.

Köstenberger, Andreas J. with T. Desmond Alexander, *Salvation to the Ends of the Earth: A Biblical Theology of Mission*. 2nd ed. Downers Grove: InterVarsity Press 2020.

Lam, Joseph. *Patterns of Sin in the Hebrew Bible: Metaphor, Culture, and the Making of a Religious Concept*. Oxford: Oxford University Press, 2016.

Leithart, Peter J. "Attendants of Yahweh's House: Priesthood in the Old Testament." *JSOT* 85 (1999): 3–24.

Levenson, Jon D. "Covenant and Commandment." *Tradition* 21.1 (1983): 42–51.

———. *The Death and Resurrection of the Beloved Son: The Transformation of Child Sacrifice in Judaism and Christianity*. Yale: Yale University Press, 1993.

Lewis, Gilbert. "A Lesson from Leviticus: Leprosy." *Man* 22.4 (1987): 593–612.

Liddel, Henry G. and Robert Scott. *A Greek-English Lexicon*. Rev. and aug. by H. S. Jones with R. McKenzie. Oxford: Oxford University Press, 1996.

Lindsay, Dennis R. "What is Truth? Ἀλήθεια in the Gospel of John." *RQ* 35.3 (1993): 129–45.

Maier, Christl M. "Psalm 87 as a Reappraisal of the Zion Tradition and its Reception in Gal 4:26." *CBQ* 69.9 (2007): 473–86.

Malbon, Elizabeth Struthers. "Galilee and Jerusalem: History and Literature in Marcan Interpretation." *CBQ* 44.2 (1982): 242–55.

Marcus, Joel. "Rivers of Living Water from Jesus's Belly (John 7:38)." *JBL* 117.2 (1998): 328–30.

Martin, Dale Basil. "When Did Angels Become Demons?" *JBL* 129:4 (2010): 657–77.

Mauchline, John. "Implicit Signs of a Persistent Belief in the Davidic Empire." *VT* 20.3 (1970): 287–303.

Mays, James Luther. "The Self in the Psalms and the Image of God." Pages 27–43 in *God and Human Dignity*, edited by R. Kendall Soulen and Linda Woodhead. Grand Rapids: Eerdmans, 2006. McCarter, P. Kyle. "The River Ordeal in Israelite Literature." *HTR* 66.4 (1973): 403–12.

McCarthy, Dennis J. *Treaty and Covenant*. Translated into English by E. A. Speizer. Rome: Pontifical Biblical Institute, 1963.

McConville, J. Gordon. *Being Human in God's World*. Grand Rapids: Baker Academic, 2016.

McKelvey, Michael G. "1–2 Samuel." Pages 203 to 222 in *A Biblical-Theological Introduction to the Old Testament: The Gospel Promised*, edited by Miles V. Van Pelt. Wheaton : Crossway, 2016.

Mendenhall, George E. "Law and Covenant in Israel and the Ancient Near East." *BA* 17.3 (1954): 49–76.

———. *Law and Covenant in Israel and the Ancient Near East*. Pittsburg: Biblical Colloquium, 1955.

Middleton, J. Richard. *Liberating Image: The Imago Dei in Gen 1*. Grand Rapids: Bazos Press, 2005.

Newberger, Elana. "Asherah: The Israelite Goddess and the Cultic Object." *J. Theta Alpha Kappa* 29.1 (2005): 48–56.

Nyende, Peter. "YHWH, his Son, and his Spirit: A Biblical Theology of God in Outline." *AJET* 39.1 (2020): 1–20.

Olyan, Saul M. *A Thousand Thousand Served Him: Exegesis and the Naming of Angels in Ancient Judaism*. TSAJ, no. 36. Tubingen: Mohr Siebeck, 1993.

Oudtshoorn, André. "Where Have All the Demons Gone?: The Role and Place of the Devil in the Gospel of John." *Neot* 51.1 (2017):6 5–82.

Reddit, Paul L. "Daniel 9: Its Structure and Meaning." *CBQ* 62:2 (2000): 246–49.

Reeves, John C. "The Feast of the First Fruits of Wine and the Ancient Canaanite Calendar." *VT* 42:3 (1992): 350–61.

Renz, J. "שׁלשׁ," *Theologisches Wörterbuch zum Alten Testament*. Vol. 8. Edited by G. J. Botterweck and H. Ringgeren, Stuttgart:Kohlhammer, 1973.

Robertson, O. Palmer. *The Christ of the Covenant*. Phillipsburg: P&R Publishing, 1980.

Ross, Allen P. *Recalling the Hope of Glory: Biblical Worship From the Garden to the New Creation*. Grand Rapids: Kregel Academic and Professional, 2006.

Routledge, Robin. *Old Testament Theology: A Thematic Approach*. Nottingham: Apollos, 2008.

Scholer, J. M. *Proleptic Priests: Priesthood in the Epistle to the Hebrews*. JSNTSup 49. Sheffield: JSOT Press, 1991.

Schreiner, Thomas R. *The King in His Beauty: A Biblical Theology of the Old and New Testament*. Grand Rapids: Baker Academic, 2013.

Shanks, Hershel, ed. *Ancient Israel: From Abraham to the Roman Destruction of the Temple*. 3rd ed. Washington: Biblical Archaeological Society, 2011.

Snodgrass, Klyne R. "Recent Research on the Parable of the Wicked Tenants: An Assessment." *BBR* 8 (1998): 187–216.

Sommer, Benjamin D. "Did Prophecy Cease? Evaluating a Reevaluation." *JBL* 115.1 (1996): 31–47.

Stanley, Christopher D. "'Neither Jew nor Greek': Ethnic Conflict in Graeco-Roman Society." *JSNT* 19.64 (1997): 101–24.

Steiner, Richard C. "Four Inner-Biblical Interpretations of Genesis 49:10: On the lexical and Syncatic Ambiguities of רע as Reflected in the Prophecies of Nathan, Ahijah, Ezekiel, and Zechariah." *JBL* 132.1 (2013): 33–60.

Stokes, Ryan E. "Satan, YHWH's Executioner." *JBL* 133.2 (2014): 251–70.

Taggar-Cohen, Ada. "Biblical Covenant and Hittite *ishiul* reexamined." *VT* 61 (2011): 461–88.

Thompson, J. A. "Israel's 'haters.'" *VT* 29.2 (1979): 200–205.

Vlassopoulos, Kostas. "Ethnicity and Greek History: Reexamining our Assumptions." *BICS* 58.2 (2015): 1–13.

Wacholder, Ben Zion. "Chronomessianism: The Timing of Messianic Movements and the Calendar of Sabbatical Cycles." *HUCA* 46 (1975): 204–209.

Walton, John H. *Genesis*. The NIV Application Commentary. Grand Rapids: Zondervan, 2001.

Watts, John D. W. *Isaiah 1–33*. WBC. Vol. 24. Waco: Word Books, 1985.

Way, Kenneth C. "Donkey Domain: Zechariah 9:9 and Lexical Semantics." *JBL* 129.1 (2010): 105–14.
Weinfeld, M. "The Covenant of Grant in the Old Testament and in the Ancient Near East." *JAOS* 90.2 (1970): 184–203.
Wenham, Gordon. *Genesis 1–15*. WBC. Nashville: Nelson, 1987.
Williams, Michael. *Far as the Curse is Found: The Covenant Story of Redemption*. Phillipsburg: P&R Publishing, 2005.

Subject Index

A

Abraham 7–8, 32, 34, 42, 55, 61, 74, 94, 101, 117, 202–203, 207–208, 217, 237, 243
  blessing-to-all-nations, promise to 32–35, 37, 58, 63, 97, 128, 137, 199, 214, 216, 243, 245
  God's promises to 9, 32–35, 37, 44, 50, 61, 117, 197, 228, 244
  promise of kings to 63, 66-70, 72-73, 79, 95, 97
  offspring of 33–34, 42, 44–45, 52, 97, 107, 114, 127, 135, 137, 187, 198–199, 201, 208, 211, 213–214, 216, 245

B

biblical theology 1, 3–4
  approach to 5
  discipline of 1–2
  need for 3–4
blessings 6, 28, 40, 47–48, 61, 67, 71, 110–111, 127–130, 132, 137, 139, 168, 170, 173, 180, 194, 197–200, 206–207, 211, 213, 219
  of abundant life 8–10, 27, 29, 40–41, 43–44, 51, 60–61, 63, 89, 92, 95, 97, 107, 110–111, 114, 120, 127–132, 135, 137–140, 142, 145–146, 151, 161, 166–171, 180, 194, 196–198, 211–212, 217, 219–221, 233–234, 240–241, 243–245
  of abundant life attracting nations to YHWH and his dwelling in Zion 33, 43, 107, 114, 127, 137, 145
  of abundant life in the land 49
  to-all-nations 128, 130–131, 199, 243, 245

C

cosmology 55, 234, 237–238, 240
  as tripartite in the Old and New Testament 234–235, 237–239
  with dual emphasis in the Second Temple period 147
covenant
  ark of the 18, 55, 193
  between God and David 70–71, 89–90, 94, 203
  between God and Israel 36, 41, 45–48, 51–52, 63–64, 75, 83, 95, 104, 114, 121, 144, 203, 243
  breaking/keeping/rejection of 47, 49, 65, 103–104, 111, 120, 135, 240
  new 9–10, 120–122, 125, 127
  Sinai 45–46, 48, 203
  with David 115

D

Davidic king
  and justice 173
  God's servant 172
Davidic kings
  and justice 80–83, 85–87, 172–173, 243
  as God's anointed 8, 80, 97, 105, 115
  as God's servants 131
  as priest-kings 93–95, 105, 174
  as warrior-kings 87, 89–90, 92, 95, 145, 153, 243
  as YHWH's firstborns 78–79, 94
  as YHWH's sons 77
  God's servants 76
  idolatry committed by 102, 106
  universal reign of 79, 91
Davidic kingship 32, 79, 81, 135, 145, 150, 188
  and justice 82

a new David and restoration of 9,
  124, 131, 133, 159
 dethronement of 152, 244
 restoration of 9, 82, 91, 124, 136,
  145, 151–155, 157–160, 165,
  172, 177–178, 187, 222, 232, 244
 universal reign of 143, 151

G
God's dwelling 11, 19, 21
 above the firmament (*raqia*) 236-7
 creation 15–16
 creation intended to be 14
 Eden 14–15, 53
 heavenly nature 141–147, 149
 heavenly restoration 150
 in believers 229, 233
 in Heaven 238–240
 in Jesus 10, 229, 232
 inseparability of God's kingdom with
  17
 in temple/Mount Zion 53
 in the new Jerusalem 245
 in the world 234
 Mount Sinai 54
 Mount Zion 56, 60, 128, 221, 233
 restoration (enlargement/expansion
  of) 9
 restoration of 7–8, 32, 45, 61, 70, 95,
  219, 233, 245
 restored in believers 11, 145,
  232–233
 restored in heavenly Jerusalem/
  Jerusalem above/new Jerusalem
  9, 21
 the land 43, 56–58, 63
 the world 16–17, 219, 241, 245
 Zion 233
God's glory 54
 earth full of 16, 241, 243, 245
 filled the temple 16
 seen in Jesus 223, 228
God's kingdom
 creation intended to be a part of 21

restoration of 43, 45, 73, 135, 179,
  198–199, 214, 233
 spiritual restoration of 178

H
human beings 7, 9, 11, 13–15, 19,
  21–22, 24
 as God's representatives 24, 26, 28
 created in God's image 22–25
 rebelled against God's rule 26, 28, 31
 ruling over creation 22–25

I
idolatry 65, 98, 100, 102–104, 107
 abomination 105, 108
 child sacrifice 101
 consulting mediums 98, 123
 forsaking God 103–104, 106
 on high hills and under green trees
  102
Israel 38
 a new 209–211, 213–214, 216–217,
  219, 229, 240, 245–246
 as a holy people 37
 as a royal priesthood 36–39, 50, 127,
  137, 197, 210
 as a son of God 45, 49–52
 as God's kingdom 9, 76, 78, 80, 92,
  95, 97, 106, 115, 127, 138, 161
 as God's special possession (*sᵉgūllâ*)
  36, 38, 51
 historical 202–204, 209–211, 213,
  217, 245–246
 people of 7, 10
 punishment of 29, 143
 restoration of 7, 9–10, 202
 vocation of 35, 37, 39, 41, 44–46,
  51–52, 104, 201, 214

J
Jesus
 as the promised Davidic king 157–
  160, 163, 167, 169, 172–174,
  177–178, 181–182, 190, 194,
  197, 213, 220, 222, 232, 244

God's anointed 155–156
son of David 152, 173, 246
Son of God 215, 231
John the Baptist
as the promised Elijah 188
prepared the Israelites for their
restoration 197
justice
and righteousness 8, 81, 83, 86, 126,
244
as social justice 84–85

S
spiritual
enemies of God 93, 146, 161

T
typology 7, 149–150, 246

Scripture Index

OLD TESTAMENT

Genesis
1:1 136
1:2 19
1:14–19 236
1:20 235–236
1:26 23
1:26–27 22
1:26–28 23
1:27–28 25
1:28 24
1:31 29
2:2 15
2:4–24 13
2:7 122
2:9 .... 20–21, 27, 52
2:10–14 21
2:11–12 53
2:12 20
2:15–17 .... 24, 53
2:17 .... 24, 28
3:5 28
3:8 .... 13–14, 26
3:17–19 27
3:18 27
3:19 27
3:22 26
3:23 27
3:23–24 26
3:24 .... 15, 53
4 191
4:8–16 29
4:23–24 29
5:3 207
5:4–31 29
6:3 122
6:5 29
6:8 30

6:11 29
6:12 29
8:1 122
9:1 30
9:2 30
9:3–5 30
9:3–6 30
9:6 30
9:7 30
9:25 31
11:4 31
11:6 32
11:26 32
12:1–3 32
12:10–20 34
13 34
13:10 15
14:17–20 94
15:18–19 33
16:13 26
17:4–6 32
17:7 74
17:13 74
17:15–16 33
20:1–18 34
21:33 74
22:1–14 101
22:2 101
22:9–14 55
22:11 237
22:15 237
22:18 34
25:19 34
25:21–23 34
25:23 50
26 34
26:4 34

28:12–17 228
28:20–22 100
32:28 34
35:13–14 100
37:35 235
37–46 34
49 34
49:3 50
49:10 .... 67, 72, 79

Exodus
1:1–7 35
2:23–25 35
3:1 54
3:1–12 54
3:7–9 88
4:22 49
8:19 162
13:2 51
15:3 87
15:4–10 88
15:5 88
15:10 88
15:17 .... 43, 57
15:18 74
19 35
19:4 49
19:4–5 .... 36, 39, 210
19:5 .... 45, 47, 51, 210
19:5–6 210
19:6 210
19:7–8 47
19:12–22 240
19:16–25 54
19:24 54
20:1–5 103
20:1–17 41

20:1–23:33 54	31:1–3 123	24:5–9 37
20:5 .... 104, 223	32:1–9 41	25 41
20:12 139	33:18 54	25:1–4 143
20:22 237	34:5 54	25:4 16
20–23 48	35:19 37	25:8–55 .... 85, 109
21:1–9 41	39:1–31 94	26:1 223
21:12–17 41	39:14 192	26:3–13 .... 29, 60, 120
21:15 139	39:41 37	26:11–12 14
21:17 139	40:34 54	26:11–12 .... 57, 61
21:18–32 41	40:36–37 55	26:14–39 .... 29, 42, 113
21:33–36 41		27 41
22:1–15 41	**Leviticus**	
22:16–17 41	1:1–6:7 41	**Numbers**
22:18–20 41	1:1–7:19 58	1:4 192
22:21–24 .... 85, 109	1–7 38	1:4–16 192
22:28–29 51	6:8–7:37 41	1:44 192–193
23:9–11 .... 85, 109	8:8 38	1:51 93
23:10–12 41	10:11 38	1:53 .... 14, 53
23:14–17 41	10:12–20 41	3:6–8 94
24:1–3 54	11 41	3:8 14
24:3 48	12 41	3:12–13 51
24:4 192	13:1–40 168	3:23 53
24:7 47	13–14 41	3:29 53
24:7–8 48	13:45–46 168	3:35 53
24:8 48	13:47–59 168	4:23–26 14
24:9–10 237	14:1–32 169	6:16–17 94
24:12–18 54	15 41	6:22–27 94
25:8 57	16 41	7:2 192–193
25:8–9 52	17 41	7:84 192
25:11 53	18 41	7:87 192
25:18 15	18:21 101	7:89 18
25:19–22 18	18:28 .... 42, 113	8:14–26 94
25:22 52	19 41	8:17 51
25:24 53	19:2 50	10:4 193
25:31 53	19:9–10 .... 85, 109	11:25 123
25:31–40 52	19:26 102	11:29 123
26:1 .... 15, 52	20 41	11:31 122
28:29 38	20:7 50	12:12 169
28:30 38	20:9 139	14:21 .... 16, 229
28:43 37	20:22 .... 42, 113	17:2 192
29:10–18 37	20:26 50	18:2 37
29:38–46 37	23 41	18:4 14
30:1–10 37	23:3 16	19:2 159
30:7–8 37	23:39–44 226	21:18 193
30:20 37	24:1–4 37	22:31 223

24:2-3 ... 123	28 ... 48	6:34 ... 123
24:7 ... 67, 79	28:1–14 ... 29, 60, 120	8:22–23 ... 65
24:7–9 ... 91	28:15–68 ... 29, 42, 113	8:29–9:57 ... 65
24:17–19 ... 67	28:29 ... 182	9:6 ... 65
27:2 ... 193	28:36 ... 42	9:56–57 ... 66
27:21 ... 38	28:45 ... 42, 114	10:1–16:31 ... 65
29:2–38 ... 226	28:49–57 ... 42	11:29 ... 123
32:2 ... 193	28:61 ... 49	11:29–40 ... 101
33:52 ... 22	28:63 ... 42	17:6 ... 65
35:34 ... 57	29:21 ... 49	19:1 ... 65
	30:10 ... 49	21:25 ... 65

Deuteronomy

1:5 ... 41	30:12 ... 235	**1 Samuel**
4:1 ... 41	30:15–16 ... 29	2:1–10 ... 67, 80
4:5–9 ... 40	31:26 ... 48–49	2:3–9 ... 80
4:9 ... 42	32:4–6 ... 50, 207	2:6–7 ... 84
4:11 ... 136	32:6 ... 50	2:8–9 ... 84
4:19 ... 223, 235	32:8–9 ... 51	2:10 ... 68, 78, 81, 156, 237
4:36 ... 237	32:15 ... 64	4:4 ... 18
6:6–8 ... 42	32:17 ... 149	5:12 ... 237
6:17 ... 27	32:22 ... 235	6:7 ... 159
6:18 ... 27	33:1–5 ... 64	7:16 ... 70
7:6 ... 36	33:8 ... 38	8:5 ... 66
10:8 ... 94	33:10 ... 37–38	8:7 ... 66, 68
12:9 ... 43, 56	33:15 ... 75	8:10–18 ... 66, 68
12:31 ... 105	33:27 ... 74	10:1 ... 68, 152
14:2 ... 36		10:6 ... 123
14:4 ... 51	**Joshua**	10:10 ... 123
15:4–11 ... 85, 109	1:8 ... 49	10:19 ... 68
16:13–17 ... 226	5:13–15 ... 87	10:24 ... 68
17:3 ... 235	8:34 ... 49	12:1 ... 68
18:10 ... 101	13–19 ... 192	12:12 ... 66
18:10–18 ... 102	18:21–24 ... 192	12:13 ... 68
18:12 ... 105	19:15 ... 192	12:17 ... 68
20:10–20 ... 90	21:7 ... 192	13:14 ... 73
21:3 ... 159	23:7 ... 223	15:8 ... 67
21:5 ... 37	24:2–13 ... 48	15:11 ... 69
21:18–21 ... 139	24:25 ... 48	15:23 ... 104
21:23 ... 183		15:26 ... 69
23:17 ... 103	**Judges**	15:28 ... 69
23:18 ... 105	2:11–14 ... 89	15:32 ... 67
23:25–26 ... 85, 109	2:16 ... 64	15:35 ... 69
24:19–22 ... 85, 109	3:7–8:28 ... 65	16:1 ... 69
26:15 ... 237	3:10 ... 123	16:13 ... 123, 152
26:18 ... 36	5:20 ... 148	16:14–23 ... 147
	6:2–6 ... 166	

19:20 123
19:23 123
25:28 89
28:3–24 102
28:6 38

2 Samuel
2:4 69
5:3 69
5:6–10 69
6:2 18
6:12–19 93
6:13 93
6:14 94
6:17 93
6:18 94
7:5 94
7:8 94
7:10 57
7:11–16 70–71
7:13 70
7:15 70
7:16 70
7:26 94
7:29 94
14:17 28
19:27 28
22:6 235
22:10 237
22:10–12 136
22:14 237
23:1 .... 78, 156

1 Kings
2:6 235
3:3 99
3:3–9 28
3:9 82
3:28 83
4:21 92
4:25 90
6:12–13 .... 61, 219
6:19–22 53
6:29 53
6:29–35 52

7:15–22 53
7:23–26 53
7:27–38 .... 15, 52
7:27–39 53
7:51 55
8:1 .... 56, 193
8:6 18
8:10 55
8:16 69
8:22 237
8:24–26 94
8:30 58
8:30–39 237
8:42–43 60
9:25 94
10:5 94
10:9 .... 74, 83
11:7 105
11:7–8 99
12:12–20 106
12:28 100
12:30 .... 98, 100, 102
12:32 99
14:23 102
14:25–28 106
14:30 106
15:3 98–99
15:7 106
15:13 100
15:16 106
15: 17–20 106
15:26 .... 100, 102
15:34 .... 100, 102
16:19 102
16:26 100
16:31 .... 98, 100
16:32 99–100
16:33 100
17:17–24 147
18:18 98
18:45 235
19:18 223
21:5–16 106
22:19–20 17
22:43 99

22:52 102

2 Kings
1:10 237
3:24–27 101
4:32–37 147
9:12–13 158
10:31 98
11:17 48
11:18 22
11:32 94
11:38 94
12:3 99
12:17–18 106
12:28 98
13:6 100
14:6 98
14:8–14 106
15:4 99
15:19–20 106
15:35 99
16:3 101
16:5–9 106
16:10 .... 22, 99
16:15 .... 99, 105
17:4–5 .... 106, 165
17:6–8 .... 112, 134
17:8 102
17:13 98
17:16–17 102
18:4 99–100
18:6 98
20:12–15 106
21:3 99–100
21:5 99–100
21:6 101
21:7 100
21:16 106
21:22 98
22:11 49
23:3 48
23:10 101
23:13 99
23:14 100
23:19 99

Scripture Index

23:26–27 112
23:31–35 106
24:1 106
24:20 58
25:8–17 134

1 Chronicles
15:1 95
15:2 95
15–16 95
15:16–24 95
15:25–29 95
16:1–3 95
16:4 95
16:7–43 95
21:1 146
23:1–2 193
23:2 192
28:5 78
29:3 36
29:6 193
29:11 78

2 Chronicles
3:1 55
13:8 78
20:6 237
20:30 142
30:2 193
30:12 193
30:27 237
36:21–23 134
36:23 134

Ezra
1:2–4 134
2:43 37
2:58 37
2:63 38
3:1–5:1 135
6:13–22 135
9 135

Nehemiah
3:26 37

7:1–4 135
8:9 176
9:1–10:39 135
11:1 135

Job
1:6–12 146
10:21 .... 136, 166
11:8 235
16:19 237
17:12–13 .... 136, 166
17:16 235
22:14 236
26:10–14 20
26:13 122
27:3 122
28:25 122
34:14–15 122
37:18 236
37:21 236
37:23 81
38:7 148
38:8 87
38:8–11 20

Psalms
2:1–3 90
2:2 .... 78, 156
2:4 237
2:4–8 90
2:6 .... 55, 78, 156
2:7 .... 77, 152, 184
2:9 90
2:10–11 90
3:1–2 58
3:3–4 56
6:5 235
8:1 58
8:3 235
8:3–8 24
10:16 .... 27, 74
11:4 18
13 58
14:2 237
15:1 56

15:1–5 60
16 58
16:10 235
16:11 .... 21, 74
18:7–15 87–88
18:9 237
18:28 .... 136, 166
18:34–39 89
18:43–45 91
18:50 .... 74, 78, 89, 156
19:1 235
20:6 .... 78, 89, 156
21:1–4 76
22 58
22:27–28 61
23 58
23:6 59
24 60
24:3 56
24:7 74
24:8 87
25:10 49
26:8 59
27:4 59
27:4–5 59
29 58
29:10 .... 27, 74
33 58
33:5 81
33:6 122
34:9 142
36:7–9 .... 59, 221
37:28 81
42:1–2 59
44:4 66
45:5 89
46:4 .... 15, 56, 221, 233
46:4–5 53
47:2 27
47:2–3 92
47:6–7 66
47:7 27
47:8 17
47:8–9 92
48:1–2 .... 55–56, 60

Reference	Page
48:2	66
48:8	56, 74
50:1–2	61
50:4	235
50:5	48
52:5	75
52:8	15, 53
61:6–7	76
65	58
65:4	59
65:7	87–88, 170
68:8	54
68:15–17	56
68:17–18	87
68:18	235
68:24–27	58
69:3	88
69:16	88
71	58
71:15	212
72:1–2	82
72:1–4	86
72:1–11	90
72:5	76
72:7	90
72:8–11	79
72:9	90
72:17	31, 76
72:19	16, 229
73:17	59
73:28	212
74:2	56
74:10	131
74:12	66
74:12–14	87
74:12–17	20
75:7	84
76:1	60
76:1–2	56
76:8	237
76:9	85
77:17	235
78:10	49
78:23	236
78:26	122, 235
78:66	75
78:67–70	73
78:70	94
78:70–71	69
79:8–10	131
80:14	115, 237
80:17	77, 115
81:11–16	93
82:2–4	84
82:5	136
84:1–7	59
85:9	57
86:16	94
87	60
87:2–3	56
87:5	239
88:12	166
88:13	136
89:2	74
89:3	69, 94
89:3–4	71
89:4	70
89:9	87
89:9–10	87
89:9–11	20
89:14	81
89:18	66
89:19	69
89:20	94
89:20–23	71, 91
89:22–23	89
89:24	71
89:25	71, 91, 170
89:27	78–79, 94
89:29–33	71
89:39	115
90:1–2	74
92:12–13	15, 53
93:3–4	88, 170
93:4	235
93:5	74
95:10–11	43
95:11	56
96:5	149
97:1–2	81
98:6	66
99:1	17
99:1–3	61
99:4	81
99:5	18
99:9	56
101:8	56
102:25–27	75
103:11	235
103:17	74
103:18	49
103:19	17
104:1–4	87
104:2	136, 236
104:5–9	20
104:9	87
104:10–13	88
104:29–30	122
105:37	149
105:41	227
106:40–42	89
106:44–45	42
107	58
107:1	74
107:10–11	136, 166
107:22	212
108:4	235
110:1	77, 160
110:2	89, 91
110:4	75, 94, 174
110:5	91
112:6	31
113:4	236
113:5–9	84
113:6	237
115:3	237
115:16	25
116:1	58
116:3	235
118	58
118:25	238
119:89	74
122:1–2	58–59
123:1	237
125:1	56, 74

132:6–7 58	**Isaiah**	11:1 124
132:7 18	1:2–3 122	11:1–3 123
132:8 16	1:2–6 108	11:3–4 .... 87, 126
132:10 .... 78, 94, 156	1:7–9 113	11:4 126
132:13 56	1:12–17 110	11:4–5 146
132:14 .... 16, 74	1:17 85	11:6–8 126
132:17 .... 78, 156	1:21 .... 110, 123	11:9 .... 17, 21, 229
132:18 89	1:23 110	11:10 129–130
134:1 37	1:24–27 123	11:11 118
135:1–2 37	2:2–3 128	11:12–13 120
135:5–7 88	2:2–4 .... 55, 60	11:14 133
135:7 122	2:3–4 234	12:3 227
135:21 .... 56, 233	2:4 129	13:9–10 .... 136, 183
137:1 115	2:5–22 113	13:13 113
138 58	2:6 120	13:13–22 113
139:8 235	3:5 140	13:17–22 88
139:24 74	3:13–15 110	14:1 .... 119, 129
144:5 237	3:14–15 109	14:12–20 148
145:13 74	4:2 124	14:14 32
148:13 236	4:5 56	14:15 235
	5:8 110	14:20 235
Proverbs	5:8–10 108	16:5 124
7:27 235	5:9–10 113	17:12–13 .... 91, 170
8:20 81	5:14 235	18:3 129
10:1 139	5:20–24 .... 28, 83	18:7 129
13:1 139	5:25 113	19:3 102
13:24 139	5:26–30 112	19:16–24 129
15:5 139	6:1 17	25:6–8 21
15:24 235	6:3 .... 16, 229	25:6–12 124
17:21 139	6:5 26	26:4 74
19:18 139	6:8–9 17	27:6 119
19:26 139	6:11–13 113	27:12–13 118
20:20 139	7:11 235	28:1 235
23:13–14 139	8:18 56	28:13 110
28:24 139	8:19 107	28:16–17 123
30:4 .... 122, 235	9:1–7 .... 133, 165	29:4 102
30:17 139	9:2 .... 136, 166	29:13 110
	9:4 166	29:21 109
Ecclesiastes	9:5 166	30:18 81
2:8 36	9:6 .... 82, 126, 184	31:8 119
2:13 136	9:6–7 .... 124, 126, 166	32:12–30 123
2:14–16 31	9:7 .... 81, 126, 142, 166	32:15 122
5:2 237	10:1–2 109	32:16 81
	10:1–3 85	32: 16–17 110
	10:20–23 118	33:13–15 85

33:20 .... 119–120, 233	56:6–7 56	**Jeremiah**
33:21 119	56:7 138	2:8 38
34:4 236	56:8 135	2:20–28 108
35:1–2 119	56:9–12 138	2:29–32 108
35:6–7 119	57:1–10 138	2:34 110
37:15 59	57:9 235	3:1–2 108
37:16 18	57:13 138	3:5–9 113
37:21–34 59	58:1–8 138	3:17 .... 129, 234
37:31 142	59:1–5 138	3:18 120
37:31–32 118	59:15–19 .... 139, 188	3:20 108
38:18 235	59:20 138	4:1–2 44
40:3–11 129	60:1–6 138	4:17 108
40:5 129	60:13 19	4:22 .... 41, 122
40:18 22	60:14–15 137	4:23–26 113
40:22 236	60:18 136	4:23–28 120
40:28 74	60:19–20 136	4:27 117
42:1–4 .... 82, 126	60:22 135	4:28 183
42:6 .... 44, 129	61:1–2 .... 86, 136	5:1–2 110
42:7 44	61:1–3 123	5:7–9 108
43:10 44	61:2 136	5:10 117
44:1–5 198	61:5–7 137	5:17 113
44:1–5 120	61:7 74	5:18 117
44:2 64	61:8 .... 74, 81	5:19 107
44:3–4 122	61:9 137	5:22 20
44:23 129	62:6–9 135	6:8–20 110
44:24 236	62:10 129	6:13 109
44:26–28 120	62:12 137–138	6:15 .... 105, 108
44:28 134	63:15 237	6:19 108
45:13 134	64:1 237	6:22–26 89
45:17 74	65:8–16 138	7:8–11 110
47:13 102	65:17 136	7:12–14 114
49:6 .... 44, 129	65:18 137	7:28 120
49:22–23 130	65:20 135	7:29 .... 114, 120
51:3 .... 15, 119	65:22–23 135	7:30 .... 105, 108, 112
51:4–5 234	65:23 135	7:31 107
51:9–10 20	65:25 136	8:2 235
51:11 74	66:1 .... 19, 237	8:5 110
51:16 .... 120, 198	66:1–2 138	8:19 107
52:7–8 .... 132, 234	66:12 135	9:1–6 .... 41, 122
52:9–10 130	66:13–16 188	9:3–6 110
54:11–17 .... 120, 233	66:15–16 136	9:11 113
55:4 .... 79, 134	66:15–17 .... 139, 188	9:24 81
55:5 130	66:18–21 138	10:10 74
55:9 235		10:13 122
56:1–2 138		11:10 .... 49, 111

11:13 107	31:38–40 120	6:14 113
11:15 114	32:21 112	7:14–27 .... 113, 120
11:17 114	32:29 107	8:9 105
12:7 113–114	32:34 108	9:1–11 89
13:11 40	32:35 107–108	11:17 119
13:18 114	32:37 119	11:18 108
15:5–9 112	32:38 .... 120, 198	11:19–20 122
16:14–15 118	32:39–40 122	11:20 .... 120, 198
16:18 .... 105, 108	32:40 .... 74, 121	11:21 108
16:21 121	33:5 112	12:1–3 108
17:2 107	33:6–9 119	14:6–11 122
17:2–3 107	33:9 130	16:2 105
18:18 38	33:15 .... 82, 124, 126	16:20 107
19:5 107	33:21 37	16:47 108
20:4 112	33:22 119	16:50–52 108
21:7 113	33:26 94	16:59–63 121
21:9 113	34:8–17 109	17:18–19 .... 49, 111
21:11–12 86	39:1–10 134	17:22–23 55
22:1–3 86	46:27 119	20:28 .... 102, 107
23:3 118	50:2 129	20:33–38 122
23:5 .... 124, 126	50:20 118	21:21 102
23:5–6 82	52:3–30 134	22:1–6 110
23:7–8 118		22:4 113
23:13 107	**Lamentations**	22:27 109
23:40 75	2:22 113	22:29 109
24:7 .... 120–121, 198	3:1–2 .... 136, 166	23:22–29 112
24:9 113	3:6 235	23:37 107
24:10 113	3:22 74	23:46-49 112
25:9 75	3:50 237	26:20 235
25:11–12 .... 118, 143	4:20 .... 78, 156	28:11–19 148
27:9 107		28:12–15 148
29:10 .... 118, 143	**Ezekiel**	28:13 15
30:1–3 118	1:26–28 236	28:14 55
30:9 124	1:28 54	28:25–26 121
30:10 119	3:9 108	28:26 119
30:11 117	3:23 54	30:24 88
30:18 120	4:16–17 113	31:1–11 88
30:19 119	4:25 52	32:8 235
30:22 .... 120, 198	5:14–15 113	32:18–32 235
31:3 74	5:16–17 113	33:26 105
31:9 .... 50, 120	6:4 113	34:1–10 127
31:31–32 .... 49, 111	6:4–7 113	34:17–19 127
31:31–34 121	6:8–10 118	34:23 .... 124, 127
31:35 88	6:11 110	34:25 119
31:35–37 118	6:13 107	34:26–27 119

34:30 121	**Daniel**	2:19 81
34:30–31 .... 120, 198	2:36–45 .... 143, 157	2:19–20 108
36:10 119	2:39–40 141	2:20 122
36:11 .... 119, 121	4:3 74	2:23 .... 120, 198
36:23 130	4:34 74	3:1 108
36:24–31 130	7:2–14 .... 141, 156	4:1–3 .... 41, 122
36:26–27 122	7:7 .... 141, 156	4:4–6 38
36:27 122–123	7:9 .... 74, 125	4:6 .... 114, 120
36:28 .... 120, 198	7:10 17	4:10 103
36:29 119	7:13 .... 17, 125, 141, 156	4:12 .... 102, 104, 107–108
36:35 119	7:13–14 17	4:13 .... 102, 107
37:12–13 147	7:14 .... 141, 143, 156	5:3–4 108
37:23 120	7:17–18 142	6:7 49
37:24 124	7:19–27 141	6:8–9 110
37:26 119	7:22 .... 125, 142	7:13 110
37:26–27 74	7:25 142	8:1 .... 49, 111
37:27 232	7:27 142–143	8:4 107
39:27 130	8:9–13 142	9:1–2 108
39:28 121	8:12 142	9:1–3 111
39:29 122	9:2 143	9:3 112
40:31 53	9:7–14 143	9:14 107
40:34 53	9:24 .... 75, 143	9:17 120
40:37 53	9:25 143	10:1 107
41:18–20 .... 15, 52–53	9:27 143	10:1–8 113
41:24–26 53	10:13–21 146	10:7 114
42:12 .... 14, 53	10:16 22	11:1 49
43:1–4 53	11:21–39 142	11:2 107
43:1–4 14	11:32 144	11:5 112
43:7 19	11:33 144	11:11 119
44:1 .... 14, 53	11:39 147	12:1 110
44:16 37	12:1 .... 144, 146	12:7–8 109
44:16–17 37	12:2 .... 75, 147	13:1 107
44:23–24 38	12:3 144	13:2 107
45:4 37	12:10 144	13:9–11 114
45:9–10 193		13:10 107
46:12 .... 14, 53	**Hosea**	16:18 107
46:24 37	1:2 108	
47:1 .... 14, 53	1:4 142	**Joel**
47:1–2 .... 53, 220	1:9 .... 114, 120	1:9 37
47:1–12 .... 15, 21, 53, 119	1:10 119	1:13 37
47:8 220	1:11 120	2:1–2 136
47:9 220	2:1 50	2:1–13 113
47:12 220	2:1–5 108	2:10 .... 183, 235
48:15–20 120	2:8 107	2:17 37
48:30–35 120	2:18 119	2:26–27 .... 41, 122

2:28 123	**Jonah**	3:16 124
2:31 .... 113, 123	1:4 122	
2:32 124	2:2–3 235	**Zephaniah**
3:1 .... 120, 123	2:4 88	1:7–18..................... 113, 120
3:1–3 88		1:15 183
3:2 88	**Micah**	1:18 113
3:2–8 124	1:6–7 113	3:1 123
3:9-12 88	2:1–2 109	3:1–2 108
3:12 124	2:12 119	3:11–13 122
3:15 136	2:13 131	3:13 119
3:16 124	3:1–3 109	3:17 87
3:17 .... 56, 121, 123,	3:8 123	
233–234	3:9–12 111	**Zechariah**
3:18 .... 119, 123, 220	3:10 110	1:1–6 138
3:19 124	3:11 ....38, 110	1:12–17 134
3:20 123	3:12 113–114	2:11 137
3:21 124	4:1–2 ....55, 128	3:1–2 146
	4:2 60	3:7 53
Amos	4:3–4 129	8:12 135
1–2 133	4:7 19	8:13 137
1:13–15 88	4:10 112	8:14–18 138
2:4 .... 108, 110	4:11 134	8:22–23 138
2:6–8 109	5:2 184	8:23 137
3:10 110	5:4–5 126	9:9 .... 136–137, 158
4:2–3 112	5:7–8 132	9:9–10 91
4:4–5 110	5:9 126	9:10 138
4:13 122	6:10–12 109	14:8 .... 135–136, 221
5:13–14 ....28, 83	6:12 110	14:11 135
5:18 136	6:16 113	14:12–15 .... 136, 188
5:20 136	7:5–6 139	14:16–19 138
5:21–23 110	7:8 .... 136, 166	
5:24 81	7:11–12 134	**Malachi**
5:25–26 22	7:15–17 130	1:6–10 138
5:27 112	7:18–20 118	2:1–9 53
6:3 110		2:1–17 138
8:3 113	**Habakkuk**	2:7 38
8:4–6 109	1:5–11 89	3:5 .... 139, 188
8:9 182	1:12 74	3:6–10 138
8:9–10 113	2:14 ....17, 229	3:16–18 138
9:2 235	3:3–14 124	3:18–4:1 .... 136, 188
9:8 117	3:6 75	4:1 .... 139, 188
9:11 124	3:10 75	4:4 138
9:11–12 133	3:12 124	4:5 113
9:13–15 119	3:13 124	4:5–6 .... 136, 139, 178, 188
	3:15 170	

NEW TESTAMENT

Matthew

Reference	Page
1:1	152, 155
1:11	152
1:16	152, 155
1:20–23	184
1:21	182
2:2	156
2:4	155–156
2:22	166
3:2	189
3:7–10	189
3:9	209
3:11	190
3:13	166
3:16	238
4:12	167–168
4:12–16	167
4:17	168, 179
4:23–25	167
4:24	161, 164
5:34	239
5:34–35	19
5:48	239
6:1	239
6:9	239
6:10	179, 239
6:13	163
6:19–20	239
6:26	239
7:12	176, 185
7:28	176
8:5–13	168
8:16	161
8:23	170
8:28–34	164
8:29	162
9:2	180
9:14–17	177
9:18–26	168
9:22	180
9:27	173
9:27–31	168
9:32–33	161
10:1	191
10:1–15	194
10:2	191
10:6	195
10:7	194
10:14–15	194
10:15	171
11:1	176, 191
11:2	155
11:13–14	187
11:18–19	190
11:20–24	181
11:22	171
11:24	171
12:9–14	168
12:15	168
12:15–21	172
12:22	164
12:24	162
12:26	162
12:27	162
12:28	162
12:29–30	163
12:36	171
12:38	176
13:1–50	178
13:18–23	180
13:24	179, 239
13:31–32	178
13:33	178
13:39	163
13:45	239
13:47–50	179
13:52	178
13:53	176
13:58	180
14:14	168
14:15–21	169
14:36	168
15:1	176
15:1–20	203
15:3–7	181
15:13	239
15:21–28	164, 198
15:22	173
15:28	180
15:30	168
15:32–38	169
16:16	155
16:20	155
16:21–28	182
17:5	185
17:15	173
17:18	164
17:22	157
17:22–23	182
17:24–27	169
18:1–4	181
18:12–14	181
18:35	239
19:2	168
19:28	193
20:18	157
20:20–28	181
20:28	182
20:30	173
21:1–11	158
21:2	158
21:4–5	159
21:9	238
21:14	168
21:32	191
22:36–40	185
23:37	198, 215
23:39	215
24:1	221
24:30	157
26:1	176
26:14	191
26:61	222
27:17	155
27:22	155
27:45	182

Mark

Reference	Page
1:1	155

1:1–3 189	6:30 191	15:38 183
1:5 189–190	6:48–49............................ 170	16:19 .... 160, 238
1:7 190	6:49–52............................ 171	
1:9 166	7:1–5 203	**Luke**
1:10 238	7:24–30 .... 164, 168, 198	1:16–17............................ 187
1:11 .... 152, 238	7:27 198	1:26 166
1:12–15............................ 162	7:31–37............................ 168	1:30–33............................ 153
1:14 .... 166, 168	7:34 238	1:35 184
1:15 179	8:22–26............................ 168	1:39–45............................ 188
1:22 176	8:29 155	1:68–71............................ 153
1:23–26............................ 161	8:31 157	1:76–77............................ 153
1:24 .... 162, 173	8:31–32............................ 182	2:11 155
1:30–31............................ 168	9:7 185	2:14 238
1:32–34............................ 161	9:13 190	2:26 154–156
1:34 168	9:20–25............................ 161	2:29 154
1:37–9.............................. 167	9:31–32............................ 182	2:30–32............................ 154
1:38–39............................ 161	9:33–35............................ 181	2:36 154
1:39 166	9:35 191	2:37–38............................ 154
1:40–45............................ 169	9:38–40............................ 163	3:3 189
2:1–12.............................. 168	9:41 155	3:7–9 189
2:5 180	9:42–43............................ 161	3:10–14............................ 190
2:6 176	10:17–21.......................... 185	3:10–15............................ 190
2:20–22............................ 177	10:17–23.......................... 180	3:16 190
2:28 157	10:32 191	3:21 238
3:7–11 161	10:35–45.......................... 181	3:21–22............................ 152
3:11 162	10:45 182	4:14 .... 155, 162, 167
3:14 191	10:46–47.......................... 173	4:18–21............................ 155
3:22 176	10:47 173	4:31–42............................ 167
4:10 191	10:52 180	4:32 176
4:11 176	11:2 158–159	4:34 173
4:13–20............................ 180	11:3 159	4:40 168
4:15 163	11:4–5 159	4:41 155
4:26–29............................ 179	11:9–10............................ 158	5:1–11.............................. 169
4:30–32............................ 178	11:10 238	5:20 180
4:39 170	11:17 222	5:21 176
5:1–13.............................. 164	12:9 215–216	5:24 157
5:7 162	12:10 215	5:36–39............................ 177
5:15 164	12:12 215	6:13 191
5:34 180	13:1–2 221	6:18 164
6:2 176	13:4 222	7:11–16............................ 168
6:5–6 180	14:58 222	7:21 164
6:7 191	14:61 157	7:22 169
6:7–13.............................. 194	14:62 157	7:29–30............................ 191
6:11 194	15:32 156	8:1 191
6:12 194	15:33 182	8:1–2 164

8:11–15 180	21:5–6 221	7:37–39 .... 222, 227
8:22–25 170	21:36 157	7:39 224
8:26–39 .... 161, 164	22:28–29 193	7:41 166
8:28 162	22:31 163	8:24 180
8:48 180	23:2 155–156	8:28 .... 176, 185
9:1 191	23:5 166	8:32 224
9:1–6 194	23:44 182	8:39 207
9:2 194	24:26 155	8:40 224
9:5 194	24:51 238	8:42–44 163
9:11 168		8:45 224
9:12 191	**John**	9:1–41 168
9:20 155–156	1:14 .... 223, 228	10:10 163
9:22 176	1:17 224	10:33 184
9:35 185	1:32 224	11:12 158
9:42 164	1:33 224	11:26 180
9:43–45 182	1:35–37 191	11:27 155
9:46–48 181	1:36 182	11:33 224
10:12 171	1:41 155	11:38–44 168
10:12–15 181	1:51 .... 223, 228	11:49–51 182
10:14 171	2:1–11 169	12:12–19 158
10:17 162	2:19 .... 222, 229	12:14 158
10:18 162	2:20–22 222	12:14–15 159
11:13 239	2:21–22 229	12:16 160
11:20 162	3:3 179	12:20–24 198
11:31-32 171	3:14–18 179	12:20–26 183
13:3–5 181	3:16 180	12:31 183
13:10–17 168	3:34 176	12:31–32 163
13:16 .... 164, 198	4 223	12:32 184
13:18–19 178	4:10–14 .... 222, 226	12:49 176
13:20–21 178	4:20 223	13:2 163
13:32 161–162	4:23–24 222–223	13:5–15 181
13:34–35 .... 198, 215	4:24 225	13:21 224
14:1–6 168	4:39–42 226	14:6 224
14:7–11 181	4:46–54 168	14:16 224
15:8–10 181	5:1–18 168	14:17 224
15:11–32 181	5:18 184	14:26 176
18:6–8 171	5:19–21 185	15:7 225
18:31 157	5:26–27 171	15:16 225
18:35–43 168	5:27–28 171	16:11 173
18:37 173	5:36 185	16:13 224
18:42 180	6:40 180	16:14–15 224
19:9 198	6:67 191	16:23–24 225
19:29–44 158	6:71 191	16:26 225
19:36 158	7:2 226	17:1 238
20:41 155	7:16–17 .... 176, 185	17:8 .... 176, 185

18:37 224	10:34–42.........................200	14:17 21
19:30 224	10:36–38.........................164	15:16 39
20:24 191	10:39 183	
20:30–31 180	10:39–41.........................196	**1 Corinthians**
20:31 155	10:42 171	4:4 163
21:1–14 169	10:44–45.........................200	6:1 179
	10:45 214	6:9 179
Acts	11:15–17.........................200	6:15 230
1:8 ....194–195, 217	11:19 195	6:16–17...........................230
1:9–11 238	11:19–27.........................195	6:19 230
1:21–23 196	11:22 197	10:4 227
2:1–8:3 195	13:4–5..............................201	12:2 209
2:5–18 196	13:13 201	15:25 185
2:11 196	13:29 183	15:42–44...........................21
2:22 195	13:48 201	15:50 21
2:29 195	13:48–49.........................201	15:50–57...........................21
2:36 195–196	14:1 201	
2:43 197	14:1–8..............................201	**2 Corinthians**
3:1–9 197	15 ....199, 203	4:6 212
3:25–26 198	15:1 204	5:10 172
4:4 196	15:14 213	6:14–15...........................212
4:10 195	15:16–17.........................199	6:18 232
4:11 215–216	16:6 201	
4:20 196	16:9–10............................201	**Galatians**
5:12 197	16:11–12.........................201	1:2 206
5:14 196	16:30–34.........................201	1:6 ....206, 239
5:16 197	17:1–15............................201	2:12–21...........................206
5:27–32 196	17:16–34.........................201	3:1–5 ....206, 239
5:30 183	17:31 172	3:1–14...............................206
5:31 196	17:34 201	3:2 206
7:56 239	18:1 201	3:2–22...............................207
8:4–7 197	19:10 201	3:6–7.................................207
8:4–12:25 195	20:32 179	3:8–9.................................207
8:14 197	22:28 205	3:10 206
9:1–9 201	26:18 212	3:13 183
9:1–22 195		3:19–22...........................206
9:15 201	**Romans**	3:25–29...........................208
9:35 196	1:16 200	3:26 206
9:36–40 197	3:25 183	4:8 209
10 200	4:9–12..............................208	4:8–11...............................206
10:1–7 200	4:11 208	4:13–15...........................206
10:11 239	4:13 217	4:21 206
10:15 213	8:16 206	4:24–25...........................239
10:28–29 200	8:33–34............................175	4:26 240
10:33 201	14:10–11.........................172	4:28 239

4:28–31 206	4:16 238	2:4–5 231
5:1 206		2:5 232
5:21 179	**2 Timothy**	2:6–7 215–216
6:12 .... 206, 239	4:1 171	2:7 209
6:16 209		2:9 .... 39, 210–211
	Hebrews	2:10 210
Ephesians	1:3 .... 160, 175, 238	2:11 209
1:1 205	2:14–15 184	2:12 212
1:13–14 179	2:17–18 39	2:24 .... 183, 212
1:20 .... 160, 238	4:14 175	3:7 212
1:22–23 230	4:14–15 176	3:21–22 212
2:11–12 209	4:14–16 39	3:22 160
2:11–19 203	4:16 176	4:4–3 209
2:11–22 202	5:1 39	4:4–5 212
2:12 205	5:1–6 174	5:10 212
2:15 204	7:23–25 175	
2:19 205	7:24 185	**1 John**
2:20 231–232	8:1 .... 160, 175, 238	2:1 175
2:20–22 231	8:2 175	
2:21–22 232	8:5 174	**Revelation**
4:12 205	9:1–10 175	3:12 241
4:13 231	9:11 175	5:10 25
4:15–16 231	9:12 175	21:2–4 241
4:17–19 209	9:23 175	21:4 21
5:3 205	9:24 175–176	22:5 25
5:5 179	10:10 175	
5:8 212	10:11–14 175	**1 Maccabes**
6:3 217	12:2 175	13:51 158
6:18 205	12:18 240	
	12:22 240	
Philippians	12:27 175	
2:10–11 185		
3:20 .... 206, 240	**1 Peter**	
	1:1 209	
Colossians	1:4 .... 179, 212	
1:13–14 212	1:5 212	
1:19 229	1:9–10 212	
2:9 229	1:12 212	
2:16–19 230	1:13 212	
3:1 160	1:14 .... 209, 212	
3:1–2 240	1:17 209	
3:2–3 240	1:18 209	
	1:25 212	
1 Thessalonians	2:3 212	
4:5 209	2:4 231–232	

Langham Literature and its imprints are a ministry of Langham Partnership.

Langham Partnership is a global fellowship working in pursuit of the vision God entrusted to its founder John Stott –

> *to facilitate the growth of the church in maturity and Christ-likeness through raising the standards of biblical preaching and teaching.*

Our vision is to see churches in the Majority World equipped for mission and growing to maturity in Christ through the ministry of pastors and leaders who believe, teach and live by the word of God.

Our mission is to strengthen the ministry of the word of God through:
- nurturing national movements for biblical preaching
- fostering the creation and distribution of evangelical literature
- enhancing evangelical theological education

especially in countries where churches are under-resourced.

Our ministry

Langham Preaching partners with national leaders to nurture indigenous biblical preaching movements for pastors and lay preachers all around the world. With the support of a team of trainers from many countries, a multi-level programme of seminars provides practical training, and is followed by a programme for training local facilitators. Local preachers' groups and national and regional networks ensure continuity and ongoing development, seeking to build vigorous movements committed to Bible exposition.

Langham Literature provides Majority World preachers, scholars and seminary libraries with evangelical books and electronic resources through publishing and distribution, grants and discounts. The programme also fosters the creation of indigenous evangelical books in many languages, through writer's grants, strengthening local evangelical publishing houses, and investment in major regional literature projects, such as one volume Bible commentaries like *The Africa Bible Commentary* and *The South Asia Bible Commentary*.

Langham Scholars provides financial support for evangelical doctoral students from the Majority World so that, when they return home, they may train pastors and other Christian leaders with sound, biblical and theological teaching. This programme equips those who equip others. Langham Scholars also works in partnership with Majority World seminaries in strengthening evangelical theological education. A growing number of Langham Scholars study in high quality doctoral programmes in the Majority World itself. As well as teaching the next generation of pastors, graduated Langham Scholars exercise significant influence through their writing and leadership.

To learn more about Langham Partnership and the work we do visit **langham.org**

www.ingramcontent.com/pod-product-compliance
Lightning Source LLC
Chambersburg PA
CBHW071423150426
43191CB00008B/1026